I leave them the curse of the dying;
I leave them their own fetid crowd;
I leave them the voices at midnight;
I leave them the hope of a shroud;
I leave them the groans of the fallen;
I leave them the culture of swine…
All these but another — bear witness, good brother —
I leave them the fate that was mine.

—*The final verse of "The Testament of a Dying Ham" by Gene Fowler, the favorite poem of the Bundy Drive Boys*

The Hellfire Club Comes to Hollywood

The Bundy Drive Boys never belonged to an organization called the Hellfire Club, but they very well could have.

The original Hellfire Club was an aristocratic British group that met throughout the middle of the eighteenth century to drink, whore and raise hell. The club motto, taken from Rabelais and later appropriated by Aleister Crowley, was "Do What Thou Wilt."

The Hellfire Club, like the Bundy Drive Boys, enjoyed reading blasphemous and often seditious pornographic poetry and skits. Original Hellfire Club member William Hogarth — like Bundy Drive boy John Decker in his portraits of W.C. Fields and Sadakichi Hartmann — enjoyed parodying religious iconography substituting Hellfire Club members for historic holy men.

It has also come to our attention though a conversation with John Barrymore III that his great-grandfather, born Herbert Blythe, renamed himself Maurice Barrymore after an historical character named Richard Barry, the 7th Earl of Barrymore (1769 - 1793). The Earl of Barrymore was born a little too late to become involved in The Hellfire Club, but on his own went against the rules of aristocracy by acting and becoming known as "The Rake of Rakes," and like Hellfire Club members, was an enthusiastic womanizer.

The Bundy Drive Boys are the true latter-day versions of the Hellfire Club.

Fait ce que vouldras.

HOLLYWOOD'S

The Bundy Drive Boys gather at John Murray Anderson's Fall 1941 gala opening, weeks prior to John Barrymore's death.
W.C. Fields, Gene Fowler, John Barrymore,
John Carradine, Jack LaRue, John Decker

HELLFIRE CLUB

THE MISADVENTURES OF JOHN BARRYMORE, W.C. FIELDS, ERROL FLYNN AND "THE BUNDY DRIVE BOYS"

BY
GREGORY WILLIAM MANK

WITH
CHARLES HEARD
AND BILL NELSON

CONTENTS

07 **Prologue**

Part I: The 1920s

18 Chapter One : The Old Toymaker,
"That Red-Haired Whore" and the Master Poisoner
30 Chapter Two: Mad Jack's Travelin' One-Man Freak Show
50 Chapter Three: The First Hippie
62 Chapter Four: The Great Charlatan
70 Chapter Five: "The Devil Can-Cans in Their Souls"
80 Chapter Six: Father Confessor
88 Chapter Seven: Maloney and Other Vultures

Part II: The 1930s

96 Chapter Eight: The Glory Days and Nights
128 Chapter Nine: Captain Blood
146 Chapter Ten: The Featured Players
164 Chapter Eleven: The Last of the Twittering Vaginas
180 Chapter Twelve: The Greatest Year of the Movies, "The Spiritual Striptease of Gypsy Rose John," and John Decker's Biggest Caper

Part III: 1940–1947

- 200 Chapter Thirteen: 1940: Bundy Drive
- 226 Chapter Fourteen: 1941: "A Match for the Tribes of Hell"
- 242 Chapter Fifteen: The Death of John Barrymore
- 266 Chapter Sixteen: In Like Flynn, Courtroom Melodramas, Jane Russell's Brassiere, Ghosts from the Past, Dream-Turned-Nightmare, "Am I Supposed to Eat This — or Did I?"
- 286 Chapter Seventeen: 1944: "A Superbly Weird Imagination," Farewell to Bundy Drive, "Jesus" Walks the Pool, W.C.'s Last Popinjay, and the Passing of "Chrysanthemum"
- 298 Chapter Eighteen: 1945: End of a War and "The Five Million Virgin Cunts from Heaven"
- 304 Chapter Nineteen: 1946: Mona, Peeing in the Wind, A Female Captain Bligh, and the Passing of the Great Charlatan
- 324 Chapter Twenty: 1947: Raphael's Angels

Part IV: The Aftermath

- 340 Chapter Twenty-One: Shuffling Off the Mortal Coil
- 364 Chapter Twenty-Two: Useless. Insignificant. Poetic.

- 366 Acknowledgements

- 370 Bibliography

- 381 Index

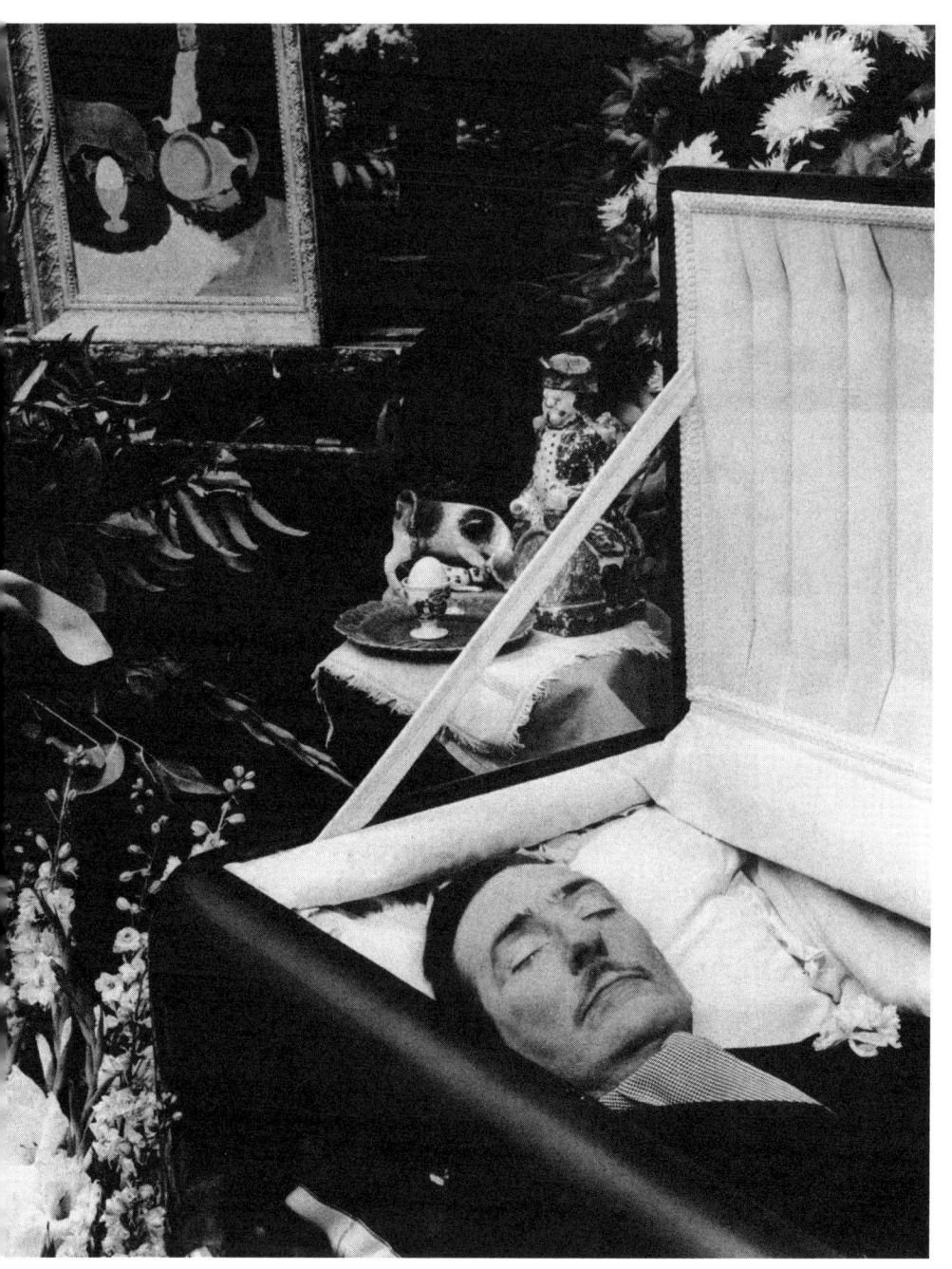

John Decker's cadaver, soft-boiled

PROLOGUE

JUNE 10, 1947: IN his art studio at 1215 Alta Loma Drive in Hollywood, the corpse of John Decker — artist, forger, and profane figurehead of Hollywood's "Bundy Drive Boys"— lay in state, flanked by his paintings, his widow and approximately 250 weeping, drunken mourners. The art studio-turned-funeral parlor was only a bottle's throw from the trashcans of the Mocambo nightclub on the Sunset Strip. His favorite drink never more than an arm's reach away, Decker created his final masterpieces and forgeries while other whiskey-soaked revelers danced in Conga lines only yards away. At the wake, Decker's cadaver looked strikingly like John Barrymore made up as Lucifer. This surely would have pleased the deceased. "The Great Profile" had been the most celebrated of the hard-drinking pack who once gathered at Decker's previous home and studio, 419 N. Bundy Drive, an English Tudor cottage in then-pastoral Brentwood. The oaken door had a magical fairy-tale look, for Decker had painted his coat-of-arms unicorns below its "peep hatch," and had added his ironic motto:

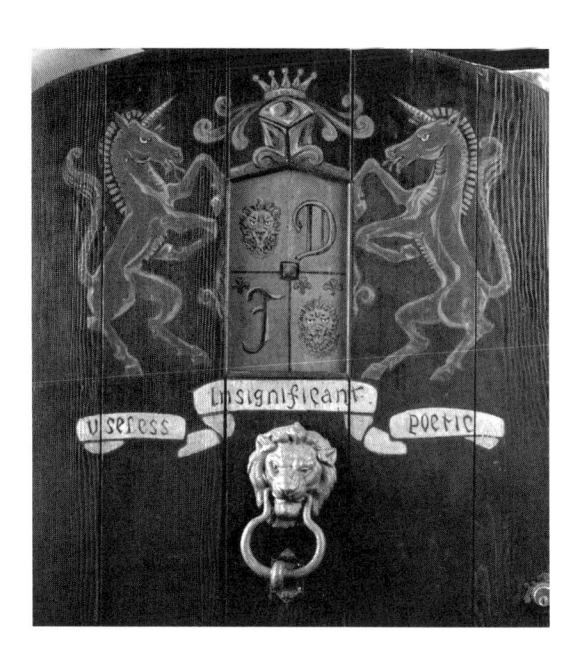

Useless. Insignificant. Poetic.

Barrymore had likely been the greatest actor of his century. He'd made cinema history, changing from Dr. Jekyll to Mr. Hyde without makeup. He had triumphed as Hamlet on both the New York and London stage. In their *Grand Hotel* love scene, Greta Garbo impulsively kissed him, forever after praising the man's "divine madness."

"I like Decker," Barrymore once said. "He hates sunsets and his mother."

They had degenerated together. By the time John Barrymore had died in 1942, the star was trashing his talent, pissing in public, and trying to seduce his 21-year-old daughter Diana.

The Bundy Drive Boys called Barrymore — affectionately — "the Monster."

For many, John Decker was the devil who perched on John Barrymore's shoulder, appealing to the actor's real-life Hyde and cheerleading the man's final debauchery. Decker's major fame had come through his paintings of Hollywood stars in Old Masters style — e.g., Garbo as da Vinci's Mona Lisa, and Harpo Marx as Gainsborough's Blue Boy. Decker painted them as he saw them, and as brilliant writer/Bundy Drive Boy Ben Hecht expressed it,

> Decker not only gets a true likeness down — with one of the swiftest, sharp-shooting brushes in modern art — but he also introduces into his portraits a full Freudian biography of the celebrity involved

His subjects weren't always pleased. When Katharine Hepburn played *Mary of Scotland* (1936), she sat for Decker, who gave the actress an aura so radiantly evil that the spooked actresss immediately gave away the picture and was allegedly reluctant to sit for a portrait ever again. The long-disowned painting only emerged again in 2006 after the star's death.

The Bundy Drive Boys — gifted, world-famous men — smiled like pirates, cavorted like the Marx Brothers and had dark sides worthy of Dracula. The pre-Rat Pack gang had created a crazy Hollywood peep show, a wild midnight carnival, a modern *Canterbury Tales*.

Supporting Cast:

- **W.C. Fields:** "It's a funny old life," the curmudgeon once said. "Man's lucky if he gets out of it alive." The bulbous-nosed comedian managed in a superb irony, considering his known dislike of the holiday, to die on Christmas Day, 1946. He was also the inspiration for one of John Decker's most famous works — Fields as Queen Victoria. "Sabotage!" rejoiced Fields of this incarnation. "Decker has kicked history in the groin!"

- **Errol Flynn:** The star who was forever Robin Hood — despite barely escaping conviction in 1943 for statutory rape — had a tragic aura that Decker caught in a casual portrait with almost startling perception. Flynn, just before his death in 1959, spent his final moments entertaining his doctor with tales of Decker and the Bundy Drive Boys.

- **Thomas Mitchell:** The great character actor won the 1939 Best Supporting Actor Academy Award for John Ford's *Stagecoach*, giving one of the shortest and most refreshing acceptance speeches in Oscar history: "I didn't think I was that good!" He was the victim of (or perhaps a collaborator on) Decker's now infamous alleged forgery — the Rembrandt Bust of Christ that has awed the faithful for decades in Harvard's Fogg Museum.

- **Sadakichi Hartmann:** Ancient and unwashed, he was once New York's "King of the Bohemians," with the colossal misfortune in World War II Los Angeles of having Axis Powers ancestry, half-German and half-Japanese. Regularly compared to looking like a praying mantis, he wrote about a tempted-by-the-flesh Jesus Christ over 100 years before *The Da Vinci Code*, and amazed and appalled the not-easily-impressed Barrymore, who described Hartmann as "a living freak presumably sired by Mephistopheles out of *Madame Butterfly*."

• **Ben Hecht:** The fireball newspaper reporter and prestigious stage and screenwriter of such hit plays (with co-author Charles MacArthur) as *The Front Page*, won the very first Academy Award for Original Screenplay for 1927's *Underworld*, and used his Oscar for a doorstop. He later contributed to such classic films as *Stagecoach, Wuthering Heights* and *Gone With the Wind*, all in the same year. Sharing an office in Hollywood for a time with fellow Bundy Drive Boy Gene Fowler, the duo engaged a blonde showgirl ("Bunny") who performed her secretarial duties wearing only high heels and a smile.

• **Gene Fowler:** The Denver-born journalist/Hollywood writer, hailed as "The Rabelais of the Rockies," was once the tenth best-paid man in the United States — yet had such contempt for his film studio work that he demanded he be paid daily, as would a day laborer. "The truth — Fowler was as out of place in Hollywood as a third leg on a rumba dancer," said Ben Hecht. "As what man of talent isn't?" Regarding his cronies with both simpatico and compassion, Fowler preserved the frivolities and genius of these men in books such as *Good Night, Sweet Prince* and *Minutes of the Last Meeting*.

• **John Carradine:** The cadaverous character player first won notice parading up and down Hollywood Boulevard, wearing a cape and slouch hat, roaring Shakespeare. Success would not tame his eccentricity. He'd announce one night at the Garden of Allah that he was Jesus Christ and would prove it by walking across the swimming pool. He sank.

• **Alan Mowbray:** The British thespian tallied up a remarkable amount of film and TV appearances yet despised the sight of his own face on screen and avoided all his own credits. A popular toastmaster and admitted scoundrel, he was also a pioneer of the Screen Actors Guild, writing the check so that the rebellious group (regarded in 1933 as subversive) could gain legal representation.

• **Roland Young:** The mousy actor, also a Britisher and Topper of the movies, sported a mustache and monocle and specialized in scene-stealing larceny. Barrymore used to laugh that, when Young played Dr. Watson to Barrymore's Sherlock Holmes in the 1922 film, the star felt so sorry for his meek little co-player that he suggested bits of business for him. Later seeing the film, Barrymore realized Young had stolen virtually every scene.

• **Anthony Quinn:** Once denounced by Cecil B. DeMille as "a half-breed," he bounced back by marrying DeMille's daughter Katherine. Destined for two Oscars, the young and stalwart Quinn — who fathered a child at 81 ("Zorba the Stud," read a tabloid headline) — inspired the joke that he was primarily a Bundy Drive Boy because he had Decker's blood type and willingly reported for emergency transfusions.

• **John Barrymore:** "The Monster." The Boys practiced swordplay in front of the roaring fireplace, gave a spirited midnight reading of *Macbeth* (Decker, in top hat with flour on his face, creating a ghostly effect), swapped tall tales, and protected each other from the horrors of their own private demons. Each man had a quixotic defiance of the Film Industry and a loyal, almost child-like devotion to the others. After Barrymore's funeral, Decker, who had painted his portrait numerous times, unveiled his latest evocation. It was a Calvary-esque Barrymore, in loincloth, crucified between two naked women — his sloe-eyed last wife who had fleeced and divorced him, and her mother.

"These men lived intensely," wrote Gene Fowler, "as do children and poets and jaguars."

If John Barrymore had been the Bundy Drive Boys' center-ring attraction, John Decker had been their demonic ringmaster. He'd been the man who kept the calliope shrieking away, long past the witching hour.

The bier at Alta Loma was based on the deceased's painting of Van Gogh's funeral, with casket on a pool table and Decker's famous deathbed sketch of Barrymore, suffering a mortal's final death agonies. The sketch, crowned with a spray of red roses, stood propped on Decker's coffin, an evocation of his art, their friendship, and Barrymore's prophecy of coming back as a ghost.

"If you think I'm joking about the visitation," Barrymore had warned one rainy night, pointing a dramatic finger in the firelight, "wait!"

John Decker's widow, his third wife — he never legally divorced the first two — was nearly hysterical with grief. Blonde, attractive Phyllis Decker carried the soignée look of a leading lady in a Bogart melodrama. Once more she admired Decker's large, broken, almost phallic nose — and further damaged in recent years by a pet parrot — but winced as she regarded his mustache. It was a naturally red color, and reminded him of the two things that, as Barrymore had expressed, Decker despised most: sunsets and his auburn-haired mother. Phyllis knew why he had hated them; so had Barrymore and the Bundy Drive gang.

Using her mascara wand, Phyllis darkened the cadaver's mustache one last time.

A recording of Decker reciting Cyrano de Bergerac's defiant "No thank you" speech played over and over at the bier — another of the deceased's requests:

To sing, to laugh, to dream, to walk in my own way and be alone...

Many mourners had come only for the booze, and for a morbid proximity to the diminishing legend of the Bundy Drive Boys. Donations were necessary to pay for the wake. Few were forthcoming.

> Then... as Gene Fowler wrote in a personal letter to Ben Hecht (not present at the funeral):
> There was a spray of red roses hanging on the Barrymore deathbed sketch and, so help me, God! I am told that at the very moment the minister said, "Let us pray," this spray of flowers came down with a plop upon the unopened half of the casket lid. I remember that you once said that if anyone could come back from what is known as the Great Beyond, that Barrymore could do it. Perhaps this was some kind of a benediction, or its antithesis...

The shocker nearly caused the widow to faint and scared the hell out of tipsy mourners who screamed at the spectral surprise. It was as if Hamlet's ghost had conjured itself at the bier, as if "Mad Jack" had fled his tomb at L.A.'s Calvary Cemetery to fulfill his ghostly promise and to pay his final respects.

Yet the true ghostly spectacle was still to come.

The hearse left the Strip, heading south to Inglewood Cemetery. The pallbearers, including actor/art collector Vincent Price, artist Philip Paval, and Alan Mowbray and Anthony Quinn bore the coffin to the crematory. As was the custom at Inglewood, the pallbearers received the invitation to watch the actual cremation, and they reluctantly agreed. The open casket and the corpse headed for the fire.

And then, as Paval later wrote in his memoir, it happened. As if by some horrific final prank, the satanic-looking corpse with mascara on its mustache suddenly sat up in flames. It was as if the cadaver were on a carnival joyride into hell, enjoying its own fiery immolation. It was, by the law of physics, a reaction of the body to the blast of heat, but the Bundy Drive Boys imposed their own mystical spin on John Decker's Phoenix-like resurrection.

Barrymore and other deceased Bundy Drive Boys would rally and join him.

Part I
The 1920s

New York, Hollywood, The Isle of Man, Weimar Berlin, London, the Boston Charles Street Jail, The Denver Market Street Whorehouse, The Pornographic Doll House, The California Desert, Elsinore on 42nd Street and Points Between and Beyond

I painted a lot of pictures, both serious and satire, in the last three decades, and I never got rich. Yet, I have been wealthier than most — because in all these maddening, dizzy and daffy decades, I have had Friends — great actors, great writers, great painters, great singers, great creditors and great heels. In New York, before the Second World War, I was the center of a streamlined ale-guzzling, word-baiting coffee-house group, the kind that Doc Johnson and Addison and Swift and Steele belonged to in the early 18th century, and I heard things ordinary humans would pay fortunes to see, and always I was a part of big and screwy events.

— John Decker, as told to Irving Wallace in "Heroes with Hangovers," a projected three-part feature for *Liberty* Magazine, May 1941

John Decker, extreme left, postwar Germany

Chapter One

The Old Toymaker, "That Red-Haired Whore" and the Master Poisoner

"We are too big for our bodies. We spring the seams, then blow to pieces."
— John Decker

The wind blows cold off the Irish Sea at sunset on the Isle of Man.

The Isle, an archipelago, has a fascinating history. Between 700 and 900 A.D., "Mann" was a Viking outpost; today, it's a self-governing crown dependency. Pop music disciples honor it as the birthplace of the Bee Gees. Motorcycle enthusiasts acknowledge it for the "Isle of Man TT," an annual cycle race that dates back to 1907. In ancient times, there was the belief one could stand on "Snaefel," the Isle's highest mountain, and from its 2,036'-high crest, behold seven kingdoms: Mann, Scotland, England, Ireland, Wales, the Sea — and Heaven.

What John Decker observed on the Isle of Man was the kingdom of Hell.

For two years, John Decker, Prisoner-of-War via freakish circumstance, defiantly survived in the Isle of Man's World War I internment camp. There he watched the sunset from behind the electric barbed wire, feeling the cold and approaching darkness, anticipating the weeping in the night from his fellow prisoners, the wails of hopelessness, the screams from their nightmares.

Among his fellow prisoners was an old German toymaker. Some of the incarcerated clung to God, others to the vision of the sweetheart at home, but the toymaker's beatific image was his son. Now grown, the son — the toymaker claimed — would surely write to him, maybe even enter the stockade and visit him. The old man cherished the boy's frayed picture, until the day that some bitter men, weary of the tales of the wonderful boy, ripped the picture from the father's hands and spitefully tore it to pieces.

As John Decker remembered it, the old toymaker cried all day.

Some time later, the miracle feast day came. A guard brought the man's son into the stockade — not as a visitor, but as a POW. This didn't enter the old man's mind. "I knew you'd come!" he cried, joyfully staggering to the boy who'd been his inspiration to survive. In *Minutes of the Last Meeting*, Gene Fowler recorded Decker's climax of the saga:

> The son just stood there glaring at his father, not making a move. When the old man opened his arms to embrace his son the young fellow began to curse him. It was terrible. He blamed his father for his arrest, saying that the letters written by the old man had been intercepted and had incriminated him. He spat in the old man's face. And then, my God! The feeble old fellow stood as if stunned by a sudden blow. After a few moments he got some kind of weird strength. He turned, ran, and threw himself against the high voltage wire. He shook in a great spasm. He did not scream. His body turned halfway around, then hung there against the wire and setting sun, like God on the cross.

"I saw too much and learned too much — most of it degrading," said John Decker. "Only when I paint or drink can I forget it now."

John Decker was born November 8, 1895, in San Francisco — or so went the legend in his lifetime. After his 1947 death, his widow Phyllis told the Los Angeles press that John Decker was actually Baron Leopold Wolfgang von der Decken. The widow Decker (or von der Decken) revealed:

> None of his close friends — John Barrymore, Errol Flynn, any of them — knew about it. After his reputation as the great American artist grew so rapidly, he just decided to say nothing about it.
>
> At the outbreak of the second World War, John was quite worried. He destroyed all his German correspondence and papers.
>
> Of course, his biographers will tell about it and that's one reason why I decided to go ahead now.

Phyllis Decker's words reveal a certain delusion about her husband's ability to keep secrets from the Bundy Drive Boys. In *Minutes of the Last Meeting*, Gene Fowler describes a desperate Decker pouring out the true story of his ancestry to his cronies, fearful of yet another wartime incarceration. As for her trust in her husband having "biographers," Phyllis Decker would live more than 40 years longer than her husband and die long before anyone expressed interest in the life story of "the great American artist."

Count von der Decken, John's father, was a Prussian Guards colonel. His mother was a singer with the Berlin opera. They came to London when the boy was small, and Decker's nightmare image of his mother was always that of a red-haired, vainglorious diva. The memory took on horrific size after she abandoned her son when he was only 13 years old. His father, heartbroken, soon disappeared too.

"That red-haired whore!" John Decker would roar in his Bundy Drive studio over 30 years later, often as the night approached. The Bundy Drive familiars surely knew a variety of bastardly whores, but they were distinctly aware of whom he spoke. The sunset conjured up not only the dead, hanging toymaker on the Isle of Man, but the red tresses of his monstrous mother.

The Boys knew when it would be another rough night for John. Such nights came frequently — even though Phyllis vigilantly closed the curtains every evening, in hopes of sparing her husband the agonies of his tormenting reminder.

Life as an orphan was suddenly Dickensian, as Baron Leopold scrambled for survival in the London streets. He painted scenery at His Majesty's Theatre, and studied at the Slade School (where John Barrymore had once studied) with noted artist Walter Sickert. In her 2002 book, *Portrait of a Killer: Jack the Ripper Case Closed*, Patricia Cornwell names Sickert (who died in 1942) as the Ripper himself. "By age five," wrote Cornwell, presenting Ripper motivation, "Sickert had undergone three horrific surgeries for a fistula"— a genital deformity. Ms. Cornwell goes on:

> Sickert's early boyhood was traumatized by medical violence... it can create fears of castration. Sickert's operations would have resulted in strictures and scarring that could have made erections painful or impossible. He may have suffered partial amputation....

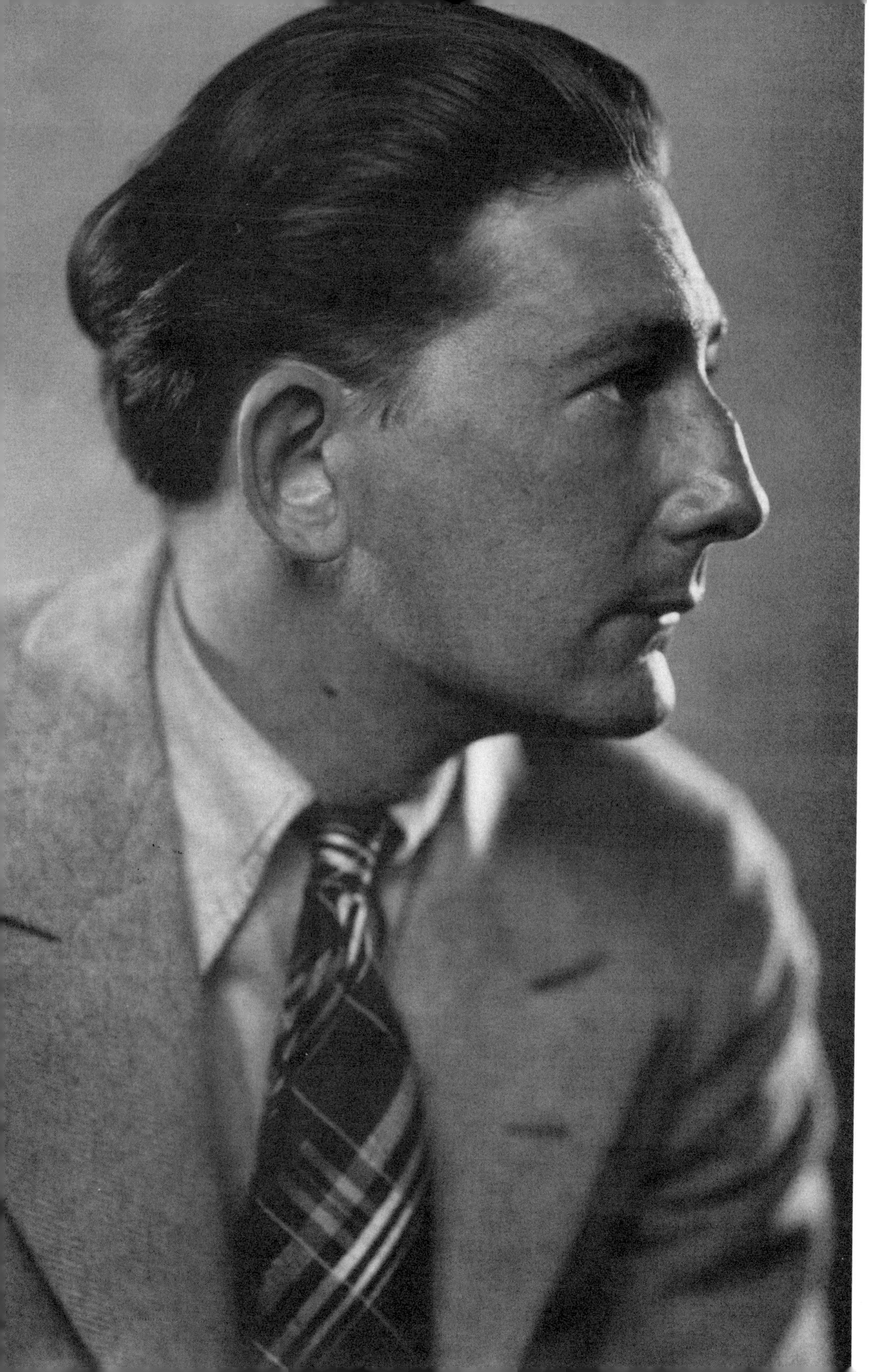

If Walter Sickert was the Ripper, Decker would have been his student a quarter-century after the Ripper's 1888 reign of terror.

Decker was soon to meet his Fagin. He was a London art forger, and under the rapscallion's tutelage, Decker learned to dash off Old Masters. By now, Decker was an adult —lean but powerfully built, handsome profile with prominent nose, and a mane (to his distress) reminiscent of his mother's auburn hair. It's easy to conjure Decker and his old forger tutor, buying old frames from sooty antique shops to brace the "Van Gogh" or "Gauguin" or "Modigliani" one or the other had dashed off the previous night. The tourists proved easy prey, and many would bequeath the paintings to their families or favorite museums who, to this day, believe they possess genuine Old Masters paintings.

John Decker, with a voracious appetite for hedonism, celebrated his success with ample samplings of liquor and prostitutes. Punishment would follow, but not for the expected reason. A sandy-whiskered patron of Decker's talent had been buying his paintings, only to include espionage messages inside the canvas and send them to the Fatherland. Authorities denounced John Decker as a German spy, and off he went to the Tower of London — and from there to his horrific two years on the Isle of Man. Nightmares abounded. John Decker later told Dolores Costello, John Barrymore's wife, that he and his fellow POW prisoners only survived because they ate the bodies of those who had died from malnutrition.

The Armistice. Freedom. John Decker, painter/forger/former POW, traveled the world, much of which was in a dizzying postwar spiritual free-for-all. "I painted my way through France, Germany, Austria, Italy and Africa," said Decker. His cavalier attitude about life battled with a desire (and genius) for survival, and some of what Decker saw in his travels had lasting impact on the impressionable man.

First he went to his birthplace Germany, just in time for the Weimar era and the rise of such attractions as Anita Berber, "the Priestess of Depravity," who — as noted by her biographer Mel Gordon — "scandalized Weimar Berlin, appearing in nightclubs and casinos, radiantly naked except for an elegant sable wrap, a pet monkey hanging from her neck and a silver brooch packed with cocaine."

In 1921, Decker sailed as a stowaway to the United States on the *La Lorraine*. New York City offered its own fascinations. It was the era of the "Jazz Baby."

John Decker, early '20s, New York

The Roaring '20s, the Big Apple, Prohibition — it was a time fascinating for the stylistics of its fashion, the brazenness of its entertainment and the ferocity of its amusements. For a night in New York, the Jazz Baby might adorn herself in a Netheralls corset (a beauty secret of the Follies girls, or so the advertisement promised), black silk $1.75-per-pair stockings, a Paris frock, a string of pearls, black satin "opera pump" high heels, and to crown it all, a "Chapeau Nouveau de Paris," worn with the brim up in the front, like a pirate female impersonator.

Thus did the Jazz Baby, resplendent in all her stylistic fashion, prowl New York at night for sensation.

On Broadway, 1922 was the Year of the Voluptuary. Jeanne Eagels slinked and vamped as immortal tropics hooker, Miss Sadie Thompson, in Somerset Maugham's *Rain*. David Belasco, the "Bishop of Broadway" (who dressed the part in black suit and clerical collar) was offering his sexpot attraction Lenore Ulric as Kiki ("Miss Ulric outdoes all expectations — even the wildest," reported *The New York Times*).

The musical revues also took a racy tone. Florenz Ziegfeld glorified the American girl via The Ziegfeld Follies, starring Will Rogers, while George White promised a "Rare Collection of New Beauties" in his Scandals, with headliner W. C. Fields.

There were horror melodramas — *The Cat and the Canary*, *The Monster*, *The Bat*. John Barrymore would climax the 1922 season as Hamlet, spicing up Shakespeare's Melancholy Dane in a virtuoso display of sex, perversity and horror.

Then there were the movies, offering the same "hot" sell — a smoldering Rudolph Valentino in *Blood and Sand*, an athletic Douglas Fairbanks as Robin Hood. There was Erich Von Stroheim's *Foolish Wives*, a sex spectacle advertised by Universal Studios as the first million dollar picture, starring "Von" ("The Man You Love to Hate!") as a depraved count, flanked by two female villains, and featuring a climax in which the star, in a final flash of perversity, tries to rape a retarded girl.

At least as titillating as the films were the 1922 headlines from Hollywood. There was the February murder of William Desmond Taylor, shot in his Los Angeles bungalow; the never-solved homicide wrecking the careers of "Female Chaplin" Mabel Normand (seen leaving the bungalow shortly before the shot) and Mary Miles Minter (whose lingerie and at least one love letter were found at the murder site). Then there was Fatty Arbuckle, who in April of '22 won a "Not Guilty" verdict (after three trials) in the charge of his rape/murder of starlet Virginia Rappe. He even received an official apology for the accusation. Nevertheless, the movie fans remembered more vividly the popular account of a giggling Arbuckle leaving Rappe's bedroom at San Francisco's Saint Francis Hotel, wearing his pajamas and Virginia's hat, complaining that the screaming woman in the boudoir whom he had allegedly squashed under his 320-lb. girth (and, again allegedly, violated with a Coca-Cola bottle) "makes too much noise." And there were reports that "the sad-rum-and morphine-wracked body" of movie star Wallace Reid was slowly rotting away, strapped down in a padded cell in a Los Angeles sanitarium, where he died in 1923.

There were racy books such as James Branch Cabell's *Jurgen, a Comedy of Justice* and Ben Hecht's *Fantazius Mallare* — both Medieval fantasies banned for obscenity. All in all there was plenty to savor, and to make one forget or ignore entirely such facts of life as Mussolini marching on Rome, or the unleashed "curse" of King Tut's newly-discovered tomb, or Henry Ford warning workers that any of his employees caught with liquor on their breath faced immediate firing.

And there were the speakeasies, the on-the-rise gangsters, the temptations of what Frederick Lewis Allen purple-prosed as "champagne baths, midnight revels, petting parties in the purple dawn ... white kisses, red kisses, pleasure-mad daughters, sensation-craving mothers ... the truth — bold, naked, sensational."

The era rivaled the 1960s and in many ways was more exhilarating and dangerous. Enter into the exotic arena 26-year-old aspiring actor/scenic designer John Decker, who relished a story that captured the mad, Barnum & Bailey atmosphere of the U.S. 1920s:

> Two Englishmen, in London, were standing outside a store looking at some bottled merchandise. Near the goods was a sign reading, "Buy Snyder's Vinegar."
>
> Said one Englishman to the other, "Here in England we don't know how to advertise. Look at that tiny sign, 'Buy Snyder's Vinegar.' Now in America it's different. If they were advertising the same product, they'd rent space atop a building at Times Square. Have a huge cross, a hundred feet high, in neons, and on the cross, in electric bulbs, outlined the crucified figure of Christ. Beside him, forty feet high, also in dazzling electric bulbs, a Roman soldier holding a spear with a sponge dipped in vinegar at the end. And a huge flashing sign, illuminated, with Christ saying, 'Take it away. It ain't Snyder's!'"

At first, Fate was kind.

Surely due at least partially to his rather sinister handsomeness, Decker landed a plum part in which he would portray the title role of "The Master Poisoner," a Grand Guignol playlet by Ben Hecht and Maxwell Bodenheim — a team of irreverent rebels who were soulmates with their newly-discovered star. As Chicago newspaper reporters, Hecht and Bodenheim were already carving their legends — one of which was a debate they once waged for the Chicago Book and Play Club: "Resolved: People Who Attend Literary Debates Are Fools." Hecht, taking the affirmative, stood up, stared silently at Book and Play clubbers in their tuxes and evening gowns, then turned to Bodenheim.

"I rest my case," he said.

Now Bodenheim stood, stared at the crowd silently for a full minute, and turned to Hecht. "You win," he shrugged.

"The Master Poisoner" told a terrible tale, as described in William MacAdams' Hecht biography:

> ... the play's master poisoner ... has created his masterpiece, a poison he believes will arrest Death. He administers the poison to his wife Fana, who becomes inhumanly beautiful but doesn't die as expected. Death takes the master poisoner instead....

It came complete with richly morbid dialogue such as:

> Your last poison of moth blood produced an effect so exquisitely monstrous that even death was appalled. Ah, the bones of an old woman, dissolving within her, left her body a loose grimace...

Bodenheim (fated to be found murdered with his wife in 1954 in a cheap Bowery room, after being reduced to begging with a bogus "I Am Blind" sign around his neck) allegedly based his villain on poet Sherwood Anderson, whom he despised. "The Master Poisoner" was just a part of *A Fantastic Fricassee*, "A New Sparkling Revue," which was set to open at the Greenwich Village Theatre September 11, 1922. A grab bag of bizarre skits and songs, the offerings included young baritone Jimmie Kemper performing a Japanese dirge as he faked hara-kiri — an act so tastelessly creepy that it was dropped during the show's run. Then there was the climactic "Virgins of the Sun," a near-nudity spectacle (with scenery by Decker) featuring (as Alan Dale of the *New York American* described it) "sinuous young women" who "wiggled their shapes,

tossed their manes, and behaved altogether like sufferers from delirium tremens."
The ... *Fricassee* won a splash of New York infamy Sunday, November 19, 1922, after the company visited Sing-Sing to perform the show for prisoners — only to have the warden cancel the show after fearing what effect those wiggling, mane-tossing Virgins of the Sun would have on the restless inmates.

Lasting 112 performances, *A Fantastic Fricassee* is notable in theatre history primarily for the presence of Jeanette MacDonald, MGM's super diva of the 1930s, who joined the show after its opening in October of 1922. Decker was still in the show when 'The Iron Butterfly' arrived, but later editions of the ... *Fricassee* program fail to list his name as an actor, or *The Master Poisoner* playlet. As *Newsweek* reported:

> One night, after five or six bourbons, he walked on the stage and fell flat on his face. After that, as he tells it, he gave up the theatre and took up drinking.

Inevitably, the accident took on mythic proportions — the yarn eventually spinning that Decker toppled over the footlights, fell head-first into the orchestra pit and landed with his face in a tuba. *A Fantastic Fricassee* was John Decker's only New York stage appearance.

Truly strange is the fact that *The Greenwich Village Follies of 1922*, for which Decker claimed to have been set designer, opened September 12, 1922 — exactly one day after the premiere of *A Fantastic Fricassee!* How Decker juggled his *Follies* scenic duties with his *Fricassee* rehearsals is baffling.

The Greenwich Village Follies of 1922 was a hit, with the redoubtable Alexander Woollcott of *The New York Times* praising the show "as festive and good-looking and entertaining a revue as these eyes have seen." The production ran an impressive 209 performances.

Decker's apparent double-dipping, along with his falling-face-first-into-a-tuba saga, effectively blackballed him from any major future Broadway assignments. In 1922, he had married 18-year-old Helen McChesney. Considering that their daughter Gloria (soon separated from her father, only to pursue him 20 years later in Hollywood) was born May 19, 1923, the Deckers must have been expecting during his Broadway misadventures.

Soon he turned to sketching. For a time he did drawings for Walter Winchell on the old *New York Graphic*. John Decker also devoted himself to caricature work for the *New York Evening World*, working at the desk next to famed critic Heywood Broun.

Decker was creating his *Evening World* sketches just in time for the most historic theatre event of the 1922 season. The star of the play was a man John Decker hailed as "brilliant" and "profane." "I have never had a better friend nor known a human more thoroughly nor enjoyed one's comradeship more," said John Decker of John Barrymore.

To Mickey
best love

John Decker
in *The Master Poisoner*

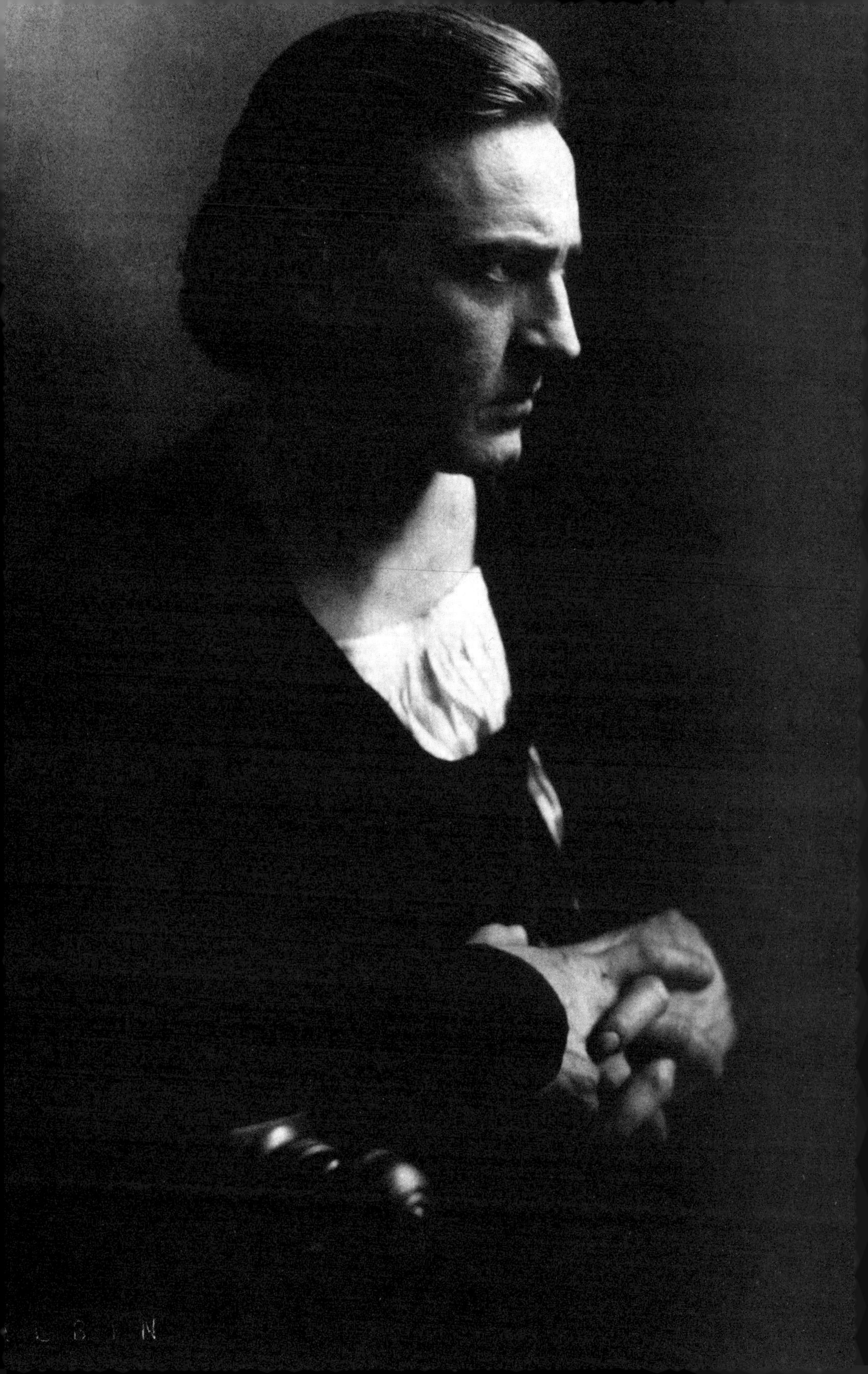

Chapter Two

Mad Jack's Travelin' One-Man Freak Show

> That dirty, red-whiskered son-of-a-bitch!
> That bastard puts his prick in my mother's cunt every night!
> —John Barrymore, musing on Hamlet's motivation

The world hailed him as "The Great Profile," but his most remarkable feature was his eyes.

John Barrymore had mad, bright, distant eyes — the eyes one sees in portraits of saints and photographs of serial killers. In *Svengali* (1931), perhaps his greatest cinema performance, Barrymore's eyes chillingly dilated as he bewitched Marian Marsh, the blonde-wigged heroine. Warner Bros. added primitive contact lenses for intensity.

Barrymore didn't need them.

It was his eyes that inspired John Barrymore — whose most profound nightmare was to die mad in an asylum, as had his own father — to prefer showcasing his left profile. His right side, he claimed, had "all the nuance of a morbid deep-sea fish." Those tell-tale eyes, directly gazing out into an audience from a giant screen, risked far too much exposure ... possibly gave away too many secrets of a man whose Paradise Lost fall surpassed that of any Golden Age star, both in its spectacular sordidness, and the man's masochistic revelry in his own ruin.

Barrymore as Hamlet

On the night of November 16, 1922, on the stage of New York's Sam H. Harris Theatre, John Barrymore exposed his tormented spirit and made theatre history. As John Corbin reported the next morning in the *New York Times*:

> The atmosphere of historic happening surrounded John Barrymore's appearance last night as the Prince of Denmark; it was unmistakable as it was indefinable. It sprang from the quality and intensity of the applause, from the hushed murmurs that swept at the most unexpected moments, from the silent crowds that all evening long swarmed about the theatre entrance. It was nowhere — and everywhere. In all likelihood we have a new and lasting Hamlet.

The *Hamlet* of 1922 was a new model, one for the era. Barrymore's melancholy Dane was sly, demonic, garbed all in black, a fallen Lucifer.

"Here, if ever, was a scurvy, mother-loving drip of a man!" Barrymore exulted of his Hamlet at his final birthday party in 1942. "A ranting, pious pervert! But clever, mark you! Like all homicidal maniacs! And how I loved to play him. The dear boy and I were meant for each other."

The most striking aspect of Barrymore's Hamlet was the Dane's incestuous love for his mother, Queen Gertrude, played by Blanche Yurka as a voluptuary in cascading fair hair and alluring scarlet gown.

John Barrymore provided the awed Broadway audiences another of his "spiritual striptease" performances (an expression coined by Chicago historian Lloyd Lewis) flashing his personal torments and obsessions wide and far..

Mad Jack had a laugh, a wild cackle that his late-in-life crony Phil Rhodes likened to "a mad insect." There was his cry when he sexually climaxed — a banshee scream that not only saluted that evening's lady, but often succeeded in making her forget that she herself had not yet climaxed. There was his rapier-sharp wit. One night in 1920, as Barrymore's Richard III howled "My kingdom for a horse!" a heckler dared to whinny.

"Hold, make haste," volleyed Barrymore, staring and pointing at the heckler, "and saddle yonder braying ass!" The audience cheered.

Audiences loved John's brother Lionel, chuckling appreciatively at his grab bag of mannerisms that in time reduced the stage and cinema's top character star to a wheezy cliché in a wheelchair. They revered his sister Ethel, who late in life overcame her own sins to become a saintly First Lady of the Cinema, professing off-screen that suffering was desirable, for it brought one to his or her knees. ("And isn't that the best place from which to pray? On your knees?") But audiences feared Jack. He was the Mad Genius, so much so that Warner Bros. starred him in a 1931 film of that title. Candid pictures of Mad Jack in the 1920s frequently reveal him in stylishly cocked hat and flowing coat, almost always with a cigarette, posing in a mix of vanity and mockery, seemingly radiating the "half-crazed actor" pejorative used to describe John Wilkes Booth. In his most beautiful era, Barrymore truly resembled, as his second wife once sighed, "an archangel," but gave the startling impression of being an archangel taunted and possessed by a demon.

He seemed dangerous. One of the reasons audiences laughed so raucously at John Barrymore in his pitiful final act was that his danger seemed safely drowned in deep seas of alcohol and long-lost women — or as Barrymore called them, "twittering vaginas." Yet even in the dregs, he at times would rally, resurrect his old demonic splendor and be ominous to behold.

John Barrymore also possessed talent as a visual artist and a lifelong fascination with the strange and the bizarre. His first dream was to illustrate the works of Edgar Allan Poe. A drawing he made of himself as Dr. Jekyll and Mr. Hyde is hauntingly good. Much later, in California, he sketched John Decker's "Astral Self" — a slavering, pinheaded, leering monster.

The Barrymore family can trace its dramatic tradition to 1752. It was also a family of addictions — with various inspirations for the dependencies. His father was Maurice Barrymore, the handsome stage star, born of English parents in India in 1847; the legend goes that he was suckled there by a goat, and the joke went that he spent the rest of his life proving it. In a letter dated January 12, 1943, Dr. Harold Thomas Hyman, M.D., wrote to Gene Fowler, aware of the coming Barrymore biography *Good Night, Sweet Prince*. Hyman claimed "many illuminating conversations" with Barrymore, writing that he

> ... had a hatred of his father that was not erased by the passage of time. One of the things that impressed him in this animosity was the hairiness and smell of his father, who was apparently a very hirsute individual who was addicted to tobacco and had a combination stink of masculine secretion and the noxious weed.
>
> To add to Jack's disgust, his father was apparently fond of embracing him and this would almost make him sick to his stomach.

Above, Barrymore's illustration of Jekyll and Hyde; right, Barrymore's Mr. Hyde, with finger extensions

34 Hollywood's Hellfire Club

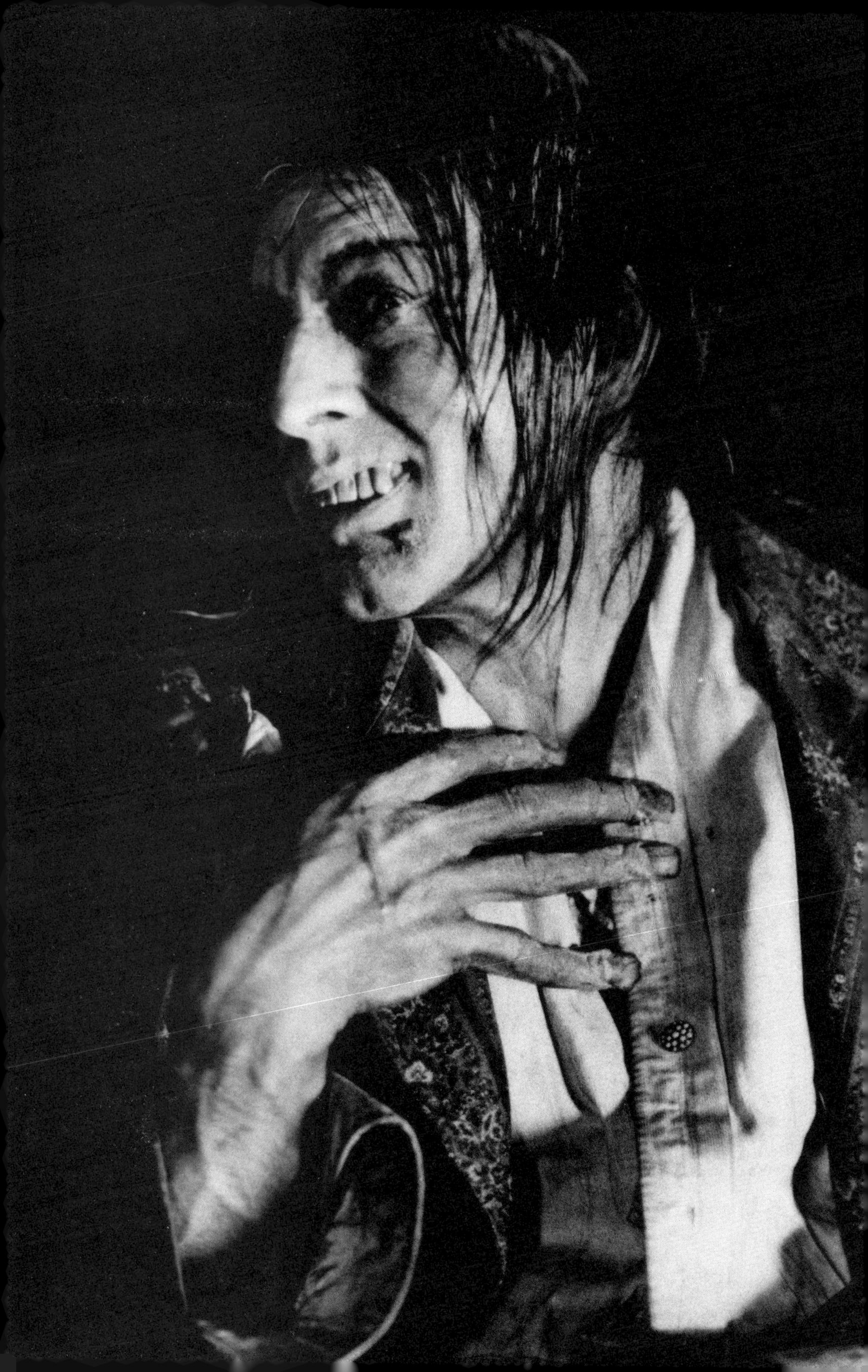

The memory of Maurice Barrymore's death in 1905 at the Long Island Home for the Insane at Amityville haunted his son mercilessly. Wracked by syphilis, strapped down to a table in an asylum, hopelessly, wildly insane, so ravaged that his corpse was unrecognizable, Maurice Barrymore had played a real-life death scene that forever terrified his son, who had nightmares of suffering the same fate.

The demons had come early. John's mother had died when he was 10, and his father remarried Mamie Floyd, a young sensualist who, so the legend goes, had a taste for exotic sex. Phil Rhodes, actor and Marlon Brando's longtime makeup man, had met Barrymore in the twilight years, and says:

> Barrymore was in love with his father's second wife, a very young actress. She had turned him on to sex. As soon as Maurice would come home from a play, John could hear him as he fucked this young girl. The father had picked up all kinds of diseases, and he was dirty and filthy now, and Barrymore would hear them, his father grunting and jerking her around the bedroom...
>
> Yet Barrymore loved his father. There is a photograph of him kissing his father's picture. And he wanted to be buried with him in Philadelphia.

Another major trauma came at age 15 with the death of his grandmother, Louisa Drew, "Mummum," probably the only adult with whom he had felt safe and secure. When Barrymore died 45 years later, "Mummum" was his final utterance. Yet, by the time of Mummum's death, John was already twisted — Dr. Samuel Hirshfeld wrote in a 1934 medical report that Barrymore "since the age of 14 has been more or less a chronic drunkard."

John Barrymore ascended as an actor, at his best with brother Lionel. *Peter Ibbetson* (1917), based on George du Maurier's novel, saw matinee idol John in the lushly romantic title role and a climax in which John's Peter, learning from Lionel's Colonel that Peter's mother had been the Colonel's mistress, and that he is the Colonel's natural son, kills the villain, beating him to death with a cane. It overwhelmed the audiences; a woman was hospitalized for "an unaccountable weeping hysteria."

John was underwhelmed, describing his Peter Ibbetson as "a marshmallow in a blonde wig."

Even more awe-inspiring was *The Jest* (1919). The play was set in the era of Lorenzo the Magnificent in Renaissance Florence, with John as Gianetto, a spiritual yet kinky painter of Madonnas, costumed in fire-red wig and green "symmetricals" (padded tights), singing "Madrigal of May." Lionel was Neri, a mustached, glowering bully, who has "pricked grotesqueries" into Gianetto's skin and tossed him into the Arno River. John's Gianetto tricks Lionel's Neri into killing his own brother, and Neri goes horrifically mad.

"*Ave Maria gratia plena!*" climaxes the triumphant Madonna painter, reveling in his nemesis' insanity.

The Jest was a sensation, and a panel of 12 women voted John Barrymore the second most fascinating man in the world (with first place going to the Prince of Wales). Yet he was contemptuous of his own handsomeness and called his Gianetto a "decadent string bean."

Barrymore was starring in silent movies too, such as *Raffles, the Amateur Cracksman*, (1917), but was cynical about his work there as well:

> In the silent days, I found myself continually making frantic and futile faces to try to express unexpressable ideas — like a man behind a closed window on a train that is moving out of a station who is trying, in pantomime, to tell his wife, on the platform outside, that he forgot to pack his blue pajamas and that he wants her to send them to him care of Detweiler, 1032 West 189th Street, New York City!

In March 1920, John Barrymore opened at Broadway's Plymouth Theatre as Richard III. Always fascinated by animals, Barrymore based his "foul lump of deformity" on a red tarantula with a gray bald spot, which he admired at the Bronx Zoo:

> I have oft heard my mother say
> I came into the world with my legs forward…
> The midwife wonder'd, and the women cried,
> O! Jesus BLESS us, he's BORN with TEETH!
> And so I was; which plainly signified
> That I should snarl and bite
> And play the dog…

Barrymore's Richard III was a cackling Prince of Darkness, and surviving photographs of him in the role are fascinating. Spidery, yes, but demonic, sporting a long black wig with bangs, a vulture's smile and a come-hither stare. His black copper armor became so hot under the stage lights that the crew had to spray it with a hose before the star could remove it. He performed an acrobatic death scene, and on opening night, Barrymore became a bit too acrobatic — his wig went flying. Yet nobody in the Plymouth Theatre laughed.

Nobody dared to.

John Barrymore captured the warped, tortured soul of Richard III. He later claimed in a rare mood of artistic reflection, that it was his finest performance. "It was the first time I ever actually got inside the character I was playing," he told Gene Fowler. "I mean I thought I was the character, and in my dreams I knew that I was he."

His star kept rising. And then on Sunday, March 28, 1920 — while *Richard III* was still playing — Barrymore inspired sensation worthy of a rock star: Paramount's *Dr. Jekyll and Mr. Hyde* premiered at New York's Rivoli Theatre. So hell-bent was the crowd to see the film that hysteria erupted outside the theatre as the crowd broke the Rivoli's door and shattered two windows.

Barrymore had vowed to transform into the horrible Hyde as Richard Mansfield had done on stage in 1887 — with no makeup. After his Jekyll (handsome as an archangel) drinks his unholy elixir, he suffers manically (and again, acrobatically) then aims his leering, hideous face at the camera. Camera cuts and trickery actually allowed makeup: a conical skull, a scraggly wig, large horse teeth, and long skeletal fingers (a special delight for Barrymore — his own fingers were stubby and he hated them).

Perhaps the most evocative word-picture of Barrymore's Hyde transformation came via the actor's vampy fourth and final wife, Elaine Barrie Barrymore, in her 1964 memoir *All My Sins Remembered*. The notorious "Ariel" to his "Caliban" in the scandalous headlines (and whose own infamy included the star role in the 1937 short subject *How to Undress in Front of Your Husband*) remembered a pre-divorce night in Hollywood when she promised Barrymore a beer if he'd "do Jekyll and Hyde for me." Barrymore's Jekyll posed at the fireplace, downed his elixir from an empty glass, wildly clutched his throat and heart — then turned to Elaine:

> My blood ran cold. There wasn't a feature that was recognizable. His face was contorted by the presence of sheer evil. No! It wasn't even evil. This was no cliché of cruelty or bestiality... This was utter amorality. The smile made you crawl with its obscenity. The secrets of hell were unlocked... I sat frozen in terror as he slowly hobbled toward me like a giant crab. One wasn't frightened of death at this monster's hands but of the unknown. The look of lechery did not spell rape or violence but something unheard of, so loathsome that man had still to articulate it. I almost fell into a faint....

Barrymore played up the sexuality of *Dr. Jekyll and Mr. Hyde* with his two leading ladies — "virginal" Martha Mansfield and "voluptuous" Nita Naldi. Ms. Mansfield was fated for

The Beloved Rogue
is burned alive

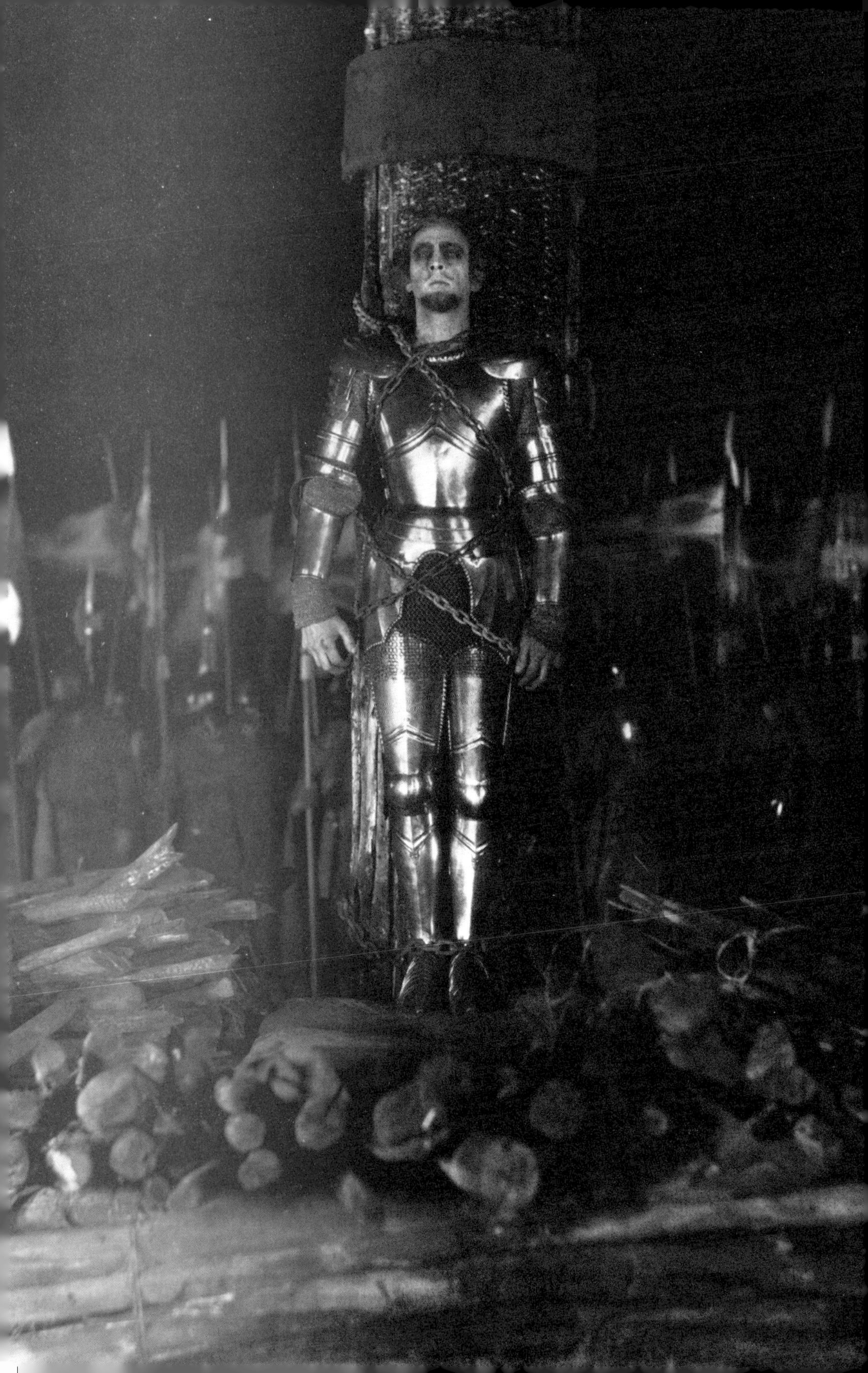

a terrible real-life death; in 1923, on location in Texas filming *The Warrens of Virginia*, her dress caught on fire from a carelessly tossed match and she burned to death. Yet watching her most famous performance in *Dr. Jekyll and Mr. Hyde*, one imagines her near-desecration at the claws of Barrymore's Hyde might have been an even more horrible fate.

Audiences applauded thunderously at the finale of *Dr. Jekyll and Mr. Hyde* and left the Rivoli stunned, as if they had truly witnessed a miracle. John Barrymore, characteristically, was unimpressed by his own virtuoso triumph:

> The critics said my portrayal of the horrible Hyde was something magnificent. All I did was put on a harrowing make-up, twist my face, claw at my throat, and roll on the floor. That, the critics said, was acting. And, may my worthy ancestors forgive me, I began to agree with them!

The words, again, hid the truth of the actor's passion. *Richard III* closed a few days after *Dr. Jekyll and Mr. Hyde* opened, and Barrymore — exhausted from playing Hyde, Richard III and battling his second wife, poetess Michael Strange — suffered a breakdown, entering a sanitarium in White Plains to recover. Surely there he remembered his father's downfall, and despaired about his own potential fate.

Barrymore's *Dr. Jekyll and Mr. Hyde* stage performance remains, 87 years later, an astounding piece of acting, and poetically prophetic of the sordid variation of the roles he'd play offscreen in his tragic later life. Even before his 1922 *Hamlet*, it was his first great public "spiritual striptease."

Barrymore's Hyde spooked not only wife number four, Elaine Barrie, but their dog Timmy, who barked so hysterically that Elaine feared it would go mad. As Elaine screamed at Barrymore to stop, he turned off his Hyde like a man turning off a light and hugged Timmy.

"Best audience I ever played to," said Barrymore, consoling the dog.

> 'Tis now the very witching time of night,
> When churchyards yawn, and hell itself breathes out
> Contagion to this world: now could I drink hot blood,
> And do such bitter business as the day
> Would quake to look on...
>
> —*Hamlet*, Act III, Sc. ii.

Shakespearean incest: Blanche Yurka as Gertrude,
John Barrymore as her devoted son

The John Barrymore *Hamlet* was sure to be the apogee of Broadway's legendary 1922. As with *Richard III*, the illustrious Arthur Hopkins would direct the production, and the esteemed Robert Edmond Jones would design Castle Elsinore.

The real show, naturally, was its star.

"... so paralyzing was the intensity of the wild-eyed Hamlet, so compelling his biting scorn, so poignant his pathos..." recalled Blanche Yurka, who played a very alluring Queen Gertrude. The 35-year-old actress was vain about playing the mother of a 40-year-old Hamlet, and thusly glamorized herself, as she expressed it, "striving to look as much as possible like a candidate for Ophelia ... a silly thing to do." Perhaps, but it sensually suited the Oedipus angst of this production. In rehearsal, Barrymore told Yurka how he envisioned the first scene:

> A hunt dinner is in progress; it's a drunken orgy ... tankards roll off the table... slabs of meat are thrown to great hunting dogs... court ladies loll with their shoulders and bosoms half bare... it is to be a sensuous, dissolute

court, dominated by a lecherous king. In the midst of it, Hamlet sits, a mute black figure, bathed in firelight…

"I expect it was the frustrated painter in him speaking," wrote Ms. Yurka. "It sounded marvelous. It never happened." Arthur Hopkins wasn't daring enough to stage the orgy his star wanted, but he allowed Barrymore his own way. As Yurka noted, "Certainly Jack's own passionate, bitterly humorous reading of the part, his almost incestuous handling of the closet scene, bore out what he had told me of his concept of the play."

In his book *John Barrymore, Shakespearean Actor*, Michael A. Morrison, based on far-flung research of prompt books, reviews, and reminiscences, writes that the star played part of the "closet scene" with Gertrude as if the Ghost had possessed him — in "a beam of sharp-greenish light from above," "rigid, trembling and transfixed," eyes "wide and staring," hands "stiff at his sides," speaking "in a strange, deep, hoarse, measured voice like that of the Ghost." Thusly did Barrymore attack his stage mother with some of Shakespeare's most vile and daring language:

Nay, but to live
In the rank sweat of an enseamed bed,
Stew'd in corruption, honeying and making love
Over the nasty sty

As Morrison described the scene, "Hamlet falls to his knees left of the Queen as if unable to support himself. As he kneels he gasps, then he shrieks wildly in terror and hysteria, as though released from the grip of his father's spirit…"

Blanche Yurka called the scene Barrymore's "epileptic fit," yet she accepted its intensity. During Christmas week, Ms. Yurka sent a card to his dressing room, expressing Yuletide cheer and adding, "To my son, from his mildly incestuous mother." Barrymore replied with his own Christmas card, a reproduction of his famous Hamlet drawing by John Singer Sargent, noting:

To my mother with much love from her wildly incestuous son – John Barrymore

What truly motivated what can be described, without hyperbole, as the most shattering stage performance of the twentieth century?

"If the dear old schoolteachers, who used to come to the Sam Harris Theatre, knew what was going through my mind while I was saying my lines," Barrymore remembered, "well, they would have run screaming into the street, either to escape what was going on, or to hunt a sailor." Gene Fowler later wrote in his private correspondence with Dr. Hayman that he talked with Barrymore about his Hamlet when the actor was "at a sanitarium in Westwood in 1937." He quoted Barrymore's inspiration for Hamlet, and his motivation for hating Claudius, this way: "That dirty, red-whiskered son-of-a-bitch! That bastard puts his prick in my mother's cunt every night." (From a letter Gene Fowler sent to Dr. Harold Thomas Hyman, January 13, 1944.)

Was John Barrymore envisioning his own, foul-smelling father, whose raving asylum death tormented him, and whose debauched downfall he possibly could never forgive? In his passion with stage mother Gertrude, was he imagining his stepmother Mamie, and her capricious seduction of him as a young teenager?

Whatever the motive, it wreaked its toll — and Barrymore found an escape hatch from the eight-shows-a-week torment. After the scene with Gertrude, Barrymore took an early curtain call; actress Josephine Hutchinson, who saw a performance, remembered that Barrymore "told colored jokes" — i.e., jokes about his mulatto dresser, Paul, and his remarks about Barrymore's performance. The jokes were affectionate toward Paul, mocking toward himself, delightful for the audience — and a relief for an actor who otherwise might have been overwhelmed by his own raging emotions.

There were a variety of escapes. J. Lark Taylor, who played a variety of small roles in this *Hamlet*, remembered the burial of Ophelia scene, with Whitford Kane as the First Gravedigger:

> Barrymore used to "kid" the life out of him, and break him up so he could hardly go on with his lines. On one occasion, Barrymore painted a comic face on the dummy which Kane and the second gravedigger — Cecil Cloville — had to lower into the grave, and Barrymore was a clever enough artist to make the thing resemble Rosalind Fuller [who played Ophelia]. When Kane caught sight of it, he nearly had hysterics. Blanche Yurka also went to pieces, and Barrymore himself was broken up by his own joke. 'Twas rather a jolly funeral that night, and I wondered what the audience must have thought of it all.

Taylor also recalled Barrymore smoked constantly in the wings — "One could trail him about the stage by the half-consumed cigarette butts" — and that Michael Strange, Barrymore's madly jealous wife, had taken both children to Paris and never returned to see her husband's historic performance. After Barrymore wished him a Merry Christmas, Taylor said he hoped the star's day had been happy.

"Yes, I was with the animals," Barrymore replied. "I spent the day at the Zoo."

Then there was the night a replacement for one of the men who bore the dead Hamlet off stage, let the body slip. As Taylor recalled:

> One of the other fellows grabbed to save him, and evidently tickled him, for Hamlet's limp, dead body gave a sudden, spasmodic jerk, and the dead lips ejaculated, quite loud enough to be heard in the last row of the balcony: "JESUS!"

Barrymore played Hamlet 101 times on Broadway — just long enough to surpass Edwin Booth's 100-performance New York run. He reprised his success in New York the following season and, in 1925, played Hamlet in London — a stunning success for an American actor.

Yet it was, aside from his 1940 return to Broadway in the shoddy comedy *My Dear Children*, his final stage work. Hamlet told the players to "Hold the mirror up to nature," and Barrymore, as Hamlet, held up a mirror to himself, a mad, funhouse mirror that reflected all his demons and tortured spirit.

The World's Greatest Living Actor
—Warner Bros. Publicity for John Barrymore, 1925

The HOLLYWOODLAND sign loomed like a pagan god atop Mount Lee, its 50'-high letters glowing in the night, exalted by its 4,000 light bulbs.

The Hollywood of 1925 had a population of 130,000. There were big, booming, classic films that year, such as *The Gold Rush*, in which Charlie Chaplin ate his boots (actually made of chocolate), and *Ben-Hur*, in which Ramon Navarro's title hero defeated Francis X. Bushman's Messala in the classic chariot race (filmed by 42 cameras on 200,000 feet of film — 750' of which appeared in the release print).

There was an unbridled, Barnum & Bailey-style showmanship in Hollywood, and the accent, of course, was on sex. Erich von Stroheim was directing MGM's *The Merry Widow*, his genius fashioning minimal operetta, maximum sex spectacle. Anielka Elter, once publicized as "The Girl with the Wickedest Eyes in the World," played the masked musician in *The Merry Widow*'s famous seduction scene. Almost 40 years later, Ms. Elter told the *Los Angeles Times*:

Barrymore as Captain Ahab
in *The Sea Beast*

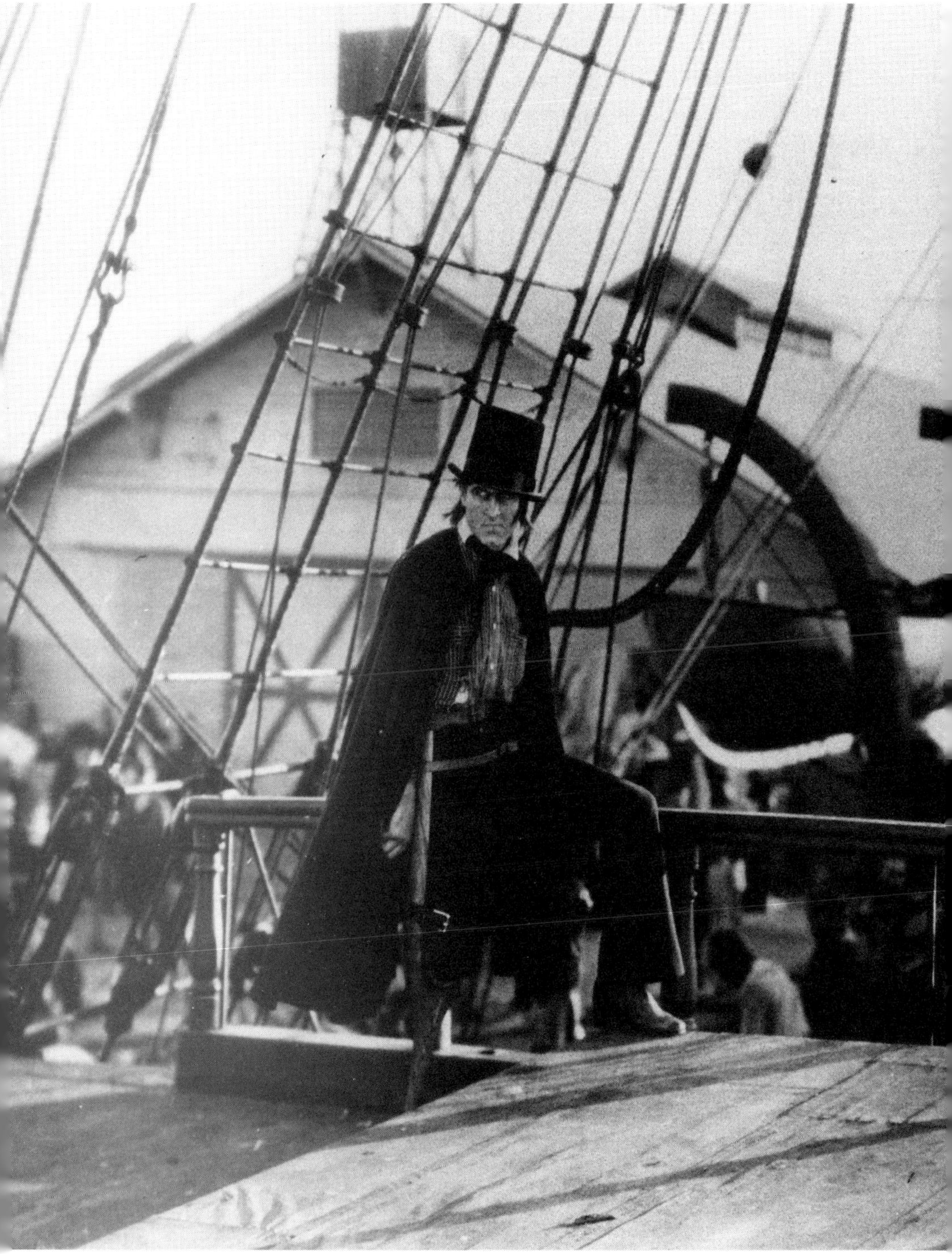

> What a shame that one gets to be old and the wicked eyes are not so wicked any more. I was a Hollywood girl when the going was good and the most interesting or the craziest people were always interested in me. Stroheim saw me as a temptation of evil. I wore what in those days we used to call "a couple of flowers and nothing to pin them on." He shot a cigarette out of my mouth in that picture. I was insured at Lloyds for one day but the scene wasn't shown.

The corset of restraint, the gleeful crushing of genius by moguls and front-office lackeys — not to mention Will Hays — was already in play. Moguls, moralists and the prejudices of the great unwashed would soon have their own wicked way with the movies.

John Barrymore, originally rejoicing in this "God-given, vital, youthful, sunny place," had arrived in style, complete with a Warner Bros. contract promising $76,250 per picture, story approval, and train traveling expenses for himself, his English valet Blaney, and Clementine — his adored pet monkey. He had his own ideas as to the roles he'd portray on film, and as film historian James Card wrote:

> As a person, John Barrymore seemed to some of his admirers to be a living synthesis of Lord Byron and Dorian Gray: an embodiment in one player of all the mysteries and excitement of Gothic romanticism. And the Gothic in Barrymore that leered out of the wings to mock the classic beauty of the famous profile, led him gleefully into such wild excesses…the cauterized amputee of Melville, a supernatural Svengali, and of course, the progressively more nauseatingly monstrous Mr. Hyde. One forgives Mr. Barrymore, the actor, for these frenetic digressions, remembering that he was an actor reluctantly and would have preferred to have indulged his Gustave Dore nature as an illustrator.

It was "the cauterized amputee of Melville" whom Barrymore first played on his new Warner pact — Captain Ahab of *Moby Dick*, here retitled *The Sea Beast*. Barrymore made Ahab the fallen angel beautifully, almost divinely handsome pre-loss of leg, with a pet monkey (played by Clementine herself). After Moby's big bite, Mad Jack's Ahab is a peg-legged Lucifer scuttling about with Hyde-like leers, wild eyes, lanky hair and even a Gothic top hat.

Captain Ahab was an appropriately classic role for "The World's Greatest Living Actor," but Warner Bros. saw one big problem: no love interest!

Barrymore, amused by this prosaic concern, made a suggestion typical of his humor — he'd play mad love scenes with the whale. His artistic contempt abandoned ship

Dolores Costello ("Jiggie Wink") in *The Sea Beast*

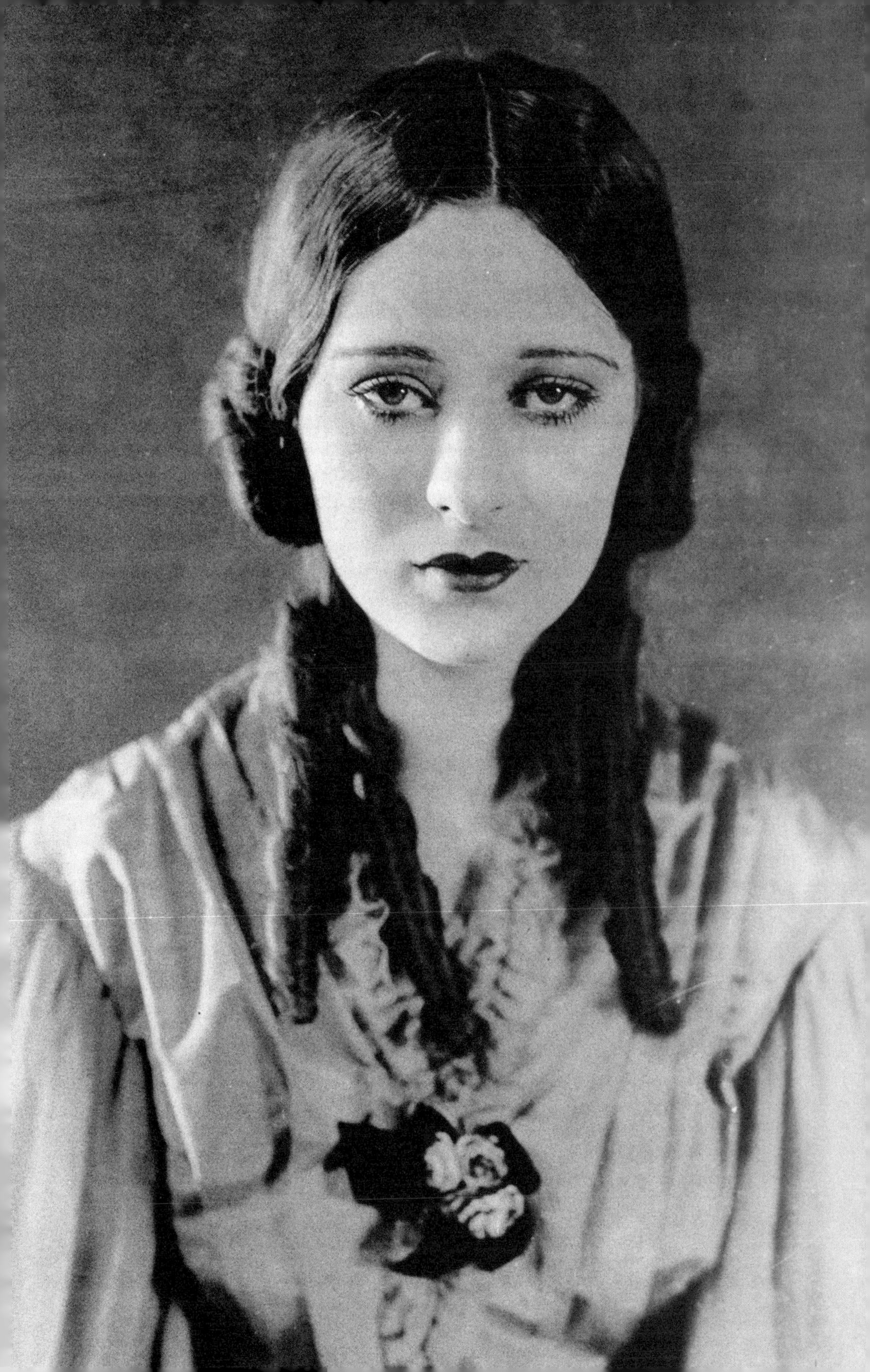

when he saw the screen test of blonde Dolores Costello, whom he instantly proclaimed "the most preposterously lovely creature in all the world!" She became *The Sea Beast*'s ingénue, included to provide Ahab with a Happy Ending and fated in real life to be Barrymore's third "bus accident" (as he referred to his marriages).

Released in January of 1926, *The Sea Beast* was a box office smash. Despite his lovesick sellout acceptance of Dolores as leading lady, he makes the White Whale his true co-star — madly riding atop it come the climax, wildly harpooning it, flashing his crazy eyes, screaming (he appears to be screaming in this silent film), reveling in the whale's blood spraying in his face. Barrymore's climactic revenge seems more like an insane rape — very likely what he had in mind the day he played the scene. Sadly, poor "Moby Dick" himself looks like a giant, glistening prophylactic, a sea-going phallus of incredible size and conceit.

More cinema triumphs followed, the most notable ones featuring dashes of baroque Barrymore flourish. There was Warner Bros.' *Don Juan* (1926), a lavish costumer and the first fully-synchronized music Vitaphone sound feature, complete with Mary Astor (a former lover of Barrymore's), Myrna Loy (who, padded for her vamp role, recalled Barrymore slyly sticking pins into her false bosom between scenes) and a vignette in which the star, à la Hyde, transformed himself (with no makeup) to resemble the film's axe-faced villain (Gustav von Seyffertitz). There was *The Beloved Rogue* (1927), which Barrymore did as one of the original "United Artists" (with Douglas Fairbanks, Mary Pickford, and Charlie Chaplin), playing a dashing François Villon, especially vivid in his "King of the Fools" makeup, resembling a decaying clown from Hell.

There was also a reprisal of sorts of Mr. Hyde. Seeking a house, Barrymore feared the sale price would inflate if the seller knew the famous identity of the buyer. Hence, Barrymore and his business manager Henry Hotchener visited the for-sale hacienda of King Vidor at 6 Tower Road, high above Beverly Hills. Their roles that day: maniac and his keeper. Barrymore dressed in his old Hyde hat, wig and cloak, hid on the car floor as Hotchener met the real estate agent at the grounds, and then leeringly peeked out the car window at the agent — rolling his eyes, cackling madly, and kissing his monkey Clementine.

"Have to humor him with pets," said Henry Hotchener.

The agent, doubting if maniac and keeper were men of means, cut $10,000 off the price, and Barrymore now had his mountain estate — which he christened "Bella Vista" — complete with a tower with trapdoor and ladder, and a view of the ocean.

Life was seemingly idyllic. John Barrymore wed Dolores Costello November 24,

1928. They honeymooned on his yacht, *The Mariner*, along the coast of Panama. Barrymore called his new bride "Jiggie Wink." He wrote in his diary during the honeymoon, "The small egg is very happy I think — I love her more and more every day…" Bella Vista had a pool with a giant antique sundial in its midst, an $8,500 pink Meissan chandelier, a mahogany Klondike bar, a trout pond, Italian cypresses…

It was his own, personal, Hollywood-financed Paradise. Yet most tellingly, as John Barrymore, whose real name was Blyth, created a Barrymore "coat-of-arms," hanging it on the gates and walls of Bella Vista, he self-designed his own symbol — a snake, wearing a crown.

The serpent was loose in Barrymore's Garden of Eden.

Meanwhile, the man whom many would come to see as John Barrymore's devil had come to Hollywood, shortly before the star's marriage to Dolores Costello.

John Decker had met Barrymore in New York during the run of *Hamlet*. His own marriage had crashed in New York City and in 1928 he came west to seek his fortune. He was still a young man — only 33 — and apparently arrived with a new wife, Julia, without benefit of any legal divorce from Helen.

Decker's plan: sell his services to the movie industry and the layman/laywoman. He'd paint anything … for anybody … in any style … and for any purpose.

Meanwhile, there was another future prominent "Bundy Drive Boy" also in California by 1928, but he was rarely in Los Angeles. He was, quite literally, "a voice in the desert" — Beaumont, California, to be precise — and had summed up the year of 1927 in three words: "Wrestling with Fate." His 1928 summary: "Started to write book on esthetics."

The affection John Barrymore and John Decker would have for the brilliantly eccentric Sadakichi Hartmann would be lasting and profound.

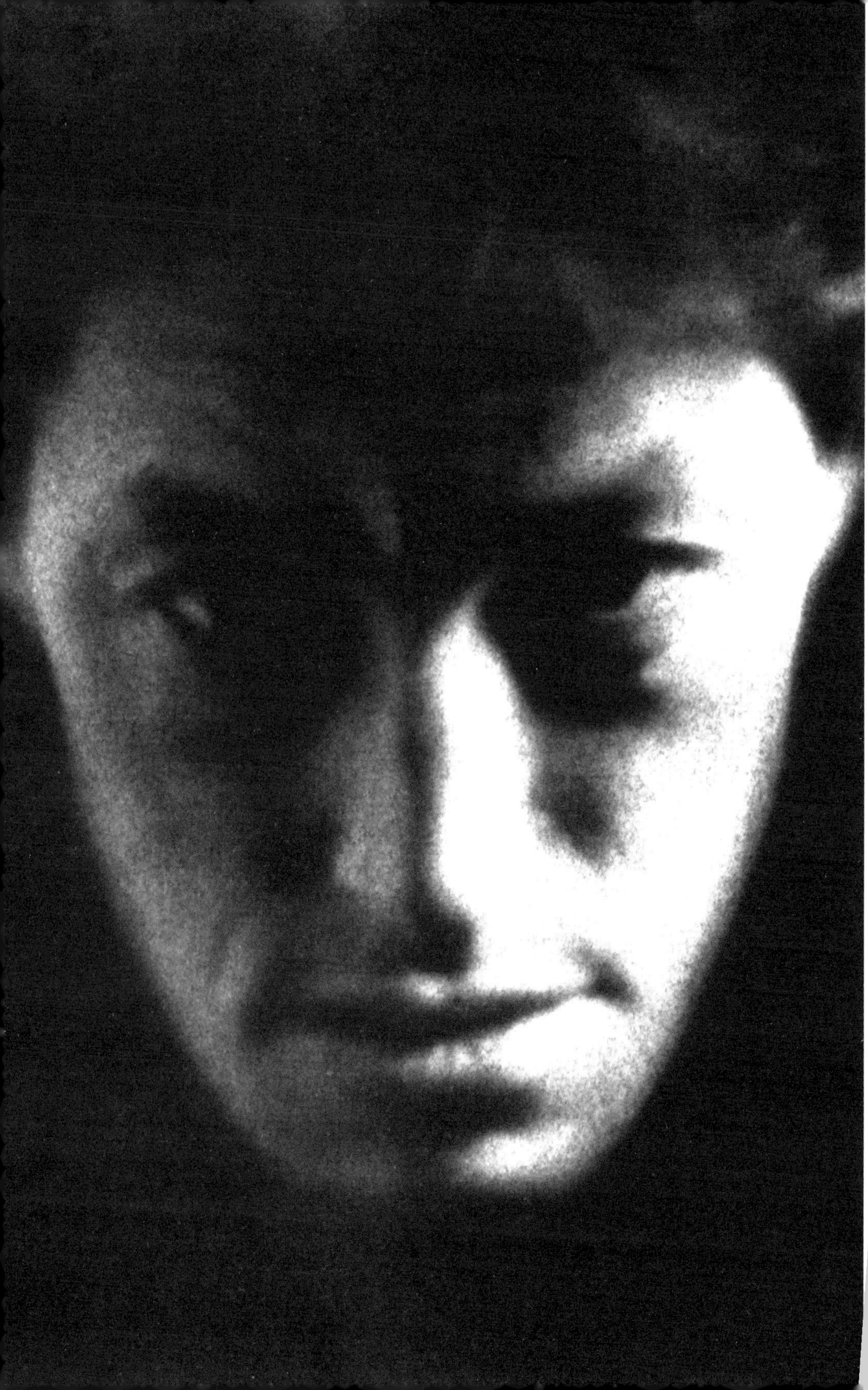

Chapter Three
The First Hippie

> Sadakichi Hartmann, who once told his friend, John Barrymore, that he was a lousy actor, and on another occasion procured a gun for a penniless sculptor who wanted to kill himself — and did — is dead.
> —"Hartmann, 'King of Bohemia,' Taken by Death,"
> *Los Angeles Times*, November 23, 1944

Thus did the *Los Angeles Times* lead off its obituary when Sadakichi Hartmann finally gave up his profane ghost at the Florida home of his daughter Dorothea — just one of his 12 or 13 children (accounts vary) most of whom he'd named after flowers. He was, according to his death certificate, 77 years, 11 months and 13 days old. The *L.A. Times* gave his age as 78, but John Decker had no faith in either number.

"He must have been at least 178," Decker told the *Times*. "He'd been knocking years off his age at every birthday for years."

"HA!" was the battle cry of Sadakichi, the tall, tousle-haired half-German, half-Japanese scholar/critic/author/poet/artist/actor/dancer/moocher/pickpocket/Peeping Tom/pants-wetter/Renaissance Man, hailed by many pre-World War I savants — and by some disciples to this day — as the patron saint of the American avant-garde. The canonization is no joke; indeed, the University of California in Riverside, which houses the old boy's archival collection, reverently includes in its 46 boxes of Sadakichi material a bust of his head and a lock of his hair.

Sadakichi Hartmann

Of all the Bundy Drive Boys, Sadakichi was farthest out on the perilous edge and perfectly delighted to roost there. John Barrymore proclaimed Sadakichi "the last of the Pharaohs, and nicely mummified at that...." Gene Fowler, who awarded Sadakichi the star role of his 1954 book, *Minutes of the Last Meeting*, made valiant stabs at a proper evocation — an "eerie Jack-of-all-arts," an "aged warlock," a "fugitive from an embalming table" and "the most prodigious sack of sticks ever faggoted by the Almighty." John Decker said in his review of *Minutes*, that Sadakichi was "a worshipper of the God of perversity." The *L.A. Times* book critic wrote of Sadakichi:

> He seems to have inherited the worst of physical characteristics. In appearance he was tall, gaunt, wraithlike, looking less like a cornfield scarecrow than a caricature of all the scarecrows in the world. But one must admit that he was, in motion, a graceful scarecrow.

Known to all who encountered him, Sadakichi always sported a self-made truss, a virtual hammock, that not only provided support to his oft-siring genitalia but gave it a pronounced accent. The protuberance once caused Sadakichi to be tossed out of a debutante ball when the host saw Sadakichi doing the Bunny-Hug with his coming-out daughter. It was also this truss that inspired John Barrymore to proclaim that Sadakichi Hartmann, and not he, truly deserved the title "The Great Profile."

Of all the purple prose heaped upon him, the appellation that Sadakichi probably would have most approved was the title Richard Hill used in a *Swank* magazine profile in April of 1969: "The First Hippie."

Born on November 8 (a birthday he shared with John Decker) on Deshima Island near Nagasaki, 1867, he was disowned by his German industrialist father Carl Herman Oscar and Japanese mother Osada Hartmann, who exiled him to a great-uncle in Philadelphia ("not apt to foster filial piety," he said). He was freelancing stories for Boston and New York newspapers at age 14, serving Walt Whitman as a teenage secretary at 18, apprenticing in the Royal Theatre of Munich, Germany at 19, and settling in Greenwich Village at 23, where he soon wore the crown of the Bohemian King — even though he only lived there sporadically.

Come Yuletide of 1893, the 27-year-old Sadakichi penned his first play, *Christ*. The drama presented Mary Magdalene as the sister of Jesus (or "Jeshua," as Sadakichi calls him). Jeshua is in love with a pilgrimess named Hannah – "we feel the burning passion of all mankind, and the body becomes as sacred as the soul!" they chorus, kissing as meteors shoot across heaven. Jeshua faces temptation via harlot queen Zenobia, who tries to seduce him, and that failing, kill him:

Jeshua: Let me go! Inordinate love can gain no power over me.
Zenobia: Behold me as I am!
  (rends her garments)
  This god-like form is yours!

Jeshua *(yields for one moment, then suddenly frees himself)*: I still resist!

Zenobia: What woman's son are you? — I see my efforts to conquer you are in vain; but in my body lives a sea of blood. Now I give vent to all inhuman feelings that find shelter in my belly's flame!
(seizes her dagger)
I'll limb and laniate the body of my wayward suitor; lacerate his selfish heart, and amidst writhing, mutilations and smoking sloughs of blood, I shall stand triumphant!
(stands for one moment transfigured as the incarnation of lust, then throws herself upon Jeshua, who disarms and forces her to the ground. A groan comes from Zenobia's lips, she murmurs)
Forgive!

Seventy-five years later, this might have been incorporated into a rock opera; 110 years later, it might have become a historic bestselling novel. As it was in 1893, *Christ* was banned in Boston, burned in public and caused its author to be convicted of obscenity and tossed into the Charles Street jail, just in time for Christmas. "Worst food I ever ate," recalled Sadakichi. (His 1920 novel version, *The Last Thirty Days of Christ*, would ignite its own firestorm of religious censorship.) He also wrote plays about Moses, Buddha and Mohammed.

His irreverence remained boundless, and almost a holy cause.

He lost his job as an architect for the famed Stanford White after publicly declaring that White's drawings were "to be improved upon only by the pigeons, after the drawings become buildings." He published an essay in defense of plagiarism, and actually made it stick:

I have always endorsed Heine's defense of plagiarism, that it is permissible to steal entire columns and porticoes from a temple, providing the edifice one erects with their aid is great enough to warrant such violent proceedings…

One night at Carnegie Hall, Sadakichi watched world-famous pianist Moriz Rosenthal, who had studied with Liszt, flamboyantly add a series of rapid scales to the Hungarian Rhapsodies.

"Is this necessary?" bellowed Sadakichi from the balcony. "I am a man needed but not wanted!" protested Sadakichi as they tossed him into the street.

His own theatrical career, especially the night of November 30, 1902, had been epically disastrous, as this *New York Times* headline suggests:

> PERFUME CONCERT FAILS
> *Scoffers Spoil It with Tobacco Smoke*
> *And Facetious Remarks – Esthetes*
> *And Deaf-Mutes Disappointed*

Sadakichi had promised "A Trip to Japan in Sixteen Minutes, Conveyed to the Audience by a Succession of Odors." Hellbent on making his mark as a theatrical impresario, Sadakichi, using the stage name "Chrysanthemum," was pioneering a new type of entertainment, a precursor to the later cinema debacle known as "Smell-O-Vision." Promising to whisk away the audience on a tour of the world via the olfactory sense, Sadakichi installed two formidable fans to blast the smells of the Orient right up the noses of the Broadway crowd. To spice up the act, Sadakichi hired the Meredith Sisters — two wild-eyed, leggy New York dancers, whose true specialty was a high-kicking Can-Can — Geisha girls and twitter about the stage amidst the music and "A Melody of Odors."

The *Times* reported that the opening night house was crowded, including a section of deaf-mutes, as well as "a man with a Cyrano de Bergerac nose, who was all eagerness for the entertainment." There was even a "hay-fever contingent," happily anticipating flowery smells that would cause no allergies. But the "Perfume Concert" was just one act on the vaudeville entertainment bill that night, and a large segment of the crowd had come (as the *Times* noted) "to be amused with horseplay, ragtime, dancing, and singing soubrettes. They had no faith in the perfume recital…"

"A Trip to Japan in Sixteen Minutes…" began with a musical overture titled "The Sadakichi March." Enter Sadakichi, wearing a chrysanthemum on the left lapel of his evening coat as he took the stage. The audience promptly began giggling, started, as one newspaper account put it, by "a lady in the right hand box" who "stopped chewing gum long enough to titter." The Geisha Girls fluttered on stage, loaded the beehive-like ovens, and the fans smelled the evening's introductory odor — a fragrance of roses, such as those tossed to first-class passengers as a steamer to the Orient.

The 1920s 55

There was "faint applause" from those folks in the front rows who could actually smell the roses. The man with the de Bergerac nose shouted "Bravo," while the deaf mutes, in the words of the *Times*, "stamped their feet and slapped their hands." Audiences farther back couldn't smell a damn thing.

Chrysanthemum carried on, with a stop in Germany. "Have you ever gathered violets on a Sunday morning in the outskirts of a village on the Rhine?" Germany was not popular with the 1902 assemblage, and it was, as one newspaper expressed it, a "Fatal Question!"

"Rot!" shouted a Philistine, starting the stampede up the aisle.

"Back the rathskeller!" howled another heckler.

"Reminds me of the time the gas meter leaked!" cried yet another, as the scoffers, in rising hilarity, began filling the theatre with tobacco smoke.

"People fell over each other in their haste to get out," noted one reporter. Sadakichi, shouting that the crowd would have been more appreciative if he'd wafted out onions and cabbage, fled the stage in a rare retreat.

"I guess I'll quit," he said in the wings.

The Meredith Sisters, valiantly trying to salvage the night, belted out their songs ("with shrill soprano defiance"), accompanied by some impromptu Geisha bumping-and-grinding, but all to no avail. As the *New York Times* (tempering mercy with justice) concluded its postmortem:

> The deaf mutes filed out, with their fingers busy telling their disgust with the audience and sympathy for the performer. The man with the big nose shoved his way through the crowd, whom he termed "pigs," and the esthetic people and the hay-fever crowd scattered like frightened sheep caught nibbling in flower-beds.

Another newspaper, less sympathetic than the *New York Times*, was considerably more blunt:

New York last night took its first sniffff (sic) at a "perfume concert." After its second sniff it got caught in the door trying to get out.

As Sadakichi conservatively wrote of his experiment with the commonality:

> 1902. Originated the Perfume Concert. Tried it on the dog at New York Theatre, November 30. The dog barked.

Bloody but unbowed, Sadakichi eventually and defiantly revived his Perfume concerts, usually to the same disastrous reception. The story goes that, during one of his abor-

SADAKICHI HARTMANN

Originator of the

Perfume Concert

THE LATEST NOVELTY IN THE ENTERTAINMENT LINE

Begs to announce that he is ready to accept engagements for Smokers, Clubs, or Private Entertainments, etc. : : : : :

For Terms, apply to

S. HARTMANN,

Erne's Cliff Place, Bedford Park, N. Y. C.

tive plays, he ventured to the lobby after Act I to hear what the critics had to say. When they denounced his effort, Sadakichi vowed to have the last word: he set fire to the theatre. "The blaze was extinguished," reported the *Los Angeles Times*, "and the play went on."

Sadakichi found more success with his writing. In 1901, he authored *Shakespeare in Art*; in 1902, he produced the textbook *History of American Art*, which covered such then-unknown painters as Winslow Homer and gave America its first serious analysis of photography as a true art form. In 1904, he published the milestone book *Japanese Art* (under the *nom de plume* of Innocence De La Salle); in 1910, he wrote *The Whistler Book*, based on the painter, who was Sadakichi's crony. In *The Whistler Book*, Sadakichi, AKA "Chrysanthemum," addressed his fondness for chrysanthemums quite beautifully:

> Whenever I gaze at a white chrysanthemum, my mind becomes conscious of something which concerns my life alone; something which I would like to express in my art, but which I never shall be able to realize, at least not in the vague and, at the same time, convincing manner the flower conveys it to me. I am also fond of displaying it occasionally in my buttonhole; not for effect, however, but simply because I want other people to know who I am; for those human beings who are sensitive to the charms of the chrysanthemum must hail from the same country in which my soul abides, and I should like to meet them. I should not have much to say to them — souls are not talkative — but we should make curtsies, and hand white chrysanthemums to one another.

"Artists must not become too respectable," opined Sadakichi, "because their mission is to teach the play phase of life." By 1917, he was a widely-traveling lecturer, "a maverick of the seven arts," offering his predictions and observations — some pithy, some funny, some unforgivable:

★ It pays to be a snob.

★ Americans don't know how to drink.

★ California will eventually secede from the rest of the union.

★ Lynching Negroes in the South is very horrible, but quite necessary.

★ All is money in this country.

★ Peace is only a dream.

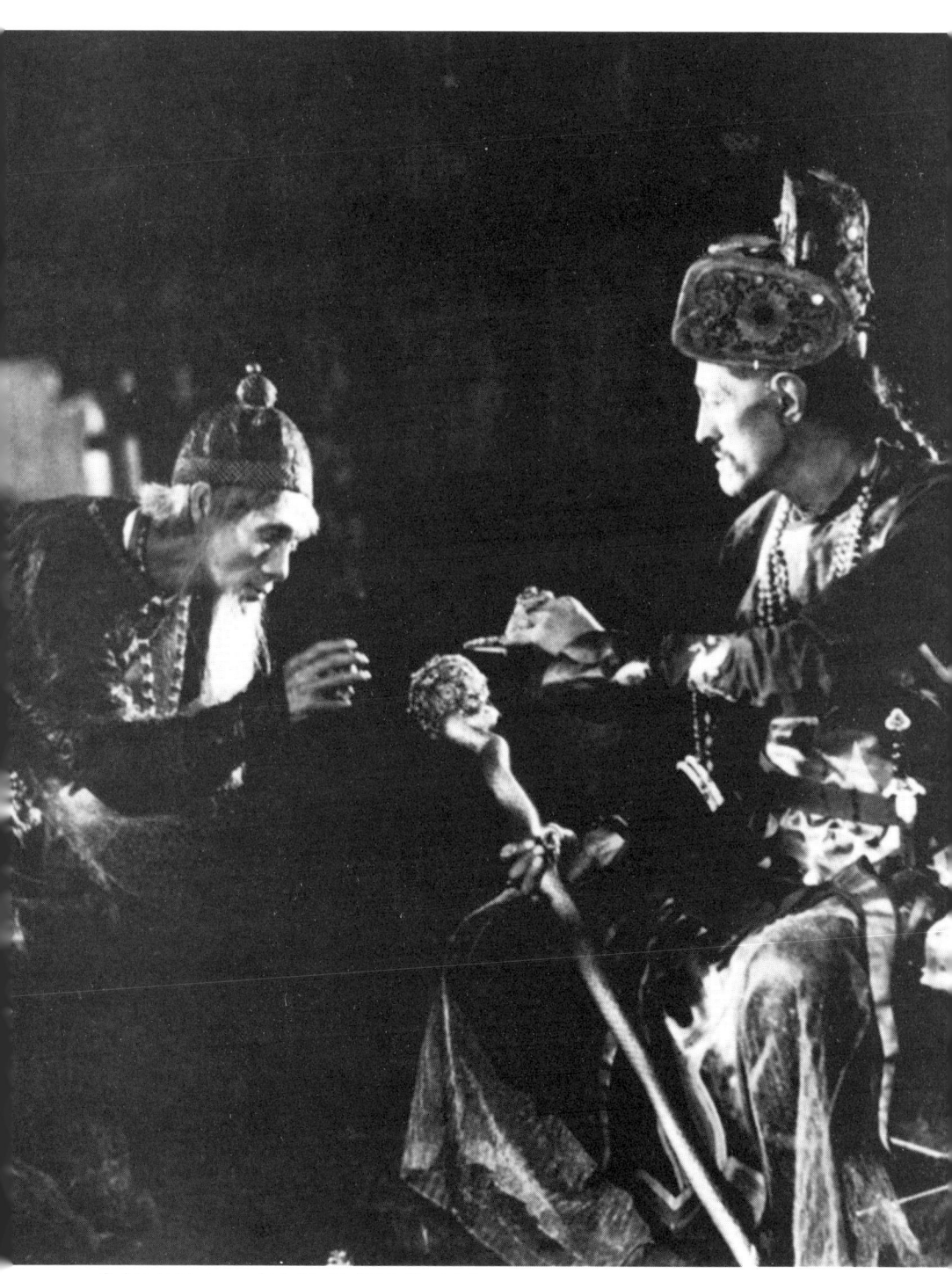

Sadakichi Hartmann (right) In *The Thief of Baghdad*

- ★ The Germans and the Japanese make me tired.

- ★ Life should consist of one new sensation after another; otherwise we might as well commit suicide.

And come 1922/1923 — the lofty era that saw John Decker falling into an orchestra pit and John Barrymore groping his stage mother — we find the first of the Decker and Hartmann sagas. The tale goes that Decker and Hartmann met, crashed the Washington Mews studio of (in Decker's words) "a would-be sculptress… one of those wretched beings with one-nineteenth of a talent and lots of alimony." While the guests ("the usual coterie of half-assed sycophants and poseurs who think that by rubbing up against bad art they can become good artists") savored the bootleg booze, Decker and Sadakichi crept upstairs to the studio, where Decker found a veiled sculpture — a giant clay hand. Decker found some plasticene in the studio and added, in the grip of the hand, an impromptu penis. Sadakichi rewrapped the aborning art.

"Now quiet, everybody, please," announced the sculptress after finally rounding up the drunken guests to behold the unveiling. "I felt truly inspired as I modeled this. And I hope you will experience the same wonderful thrill when you look upon it." She unveiled the statue.

"I call it 'The Hand of Friendship!'" she proclaimed, unveiling the penis-brandishing statue.

The guests laughed. When the sculptress looked away from their faces and saw the phallus looming in her Hand of Friendship, she nearly fainted. "Sadakichi was all for staying on," recalled Decker, "but I dragged him away when I heard someone mention the police."

By Sadakichi's own records, he was away from New York much of this era, traveling to towns in New Jersey, Alabama and Florida, pursuing his fleeing health.

Then in 1923 Sadakichi went Hollywood.

He moved his family to the desert town of Beaumont, worked on a script for Don Quixote (which was never produced) and landed the juicy role of the Court Magician in the classic *The Thief of Baghdad*, starring Douglas Fairbanks. His fee: $250 per week and a case of whiskey. The legend goes that he walked off the set after several weeks when the latest case of whiskey failed to meet his standard, and that Fairbanks had to reshoot the scenes at a cost of $65,000. (Some sources go as high as $250,000.) In fact, Sadakichi survives in the release print — looking like a mix of Poe and Fu Manchu, and seemingly enjoying his one and only film credit. Douglas Fairbanks' final estimation of Sadakichi: "An intelligent spittoon."

Sadakichi had his own insight, naturally, into the cinema:

The motion picture comes nearest to the two conditions which are destined to be the main characteristics of all future art expression: being used on a principle of motion and dependent on composite efforts. It is the youngest in the family of arts and presents the cumulative result of mechanical efficiency and economic power, guided and shoved into place by mob predilection. It is one of the best time-killing soporific entertainments the world has ever known ... a welcome narcotic sent by the Zeitgeist to mankind suffering from twentieth-century boredom.

Hartmann had a face that John Decker called "a painter's dream." There was a dignity in that mummy face, a nobility, a saintliness — and if ever a face reflected the inner soul, thus did Sadakichi's. He was, with all his eccentricities, a brilliant man, and his poetry that survives is powerful, such as this verse from his *My Rubaiyat* (1913):

> If youth would refuse to obey
> To die without cause of reason,
> If youth would refuse to bear arms
> Against brothers they do not know,
> Then like Chaldean shepherds,
> We might greet a great white dawn.

So Sadakichi Hartmann disciples survive, many in Japan, and 46 boxes at University of California, Riverside contain not only a relic of his hair, but the sheet music to "The Sadakichi March." In the eyes of his worshippers, Sadakichi had a radiant arrogant brilliance that could truly be inspiring and (yes, for some) a sexual adventure to be remembered. Gene Fowler, locating one of Hartmann's wives after his death, asked what made her forgive his many most grievous faults.

"Sadakichi," she said solemnly, "was capable." Presumably with or without his truss.

Fated to be remembered primarily as the cherished mascot of the Bundy Drive Boys, Sadakichi had his dissenters. One of the gang despised him, calling him (among other things) "Itchy-Scratchy" and "Catch-a-Crotchie." W. C. Fields was not an easy man to impress.

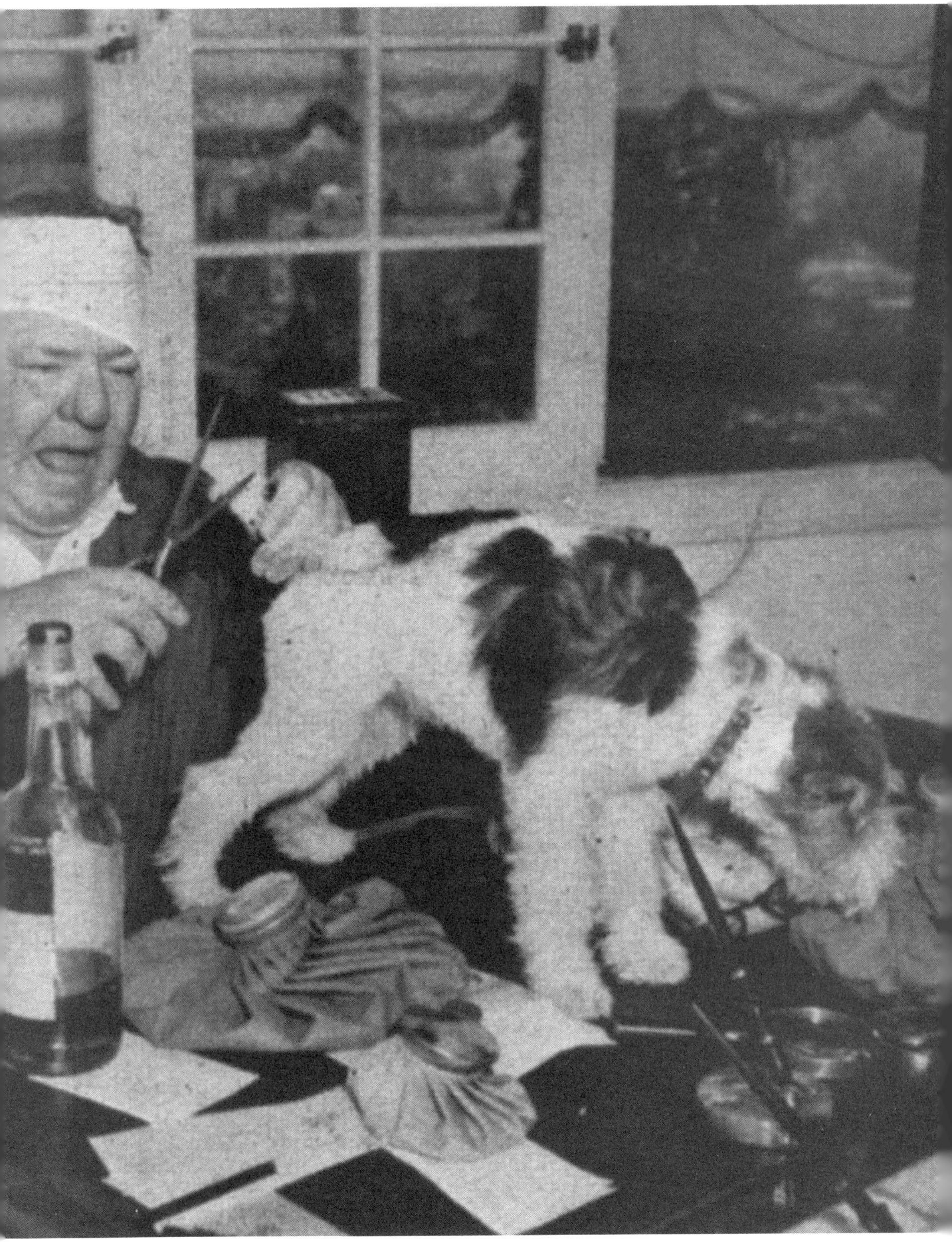

Chapter Four
The Great Charlatan

> Even in his own family, W.C. Fields was persona non grata!
> — Ronald J. Fields, interview with the author, 2006

W.C. Fields hated dogs, he said, "Because the sons-of-bitches — and they really are, you know — lift their legs on flowers."

He hated water, he explained, "because fish fuck in it."

Then there was Fields' story of Ziegfeld Follies' Hans Kunt ("one of the German Kunts; not to be confused with the Italian Cunts"). Once while Hans was rehearsing with the Ziegfeld girls, Fields came down the center aisle of the New Amsterdam Theatre and shouted, "Hello, Kunt!"

As Fields told it, the Follies girls all smiled and replied, "Hello, Mr. Fields!"

There was his letter to a Jewish Hollywood producer, with the salutation, "Dear Christ Killer," his reference to polio-stricken President Roosevelt as "grim legs." And it was Fields who inspired not only John Decker's classic Fields-as-Queen Victoria portrait, but also one of Decker's most infamous works, never exhibited in public, of W.C. and Carlotta Monti, his one-time secretary and mistress. Charles Heard, a Dallas-based Decker historian and collector, remembers the painting vividly:

> As for the naughty Decker painting at Chasen's... I visited there in 1974 and saw the famous Queen Victoria painting and the pencil Decker sketch of W.C. and Barrymore in the same hospital room together — both are hooked up to alcohol IV's.

When we entered the restaurant, I made it known to the maître d' that I was a big Fields fan making a Chasen's pilgrimage — and after dinner, he approached my table and invited me to accompany him to the Chasen's office. We walked into this richly paneled office and he said, "I'll show you something that not many have seen that used to hang in W.C. Fields' home." He then pulled out a couch from against the wall and removed a long horizontal painting of Carlotta in the buff with W.C. in miniature on her muff, with top hat on and holding a martini glass high!

If John Barrymore seemed to carry his pet devil in his eyes, W.C. Fields appeared to transport his in his nose — a red, bulbous, and seemingly ready to explode violently (indeed, it once did). What Fields got away with saying in public made him a comedy icon, a modern wit, a rebel to 1960s radicals.

★ I am free from all prejudices. I hate everyone equally.

★ Start every day with a smile, and get it over with.

★ What a gorgeous day. What effulgent sunshine. It was a day of this sort that the McGillicuddy brothers murdered their mother with an axe.

★ What fiend put pineapple juice in my pineapple juice?

★ If at first you don't succeed, try, try again. Then give up. No use being a damn fool about it.

★ Children should neither be seen nor heard from… ever again.

★ A woman drove me to drink, and I never even had the courtesy to thank her.

★ Once, during Prohibition, I was forced to live for days on nothing but food and water.

★ I always keep a supply of stimulant handy in case I see a snake, which I also keep handy.

★ My illness is due to my doctor's insistence that I drink milk, a whitish fluid they force down helpless babies.

Was the man really the dog-hating, child-despising misanthrope that legend has cranked him up to be? Ronald J. Fields, the Great Man's grandson, author of *W.C. Fields: A Life on Film*, says:

W.C. was split, really split! There were contradictory things. For example, in his will, he donated most of his money for an orphanage, but being very anti-religious, he stipulated it had to be an orphanage where no religion of any kind could be taught!

As for "Anyone who hates children and dogs can't be all bad" — well, Baby LeRoy was "over the hill" in Hollywood because he was three or four and W.C. fought cats and dogs with the studio to have him in his movie *The Old-Fashioned Way*. He basically got Baby LeRoy out of retirement at the age of four! At the same time, Ray Bradbury remembers that he'd ride his bike over to Paramount and wait outside for the stars to come out and here comes W.C., coming out in his limousine. "Mr. Fields, Mr. Fields, can I have your autograph?" W.C. grabs the book, signs it, and "There you go, you little bastard!" For just about every kind thing I could say he had for children, I could tell you something else he wasn't so kind about! It's kind of a mixed bag on that one.

As with his Bundy Drive confreres, W. C. Fields definitely had his demons — all of which had an impact on his artistry. As legendary screen beauty Louise Brooks perceived, "W.C. Fields stretched out his hand to Beauty and Love and they thrust it away."

The rejection ironically inspired one of the great comic performers of all time.

The first thing I remember figuring out for myself was that I wanted to be a definite personality. I had heard a man say he liked a certain fellow because he always was the same dirty damn so-and-so. You know, like Larsen in Jack London's *Sea Wolf*. He was detestable, yet you admired him because he remained true-to-type. Well, I thought that was a swell idea so I developed a philosophy of my own, be your type! I determined that whatever I was, I'd be that, I wouldn't teeter on the fence.
—W.C. Fields, interview with Maude Cheathamn, 1935

His birth date is a mystery, probably January 29, 1880; his birth name was William Claude Dukenfield. His father, James Lyden Dukenfield, had arrived in the U.S. from England at age 13 in November, 1854. A Civil War veteran (he had two fingers shot off in the Battle of Lookout Mountain, and still dressed up in his uniform in his old age), James wed Kate S. Felton on May 18, 1879. Doing the math, one deduces Kate was already expecting bundle of joy William Claude the day they married at Philadelphia's St. George's Methodist Church.

"I was the oldest child," said W.C. "We were all very poor, but I was poor first."

It is poetically proper that Fields grew up above a saloon, where his father tended bar. As Jon Winokur wrote in *The Portable Curmudgeon*:

His mother was a strong woman, bitter about her lot in life, and he probably inherited his wisecracking, side-of-the-mouth style from her. She would sit on the porch with her young son and entertain him with a snide, running commentary about passing neighbors.

Father and son clashed violently. "His Dad was a reformed alcoholic," says Ron Fields, "and a really pissed-off one! He and his father fought an awful lot." His father also enjoyed raising his voice in bellowing song (with his surviving Cockney accent); W.C claimed he had a lifelong hatred of music. He also harbored a hatred of Christmas. As he told Gene Fowler:

> Well, it was this way: I believed in Christmas until I was eight years old. I had saved up some money carrying ice in Philadelphia. I was going to buy my mother a copper-bottom clothes boiler for Christmas. I kept the money hidden in a brown crock in the coalbin. My father found the crock. He did exactly what I would have done in his place. He stole the money. And ever since then I've remembered nobody on Christmas, and I want nobody to remember me either. Is that clear?

The animosity reportedly reached the point where W.C.'s father once smashed him over the head with a shovel. Fathers are loathsome villains in the Bundy Drive Boys sagas.

Amazingly, considering his career-fueling rage, W.C. made peace with his hostile papa, who later came to see him in his stage appearances. In fact, W.C. would erect grave markers in honor of both his parents: he had "A Great Scout" inscribed in the granite of his father's marker, and "A Sweet Old Soul" added to his mother's.

He made his show business debut as a juggler at age 14, appearing as "Whitey the Boy Wonder" at the Plymouth Park Pavilion near Norristown, Pennsylvania. In Atlantic City, he performed as "W.C. Fields, the Tramp Juggler," as well as a "drowner" — a sideshow ruse designed to lure the crowds into a beer garden. As W.C. described the gig:

> My work was very simple. All I had to do was swim far out in the ocean, then flounder and scream for help. Lifeguards who worked for shows nearby would rescue me. Once I was brought to a pavilion, a crowd would gather. The waiters would immediately begin to yell their wares.

"The Eccentric Juggler" made his vaudeville debut at age 18 in New York, played the Orpheum circuit, and performed at London's Palace Theatre. His *New York Times* obituary reported:

It is recorded that he went abroad and performed juggling acts in Europe, Asia, South Africa, Australia and even at Pago Pago in the South Sea Islands. He was in Johannesburg while the guerrilla end of the Boer War was still on, juggling clubs and other sundry articles.

A pivotal day in the life of W.C. Fields and all lovers of irreverent comedy came April 8, 1900, as W.C. wed chorus girl Harriet "Hattie" Hughes in San Francisco. Hattie joined W.C.'s juggling act on a popular European tour, and on July 28, 1904 gave birth to their son, William Claude Fields, Jr.

W.C. made his Broadway bow in *The Ham Tree* on August 28, 1905, in which the star immortalized his ever-popular expression, "Mogo on the Gogogo." He scored a smash hit and went on tour in the show.

Cheating managers and agents ransacked his money, spawning a lifelong fanaticism for financial security. Meanwhile, his marriage toppled. Life became a domestic nightmare. Hattie, a Catholic, refused to divorce W.C.; in time, he was also alienated from his son. It all became grist for his act, which in turn became an outlet for his angst. As Ron Fields relates,

> W.C. used his pet peeves and all this stuff in his stage and screen persona, which came from a real inner feeling, his true life and his true thoughts. Hattie, was of course, very important, in a negative sort of way. Again, "A Life on Film" — his wives are always harridans. And that's how he viewed Hattie! And she was, pretty much... well, very mean...
>
> Now, in all of his movies, if he has a son, or if there's a younger generation person, they're usually lousy people. Like Claude in *The Man on the Flying Trapeze*... That's the name my father (W.C.'s son) went by, and in *Trapeze*, the stepson, "Claude," is played by Grady Sutton as kind of a sissy. That's kind of what W.C. saw in his own son... and it was interesting that he called him "Claude," because my father went by the name W. Claude Fields Jr.
>
> Also, whenever he has a daughter in a show or film, she's always a lovely daughter, like Constance Moore in *You Can't Cheat an Honest Man* — a loving, supporting daughter. In one of W.C.'s letters to Hattie he says, "You've turned my son against me... If we'd have had a daughter, she would have seen through your perfidy, Hattie." That reveals how he portrays his fictional sons and daughters in his films. So Hattie, and his belief that his son was turned against him, was part of "his life on film."

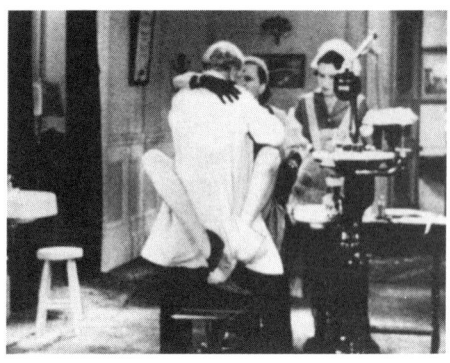

The Dentist

Now and then a revisionist tries to reassess W.C.'s relationship with the redoubtable Hattie, but letters — such as this one from 1944 — do little to support the argument for surviving affection, at least in W.C.'s case:

> Can you imagine my surprise when I read your letter and you said we had gone through life doing nothing for each other? Sixty smackers a week, year in and year out, for forty years ($124,800.00) you consider nothing. Heigh-ho-lackaday. Surprises never cease.

Hattie would haunt W.C. all his life, and beyond. After his 1946 death, she contested his will and won a large piece of his $1,000,000-plus estate.

As Winokur wrote in *The Portable Curmudgeon*, "He was naturally undemonstrative and easily hurt, so he affected a phony manorial demeanor to conceal his vulnerability … He strove to be a part of the world but was an outcast."

June 21, 1915: The new edition of *The Ziegfeld Follies* opened at the New Amsterdam Theatre. The stars were Bert Williams, Leon Errol, Ina Claire, Ed Wynn, and W.C. Fields. Taking in a performance was John Barrymore, who'd fallen for Nora Bayes, a musical comedy star. Barrymore had heard that Miss Bayes was the paramour of one W.C. Fields, and had come to glare at his competition, whom he prematurely described as a "trivial mugger." Ethel accompanied John. After the curtain, and witnessing Fields' comic genius, Barrymore turned to his sister.

"Ethel, he's one of the greatest artists of all time. I'm not in love with Miss Bayes now. Hell! I'm in love with W.C. Fields!"

W.C. became the headliner of *The Ziegfeld Follies* from 1916 through 1921. He wrote much of his own material and developed routines that became classics: the pool table routine, the croquet game, the golf specialist. He shared the stage with such stars as Will Rogers and Fannie Brice. In the 1921 *Follies*, there was lampooning of the three Barrymores, presenting them in a Camille burlesque, with Raymond Hitchcock as Lionel, Fannie Brice as Ethel and W.C. as "Jack." Meanwhile, he made his film debut in *Pool Sharks* (1915), a one-reeler for Gaumont-Mutual, performing his celebrated pool table skit.

Come 1922 when as John Decker and John Barrymore made their own contributions to New York theatre, Fields jumped ship from Ziegfeld to star in George White's *Scandals of 1922*. In the show's chorus as an "English tea girl" was Dolores Costello — soon to be Mrs. John Barrymore. W.C. added to his laurels as Professor Eustace McGargle in *Poppy*, which opened September 3, 1923, ran for 300 performances, and offered the spectacle of W.C. singing "Kodoola, Kodoola." It was at this time that John Decker, who'd previously met W.C. in England, became reacquainted when he sketched Fields' caricature for the *Evening World*.

It was a trademark portrayal, and by now, his self-creation was complete. Abused by his father, cheated by his managers, despised by his wife (whose religious zeal prevented her from divorcing him), estranged from his own son, W.C. Fields defensively became the Great Charlatan — the Olympian Con-Man, the Shyster Supreme, a carnival rogue in a top hat and lapel flower, hating children, making fools of women, eyes twinkling as he merrily cheated much of the world at large, self-righteously forgiving himself, for, as Fields put it, You Can't Cheat an Honest Man.

Rarely would such bitterness transform into such humor, and W.C. Fields' comedy, in its true essence, was as much a heartbreaking self-exposé as John Barrymore's Hamlet. W.C. Fields made his feature film bow in 1924's Revolutionary war epic *Janice Meredith*, playing a soused British soldier. But his big cinema splash was *Sally of the Sawdust* (1925), D.W. Griffith's version of *Poppy*. W.C.'s highlight: selling a fraudulent talking dog. Carol Dempster had the title role, as she did in Griffith's *That Royle Girl* (1926), with W.C. as "Dads" Royle. As Fate had it, Miss Dempster also happened to be Griffith's lover, and persuaded D.W. to cut down W.C.'s role so to build up her own.

Fields career went merrily along: *The Ziegfeld Follies* of 1925 (including his famed Drug Store skit), a series of Paramount comedy films with Chester Conklin, and a new Broadway hit in Earl Carroll's *Vanities* (August 6, 1928). which featured two of W.C.'s all-time funniest skits: "Stolen Bonds," in which he sings the title song to a crying Canadian Mountie and says "It ain't a fit night out for man or beast, and it's been a stormin' for over a fortnit!" Which is followed by a splash in the face with fake snow. Equally memorable and considerably more racy was "An Episode at the Dentist," in which W.C. ("Have you ever had this tooth pulled before?") yanks the tooth of a willowy young lady whose legs entwine themselves about the dentist until the scene resembles a hardcore stag loop. The humor survives in the 1932 Mack Sennett short *The Dentist* (highly censored in its original release).

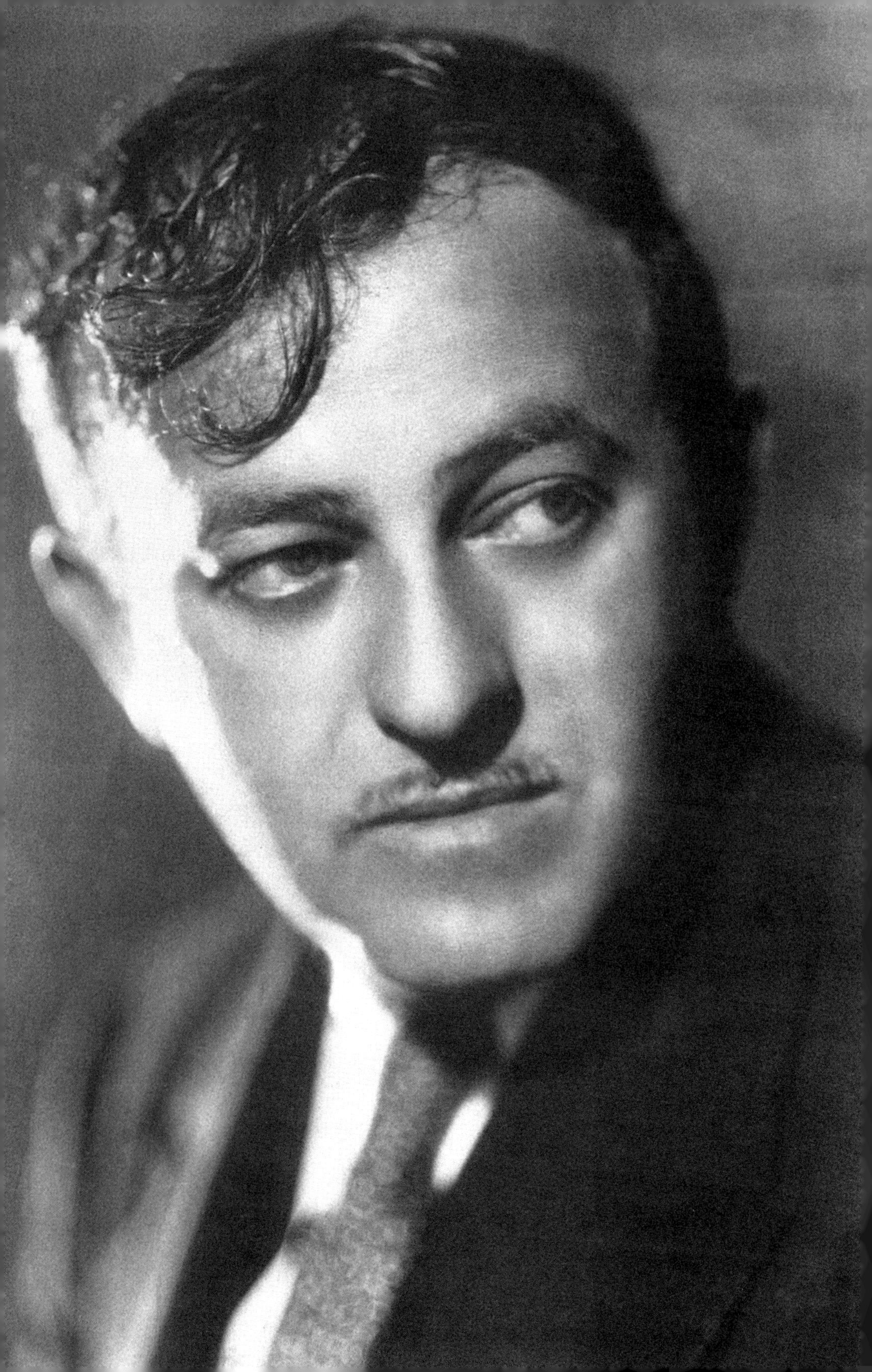

Chapter Five
"*The Devil Can-Cans in Their Souls...*"

> A hanged man dies in a few seconds if his neck is broken by the drop. If his neck isn't broken, due to the incorrect adjustment of the noose, he chokes to death. This takes from eight to fourteen minutes.
>
> While he hangs choking, the white-covered body starts to spin slowly. The white-hooded head tilts to one side and a stretch of purple neck becomes visible. Then the rope begins to vibrate and hum like a hive of bees. After this the white robe begins to expand and deflate as if it were being blown up by a leaky bicycle pump. Following the turning, vibrating, spinning, humming, and pumping up of the white robe comes the climax of the hanging. This is the throat of the hanging man letting out a last strangled cry or moan of life.
>
> — Ben Hecht, *Gaily Gaily* (1963)

8 p.m., May 19, 1929. It was the very first Academy Awards Banquet, held at the Blossom Room of the Hollywood Roosevelt Hotel.

Louis B. Mayer, grand poobah of Metro-Goldwyn-Mayer Studios, hatched the Academy Award concept. The Academy of Motion Picture Arts and Sciences was open to anyone who "had contributed in a distinguished way to arts and sciences of motion picture production." Others saw it more cynically. The Academy came to life as a rabid industry watchdog, giving Hollywood bigwigs the power to attack and devour any labor dispute upstarts in its own formidable way. The Academy planned to hop in bed with Will Hays' censorship office and host annual membership-only, let's-slap-each-other-on-the-back banquets.

Ben Hecht

There was a message/warning implied in the Academy's formation: behave yourself, stay away from those goddamned unions, and you, too, might win a prize.

As for the prize itself… Cedric Gibbons, MGM's handsome, mustached art director, then happily settled into a sado-maso marriage to Dolores del Rio, designed the statue: a naked man, jabbing a sword into a reel of film. There were five holes on the reel for each of the Academy branches. As Mason Wiley and Damien Bova wrote in their book *Inside Oscar: The Unofficial History of the Academy Awards*:

> For the production of the statuette, the Academy gave $500 to an unemployed art school graduate named George Stanley, who sculpted Gibbons' design in clay. Alex Smith then cast the 13 ½-inch, 6 ¾-pound statuette in tin and copper and gold-plated the whole thing. The Award was ready; now it was time for the first winners.

There were no surprises on Academy Award night; the winners had been announced three months before the ceremony. Douglas Fairbanks, Academy president, presented all the awards. Among them: Best Picture, a tie: *The Last Command* and *Wings*. Best "Artistic Quality of Production": *Sunrise*. Special Award for "the outstanding pioneer talking picture": *The Jazz Singer*. Best Actor: Emil Jannings of *The Last Command* (Jannings was spooked by the "Talkie" phenomenon had received his award previously, and took it home to Germany). Best Actress: Janet Gaynor, for three films: *Seventh Heaven*, *Street Angel* and *Sunrise*. Best Director: Frank Borzage for *Seventh Heaven*. Best Comedy Direction: Lewis Milestone for *Two Arabian Knights*. Best Writing (Adaptation): Benjamin Glazer for *Seventh Heaven*.

Best Writing, Original Story: Ben Hecht for *Underworld*.

Hecht wasn't there. Suspicious of the Academy, publicly accusing director Josef von Sternberg of ruining his story, Hecht boycotted the Academy Awards, Charlie Chaplin, winner of a special Academy Award for producing, writing, directing and acting in *The Circus*, was skeptical too, and stayed away the big night. The Academy sent the absentee winner his "Best Writing, Original Story" gold-plated, naked-man-with-sword prize.

Ben Hecht used it as a doorstop.

Daredevil reporter, novelist of sex-charged fantasies, and arguably the most influential screenwriter of all time, Ben Hecht, as Budd Schulberg nailed it, was all about "animal pleasure." John Decker was the artistic chameleon, and Hecht could write in any style, with the same passionate, hard-hitting flair.

Born on the Lower East Side of New York February 28, 1894, Ben Hecht claimed he was born in a toilet — as MacAdams reports in his Hecht biography, it was Ben's cousin who was born, prematurely, in a toilet. At age eight, he was riding an open streetcar when a runaway horse crashed through the car, killing a man, and the child went home and wrote his eyewitness account of the carnage. At age 13, he received a most influential gift — 167 books from his father, including the works of Shakespeare, Dickens and Twain. The boy devoured them all and moved on to Poe, Dumas, Gogol....

At age 14, Ben and brother Peter toured as a trapeze act in a circus, hailing themselves as the "Youngest Daredevils in America."

It was as a swashbuckling reporter, however, that Ben Hecht first made his mark. In his *Gaily, Gaily,* Hecht wrote of his pre–World War I days and nights, covering news for the *Chicago Daily Journal,* living in a river-view apartment, working for editor Mr. Mahoney and with photographer Bunny Hare. All variety of sordid, sensational assignments came his way, as Hecht remembered it:

> Mr. Mahoney would say to me at 7 a.m., "Here's something in your line, professor. A honeymooning banker from Cedar Rapids has kept his nude bride chained to a bedpost in the Morrison hotel for a week, feeding her only salted peanuts and whipping her hourly with a cat-o'-nine-tails. The zebra-striped bride is in the Passavant Hospital unable to speak. But the groom is holding forth in Captain Strassneider's office on the sanctity of marriage. See what you can dig up out of the financier's soul. And take Bunny Hare along."

An example of Hecht's gloriously politically incorrect sagas in *Gaily, Gaily* is "The Fairy." Fred Ludwig, a butcher, faces the Chicago gallows for having murdered his wife Irma by grinding her up into sausage; a man breakfasting on his sausage bit into her wedding ring. On the night before the execution, as a blizzard paralyzes the city, the sheriff begs Fred to confess. The butcher agrees, with a last request proviso:

"I would like a lady's vanity case, with everything complete. Face powder, lipstick, and a cake of mascara."

Hecht ventures out into a blizzard to Queen Lil's whorehouse in quest of the vanity case. Queen Lil, her coal-warmed brothel hellishly warm in the snowy night, answers the door in bare feet and kimono, so amused by the request that she wakes up her girls (all without customers on this snowbound night) to hear the request.

> Eight girls came shuffling sleepily into the parlor. Five of them were nude. The other three wore bloomers. They were variously shaped, from skinny blondes with stringy breasts to Turkish delights with watermelon udders. Two of them were startlingly attractive. They looked more like sleepwalking princesses than five-dollar whores…
>
> When Lil finished telling my story they started whooping and slapping each other with a mysterious kind of joy. One of the sleepwalking princesses obliged with a song in a piercing soprano, "Oh, it's up the rope he goes, up he goes…"
>
> I sat dizzily in this sudden Witches' Sabbath of nudes rolling on the floor with delight, kicking each other's bare behinds. Queen Lil, herself, seemed the mistress of the baffling revelry… her Chinese kimono unbelted and her antique flesh exposed….

A massive whore named "Tiny" ("obese with an infant's face") falls in love-at-first-sight with Hecht and provides the vanity case. Back at the jail, Fred Ludwig makes himself up with the rouge, powder, mascara and lipstick, confessing to the murder, relating he could only sleep with his wife after kissing his male lover's picture under his pillow. After Irma laughed at this discovery, he slaughtered her, and the man who bit into the wedding ring in the sausage was Fred's lover, to whom he sent the sausage, and who, revolted, had turned against him. The death march begins, and Fred Ludwig falls through the trapdoor in his makeup, white robe and hood….

> It was no moan or guttural cry. Out of Fred's throat came his true voice — a high-pitched, feminine wail. I shivered because I felt something triumphant in its drawn-out falsetto note.
>
> I wrote a lead on a piece of copy paper — "Fred Ludwig lived as a cowardly man but he died as a brave woman."

Hecht was the star reporter on "The Ragged Stranger Murder Case" — army hero Carl Wanderer claimed a ragged stranger had attacked him and his wife, with the wife and stranger killed in the struggle. Hecht broke the story that Wanderer, a homosexual, had actually hired the stranger, drifter Al Watson, to kill his pregnant wife. Wanderer, convicted of the murders, went to the gallows March 19, 1921.

Hecht was also a crony of the visionary Polish-American artist Stanislaw Szukalski, himself a future guest at Bundy Drive, who'd allegedly learned about anatomy by dissecting his own father. In his *Zanies*, Jay Robert Nash writes of the time Hecht brought several art critics to Szukalski's walk-up studio:

One of the art critics carried a walking cane and, as he inspected an enormous Venus executed by Szukalski, he posed and jabbed at the statue, commenting, "That's nice... That's fine."

"Excuse me," Stanislaus said, stepping up to the critic. He snatched the cane from the startled critic. "One does not poke the art of Szukalski." He broke the cane over his knee.

"Who do you think you are?" cried the offended critic.

"The greatest artist in the world," responded Szukalski in a calm voice, and, with that, grabbed the critic by the collar and the seat of the pants and ran him over to a long flight of stairs leading downward, hurling him into the air. Fortunately the critic was only bruised in the long fall, but Ben Hecht never again invited critics to appraise Szukalski's work.

And in 1922, the year John Barrymore played Hamlet, Ben Hecht was in trouble with the federal government for obscenity, defended by no less than Clarence Darrow, and loving every minute of it.

Hecht's *Fantazius Mallare, A Mysterious Oath*, was a macabre mix of spiritualism, metaphysics and pornography, its hero a mad painter/sculptor/recluse who believes he should be a God, and that a woman is essential to his deification. In his dedication, festooned with a Wallace Smith cartoon (in Aubrey Beardsley style) of two men trapped in a maze of briars, where a giant penis is about to enter a thorny vagina, Hecht addressed his "enemies":

> ... to the moral ones who have relentlessly chased God out of their bedrooms... to the prim ones who fornicate apologetically (the Devil can-cans in their souls) ... to the reformers (patience, patience) the psychopathic ones who seek to indicate their own sexual impotencies by padlocking the national vagina, who find relief for constipation in forbidding their neighbors the water closet (God forgives them, but not I) ... to the smug ones who walk with their noses ecstatically buried in their own rectums ... to these and to many other abominations whom I apologize to for omitting, this inhospitable book, celebrating the dark mirth of *Fantazius Mallare*, is dedicated...

2,000 copies of *Fantazius Mallare* circulated privately, a limited edition eventually confiscated by the Federal government for obscenity. Darrow won Hecht an acquittal, and the writer, delighted, proceeded with a sequel, *The Kingdom of Evil*.

Hecht edited (with Maxwell Bodenheim) Chicago's influential *The Literary Review*. He joined the *Chicago Daily News* and wrote *1001 Afternoons in Chicago*, which

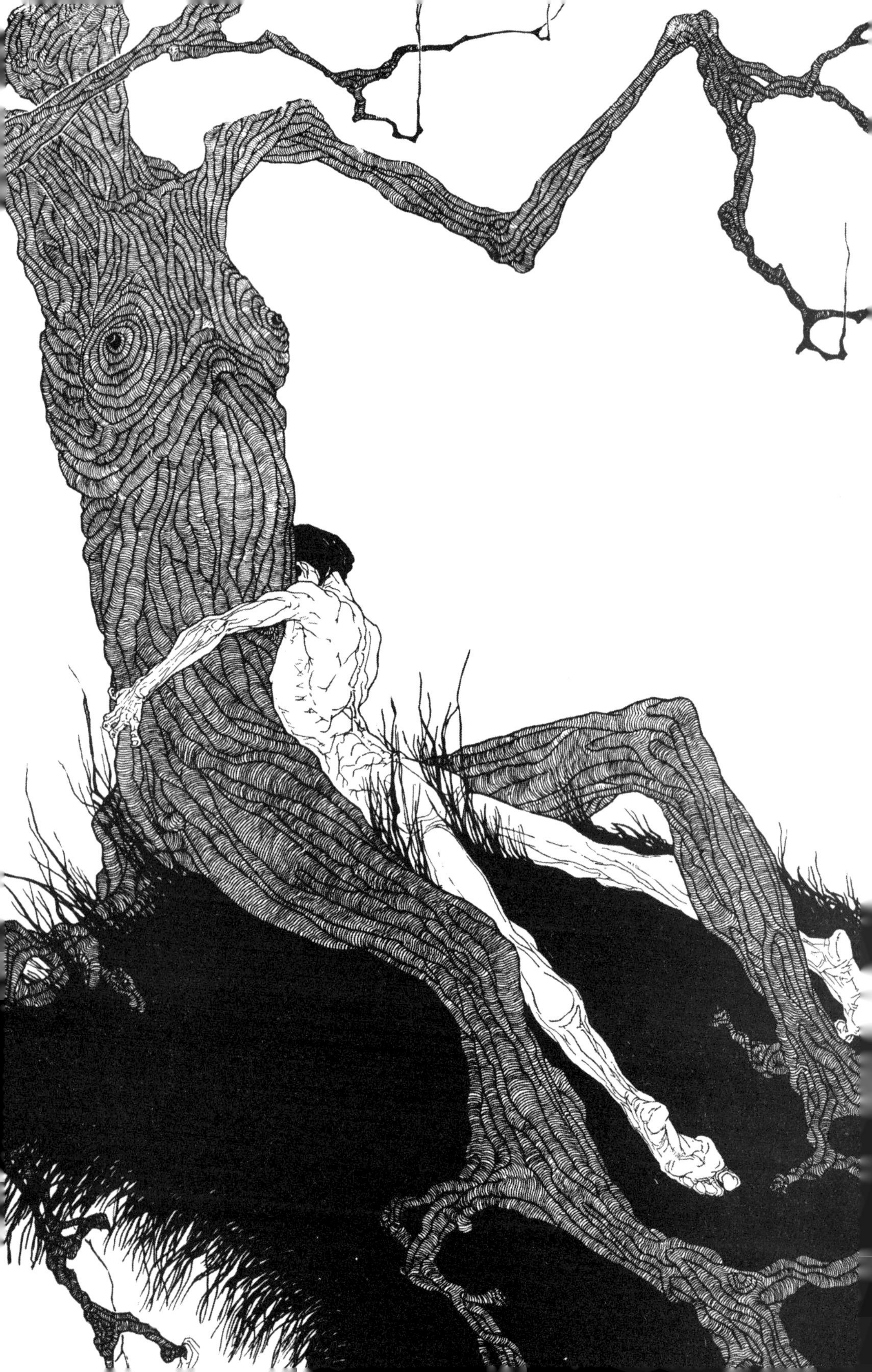

survives as classic journalism, with pen drawings by Herman Rosse (who would later design the Universal horror classics *Dracula* and *Frankenstein*). Hecht came to New York City in 1923 and later wrote in his 1954 book *A Child of the Century*, "I had arrived in New York in time to join a wild and premature *fin de siècle party*." His collaborations with Bodenheim continued, including 1924's *Cutie: A Warm Mamma*, in which part of the "First Canto" reads:

> Cutie gave St. Peter writer's cramps before she was eighteen. After she was eighteen St. Peter crossed her name out of the Judgment Book. Not taking any chances, he also threw away her telephone number…

Cutie (whom her infatuated authors claim "was as evil to look at as a spring morning") runs afoul of Herman Pupick, "a prude with one glass eye and splintered pieces of glass in what passed for his heart." When he confesses he's sinned with Cutie, Mrs. Pupick, his sex-fearing wife, kills him. Cutie takes a good look at herself in the mirror, and drops dead.

"Rest in peace, Mrs. Pupick," write the authors. "No white slaver can get you now."

Ben Hecht — always attacking prudery, censorship, the self-righteous, always in love with the outcast, the renegade.

Hecht soon joined the famed "Algonquin Round Table," it was his fame as a reporter that was his greatest celebrity. In *Letters from Bohemia*, Hecht remembered his pal and writing partner Charles MacArthur, and wrote:

> The stories we covered were part of our friendship. They remained a world out of which neither of us entirely emerged. We interviewed thieves, swindlers, murderers, lunatics, fire bugs, bigamists, gangsters, and innumerable sobbing ladies who had taken successful potshots at their married lovers.
>
> For all such evil-doers Charlie had sort of a collector's enthusiasm. Crime and disaster allured him, socially. Hangings, death beds, 4-11 fires, protracted gun battles between cops and loonies, mysterious corpses popping out of river and swamp, courtrooms and jail cells loud with deviltries, were a sort of picnic ground for MacArthur. For me, also.

Hecht and MacArthur made theater history in 1928 as the playwrights of the volcanic newspaper melodrama, *The Front Page*, in which ace reporter Hildy Johnson (Lee Tracy) is tempted away by editor Walter Burns (Osgood Perkins) from his new marriage on the night of a big hanging. An anarchist murderer is hidden in the

Wallace Smith's erotically-charged illustration from Ben Hecht's perverse novel, *Fantazius Mallare*

pressroom desk, a sad but gallant whore takes a suicide leap out of the window, and at the end Walter Burns sends off Hildy for a life of middle-class joys, and even gives Hildy a gift — his watch — which sets up a great curtain line. After Hildy and his bride leave, Burns calls the authorities and orders them to nab Hildy on the departing train's first stop:

"The son of a bitch stole my watch!"

Opening at the Times Square Theatre August 14, 1928, produced by Jed Harris, directed by George S. Kaufman, *The Front Page* ran for 276 performances, climaxing a roaring decade for Ben Hecht.

Hecht's screenplay for *Underworld*, directed by Josef von Sternberg, presents a gaudy star trio: "Bull" Weed (George Bancroft), a smilin' stud of a gangster whose mantra is, "Nobody helps me — I help them!," Rolls Royce Wensel (Clive Brook), a literate drunken derelict whose life changes after Bull hands him a stash of money, and "Feathers" McCoy (Evelyn Brent), Bull's vampy moll who has a sartorial taste for feathers.

Underworld, in the words of Paramount co-founder Jesse Lasky, "was so sordid and savage in content, so different from accepted film fare," that the studio considered shelving it. Ben Hecht, naturally, protested that the film was not sordid and savage enough, due to "a half-dozen sentimental touches" provided by von Sternberg. "I still shudder remembering one of them," Hecht recalled. "My head villain, after robbing a bank, emerged with a suitcase full of money and paused in the crowded street to notice a blind beggar and give him a coin before making his getaway."

As the Roaring '20s neared its disastrous close, Ben Hecht had conquered the world of newspapers, Broadway theatre and motion pictures. His true genius was in his irreverence, and his eventual membership as a "Bundy Drive Boy" was inevitable.

Among his controversial offerings, the book *A Jew in Love*:

> One of the finest things ever done by the mob was the crucifixion of Jesus. Intellectually it was a splendid gesture. But trust the mob to bungle. If I'd had charge of executing Christ, I'd have handled it differently. You see, what I'd have done was have had him shipped to Rome and fed to the lions. They could never make a Savior out of mincemeat!

Did Hecht have any of the Oedipal lusts/father complexes that so profoundly affected Decker, Barrymore, Hartmann and Fields? His parents had been nurturing, and come the late 1920s, he was settled into a lasting happy marriage with his second wife, Rose.

In his 1980 book *The Second Handshake*, the late Will Fowler (Gene's son) remembers an early 1930s Fourth of July at Hecht's home in Nyack. There had been fireworks, Hecht had blown up his small boat landing as a finale, then all retired, and young Will was sent to sleep in the library. In the night he noted a secret door that led to a fully-lighted, incredibly detailed doll's-house bedroom, complete with vanity table, four-poster bed with canopy, and revelers. As Fowler wrote,

> What set this display apart from being an ordinary doll's house were two well-fashioned nude figures on the bed, locked in sexual embrace. In each cubicle were two or more dolls in several venery positions. One even displayed an adult woman enjoying her pleasures with two pre-teenage boys. But the little box I was unable to understand exhibited a female doll lying in bed, her feet touching the floor. And the male doll looked as if he had tripped on the way to greet her. He had fallen, his face landing on her stomach.
>
> I was so entranced by these ravishing displays that I rose a half-dozen times during the night to re-inspect my discovery.
>
> From then on, each time we visited Ben's house, I always insisted on sleeping in the library.

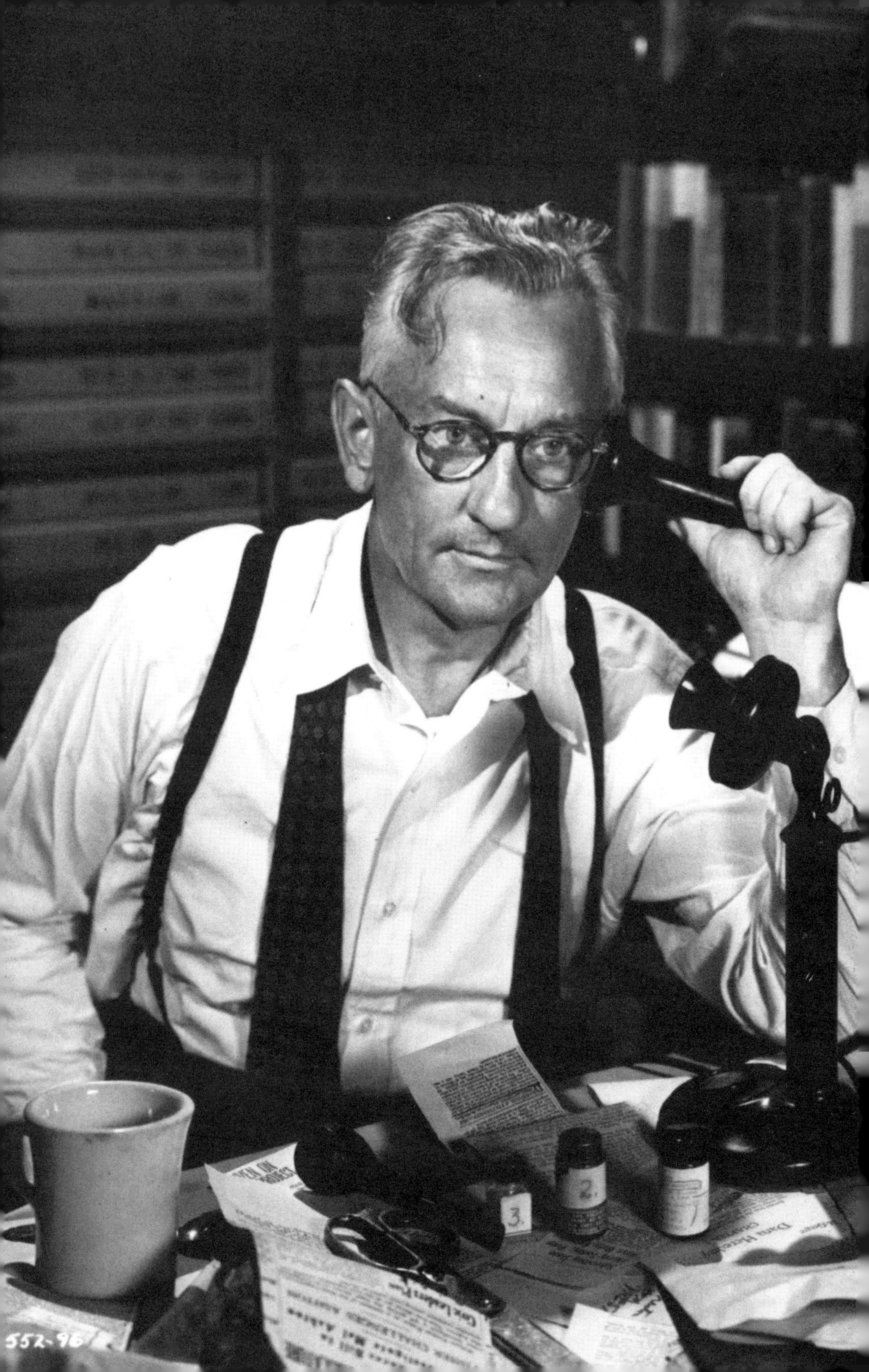
552-96

Chapter Six
Father Confessor

"Writing is easy," said Gene Fowler. "All you do is stare at a blank sheet of paper until drops of blood form on your forehead." According to his son Will (the first reporter on the murder site of the Black Dahlia), Fowler was a mix of "angels and demons," a spiritual toss-up whom key people in his life saw as worth saving. He in turn saw possible salvation for the Bundy Drive Boys he knew and loved so well, serving them as part Boswell, part father confessor.

Fowler would have enjoyed being labeled fellow sinner, and he'd tallied his share of transgressions. He had affairs with such movie stars like Ann Harding and Mary Astor and even, so the story goes, Queen Marie of Rumania. This excerpt from a letter a flu-suffering Fowler wrote to John Barrymore in Hollywood from the Hotel Delmonico in New York, circa 1941, gives evidence of his Rabelaisian humor:

> Charlie MacArthur, the Laird of Delancey Street, called on me … I told him that you had been trying to lay a midget at Earl Carroll's, and that you claimed that any venereal disease procured at such a Lilliputian source would only be half as bad as blue balls from a normal lass.
>
> Ben Hecht also called, and brought the most interesting news since the burning of Harper's Ferry. He has discovered a woman who disports four legs and two pelvic grottoes. She has had a child from either trench. One of these slits of ecstasy is a mite (not the widow's) smaller than the other. Also, the gap on the starboard beam is hairless — probably because of her Chihuahua

Gene Fowler in *The Senator was Indiscreet*

bloodstream. Mr. Hecht is writing of this blessed damsel, and I shall forward you a clipping. As a scientist, I am always glad to examine — for a nominal fee — the cavities of a lady …

Despite the foregoing, Gene Fowler's image was always one of respectability. He had the tall, noble, American eagle handsomeness, a colorful background as a gritty New York reporter who covered sports and executions, the distinction of having once been the youngest managing editor of a major U.S. newspaper. A man with a solid work ethic, a lasting marriage (and forgiving wife), a good track record as devoted father of two sons and a daughter, a Catholic conversion and a passion for writing that kept his spiritual ship seemingly safely on course.

His maxims were, in a way, brilliant:

- ★ Money was meant to be thrown from the backs of trains.
- ★ Man is an accident born of an incident.
- ★ Men who deserve monuments do not need them.
- ★ Success is a greased pig.

Gene Fowler had a bull-in-a-china shop quality. In *Letters from Bohemia*, Ben Hecht wrote of the time Charles MacArthur had introduced his wife Helen Hayes to Fowler:

The meeting had taken place in Fowler's managing editor's office… During it, Fowler had gallantly addressed Helen Hayes as Miss Menken; Helen Menken was co-starring with Miss Hayes in *Mary of Scotland*. He had also disarmed an angry gambler, come to shoot the editor for some misstatements about him in the paper. Fowler removed the indignant reader's .45 from his hand with a judo-chop, while continuing his social talk with the MacArthurs — "By God, Charles, you never told me your wife, Miss Menken, was not only a genius but a woman of staggering beauty."

Yet perhaps his most outstanding quality was compassion. The story goes that, one Christmas, when Fowler was a reporter, his newspaper gave him $500 to distribute to needy families — and Fowler spent it all on the first family. In his feature story "Rabelais of the Rockies," Charles Samuels, who himself had been financially saved by Fowler early in his career, wrote:

He can find as many reasons for forgiving people's derelictions and mistakes as can the most gentle and understanding clergyman. Fowler hates only the vengeful, the spiteful, and the holier-than-thou crowd.

Born Eugene Parrott Devlin March 8, 1891 in Denver, he was the child of a beloved mother Dodie and an abandoning father Charlie who, shortly after Fowler's birth, deserted the family and stayed a hermit for over 30 years. Fowler's filial feelings were in the bitter league of Barrymore, Hartmann, Fields and Decker, but when the old man actually appeared once again after all those decades Fowler embraced him.

Will Fowler wrote of his father in *The Young Man from Denver*, published in 1962, but he pulled his punches since Fowler's widow (and Will's mother) Dodie was still alive. In later years, after his mother's death, Will wrote *Odyssey of a Spring Lamb* (the title comes from a chapter in *Good Night, Sweet Prince*) — a more racy, revealing, and intimate account of his father's early traumas and torments. It was never published. *Odyssey* relates that Dodie, divorcing her errant husband, remarried Frank Fowler, a handsome jock ne'er-do-well, when Gene was eight. They moved to a new house, and:

> It being his first night in a new environment, the child arose in the dark. He had forgotten to put his pee-pot under his bed. He was disoriented. He brushed against strange objects and furniture. And while trying to paw his way to the stairs — and eventually to the privy outside — he blindly wandered, only to find himself in another room where a beam of moonlight shone in. There he saw his stepfather in Pilgrim-position atop his mother. Frank was pumping his body up-and-down like a twin-backed monster. And when Eugene brushed against their bed, the grunting and St. Vitus motion paused long enough for the boy to hear the awful voice of the man growl, "Get the hell out of here and go back to your bed!"
>
> "Your bed! ... your bed!" Eugene mumbled as he traced his way back to his room. The words bruised his soul.

The following Sabbath morning, the "ogre in the child's eyes" was performing calisthenics in his "long nightgown," standing on his head against the wall…

> "… his crotch augmentation hung out like a vulture's limp neck from its hairy nest…"

And Gene ran away, to the home of his Granny Wheeler, and (according to his son's account) "sobbed as though in a fit of hiccoughs: 'I … I … I don't want … want to … ever see that man again!'"

He lived for a time with his grandmother, secretly reading the classics she'd forbidden (his favorite was Mark Twain). Will wrote that "Eugene would now lay his head on his Dodie's tender breast when they were alone on few occasions; in the hills beneath the rustling leaves of the aspen trees, with only the birds and the squirrels watching." But Dodie soon died of peritonitis. "This time," wrote Will Fowler, "he felt betrayed by God."

By age 20, Gene was the top reporter of the *Denver Republican*. He was an ace sports reporter, a prize fight referee (a childhood pal had been heavyweight boxing champion Jack Dempsey) and the suitor of a wealthy socialite he called "Gloria," whose father nixed the union when he learned that Gene's reporter salary (now on the *Rocky Mountain News*) was only $30 per week.

And so, on the night of a blizzard, Gene Fowler checked into Denver's Windsor Hotel, opened a bottle of rye, stepped out of the window in the snowstorm and began walking around the Windsor's top floor ledge. Will Fowler called it his father's "gamble with life," and the always melancholy Gene Fowler, years later, would tell Ben Hecht:

To this day, after I stepped back inside, I don't quite know if I had won or lost.

His recovery from delirium tremens came via Madame Jennie Rogers, "the Queen of the Denver Red Lights," at her House of Faces and Mirrors in Denver. The Victorian-style mansion boasted sculptures of famed doxies, chiseled from stone and framed at each corner by granite penises.

- ★ Bertha the Adder
- ★ Glass-eyed Nellie
- ★ Josephine Icebox
- ★ The Galloping Cow
- ★ Three Tit Tillie
- ★ Wild Ass Nellie

And more. Gene recovered under their vigil, and became the star reporter for the *Denver Post*. Assigned to interview the legendary Buffalo Bill, Fowler sat cross-legged at his feet and fired off his first question.

"Well, Colonel," asked Fowler, "do you really believe that the girls of 40 years ago were better in the hay than the girls of today?"

Buffalo Bill leapt to his feet. "An older man demands respect, sir!" he roared. "My hair is hoary!"

"But not with years, Colonel," said Fowler.

Gene Fowler married Agnes Hubbard July 19, 1916 — immediately attractive to Gene, Will wrote, because she so resembled his mother Dodie. They wed in a Red Rock natural amphitheatre, with a gaggle of ne'er-do-wells Gene brought along as witnesses. Damon Runyon had noted Fowler's talent and invited him to New York, with a mission.

Fowler spent all his travel money on a party with his Denver reporter pals. An undertaker came to his aid by hiring Fowler to accompany the cadaver of an old crone — "Nellie," as Fowler named her — to New York for her burial. The trip was fraught with peril. In Chicago, he ran afoul of war veterans when he accidentally threw a bowl of goldfish into an electrical American flag; the veterans beat him to a pulp. It was how he met Charles MacArthur, of the *Chicago Herald-Examiner*, who was in trouble himself for having stolen from the coroner's office the stomach of a dead woman whose husband was accused of poisoning her.

"What annoys me," MacArthur reportedly said, "is that all they found in the lady's stomach were the remains of a 75-cent blue plate lunch."

MacArthur smuggled Fowler out of Chicago before charges of malicious mischief and insulting the American flag could stick. In Detroit, however, federal detectives arrested him for defiling the Mann Act — transporting an underage girl across state lines for immoral purposes. The purported victim was the cadaver "Nellie." Fowler had to show the feds that the alleged virgin-in-peril was the aged and very dead Nellie, moldering in her coffin in the baggage car.

Gene Fowler relocated to New York, the legends continued. One of his most famous involved the demise of J.P. Morgan the elder, who despised the press. As he sickened, reporters kept a deathwatch and learned that a specialist from France was sailing to New York to attempt a medical miracle. The reporters eventually saw a great car deliver whom they believed to be the French miracle man — who was Fowler disguised in a top hat, elegant suit and fake beard. Posing as the doctor, Fowler infiltrated Morgan's bedroom, shook his head sadly at the financial giant and then ran like hell — the real doctor had arrived, and Fowler scooped his rivals that Morgan was indeed a dying man.

In 1927, at the age of 36, Gene Fowler became the managing editor of the *New York American*, the youngest editor of a major paper in the country. As Fowler told the *Los Angeles Times* over 30 years later:

> When Mr. Hearst told me he wanted me to be editor, I protested. I told him, "I don't like editors." He said, "Neither do I, young man — but they are a necessary evil."

At other times, Fowler expressed his opinion of editors a bit more colorfully: "An editor should have a pimp for a brother, so he'd have someone to look up to." Nevertheless, he and Hearst worked together happily; once when Hearst telephoned late at night in a panic, Fowler reportedly lulled him into serenity by playing the concertina over the coast-to-coast telephone connection. Once, confronted by three hostile executive editors at the *American*, Fowler gave each a gift-packaged small clay model of William Randolph Hearst, with instructions:

> Practice while on vacation in order to perfect yourself in the art of kissing the Chief's foot:
>
> 1. Always bow to statue on entering room.
> 2. Salaam sixteen times to front of statue
> 3. Salaam sixteen times to back of statue
> 4. Go to far side of room, approach statue slowly and reverently, with a hypocritical smile of obeisance on your face.
> 5. Kneel before statue, purse your lips, then fervently kiss statue's foot.

Angry editors blew the whistle and informed Hearst, who laughed and told them not to take upstarts so seriously. (This was about 14 years before Orson Welles felt the Hearst wrath for his *Citizen Kane*.)

Gene Fowler soon tired of Hearst yellow journalism. He wanted to be a writer of books ... novels, primarily. And inevitably, he succumbed to the lure of Hollywood.

Above all, he missed his great friend John Barrymore.

What initially bound John Barrymore with Gene Fowler was a deep love for animals, a trait shared by many of the Bundy Drive Boys. In November of 1918, young Fowler interviewed Barrymore after a matinee of *Redemption*. Between shows they admired a pug dog, and Barrymore only really became interested in Fowler's journalistic attentions after. Fowler related that the dog had gone mad, that his uncle had killed him by trapping it under a washtub and tossing in a poison-soaked rag, "my uncle standing there like an elephant hunter being photographed after the kill."

Barrymore was eager to learn what happened afterwards. Fowler claimed he said he'd never forgiven his uncle, and told of his grandmother's displeasure.

> She was a religious woman. She told me what a sin it was not to forgive — anything. She pointed out to me that Jesus had always forgiven, even when nailed to the Cross. I remember how terribly shocked she seemed when I blurted out, "Yes, but Jesus never had a dog."

For the first time, Barrymore offered his hand. "Hello!" he smiled.
Their friendship would last until the night John Barrymore died 24 years later.

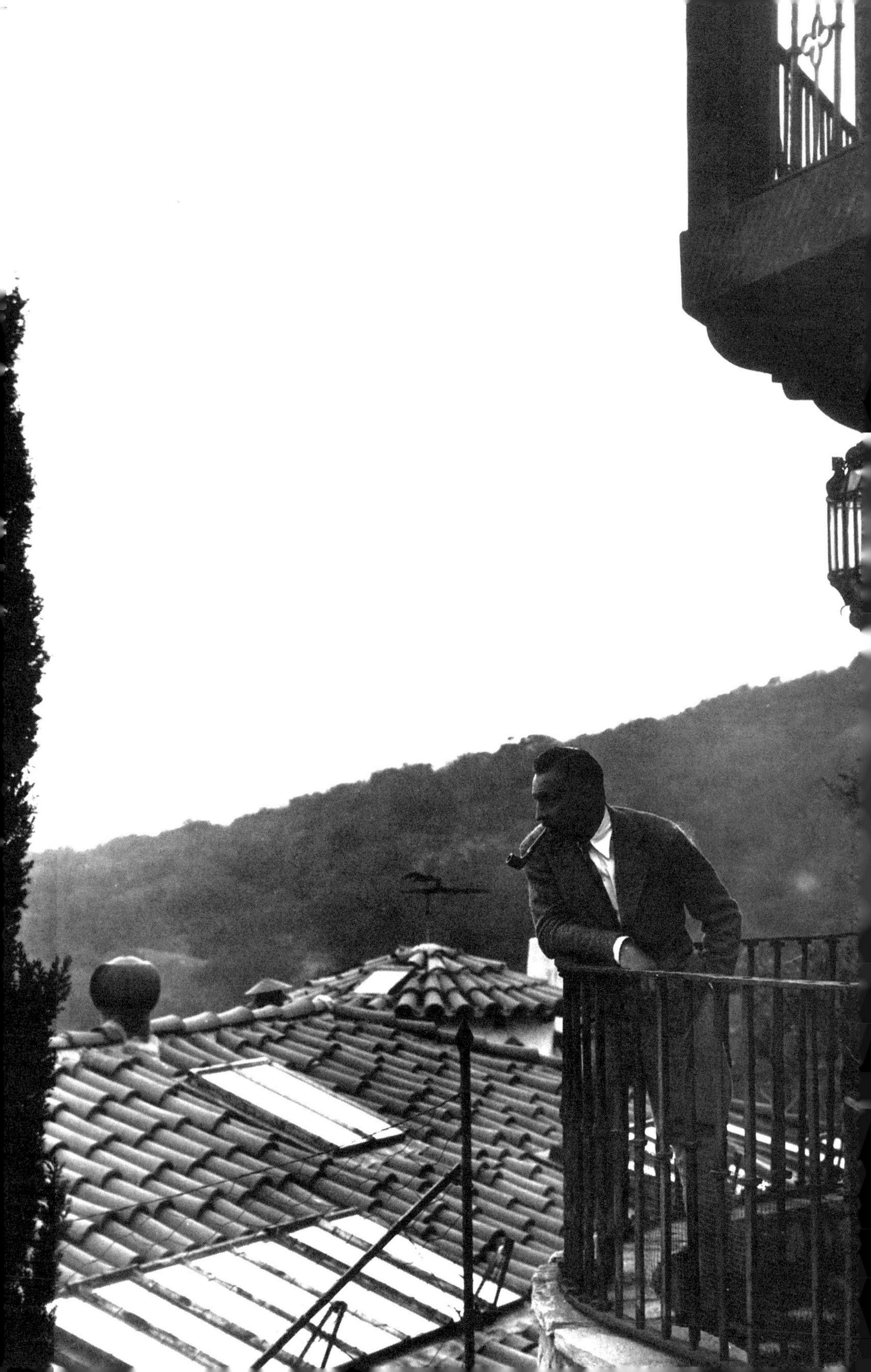

Chapter Seven
Maloney And Other Vultures

> Why, love foreswore me in my mother's womb;
> She did corrupt frail nature with some bribe,
> To shrink mine arm up like a wither'd shrub;
> To make an envious mountain on my back...
> To shape my legs of an unequal size,
> To disproportion me in every part,
> Like to a CHAOS...
> —John Barrymore as Richard III in *The Show of Shows* (1929)

Come 1929, high on his mountaintop, John Barrymore was drinking… heavily.

His Hollywood career was at a peak. He'd made his talkie debut — a new triumph for the Great Profile. His comic artistry was on dazzling display in *The Man from Blakeley's*. Yet his most exciting (if briefest) performance of 1929 was in *The Show of Shows*, Warner's all-star revue, with Barrymore reprising his Richard III. He wore his stage makeup of long black wig and his copper armor, made his entrance on a mountain of bodies carrying a severed head, and delivered Richard's soliloquy from *Henry VI* (which he'd added to his Richard III on Broadway). He's magnificently chilling.

Barrymore, via the magic of the movies, before a curtain in tuxedo, comparing his Richard to Al Capone — pronouncing the long "e" on the gangster's last name, every bit the dashing, brilliantly mad, World's Greatest Living Actor. He had signed a new Warners contract — five films at $150,000 per film, plus 10% of the gross. Life seemed rich and fully blessed for "The Great Profile."

Barrymore was festering. He was madly in love with his blonde bride. His monkey Clementine had become so dangerously jealous of Barrymore's passion for Dolores that Barrymore sadly consigned his pet to the Luna Park Zoo. Barrymore was jealous too, concerned about his young wife's eager sexual appetite, tormented by the knowledge she had posed naked (or nearly so) for James Montgomery Flagg, furious that Flagg had tattled that Dolores sometimes reported to pose in lingerie that was, frankly, not entirely clean.

Mad Jack and "Jiggie Wink" were lord and lady of the increasingly sinister Bella Vista, with the Barrymore serpent coat-of-arms looming over the gate and his Richard III armor keeping guard at the door. "He and Dolores were photographed in their baronial quarters," wrote Margot Peters in *The House of Barrymore*, "looking small and lost."

He added to Bella Vista, where, on sad nights, he'd climb up into his tower, alone in the moonlight. The new additions featured an aviary, and a beautiful stained glass window, worthy of a cathedral, showing John and Dolores posing à la archangels, looking off to the sea. The angelic window was at compelling odds with the serpent coat-of-arms.

His behavior with the birds in his aviary, meanwhile, was hardly reverential. Barrymore sat with worms dangling from his lips, attracting the birds to swoop down and pick them from his mouth. In *Good Night, Sweet Prince*, Gene Fowler wrote that Barrymore overheard his servants discussing this idiosyncrasy:

> "It ain't safe," one of the servants was saying…
>
> "You mean it ain't safe for Mr. Barrymore? Like germs or something?"
>
> "Hell no! I mean safe for the birds … Lookit," the first voice said. "I mean it's the booze on Mr. Barrymore's breath. It gets the worms drunky when he holds them on his lip. Then the birds eat the drunky worms, and then they get booze in their own system. Get me? The birds get dullened in their system."
>
> There was a pause, then the second voice said, "By God, you're right! I noticed how some of the birds flies sideways after he feeds 'em off his lip."
>
> Barrymore said that he promptly went on the wagon for 24 hours.

Mad Jack's new favored pet was Maloney, a king vulture. The great hissing creature, whom Fowler described as having a "torpid malevolence" and the look of "a cynical mortician," would sit on Barrymore's knee, preening his master's hair and mustache. When Barrymore suffered a serious attack of influenza, he moved his beloved Maloney into the bathroom, where it lurked, chained and hissing all the while, as if encouraging Barrymore's recovery. A vengeful nurse, suffering a bite from Maloney's wickedly hooked beak, unlocked his chain, opened a window and allowed Maloney's exit. As Barrymore put it,

When I roused from my fevered state, I asked where Maloney was. I received evasive answers. I was sad as I looked out of my window. I was weak as the devil, but I started straight up in my bed. There, soaring in slow circles in the sky, definitely waiting for me to knock off, was Maloney!

The ungrateful bastard! Predicting my death, anticipating it, wishing it! That's why he had been hissing so happily in the bathroom. Well, I recovered just to spite him...

Barrymore retrieved Maloney and gave him to a zoo. Still, he missed his scavenger pal, and sometimes nostalgically sent him a nice piece of carrion.

"Never let him know where it came from, of course," said John Barrymore.

John Decker, meanwhile, was earning some Lotusland fame as "The Poison Pen Caricaturist of Hollywood."

One of Decker's first big battles erupted with actor/director James Cruze. Part Ute Indian, Cruze had begun his show business career selling "snake oil" in a traveling patent medicine show, had played the title roles in the 1912 *Dr. Jekyll and Mr. Hyde*, directed 1923's *The Covered Wagon*, and, in 1929, was in legal trouble for an accident on one of his films in which a man was killed and various others injured. Cruze decided it was time he had his portrait painted by John Decker. The portrait caught Cruze with his mouth open and looking like a lout. Cruze, appalled by what Decker wrought, refused to pay for the portrait.

"So I was left with the oil," recalled Decker "You can't eat oil."

Decker explained his terrorist response to Cruze's recalcitrance in his *Liberty* magazine installment co-written by Irving Wallace:

> I decided that, even though artists had been kicked around for years, I wouldn't submit. I'd shame Cruze into paying me what I earned. So I had some prison bars built in front of Cruze's portrait, attached a large sign beneath reading "James Cruze in Prison for Debt!" and displayed the result in a prominent photographer's window at 6070 Sunset Boulevard.

Claiming he was the overnight laughing-stock of Hollywood, Cruze sued Decker for $200,000. He erupted to the press:

> I had heard of Decker's notorious poison-pen caricatures, but when I hired him to do a portrait of me, I didn't think he'd try any of his poisonous tactics. I in-

tended to have the portrait made for my wife, Betty Compson. But, Good Lord! If I ever showed her the picture Decker painted of me, it would scare her to death. I was the most surprised man in the world when I saw it. Mouth like a gargoyle; face like a frog! It made me look like an Apache or something worse!

The "Apache" to which Cruze referred meant one of those Spanish fellows in caps and scowls who toss their female partners around the bar. At any rate, Decker, relishing a good fight, delivered his own riposte to Cruze's tirade:

If Cruze wanted some wishy-washy, sloppy, sentimental portrait of himself, he could have had a photograph taken, or hire a two-bit painter to do it. I gave him a work of interpretive art!

Realizing the artist was a pauper, Cruze finally withdrew the suit, but refused to pay Decker. The artist claimed a triumph: "I felt I had scored a moral victory on the side of honest artistry against overly sensitive and unfair clients."

Then there was the night Decker ran afoul of Emil Jannings, the German actor best remembered as the masochist schoolteacher upon whose balding pate Marlene Dietrich cracks eggshells in *The Blue Angel*. Jannings soon returned to Germany, where he eventually allied himself with Hitler. Decker told Irving Wallace in "Heroes with Hangovers":

I recall when I was summoned to meet Jannings at the studio and discuss the possibilities of doing a humorous painting. He told me to be at his home that evening at seven.

I appeared at his home on time. His butler came to the door, told me Jannings was still eating, advised me to return in twenty minutes and slammed the door in my face. Well, I wanted the commission, so I hung around for twenty minutes, and finally was admitted.

Emil Jannings was still at the table, huge and gross, wiping his mouth. He peered at me, and then, with a lordly air, said:

"Ah, Decker, yes, I remember. So you wish to paint my picture, eh? Well, I'll tell you what. You go back to the studio, get some photographs of me in all the roles I've done, study them carefully, then sketch each one and bring the sketches to me. If I like one, I might let you paint me."

"My dear Jannings," I answered, suppressing my anger. "To be honest with you, I was just going downtown to see one of your latest movies. But if you'll kindly stand up and do a few scenes from it right now — well, I'll be able to decide whether or not I want to go!"

And I never saw him again, thank God!

John Decker painted Charlie Chaplin 12 times, who adored (and purchased) all dozen paintings. Decker enjoyed Chaplin's famous imitation of John Barrymore, contrived to show the man's sordid side. Phil Rhodes, who later worked with Chaplin, witnessed the lampoon.

"Chaplin would begin, 'To be, or not to be,'" says Rhodes, "and all the while, he was picking his ears and nose and scratching his balls!"

The Stars in Old Master-style paintings became a craze, and before long, Decker had painted Garbo as the Mona Lisa, Fatty Arbuckle as Falstaff, Lew Cody as Rembrandt, and even apparently made good with James Cruze, painting Cruze as Henry VIII and Cruze's wife Betty Compson as Queen Elizabeth.

The always adventurous artist took whatever came, and squeezed it for whatever publicity it was worth. On August 8, 1929, the *Los Angeles Times* reported that Decker was putting his "finishing touches" on his new creation, *Beauty and the Beast*. He had visited Gay's Lion Farm, where he painted Marie Romano, a showgirl at Hollywood's Pom-Pom nightclub, posing with Numa, "famous motion picture lion star." The daring painting attracted much attention, resulting in Decker's picture in the *Times* (along with Ms. Romano and Numa), inclusion in Fox and Universal newsreels, and bookings to appear in Decker's Hollywood studio, the Waldorf Gallery in New York and The Regent Art Forum in London.

Decker was also already perpetrating his forgeries, seeing the almighty poohbahs of Hollywood as wonderful targets for harpooning. Now and then the ruses backfired.

"I once bought a long-coveted Modigliani, sight unseen," related Decker, "and found out it was one I'd done myself!"

Besides Maloney, there were other vultures hovering over the men who'd become the Bundy Drive Boys. Come Black Friday, October 1929, the Stock Market came crashing down, bringing on the Great Depression. These remarkable men were in a way immune from the disaster, and their gifts gave them a sanctuary from the woes of the commonality.

Yet they paid for their blessings with torment. Barrymore suffered nightmares about his father, and his increasing fear of ever returning to the stage. John Decker, still horrified by sunsets. Gene Fowler, second-guessing whether he should have fallen off that hotel ledge on that snowy night in Denver. W.C. Fields, bitter about his father, estranged wife, son, and most of the world in general. Ben Hecht, guided by his savage misanthropy. And Sadakichi Hartmann, greeting much of 1929 life with a contemptuous laugh.

The terminal passion play of the Bundy Drive Boys would soon begin.

Part II
The 1930s Hollywood

"Hollywoodus in Latrina"
—*John Barrymore's sobriquet for the movie colony*

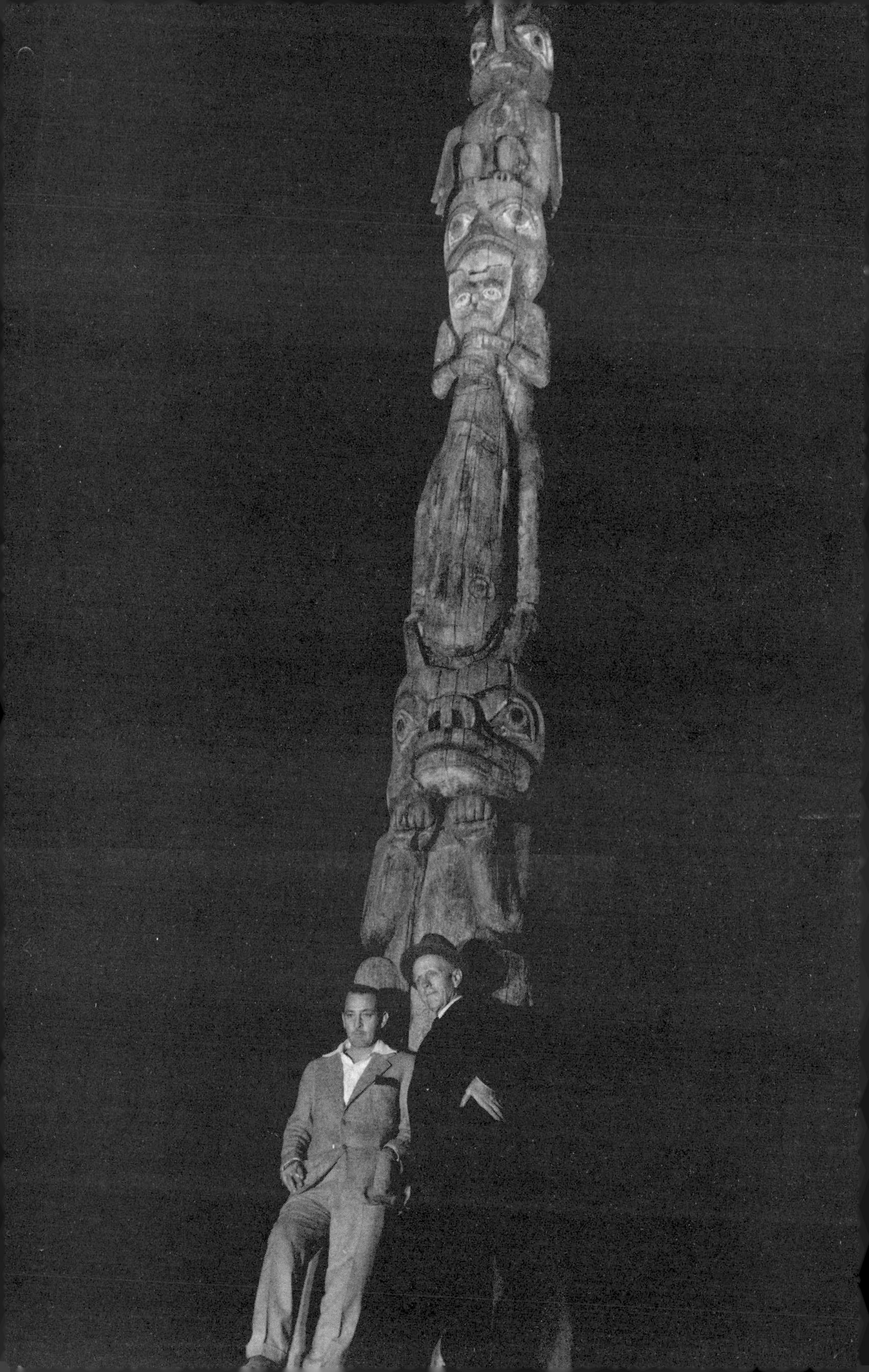

Chapter Eight
The Glory Days and Nights

In 1930, John Barrymore amassed more baroque art for Bella Vista. Below Mad Jack's crowned serpent coat-of-arms passed a treasury of religious artifacts — icons, triptychs, and silver candelabra from the Georgian Knights. There was a 13th-century *Book of Hours*, described as a "hand-executed, illuminated Catholic doctrine which chronicles the story of Jesus."

These joined the ancient Chinese wall sconces, Louis XV antique furniture, and a dinosaur egg, which, amidst such surroundings, seemed capable of miraculously hatching.

Meanwhile, on April 8, 1930, daughter Dolores Ethel Mae ("Dede") was born. Barrymore joked sourly to the press that his baby daughter looked "a little like Lon Chaney" — he had desperately wanted a boy.

The man appeared blessed in every way, yet he was restless, chain-smoking, and drinking heavily. After a sailing adventure to Alaska in 1931, Barrymore brought home a new acquisition, a towering totem pole, and he erected it to loom over Bella Vista, its painted, grotesque faces leering at anyone visiting the No. 6 Tower Road estate.

Lionel his brother was concerned. There were, John had learned, bodies of Alaskan natives entombed in the totem pole, and Lionel Barrymore feared the curse that it threatened to cast down upon the unbowed head of his brother. Years later, Lionel still blamed his brother's spectacular downfall on the Totem Pole. Lionel was too dependent, emotionally and financially, on the mercies of the film establishment — specifically his

Barrymore and friend with the notorious totem pole at Bella Vista

studio, Metro-Goldwyn-Mayer, which had financed his drug addiction — to place the blame on Hollywood.

The Hollywood of the 1930s was similar to the New York theatre of the early 1920s — racy, violent and sensational.

Greta Garbo chose to play streetwalker *Anna Christie* as her first talkie. Paramount imported Marlene Dietrich from Weimar Berlin after her "Lola-Lola" paraded her legs and garters in the S&M classic *The Blue Angel*. Sound made it possible to hear John Barrymore scream maniacally as his leg was amputated in his second go-round as Captain Ahab, which Warners now titled *Moby Dick*.

Edward G. Robinson snarling as *Little Caesar*, Bela Lugosi drinking virgins' blood in *Dracula*, James Cagney shoving a grapefruit in Mae Clarke's face in *The Public Enemy*, Dietrich facing the firing squad in *Dishonored* adorned in whore makeup and finery — all fascinated the 75,000,000 people who attended the 1931 movies weekly despite or perhaps because of the Depression woes.

The future Bundy Drive Boys were in the right place at the right time.

May 1, 1931: *Svengali*, starring John Barrymore, premiered at New York's Hollywood Theatre. Based on the George du Maurier novel *Trilby*, it's a hip *Dracula*, Gothic, subversive and rich in black comedy. As Svengali, Barrymore, in his long flowing hair and hellishly curled beard, looks like Lucifer at Woodstock, adorned in dark slouch hat and cloak, driving a lovesick woman to suicide, hypnotizing Trilby (17-year-old Marian Marsh) into becoming both his star diva and bed partner — and magically making the audience love him for it. There are even two baroque bonuses: a nude scene of Trilby (from the rear, and played by Ms. Marsh's double in a body stocking) and, for a topper, Svengali climactically succeeding in taking Trilby out of the arms of her ingénue lover (Bramwell Fletcher, Barrymore's future son-in-law) and into the grave with him.

"Oh God," Barrymore's Svengali heartbreakingly prays as he dies. "Grant me in death what you denied me in life — the woman I love!"

God, amazingly on the side of the Devil, gives the villain his final wish. The ending was similar to du Maurier's, but so unlike a conventional Hollywood happy ending as to be startling more than 75 years after its release.

Marian Marsh died at her Palm Desert house in 2006 at the age of 93, where she displayed two of the paintings of her created for *Svengali*. Years before, she had spoken to me about the joy of acting with John Barrymore:

Marian Marsh and
John Barrymore in *Svengali*

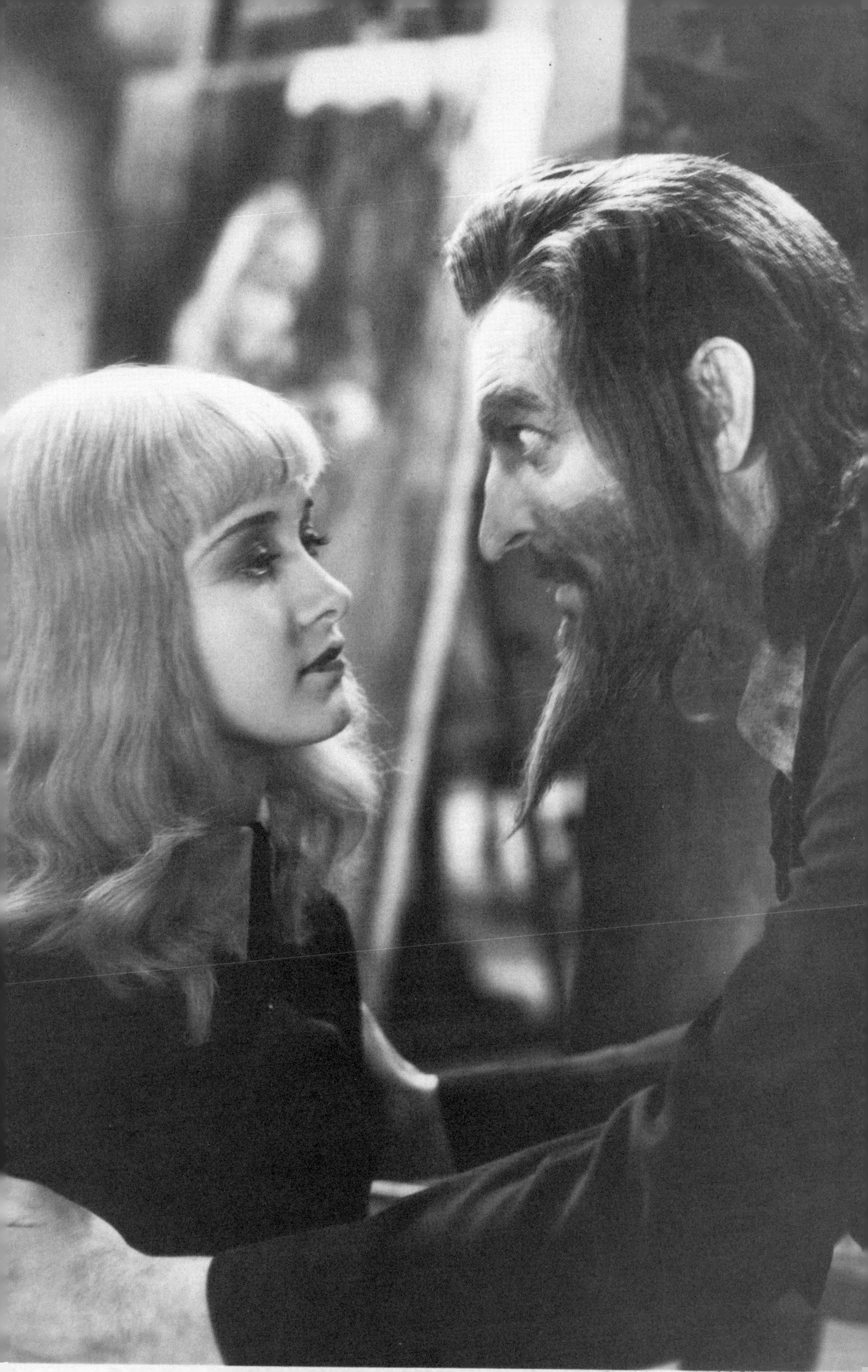

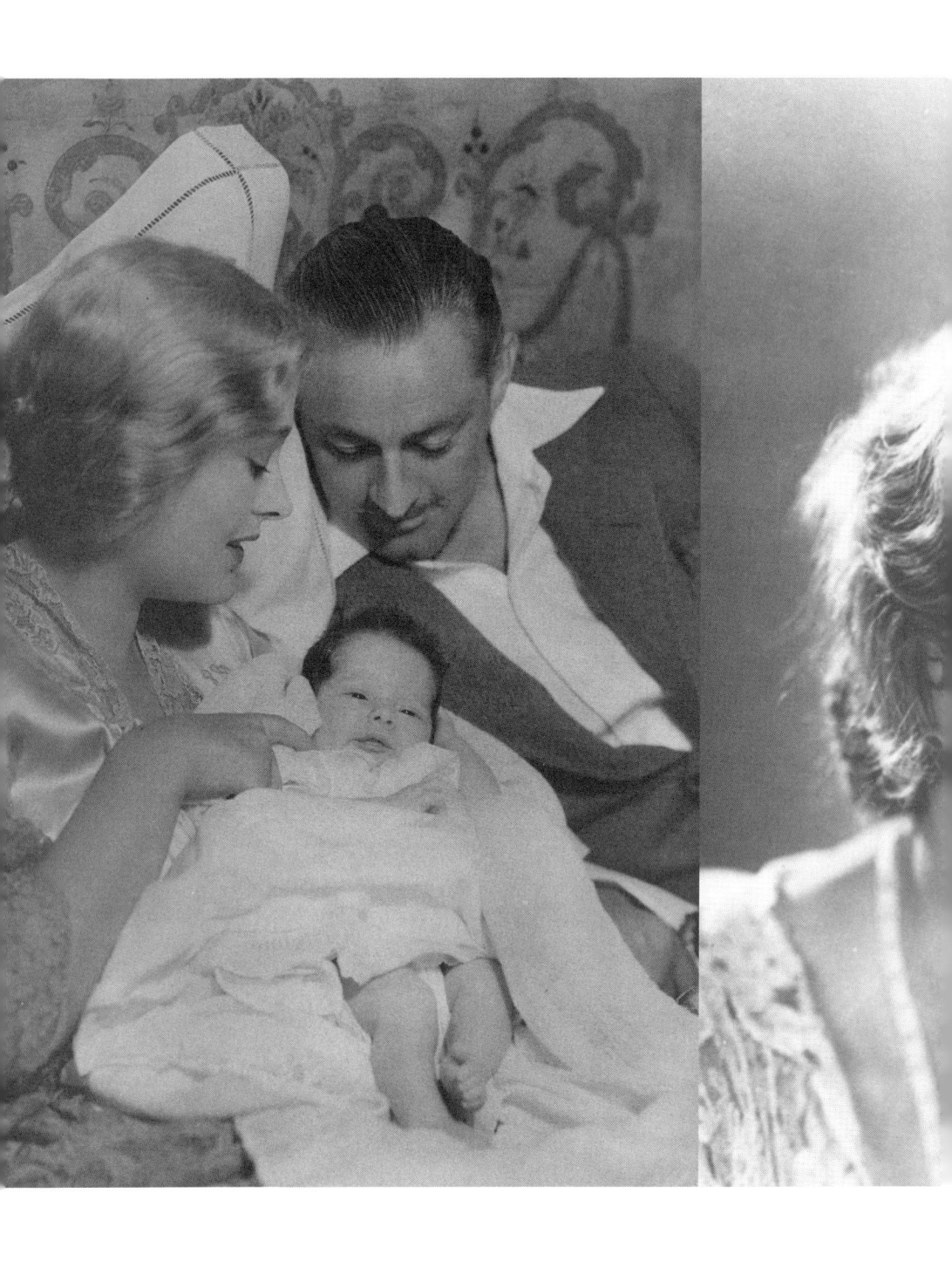

100   Hollywood's Hellfire Club

Proud, glamorous parents with John Drew

> When I first met John Barrymore, he was sick in bed, at his house, up on Tower Road ... Jack Warner and Darryl Zanuck led me upstairs to Barrymore; he was in this great big enormous bed in this great big enormous room. As I walked in, Barrymore was propped up in bed, lots of pillows around him; he sat up straighter....
>
> "Has anyone ever remarked," asked Barrymore, "that you resemble my wife, Dolores?"
>
> "Yes," I said.
>
> "Who?" asked Barrymore.
>
> And I said, "The butcher on Vine Street, who gives me liver for my cat!"
>
> Well, Barrymore just laughed his head off!

Warners fretted that the notorious, 49-year-old Barrymore might despoil their virginal starlet. The front office awaited news that Marian's panties had hit the floor. However, as Marian Marsh validated, there was no seduction:

> These were happy days for Jack Barrymore. He was on his best behavior; he was happily married to Dolores Costello, and he wasn't drinking. Dolores would visit the set with their little daughter, Dede, who was just learning to speak then. The little girl didn't like that beard! When Barrymore would want to kiss her, she didn't like that very much.

Barrymore, always enchanted by animals, paid at least as much attention to Leo, the black cat who was Svengali's familiar in the melodrama, as to his leading lady. The company soon became used to the sight of Barrymore playing with Leo, and treating the cat to sardines.

Svengali was probably Barrymore's greatest cinema performance — he's the spidery serpent from the Barrymore coat-of-arms. But Hollywood denied him an Academy Award nomination — the 1931 winner, ironically, was Lionel Barrymore, for his portrayal of an alcoholic lawyer who drops dead defending his errant daughter (Norma Shearer) in MGM's sex saga, *A Free Soul*. As Margot Peters wrote in *The House of Barrymore*:

> Lionel's performance was very good, yet it was typical of the Academy to award big and fundamentally sentimental pieces of acting. In Svengali, John Barrymore was always subtly ironic. Who was he mocking — himself, the role, the cast, Hollywood? Oscars didn't go to mockers.

Gable couldn't destroy this hated Decker painting

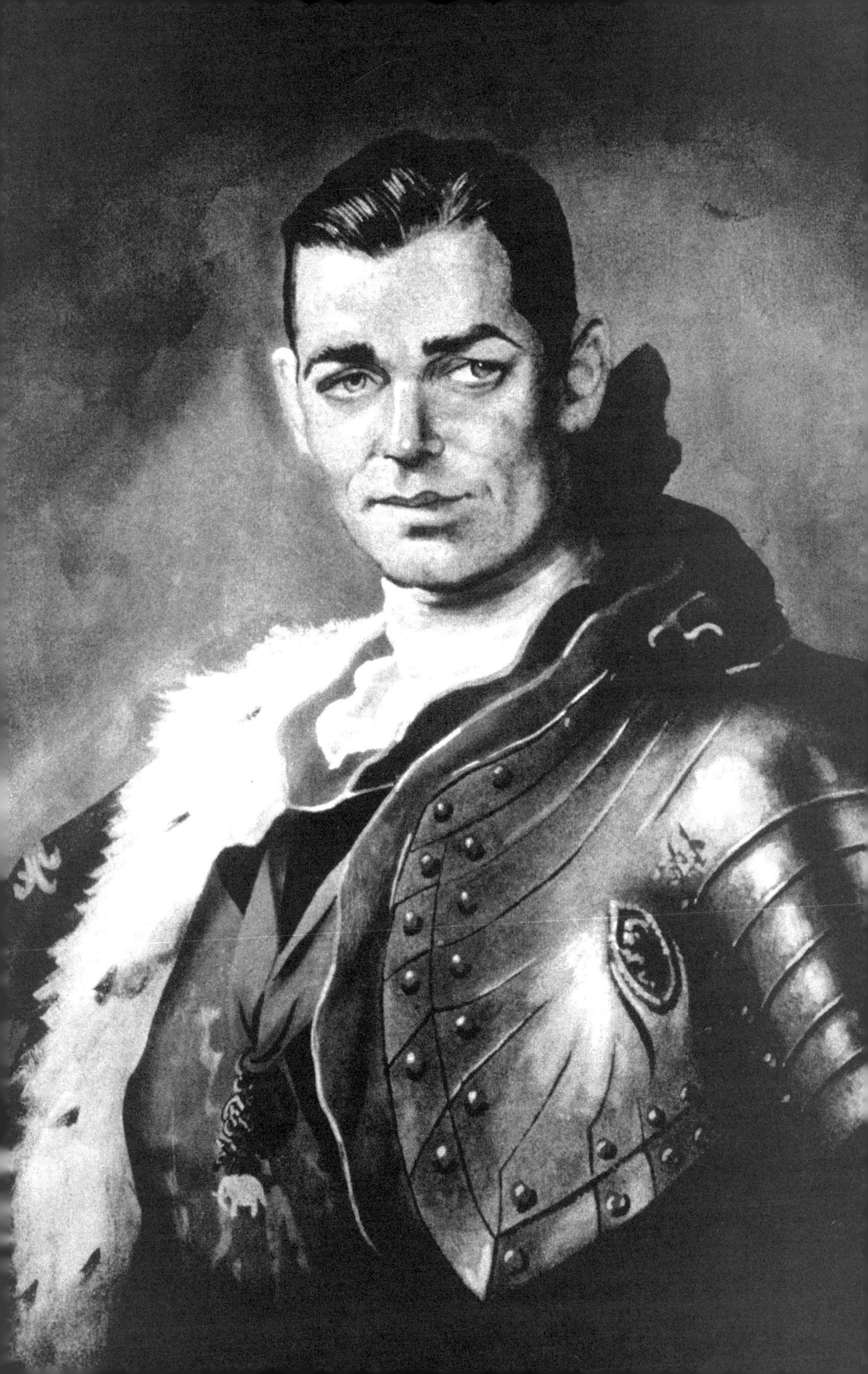

John Decker established himself in Hollywood — the 1930 census finds him living at 1058 Spaulding Avenue in West Hollywood with a new wife. Clark Gable, meanwhile, was on the rise, a sensation after roughing up Norma Shearer in *A Free Soul,* for which Lionel Barrymore had won his Academy Award. The new MGM star wanted John Decker to paint his portrait, in the armor of a cavalier.

He recoiled in horror when he saw the final result.

"You've made my ears look way too big!" protested the future King of Hollywood.

Columnist Jimmy Starr, retired in his late years to Arizona, told the *Phoenix Gazette* the whole story:

> [Decker] did this picture of Gable, and Gable seeing the finished product, said he didn't like it because it made his ears look too big. Decker was enraged and sued Gable for the money he was to have received for painting the picture. I don't think he was really that mad and probably it was just a ploy to get his name known in Hollywood, but anyway the judge ruled that Gable didn't have to pay if he didn't want to.
>
> Sometime later [the summer of 1934] the painting went on sale at an auction ... It was purchased by a man whose daughter was a fan of Gable's. But when he took it home he discovered it was too big to hang on the wall of his house.
>
> Several nights later I was out shopping for some andirons and by chance I happened to visit the man's shop. I saw the picture hanging there and, of course, recognized it immediately.
>
> "Where did you get that?" I said, excitedly.
>
> He told me about the auction and about it being too large to hang in his house. I asked him if he wanted to sell it.
>
> "Sure," he said. "I'll sell it for what it cost me — $7.50."
>
> You better believe I had the money out and quick. I took the painting home and forgot all about the andirons.
>
> A couple of days later *Variety* ran a story about Jimmy Starr being an art collector now that he had John Decker's painting of Gable. Well, Gable saw the story and came over to my house and said he wanted to buy the picture from me. He offered $500.
>
> I told him, "Okay, Clark. I'll sell the picture to you if you'll sign a paper saying you won't ever destroy it." He wouldn't agree to that.

*Barrymore sketch of
John Decker's astral façade*

John Decker's astral facade
by his friend and
well wisher —
John Barrymore

The painting still survives — part of the John Decker collection owned by Charles Heard.

For all the protests, John Decker was winning favor. Two of his most popular works of that time were his rendition of the Marx Brothers as "Burgomeisters" and a separate painting of Harpo as Gainsborough's "Blue Boy." Harpo proudly exhibited the painting ever after, and a visitor once asked him if he liked it.

"Like it?" Harpo exclaimed. "Hell, I built my new house around it!"

Decker, meanwhile, enjoyed himself observing the pomposity and the actual idiocy of the Hollywood art establishment and its bonehead *nouveau riche* collectors. As he later noted:

> By far the worst offenders in the crime of kicking-the-artist-around are the flighty wives of prominent motion picture producers. They all want to be painted in the manner of Gainsborough, because he placed big hats and flattering dresses and flowery backgrounds in his work.
>
> There was one producer's wife who came to me. She wanted me to do an imitation of Watteau to be hung over her new square fireplace. I checked on the possibilities, and learned that Watteau painted most of his work oblong because clients went in for high frames in the rococo age. But, among Watteau's efforts, I located one square masterpiece he did, which I said I could easily copy, and which would give the producer's wife something beautiful to overlook her fireplace. I then named my price. She said she'd have to think it over. Three days later she phoned me.
>
> "Mr. Decker," she said, "I must tell you honestly that I feel your price is much too high. I'm leaving for England in a few weeks — so I've decided to buy an original Watteau and cut it down to fit!"
>
> Then there was the sweet young blonde spouse of another producer. Sweet, but awfully dumb. She saw an exhibit of my work in Los Angeles, and was so impressed that she asked me to paint her. I agreed. But, an hour before the sitting, she phoned.
>
> "I'm so sorry, Mr. Decker," she cried frantically, "but my husband has suddenly made a lot of money on a movie deal, and now he's sending me to Europe. He says I should go there because then I can be painted by one of the real Old Masters!"
>
> And people wonder why artists die young!

Paul Muni in *Scarface*

March 31, 1932: *Scarface* with screenplay and dialogue by Ben Hecht premiered in New Orleans. The sexiest, most violent and flamboyantly aberrant gangster saga of them all starred Paul Muni as an Al Capone-type gangster and was produced by Howard Hughes. Hecht, who'd been in Chicago during Capone's beer wars and knew the subject all too well, was one of several writers on the picture, but its true muscle — demanding that Hughes pay him $1,000 at 6 p.m. each day he labored on the script. Howard Hawks directed, and shot the film using real bullets; reportedly Harold Lloyd's brother, while visiting the set, lost an eye due to a wayward shot.

Paul Muni starred as Tony "Scarface" Camonte, greased up and naturally scarred, while George Raft as his chief lieutenant Johnny tossed a coin and cut out paper dolls. "Look out, Johnny, I'm gonna spit!" exults Muni as he rejoices in his new machine gun. The real fireworks of *Scarface*, however, explode in the warped relationship of Scarface and his sister Cesca (played by a wild-eyed Ann Dvorak). Hecht developed an incestuous relationship between brother and sister that crackled throughout the film's death scenes and machine gun battles:

Tony: I don't want anybody puttin' their hands on you ... I'm your brother.

Cesca: You don't act like it. You act more like ... I don't know ... some kind of ... sometimes I think...

Scarface features various sensations, including Karen Morley as Scarface's platinum moll Poppy (who berates him in a restaurant for damaging her stockings with his feet), and Boris Karloff as Gaffney, a rival gangster shot down in a bowling alley as he rolls a strike. But the real show is the bristly passion of the kinky Camontes, as Tony and Cesca fight it out together against the cops and the world — Tony shot down in the street under the sign, "The World At Your Feet."

There were censorship battles for *Scarface,* which endured a title alteration: *Scarface: Shame of a Nation* and, in New York, a revised ending (Scarface going to the gallows). The censors also attempted to axe the violence and the Tony and Cesca kinky chemistry, but for the wrong reason; they felt that Tony's love for his sister "was too beautiful to be attributed to a gangster"!

April 12, 1932: *Grand Hotel,* boasting "More Stars than the Heavens," premiered at the Astor Theatre in New York City.

Based on Vicki Baum's novel, the luxuriantly melancholy *Grand Hotel* is perhaps the most celebrated movie of MGM's halcyon days, boasting a gallery of unforgettable performances: Garbo as the heartbreaking ballerina Grusinskaya, who utters the words, "I want to be alone"; John Barrymore as the sardonic Baron, who robs Grusinskaya and makes love to her; Joan Crawford as the alluring stenographer Flaemmchen; Wallace Beery as the tycoon Preysing; Lionel Barrymore as the pitiful, dying clerk Kringelein; and Lewis Stone as the scarfaced Doctor, who mutters amidst the scandal and death, "Grand Hotel. People coming, people going ... nothing ever happens."

Grand Hotel's most iconic episode is the Garbo and Barrymore love scene. From the moment John Barrymore greeted Garbo by kissing her hand and saying, "My wife and I think you are the loveliest woman in the world," she was in awe of his charm and artistry. Garbo broke one of her long-standing commandments by posing for the press with Barrymore on the set (arranging to sit so his left profile was to the camera); she prepared some "Irak punch" for him when he arrived one morning with a hangover. And after their beautiful love scene, Garbo shocked the company by giving Barrymore a passionate kiss.

"You have no idea what it means to me to play opposite so perfect an artist!" she cried.

Garbo and her beloved co-star she said
was touched with "divine madness"

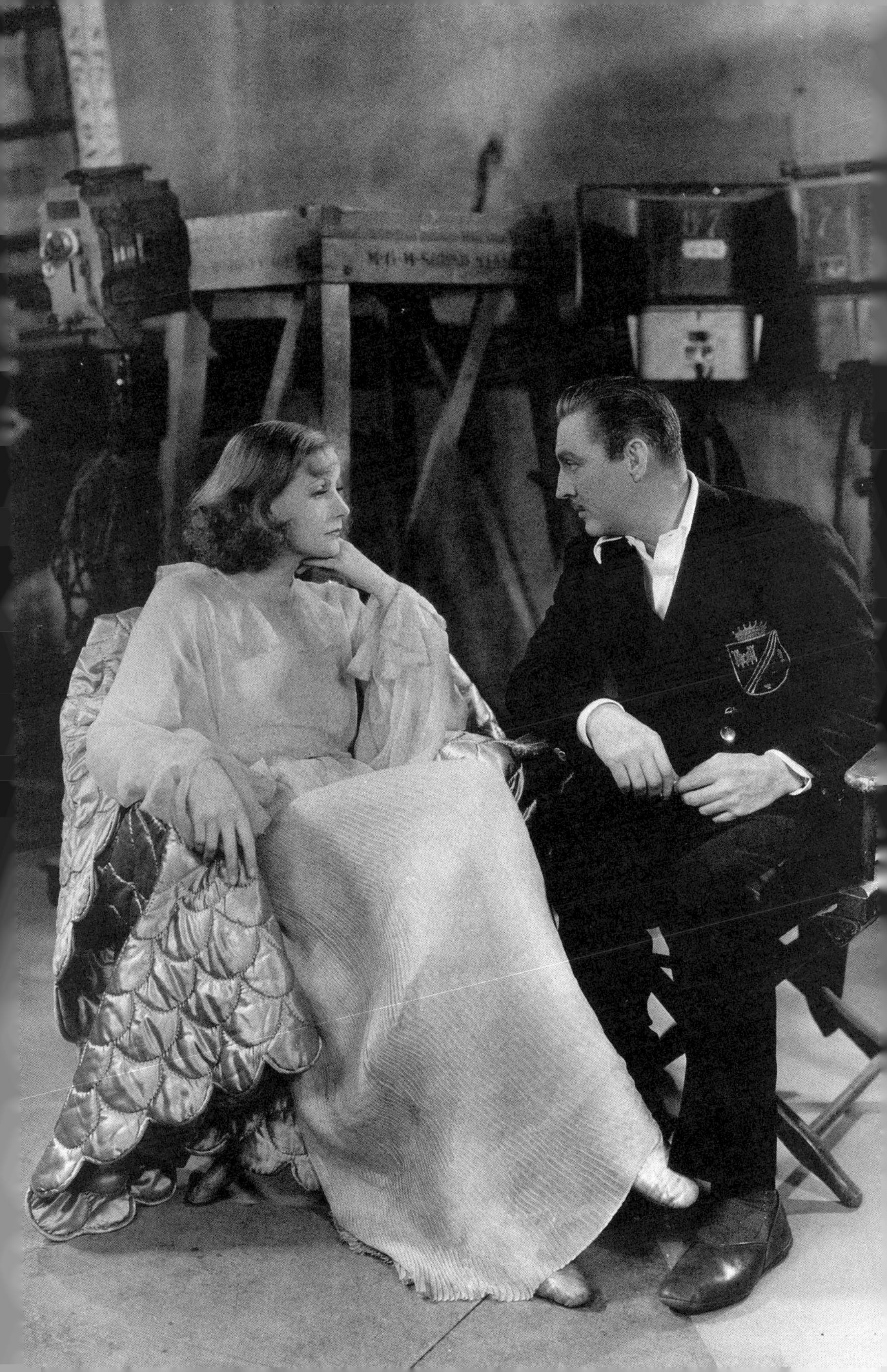

The Best Picture Academy Award winner of 1931/1932, *Grand Hotel* was a sensation, and John Barrymore's dashing Baron is one of his flagship film performances. Garbo called Barrymore "one of the very few who had that divine madness without which a great artist cannot work or live."

May 13, 1932: RKO released *State's Attorney*, starring John Barrymore and scripted by Gene Fowler and Rowland Brown. Fowler based the script on his book *The Great Mouthpiece*, concerning attorney William Joseph Fallon, the criminal lawyer who defended over 125 homicide cases and never lost a trial. The pre-Code melodrama — Barrymore defends a prostitute (Helen Twelvetrees) in night court, and ends up living with her — is a striking example both of Fowler's maverick style and the loose moral code of early 1930s Hollywood.

It was only now that Gene Fowler first saw John Decker. Rowland Brown, Fowler's collaborator on the two aforementioned films, was en route to RKO with a hungover Fowler to work on the script for *State's Attorney* when, as Fowler put it:

> We chanced to see in Gower Gulch a harried gentleman [Decker] in a condition similar to my own. He was hatless. A flock of blackbirds could be seen flying down again and again to gather hair from the gentleman's head for the upholstering of their nests. He was batting at the industrious birds, and cursing them.

Hardly settled in Hollywood, Fowler was already all too eager to lampoon it. Come June 24, 1932, and RKO released *What Price Hollywood?* — Fowler's satire on the film colony. As ham actor Max Carey, Lowell Sherman provided a superb send-up of himself and John Barrymore (who was then Sherman's brother-in-law), and the film plays as an early version of *A Star is Born*.

The leading lady of *What Price Hollywood?* was Constance Bennett, and the blonde star was just the type of pampered cinema goddess Fowler instantly despised. She hated the script. He was not very fond of her. Demanding various rewrites, Ms. Bennett received new pages one day for a scene in which she, as a movie star, was announcing her retirement from the silver screen to embrace motherhood. Not bothering to read the new lines beforehand, she grabbed the script and began rehearsing fully in character, as Fowler knew she would.

"And I'm going to have a beautiful black baby…!" announced Constance Bennett.

The stagehands burst into laughter. Constance, in a rage, threw her pages on the

John Decker sketches — on the set

floor, and demanded Fowler be fired. He wasn't. *What Price Hollywood?*, directed by George Cukor, was a hit and Gene Fowler had won a place in the movie colony while simultaneously throwing down the gauntlet at it.

To return for a moment to Lowell Sherman — it was during 1932 that he and his wife Helen Costello, Dolores' sister, divorced. Sherman had just arranged with John Decker to paint Helen's portrait, and Decker had already begun work when he read in the newspaper of the marital breakup. According to Decker:

> I raced to the phone and called the actor. "Hello, Lowell!" I exclaimed. "This is Decker. You know that portrait of your wife you ordered? Well, I heard you're divorced. I've got the picture three-quarters done, and I want to know what woman you're going out with now — I'd like to put the damn face in!"

Gene Fowler tried to keep his distance from Hollywood, spending summers in Fire Island, where he worked on his books. Nevertheless, cinema colony temptation came his way and he began an extramarital romance with actress Ann Harding. His wife Agnes forgave him and it would not be her only absolution.

June 4, 1932: John Barrymore, casting aside his fears of family madness, had vowed he'd give up drinking if Dolores bore him a boy. Dolores Costello Barrymore then gave birth to a son, John Blythe Barrymore (later to be known as John Drew Barrymore). As Phil Rhodes later learned, the pregnancy had been a troubled one, as John Decker would visit Bella Vista and loudly reminisce, in earshot of Dolores, how people in postwar Germany ate babies.

The Monster greeted the news of his son's birth with joy and hysteria, sending to Bella Vista for a revolver and vowing to stay at the hospital to protect the baby from kidnappers. When business advisor Henry Hotchener arrived at the hospital, Barrymore asked him to keep vigil as he left "for a few minutes." He returned hours later, drunk, and passed out. Dolores sent for him and wept when told of his condition.

"I swore that if God would give me a son I would never drink again," said Barrymore a few days later. "What happens to a man who makes a sacred oath — then breaks it?"

September 30, 1932: RKO released *A Bill of Divorcement*, starring John Barrymore as Hilary Fairfield, a madman who escapes his asylum one Christmas, comes home, and prompts the daughter he never knew (Katharine Hepburn, in her screen debut) to forsake her fiancé due to her fear of inherited insanity.

Not since *Hamlet* had Barrymore tackled a role so potentially catastrophic — his own terrors of his insanity and his father's must have given him nightmares during the shoot. That he began work on the film a month after the birth of his son, surely with the fear of inherited madness acute in his mind, seems disastrous, especially as his character is addressed by a doctor as "the man who ought never have had children."

As always, Barrymore hid his fears on the set. Despite rumors that he had seduced her in his dressing room and she fled crying, Katharine Hepburn remembered Barrymore as kind, funny and irreverent during the shoot. Come the famous line, "Do you know what the dead do in Heaven? They sit on their golden chairs and sicken for home," Barrymore altered the line on the first take:

> Do you know what the dead do in Heaven? They sit on their golden chairs and play with themselves.

A crocked J.B. in Havana

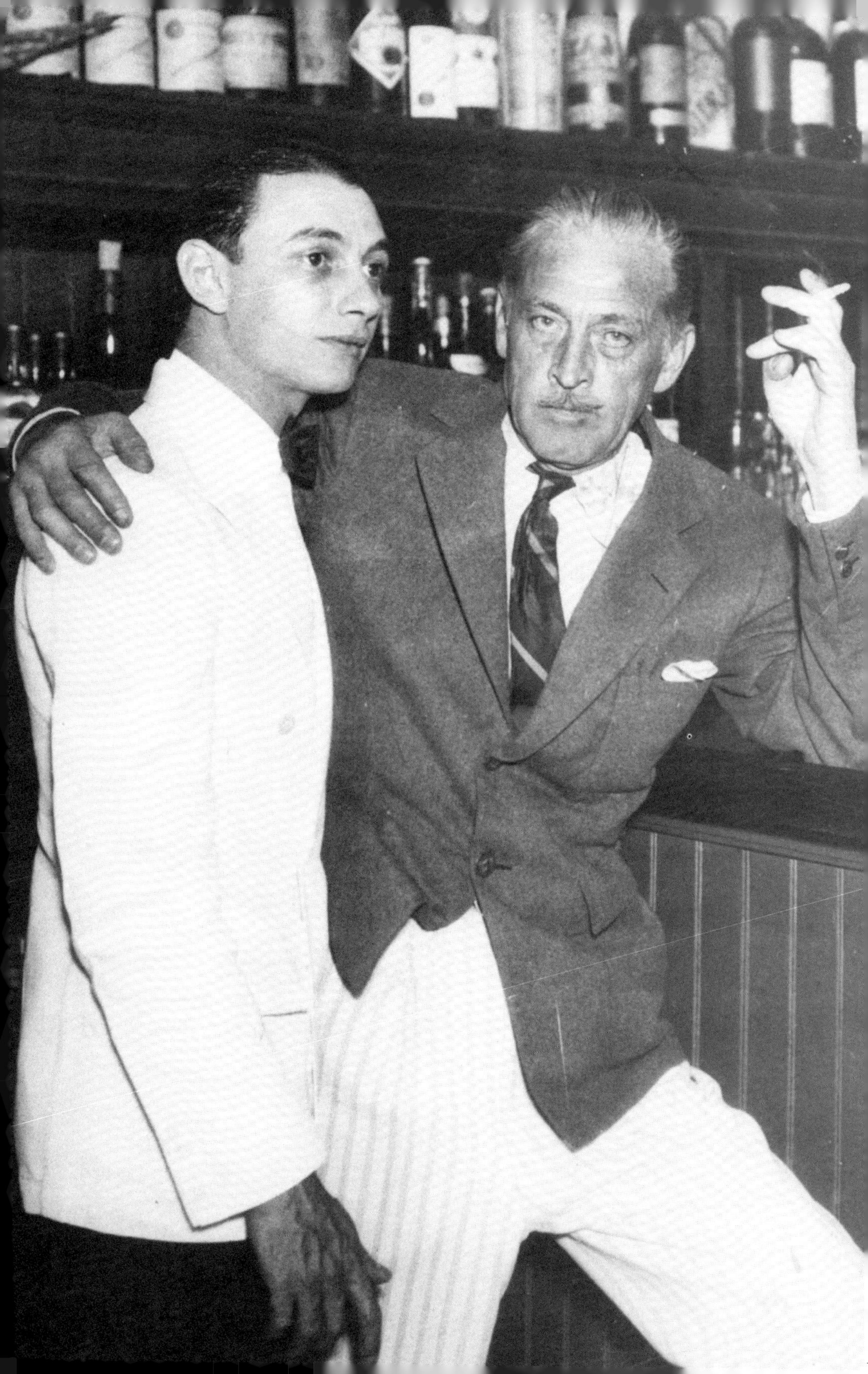

George Cukor directed sensitively; Barrymore masterfully gave the impression of being a lost child about to cry, with a few moments of almost frightening madness:

> When I talk I see a black hand reaching up through the floor. You see that widening crack in the floor to catch me by the ankle and drag, drag...!

December 2, 1932: *The Great Magoo*, a ribald play by Ben Hecht and Gene Fowler, produced by Billy Rose and directed by George Abbott, opened at Broadway's Selwyn Theatre. As MacAdams wrote in his Hecht biography:

> The play ends with Nicky and Julie leaving her squalid room, Julie exclaiming, "Oh darling, it's like a fairy tale," since she has been rescued by Nicky from a sordid fate. Tante, an old woman from Nicky's show, comes running after them holding up a douche bag, calling, "Hey Cinderella. You forgot your pumpkin!"

The opening night crowd — including Fannie Brice, Noel Coward, Sophie Tucker and Groucho Marx — roared with laughter but the critics were appalled. Brooks Atkinson of the *New York Times* wrote:

> The authors of *The Great Magoo* are not frugal. In one way or another they manage to peek backstage all the way from Coney Island to rehearsal halls in New York and the flea circus. But the formula of these picaresque slumming parties is now thrice familiar and maggoty talk is no longer a fine theatrical virtue....

The Great Magoo folded after only 11 performances. Gene Fowler, taking it all in stride, wanted to lie in a coffin at Campbell's Funeral Parlor and invite the critics to pose as his pallbearers. It was beneath the critics' dignity, if not Fowler's.

The only film to team all the famous Barrymores, John, Ethel and Lionel, MGM's *Rasputin and the Empress*, opened on December 23, 1932.

The shoot had been tumultuous. Charles MacArthur wrote the script as the film proceeded (with uncredited help from Hecht), sometimes turning in his pages the

Hepburn and Barrymore in
A Bill of Divorcement

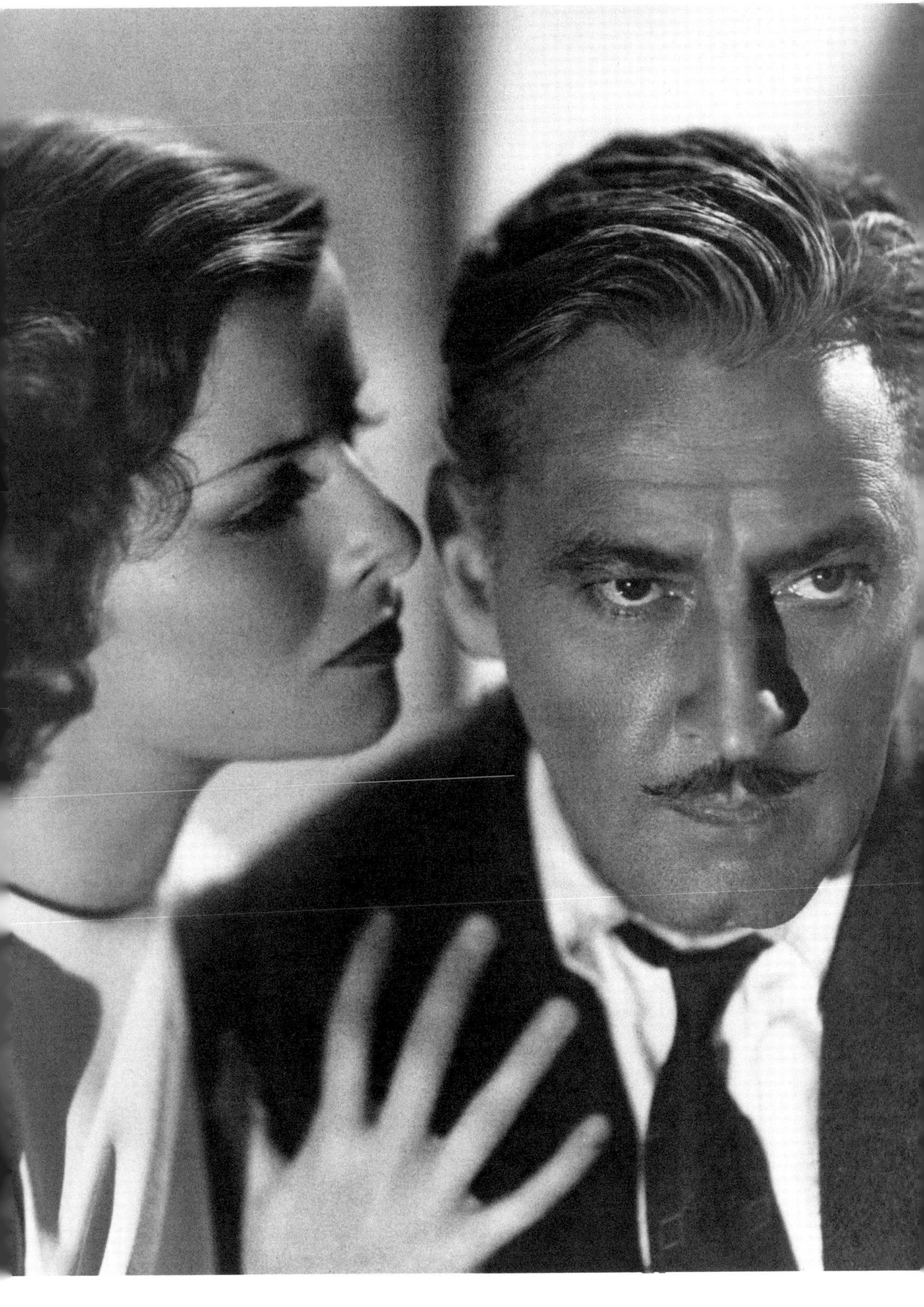

morning the scene was to be shot. Ethel hated her performance as the Czarina ("I look like Tallulah's burlesque of me"), managed to have Charles Brabin fired as director (Richard Boleslavski replaced him), and lambasted Hollywood in general ("The whole place is a set, a glaring, gaudy, nightmarish set, built up in the desert").

In the fraternal scenery gnashing, Lionel plays the Mad Monk, relishing every eye-rolling beard-stroking nuance. John, playing the dashing Prince, pops his eyes at Lionel and plays with a sword during Lionel's lines; in one scene-stealing moment, he begins to smoke a cigarette, and mugs when he realizes he's about to put the wrong end in his mouth.

The film's assassination vignette has the two stars let rip over-the-top acting. Lionel's Rasputin, having glutted on poison cakes, is a demonic monster who will not die; John, cackling and leering, virtually becomes Mr. Hyde as the assassin, spitting out a glob of vomit, smashing his victim's skull with insane glee, making the sign of the cross as Lionel's Rasputin, a bloody pulp, rises yet again from the floor to prophesy "the great day of wrath."

"Get back in hell!" shrieks John.

The finale of the scene — John drowning Lionel in an icy river — originally went awry as John, screaming, lost his balance and fell into the icy water, leaving Lionel glowering on the turf.

"It achieves one feat which is not inconsiderable," reported the *New York Herald-Tribune*. "It manages to libel even the despised Rasputin." Maybe so, but it was Prince Felix Youssoupoff (on whom John's character was based) and his wife Princess Irina who actually sued for libel, claiming the film inferred that Rasputin had raped Irina. The damages allegedly amounted to $750,000, but MGM's loss was a slight one — *Rasputin and the Empress* was a major hit and audiences flocked to see the three Barrymores in flamboyant form.

Ben Hecht began the New Year of 1933 with uncredited scripting work (with Charles MacArthur) on RKO's *Topaze* starring John Barrymore in goatee and pince-nez. In a letter dated February 8, 1933, Hecht wrote to Gene Fowler:

> I received a request from some cheap cocksucker getting up a literary magazine asking me for contributions and warning me in the same breath, not to write anything pornographic ... I mailed him back a large hand-drawn picture of a cunt — as I remember it — with the suggestion that he use it for a cover.

For all his success in the movies, Hecht had not mellowed in his feelings for Hollywood. As he added in this missive:

> You and your God damn Hollywood trollops with their quiff hair hanging like batches of seaweed from a stinking derelict!

Following their joint Broadway flop *The Great Magoo*, Hecht and Fowler decorated their office at MGM to resemble a whorehouse, hiring a voluptuous blonde named "Bunny" to perform her secretarial duties in only a pair of high heels. Some eyewitnesses to Bunny's charms also recall her wearing at times a blazing red dress. Visitors to the Hecht and Fowler office were voluminous, with Clark Gable a regular, wide-eyed caller.

The two writers kept busy producing Bunny-inspired drafts for *Farika, the Guest Artist*, to star W.C. Fields and Marie Dressler. It was never produced.

May 26, 1933: Paramount released *International House* — a mad comedy featuring such sensations as W.C. Fields, real-life gold-digger Peggy Hopkins Joyce, Rudy Vallee, Burns and Allen, Bela Lugosi, and "Girls in Cellophane."

W.C. Fields had arrived in Hollywood the previous year, with a car, cash, and a Paramount contract. He then starred in *Million Dollar Legs* (1932), followed by his guest spot in the all-star *If I Had a Million*. He settled in Toluca Lake, just down the street from Boris Karloff, hardly sharing the affection that Karloff had for the swans that sailed on the lake and eventually came to land to seek food.

"Shit green or get off my lawn!" roared W.C. Fields to his swan neighbors.

While Karloff made peace with the swans, Fields declared open war on them, including their "leader," a hostile swan with a seven-foot wingspan whom Karloff had named "Edgar." In his book, *W.C. Fields: A Biography*, James Curtis relates that Fields eventually attacked the swans with a golf club and a baseball bat — and the swans retaliated so savagely that W.C. fled Toluca Lake and moved to a ranch in Encino.

It's in *International House* that W.C. makes a spectacular entrance, his auto-gyro-helicopter crashing through a hotel ballroom roof in the village of Woo-Hoo, China:

> W.C.: Hey Charlie, where am I?
> Franklin Pangborn (as a prissy hotel manager): Woo-Hoo!
> W.C. (throwing away the flower in his lapel): Don't let the posey fool ya.

International House is packed with ribald humor, weird songs and pre-Code daring. W.C. wanders through the show in top form (pausing to peek through a keyhole, he muses, "What will they think of next?"). As the climax neared, the audience watched W.C. (as Professor Quail) and Ms. Joyce (as herself) preparing to escape Lugosi (as Peggy's ex-husband) in a car:

> Joyce: I tell you, I'm sitting on something. Something's under me. What is it?
> W.C.: It's a pussy!

The last line said as the oft-wed Peggy Hopkins Joyce moves her used-and-abused fanny and reveals she is indeed sitting on … a cat and her kittens. The censors weren't buying it, and W.C.'s exultant pussy line lit the censorship firestorm of 1933. As for the "pussy" bit, Simon Louvish reports in *Man on the Flying Trapeze: The Life and Times of W.C. Fields*, that the script had said "cat," but W.C. had changed it to "pussy," and the word somehow escaped the Breen office censors. Motion Picture Producers and Distributors of America (MPPDA) secretary Carl E. Milliken was fit to be tied when he reported to his boss Breen on the pussy matter:

> The elimination referred to above apparently escaped the notice of our office and of the public group reviewers. The dirty-minded lout who put it in the picture knew perfectly well, however, what he was doing…

The dirty-minded lout went on to a great 1933 at Paramount, following up with *Tillie and Gus,* his first film with the redoubtable Baby LeRoy. It was the fount of one of John Decker's favorite stories:

> W.C. Fields, who passionately hates kids and thinks they're brats, had to do a picture with Baby LeRoy when that youngster was the rage of Hollywood. Day after day he had to play a scene with the kid on his arm. And every day, after the kid had his orange juice, he wet his diapers on Fields' arm! Finally, Fields decided to take a vacation from this annoyance. One afternoon, while the orange juice was being prepared, Fields dropped a slug of gin in it. It was fed to the baby, who promptly passed out — and Fields had a three-day vacation!

Sadakichi by Decker

O.K'D By   Soldatik   Hartman

Fields capped 1933 as Humpty Dumpty in Paramount's Christmas release, the all-star *Alice in Wonderland*. There's still the familiar W.C. glint in this Egg Man's eyes; one keeps waiting for him to leer at Charlotte Henry's Alice from atop the wall.

July 16, 1933: "Sadakichi Hartmann, 'Ex-King of Bohemia,' Still a One-Man Show," headlined the *Los Angeles Times*. Sadakichi tossed a benefit for himself, inviting the world at large to a lawn party off the Cahuenga Pass, with admission 50 cents a head. "For years now he has ruled Hollywood's arty coteries," noted the *Times'* Arthur Millier, "adored by the 'lunatic fringe' and some who are not so loony." The story went on:

> Sadakichi is a literary legend to which he is one of the most enthusiastic contributors. Perhaps Li Po, China's greatest poet who drowned while leaning from a boat attempting to kiss the moonbeams on the water, looked like this aging Eurasian.
>
> Like Li Po, he deserves an emperor to give him money and an edict should procure him free wine.
>
> By this you gather that Sadakichi Hartmann is a one-man show, something to be seen; but what you see is the mask, what you hear issuing from his throat in strange gutturals are notes of wit and malice from a hidden soul. Under this graying crust is deep-rooted sweetness, and equally deep despair. It is not easy to be a "Man Behind the Mask" (which you cannot take off) and write exquisite English, too. "He makes Frankenstein look like a pansy," said a high school girl — yet Sadakichi seems to think that all women love him!

Sadakichi told the *Times* he had recently lectured in New York, providing a bonus act — he danced.

> "They ado-o-red it," drawls Sadakichi, then breaks out in that amazing barked laughter, like laughter from the grave.
>
> "One thing marred my life," he said, pouring another. "I arrived in Munich three years too late. King Ludwig was already quite mad. Three years earlier he would have provided for me."

For a sage always boasting of being ahead of his time, Sadakichi was truly now a visionary, with plans to advance himself via a new technology:

> Always dreaming, he has a new dream. Television is to make his fortune. He will appear for just three minutes at a time — "one must catch the swift tempo of today — a few sharp words, a few steps of my dancing, one of my laughs — it will be wonderful. The people will adore me!"

Alas, Sadakichi as the first TV evangelist never came to pass. The Gray Chrysanthemum told the *Times* of his plans to take his future television fortune and set himself up at No. 2 Fifth Avenue, "so that I can receive friends properly," with his daughter Wistaria as hostess. Then, for a finale, he'd head for a hermit's nest atop the Maritime Alps — "there to spend the last years of my life living beautifully." The *Times* wrapped up its feature with one of Sadakichi's poems:

> Nothing has changed
> Since the Dusk of the Gods
> Drift of water
> And ways of love!

And the story concluded, "... that deep organ music comes up from the soul of this strange 'Man Behind the Mask.'" The feature came complete with a caricature of Sadakichi, drawn on the back of a dinner check from Henry's Restaurant.

John Barrymore's best-known performance of 1933 was in MGM's all-star *Dinner at Eight*, which had its gala Broadway premiere on the stormy night of August 23, 1933. The star constellation was magnificent: Marie Dressler, John Barrymore, Wallace Beery, Jean Harlow, Lionel Barrymore, Billie Burke — all directed by George Cukor in a sterling David O. Selznick production.

The dramatic punch of *Dinner at Eight* is John Barrymore as Larry Renault, an alcoholic has-been star known for his profile. His meltdown as he drunkenly insults a producer (Jean Hersholt) in front of his agent (Lee Tracy) still can make a viewer squirm.

"You're through, Renault," sneers Tracy as the star's fed-up agent. "You're a corpse and you don't know it. Go get yourself buried!"

There follows Barrymore's suicide scene, almost too painful to watch: drunk, crying, tearing up the picture of his lover (Madge Evans) and tossing the scraps out the window into the night, and seating himself — after turning on the gas — so that his famed profile will be on display when authorities find his body. It's yet another of John Barrymore's spiritual striptease performances, as if prophesying the nightmare he's soon to become.

Dinner at Eight did good box-office, taking in over $2 million in rentals. Those who saw Barrymore in the film surely numbered many who believed his painfully convincing performance. Perhaps he even shocked MGM — at the time the studio considered dropping his services. But David Selznick interceded, and Jack started work on *Night Flight*, another Selznick-produced Metro-Goldwyn-Mayer all-star free-for-all with Helen Hayes, Clark Gable, Myrna Loy, Robert Montgomery and the Barrymore brothers. Based on the Saint-Exupery 1931 novel *Night Flight*, the story of pilots flying medicine over the Andes, Jack was cast as Riviere, the head of the airlines. He was so drunk on the set that director Clarence Brown tried to sack him and replace him with an unknown. Lionel, always subservient to L.B. Mayer (the widely-circulated story claims that Mayer financed Lionel's drug addiction) reportedly pleaded Jack's case, and he remained in the film. However, Jack kept drinking, and when time came for retakes, he fled with Dolores and the family once again to Alaska with his yacht *The Infanta*.

Thereafter MGM decided to dispense with his services.

After Barrymore came home from his Alaska journey, he ended 1933 impressively in Universal's *Counsellor-at-Law*, a rapid-fire, non-stop, totally natural performance.

During the *Counsellor-at-Law* shoot, Barrymore had a day in which he forgot a particular line and William Wyler spent many retakes trying to get it right. Shaken and frightened, the star went home that night having never mastered the line, and was a portrait of despair. At home he learned his Tower Road neighbor John Gilbert was contemplating suicide. Barrymore sat up with Gilbert all night, went to the *Counselor-at-Law* set the next morning and nailed the line on the first take.

Yet the worry was there. The memory lapse had its horrible effect. More than ever before, John Barrymore feared of losing his mind.

W.C. Fields carried on with his Paramount sojourn, starring in *Six of a Kind* (as Sheriff "Honest John" Huxley), *You're Telling Me!* (as Sam Bisbee, inventor of a keyhole finder for drunks), *The Old-Fashioned Way* (as The Great McGonigle, providing Baby LeRoy an audience-pleasing kick in the tail), *Mrs. Wiggs of the Cabbage Patch* (as Mr.

Carlotta Monti

C. Ellsworth Stubbins) and best of all, *It's a Gift*, released November 17, 1934. The last, with its story by Fields (under the pen name of "Charles Bogle"), has Fields playing store-owner Harold Bissonette ("pronounced Biss-o-nay"), dreaming of a new life amidst a California orange grove. Among its choice offerings is its blind man scene, as Mr. Muckle (Charles Sellon), the horrible old coot with his black, snake-like ear trumpet and rapacious walking stick, invades Fields' grocery store — smashing the glass door, upsetting various boxes of glassware, and destroying a table full of light bulbs.

"Mr. Muckle!" roars W.C. time and again. Indeed, only Fields could engineer a film so the audience hated the guts of a blind man. He also copes with a nasty Mr. Fitchmueller (Morgan Wallace) bellowing, "Where are my kumquats?" and a molasses-spilling Baby LeRoy (whom W.C. refers to at one point as "Blood Poison").

By this time, Fields had moved to a ranch in Encino (where *It's a Gift's* final orange grove exterior was shot) and had met Carlotta Monti, a 27-year-old actress then landing screen roles here and there (e.g., Madi, Priestess of Zar, in 1933's *Tarzan the*

Fearless). Carlotta of the large bonnets and profile poses became W.C.'s mistress. She called her sugar daddy "Woody." He called her "Chinaman." She moved in with W.C. at Encino, and her book, *W.C. Fields and Me*, suggests a deep, heartfelt relationship:

> Beginning with the first intimate night together when we consummated our love — I will not disclose the wonderful details except to comment briefly that it was ecstasy — I felt more intensely alive and responsive than any time before in my life, my mind quicker and honed to a fine sharpness, my energies keyed higher and stronger. Woody seemed starved for real love and affection, and I gave it to him in large quantities. During that year I blossomed into full womanhood…

Ron Fields doesn't believe it. Later when W.C. was living at 655 Funchall in Bel Air, he referred to Carlotta in a letter to a friend as "The young lady who is furnishing the poon-tang at 655."

"Women are like elephants to me," said W.C. "I like looking at them, but I wouldn't want to own one."

On March 29, 1934, the *Los Angeles Times* reports that John Decker and stage director J. Belmar Hall would create a "Tony Pastor's Theatre Club," modeled after the old New York playhouse that had presented "Gay '90s" melodramas." The club, located at 5746 Sunset Boulevard, opened in May, complete with a performance of the stage thriller *The Ticket of Leave Man* starring Sheldon Lewis and with a foyer featuring Decker's satirical paintings. There was, according to the *L.A. Times*, "a riot of forgotten variety and song acts," and the crowd sang along to songs like "The Man on the Flying Trapeze." The club was a popular Hollywood novelty for a time, but managing a club wasn't Decker's forté, and "Tony Pastor's Theatre Club" soon shut its doors.

1934 saw the publication of *Father Goose,* Gene Fowler's book concerning the rise and fall of Keystone comedy producer Mack Sennett. "An uproarious biography of Mack Sennett, the man who made America conscious of pie-throwing, Keystone cops and bathing beauties…" promised the cover jacket. The author vastly preferred book writing to script writing and hoped to devote himself full-time to such activity as soon as possible.

Barrymore and Lombard in *Twentieth Century*

April 12, 1934: *Film Daily* reviewed the Ben Hecht-scripted *Viva Villa!* starring Wallace Beery as Pancho. The film provided Hecht one of his favorite Hollywood memories: during the location shoot in Mexico, a drunken Lee Tracy (playing reporter Johnny Sykes) stood naked on a balcony and pissed on a squadron of Mexican troops. The south-of-the-border wrath and Hollywood fallout saw Jack Conway replace Howard Hawks as director and Stuart Erwin taking over for Lee Tracy (who was hustled out of Mexico in a plane and fired by Louis B. Mayer).

Hecht's rowdy script included a vignette in which Beery's Villa whipped Fay Wray's Teresa and — perhaps most memorably — a baroque death scene in which Joseph Schildkraut's villainous General Pascal was stripped, smeared with honey and tied to an anthill as a feast for the insects and vultures (all done off-screen, to the accompaniment of Schildkraut's screams). *Viva Villa!* won Hecht another Academy nomination. He'd lose to Robert Riskin of *It Happened One Night*.

Meanwhile, Hecht and MacArthur, in a daring move, co-produced, co-directed

The 1930s 125

and co-wrote their own film — *Crime Without Passion*, the melodrama of a flamboyant lawyer (Claude Rains) who kills a voluptuary (Margo), then topples into insanity. The bravura film, shot in New York at Paramount's old Astoria Studios, came complete with an opening montage of Furies (!) flying over a New York City night sky and cameos by Hecht, MacArthur, Helen Hayes and Fannie Brice.

Rains later claimed it was his favorite screen experience: "I've never done anything I like as well as this role … a role that comes once in an actor's lifetime."

This message from John Barrymore heralded *The New York Times* May 3, 1934 ad for *Twentieth Century,* one of the greatest screwball comedies. The role of Oscar Jaffe, the Greatest Ham in the World, fit Barrymore to a "T."

As Mildred Plotka, whom Barrymore's Jaffe transforms into Lily Garland, star supreme and worthy adversary, Carole Lombard came into her own. Originally intimidated by Barrymore, she was pulling punches until director Howard Hawks took her aside and asked how she'd react if some man spoke to her the way Oscar Jaffe was talking to Lily Garland.

"I'd kick him in the balls!" vowed Lombard.

At Hawks' suggestion, she did exactly that on the next take. Barrymore screamed in surprise and presumably a bit of pain. Come the next take in the film, Lombard kicked his shins. The fire was lit —*Twentieth Century* is a firecracker.

In his book *Alternate Oscars*, Danny Peary argues that Barrymore should have been the Academy's choice as Best Actor of 1934, the year Clark Gable took home the prize for *It Happened One Night*. As it was, Barrymore wasn't even nominated. He never would be. It hurt him more than he ever revealed, and he said late in life: "I think they were afraid I'd show up at the banquet drunk, both embarrassing myself and them. But I wouldn't have, you know."

The Hollywood opportunities for the Bundy Drive Boys to strut their stuff were soon to become more limited. 1934 saw the rise of the revised Production Code, as well as the Roman Catholic Legion of Decency. Barrymore's *Twentieth Century* battles with thigh-flashing Carole Lombard arrived just under the wire — the censorship office managed to nix a publicity still in which Lombard revealed her leggy charms to her all-eyes co-star.

As the movies cleaned up, John Barrymore fell apart. On his next film, RKO's *A Hat,*

Coat and Glove, Barrymore's memory totally failed him and he was replaced by Ricardo Cortez. He tried to revive himself by taking a cruise with Dolores, the children and their nurse, once again, to the always-revitalizing Alaska. During the voyage he became so desperate for alcohol he drank Dolores' perfume. Barrymore got to shore one night, went on a wild bender, returned in the morning drunk and responded to the nurse's shocked "Oh, Mr. Barrymore!" by breaking her nose — and then attacking Dolores.

Mr. Hyde was loose.

The marriage broke up. Barrymore feared Dolores would place him in an asylum. His pious and fleecing business managers, Henry and Helios Hotchener, fed his fears. He fled with them to England, where a proposed film of *Hamlet* fizzled before it even began after John saw himself in his old costume and realized he could no longer remember the soliloquies.

He fled again, this time with Helios, a spiritualist, seeking to save sanity and soul by running all the way to India.

Errol Flynn in *The Dawn Patrol*

Chapter Nine
Captain Blood

> Oh, I have seen enough and done enough and been places enough and livened my senses enough and dulled my senses enough and probed enough and laughed enough and wept more than most people would suspect.
>
> —Errol Flynn, 1959, shortly before his death

It was Marlene Dietrich who allegedly gave Errol Flynn the sobriquet "Satan's Angel." It was a considerable tribute, coming from a woman who (at least in the early 1930s) was the screen's most demonic female voluptuary; after all, in 1935, when Flynn played *Captain Blood*, Dietrich starred in *The Devil Is a Woman*. Surely it was a sensual salute to a man his friend David Niven called "a magnificent specimen of the rampant male."

There was, however, a major difference between Flynn and La Dietrich. The lady, a female Narcissus, enjoyed a lifelong love affair with herself and her cinema image that vitalized her until her death in 1991 at the age of 90. Errol Flynn despised himself and died at the age of 50.

John Decker painted Flynn's portrait. Ben Hecht saw it as

> ... the story of a troubled and ennuied soul peering out of weary eyes. Under the analytic Decker brush, the pugilistic Flynn chin grows gentle, the mouth whose smile has enchanted millions grows full of fretfulness. It is not a glamour boy who looks from the canvas, but a tormented fellow with a dislike for himself and the world.

As the painting revealed, Errol Flynn was very much a sad, kindred spirit of Decker, Barrymore and other Bundy Drive Boys. "He was a charming and magnetic man, but so tormented," said Olivia de Havilland, Maid Marian to his Robin Hood. "I don't know about what, but tormented."

Flynn was a phenomenon. An adoring Ann Sheridan called him "one of the wild characters of the world," and it was this most sex-charged male star of his era, via his 1943 rape trial, that inspired the expression "in like Flynn." Vincent Sherman, director of *The Adventures of Don Juan* (1948), remembered visiting Flynn's dressing room and finding the star wearing only a towel, which he dropped to reveal a giant phallus. It was, in fact, a fake — Flynn had engaged Warner Bros. makeup wizard Perc Westmore to create this penile prosthesis, possibly out of deference to the nickname the Warners mailroom boys had awarded Flynn: "Great Cock." After Sherman enjoyed the joke, Flynn asked his director to send in Alan Hale, who took a gander at Flynn's fabulous fake.

"I'll take a pound-and-a-half," said Hale.

Jack Warner (whom Flynn hated) eulogized him at Forest Lawn (which he also hated) as "the personification of gallantry, the essence of bravery, the great adventurer." He was Hollywood's classic swashbuckler in every sense of the word, and his classic sword duels with Basil Rathbone in *Captain Blood* and *The Adventures of Robin Hood* have storybook magic, an angel vs. devil iconography and an Astaire and Rogers dance beauty.

As with John Decker and John Barrymore, the villains behind Flynn's torment were women — in Flynn's case, a mother who had the personality of a Basil Rathbone screen villain, and a first wife who was definitely no Maid Marian.

Errol Flynn's mother told the press in 1946 that her son had not only been a "dirty little brute," but "a *nasty* little boy."

Errol's description of her, meanwhile, was "Christ-bitten."

At any rate, Errol Leslie Thomson Flynn, born in Hobart, Tasmania, June 20, 1909 was the son of Prof. Theodore Thomson Flynn, a marine biology professor who eventually became a Member of the British Empire, and mother Lily Mary (who vainly renamed herself "Marelle"), a descendant of Midshipman Edward Young, one the mutineers of the *Bounty*. As Jeffrey Meyers wrote in *Inherited Risk*:

> A sinister character, Young was a chief instigator as well as participant in the mutiny. He wound up on Pitcairn Island, where he provoked a massacre of the natives in which Fletcher Christian and other English sailors were killed. In that grisly conflict, Young was one of the two white male survivors…

The redoubtable Young had nabbed Captain Bligh's captured sword, passing it down to his family — as a child, Flynn played with it.

One fancifully imagines the sword bore a curse. Marelle seemed possessed by the ghost of Captain Bligh. An auburn-haired beauty, singer, pianist, athlete, sadist and religious zealot, she blithely cuckolded her scholar husband and viciously beat her son. Both Flynn and his 10-years-younger sister Rosemary soon realized they were unwanted children. The Flynn biographers all disdain Marelle. Charles Higham, author of *Errol Flynn: The Untold Story*, wrote that Marelle "refused to breast feed Errol because she feared her breasts might be ruined. She gave him bottled milk, which had not been pasteurized. As a result he contracted undulant fever that recurred throughout his adult life." Jeffrey Meyers, calling Marelle "a Tasmanian She-Devil," reports that, during one of Theodore's research trips, Marelle dolled herself up (as Flynn put it) in "her 1914 motoring hat, her long white veil tied under her chin and flowing in the breeze," and drove off for a rendezvous with the local cinema manager — taking along five-year-old Errol in the back seat. The exploit not only traumatized the boy, but, as Meyers writes, "eroticized both automobiles and movies."

Flynn never recovered from Marelle, who outlived him. He distrusted women, possibly even feared them, and as Higham wrote, "It was a failing which flawed his life and destroyed his marriages."

Flynn grew up loving the ocean, savoring books such as *Treasure Island* and *Moby Dick*. A natural rebel, Errol was expelled from private schools in Australia and England and embarked on various adventures as a young adult: a clerk for a shipping company, a government service cadet, overseer on a plantation, ship's cook, boxer, pearl diver, newspaper correspondent. Learning of the New Guinea gold rush, Flynn went there as a jungle guide and ended up in the 1932 documentary *Dr. H. Erbin's New Guinea Expedition*. Flynn later spoke with nostalgia about his New Guinea adventures, including the jungle dangers he faced, the wives of employers he banged and the diseases he battled — malaria and syphilis.

Flynn's dashing looks attracted the eye of Australian producer/director Charles Chauvel, who cast him as Fletcher Christian in *In the Wake of the Bounty* (1933). Finding acting the most attractive venture of all his many adventures, Flynn joined the

Northampton Repertory Company in the English midlands, which led to a role in *Murder at Monte Carlo*. Irving Asher, excited by Flynn's potential, sent a copy of *Murder at Monte Carlo* and a Flynn screen test to Jack Warner in Hollywood. Warner never even looked at it.

When Warner never responded, Hal Wallis trusted Irving Asher's judgment and signed Errol Flynn, who arrived in Hollywood on a Warner Bros. contract that paid $125 per week. His debut: *The Case of the Curious Bride*, a *Perry Mason* "B" in which Flynn appeared as a corpse in silhouette and a minute-long flashback as a blackmailer, killed by falling upon a piece of broken mirror. While shooting the violent scene, in which leading lady Margaret Lindsay fought off Flynn with a fireplace poker, Flynn accidentally knocked her out — and, as she regained consciousness, was sincerely and deeply contrite.

He seemed fated for a career as a small-part handsome heel — and then two thunderbolts struck.

First, Flynn fell madly in love with French actress Lili Damita, whose nickname was "Tiger Lil" and who has historically rated "tempestuous." Her lovers allegedly ranged from King Alfonso XIII of Spain to Marlene Dietrich. She was fiercely jealous, with a bisexual sensuality that dominated Flynn's heterosexual one. Still, they wed in Yuma June 19, 1935, and Lili clipped eight years off her age to insist she and Flynn were both 26. As Flynn wrote of "Tiger Lil" in his memoir *My Wicked, Wicked Ways*:

> She knew, however, that she was the greatest — bar none, no holds barred. I record it as a fact of any possibly interest to future historians.
>
> I do not know where she learned the arts of amour, or whether she was born gifted, but I had the feeling that she performed as if she personally was convinced that she carried with her all the legend, glory and reputation of the French.
>
> We fought. We reconciled. We fought again.

Thunderbolt Two came as Warners prepared to shoot *Captain Blood*, its extravaganza based on the Sabatini novel. The formidable Michael Curtiz was set to direct; he was Warners' most versatile and explosive director, a raging Hungarian who favored jodhpurs, high boots and a whip and was famous for his fractured language — e.g., "The next time I send a no-good son-of-a-bitch to do something, I go myself!" It was Curtiz who had directed *The Case of the Curious Bride*. Curtiz was now peacefully wed to Bess; his first wife — to whom he'd been married briefly in 1925 and 1926 — had been Lili Damita.

As Warners blueprinted its costly production, there was a major problem: they had no Captain Blood. The studio had expected Robert Donat (who later won the 1939 Best Actor Oscar for the British-made *Goodbye Mr. Chips*) to come from London and play Captain Blood, but Donat claimed his asthma prevented a trip to Hollywood. Privately, he told Irving Asher he actually couldn't bear the idea of leaving his mistress in London (and when Asher naturally suggested he simply bring her along, a weeping Donat said she didn't want to make the trip). Hal Wallis had Curtiz test George Brent, Ian Hunter and Errol Flynn for Captain Blood, and as Hal Wallis wrote in his book, *Star Maker*:

> He wasn't an admirable character, but he was a magnificent male animal, and his sex appeal was obvious. Jack and I took a gamble, and gave him a test. It seemed not to matter whether he could act. He leapt from the screen into the projection room with the impact of a bullet.

Flynn won the role. Olivia de Havilland was his leading lady. The villains were considerably better paid than the $125-per-week title role player: Lionel Atwill signed to play the whip-cracking Col. Bishop for $2,000 per week, while Basil Rathbone, as the pirate Levasseur who wages the famous swordfight in the surf with Blood, received a princely $5,500 per week. Flynn, realizing the inequity, soon demanded a raise in midproduction, and he got one — to $750 per week.

He was earning his pay. It was a volatile set, and Curtiz, directing his ex-wife's new husband, was merciless in his insults.

"Stop acting like a goddamn faggot, you no-good Tasmanian bum son-of-a-bitch!" Curtiz would scream.

"Go fuck yourself, you dumb Hungarian!" Flynn vollied.

Meanwhile, Hal Wallis, watching the rushes each night, wasn't too gentle on Curtiz, as this September 30, 1935 memo, printed in *Inside Warner Bros. (1935–1951)*, reveals:

> I distinctly remember telling you, I don't know how many times, that I did not want you to use lace collars or cuffs on Errol Flynn. What in the hell is the matter with you ... I want the man to look like a pirate, not a molly-coddle. You have him standing up here dealing with a lot of hard-boiled characters, and you've got him dressed up like a goddamned faggot...
>
> I suppose that when he goes into battle with the pirates at the finish, you'll probably be having him wear a high silk hat and spats....
>
> Let him look a little swashbuckling, for Christ sake! Don't always have him dressed like a pansy!

Come the great duel, shot at Laguna Beach, Curtiz had the protective knobs removed from the foils; Rathbone fell in the surf, and lightly scarred Flynn's face. It might have been much worse and, indeed, might have ended Flynn's career before it had begun. Understandably Flynn became tentative in the duel, and Curtiz took Rathbone (actually a master fencer) aside with a suggestion. Taking his cue from Curtiz, Rathbone taunted Flynn just before the cameras rolled:

"I'm making forty-five hundred dollars a week more than you are, you dirty little Australian!"

The math was slightly off, but the "method" worked — Flynn came afire in the duel. Hero and villain clicked, and after Flynn's death, Rathbone wrote about him in his 1962 memoir, *In and Out of Character*:

> He was one of the most beautiful male animals I have ever met. I think his greatest handicap was that he was incapable of taking himself or anyone else seriously. I don't think he had any ambition beyond "living up" every moment of his life to the maximum of his physical capacity, and making money. He was monstrously lazy and self-indulgent, relying on a magnificent body to keep him going, and he had an insidious flair for making trouble, mostly for himself. I believe him to have been quite fearless, and subconsciously possessed of his own self-destruction. I would say that he was fond of me, for what reasons I shall never know. It was always "dear old Bazzz," and he would flash that smile that was both defiant and cruel, but which for me always had a tinge of affection in it. We only crossed swords, never words....

Captain Blood was a triumph, an Academy nominee for Best Picture of the Year (losing to MGM's *Mutiny on the Bounty*). A person not thrilled with its success — and Flynn's overnight stardom — was Lili Damita. Director/writer Delmer Daves went to the opening night party, and remembered:

> Since my lady and I were among the first to arrive, we received the weeping Lili Damita Flynn who begged us again and again, "Don't ... tell him how wonderful he was…" Then more tears as she said over and over (and how true it was), "Tonight I have lost my husband." I suppose it did happen that night — for when Errol arrived, boisterously happy, exultant, it was easy to see he meant to enjoy this brave new world that brought him stardom that night. And he did.

Another competitor with *Captain Blood* for the 1935 Best Picture Oscar was *David Copperfield*, David O. Selznick's extravagant production. Heading the all-star cast was W.C. Fields as Mr. Micawber, one of his finest, warmest and best-remembered performances. However, the 1935 film for which Fields himself deserved an Academy award was Paramount's *The Man on the Flying Trapeze*. In *Alternate Oscars*, Danny Peary bestows the prize (that in 1935 went to Victor McLaglen for *The Informer*) on W.C. for his performance as Ambrose Woolfinger:

> It's a pleasure to watch Fields stumble through life and emerge, impossibly, unscathed... A strong candidate for the best moment is when Fields, in bathrobe and pajamas, is thrown into jail for having manufactured homemade applejack, and immediately sees his crazed cellmate come toward him, with twisting fingers aimed at his neck. The loony reveals his crime: "I take my scissors and stick them straight into my wife's throat." This prompts Fields to do one of his classic double takes and look for a guard. When the man adds, "I've had three wives, but this is the first one I've killed in all my life," Fields responds, "Oh, that's in your favor, yes, they have no more a case against you than a sheep has against a butcher." For playing a marvelous character no other comic could conceive, and making us laugh nonstop for 65 minutes, Fields deserves the Oscar.

The Scoundrel sounds like a title for an Errol Flynn movie. In fact, it was the new 1935 film from writers/directors Ben Hecht and Charles MacArthur, shot at the Astoria Studios and starring Noel Coward in his film debut (and title role).

The premise: a smarmy, womanizing New York publisher (Coward, who professes proudly, "I'm never nice") woos a sweet poetess (Julie Haydon) away from her fiancé (Stanley Ridges), then tosses her aside to chase a voluptuary — and has Ridges arrested for trying to shoot him. He dies when his plane crashes into the ocean near Bermuda and since "there's no rest for those who die unloved, unmourned," Coward has a month to find someone to shed a tear for him and save his soul. Of course, he seeks the poetess to plead for her forgiveness. Danny Peary writes of *The Scoundrel* in his book *Guide for the Film Fanatic*:

> A Paramount release, *The Scoundrel* (with gag cameos by Hecht and MacArthur as Bowery flophouse bums) was too avant-garde to have been a box office hit. Nevertheless, come the 1935 Academy Award night, *The Scoundrel* competed for Best Original Story with MGM's *Broadway Melody* of 1936 and

Fox's *The Gay Deception* — and won. It was Hecht's second Academy Award and MacArthur's first and only.

Meanwhile, Hecht composed a poem — "Hecht's Prayer for his Bosses." Here are a few passages, the first dealing with traditional film heroines:

> My heroine must be so nice,
> So full of dainty tweedledums –
> Her gimlet ass a cake of ice –
> So delicate she feasts on crumbs
> And full of smirking sacrifice
> Farts bonbons and shits sugar plums
>
> This Venus of cliché and slop
> Must nary imbecile affront,
> Must suffer and come out on top,
> Must love and die and bear the brunt
> While Will Hays like a traffic cop
> Barks signals from inside her cunt.
>
> And what about the dreary hick –
> My hero, with his marcelled hair –
> So noble, cute and politic,
> So winsome – Holy God is there
> In all of lit'rature a prick
> As flaccid and a mind as bare.
>
> He must be fashioned without juice
> No thinking must disturb or shock
> This last pale drop of self abuse –
> This human cipher run amok –
> Whose balls are full of Mother Goose
> With Bo Peep tattooed on his cock.

Ben Hecht made sure that Louis B. Mayer got a copy of the poem, and the Hecht and Fowler whorehouse office soon became the quarters for other talent. There's no report of what happened to Bunny.

William Powell by John Decker

136 Hollywood's Hellfire Club

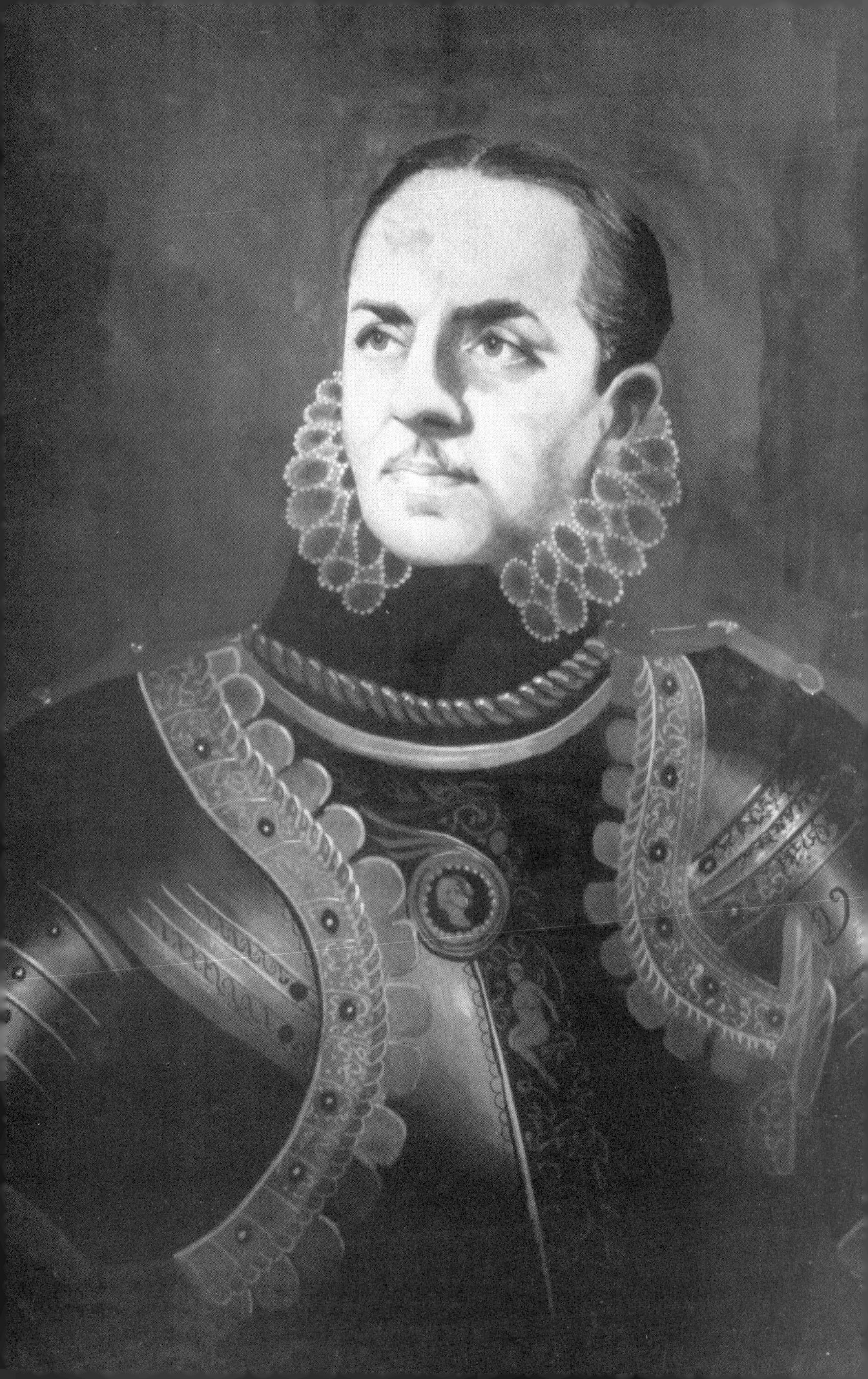

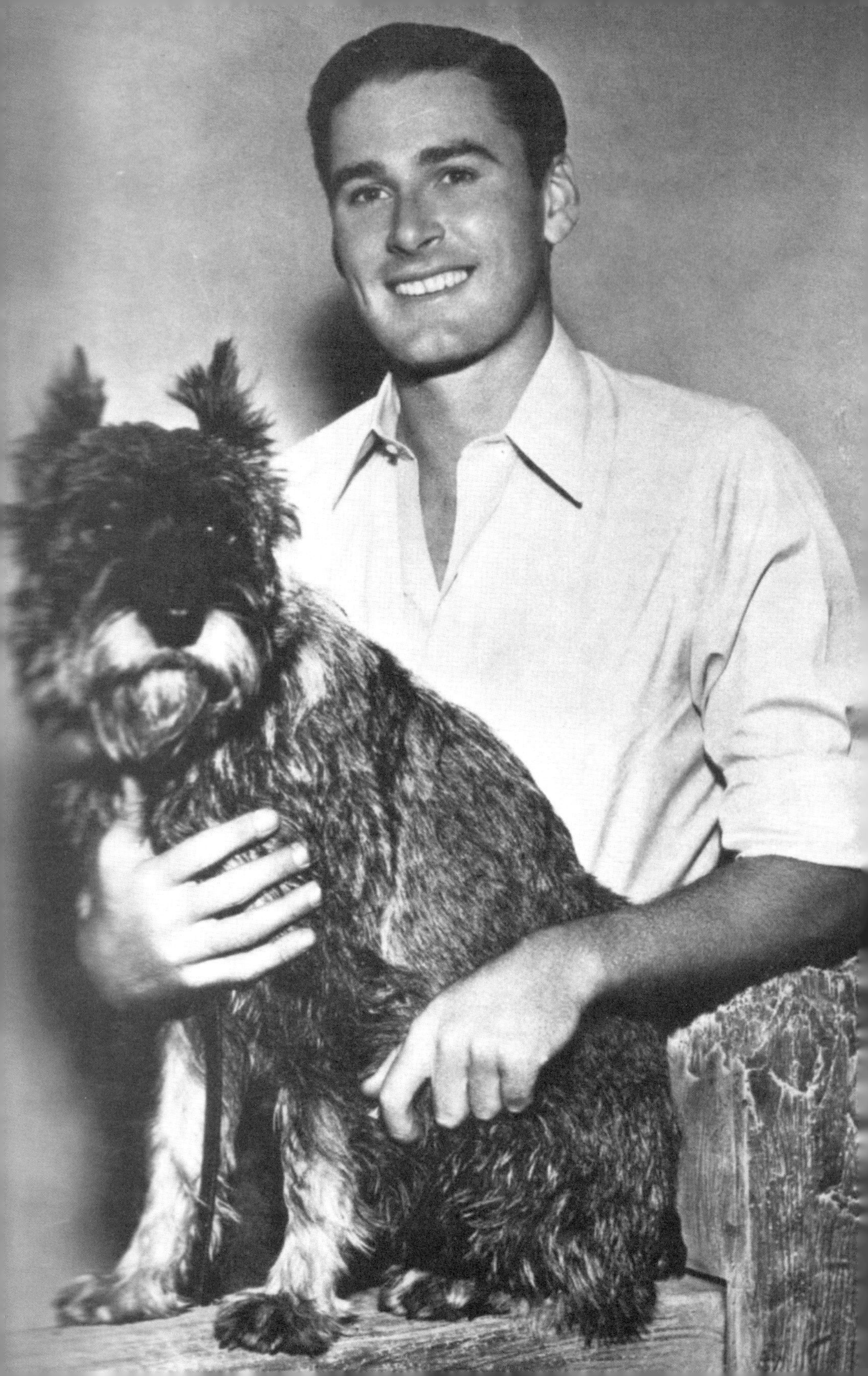

John Decker still boisterously marketed his artistic versatility, and a flyer Decker produced reads:

FOR YOUR WIFE: A painting of herself or yourself (no laughs!)
FOR YOUR HUSBAND: A painting of yourself (still no laughs!)
FOR YOU BOTH: A painting of your child (I'm perfectly serious!)
FOR YOUR FRIENDS: A caricature of himself, herself or yourself
(Now, laugh!)
Paintings or DECKER-ations suitable for the Living Room,
Library, Den or Bar.
FOR YOUR ENEMY: Let our conscience be your guide!

As Decker noted "No sittings required. Pick a favorite photograph." And he listed the styles he could provide:

Rembrandt
Gainsborough
Van Dyck
Whistler
Sargent
Picasso

Or any other artist... living or dead Including John Decker

The man would do it all — Christmas cards, place cards, bookplates, letterheads, newspaper cartoons...

In the spring of 1936, W.C. Fields made the film version of his Broadway hit *Poppy* for Paramount. During the shooting he received a tribute, as reported by the *Los Angeles Times* (April 23, 1936):

He was presented with an oil painting of himself as Shakespeare's "Melancholy Dane" done after the style of the old masters by John Decker, noted portrait painter and cartoonist.

Spending a day on the set at Paramount where Fields is making *Poppy*, Decker did a dozen sketches of the incandescent-nosed comic, and polished off the afternoon making a few linear notes for the painting.

Yesterday he delivered the portrait to Fields.

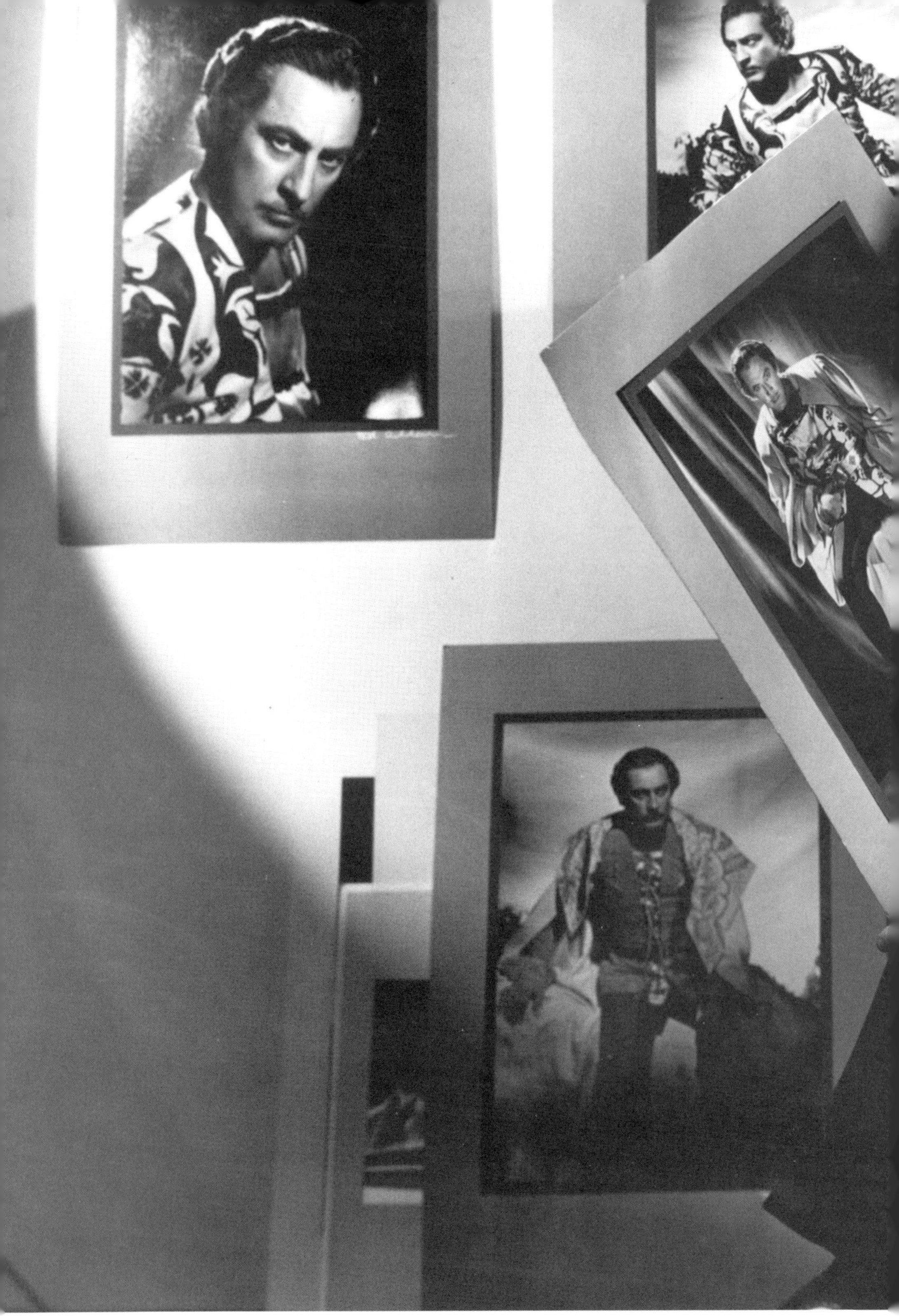

Publicity still for *Romeo and Juliet* in which Barrymore played Mercutio under duress

"As I live and breathe," exclaimed the subject regarding the work, "I'm in the wrong end of the business. As Hamlet I'd be a sensation. It never occurred to me I'd look so well in tights."

He also seemed to be very much taken with the sword hanging at his side in the painting.

Errol Flynn followed *Captain Blood* with Warners' *The Charge of the Light Brigade* (1936), again with Olivia de Havilland, whom he tormented with practical jokes, such as sneaking into her dressing room to place a snake in her underwear (accounts disagree as to whether the snake was alive, dead, or rubber). The despised Michael Curtiz directed again, and David Niven, Flynn's new pal, had a featured role. Flynn had a truly violent streak, and was challenged to prove his manhood time and again, which he had no trouble doing. One day on location for *The Charge of the Light Brigade*, as the British ambassador and guests watched the shoot, an extra stuck his rubber-tipped lance tip up the tail of Flynn's horse. As Niven wrote in *The Moon's a Balloon*:

> The animal reared up and Flynn completed the perfect parabola and landed on his back. Six hundred very muscular stunt men roared with laughter.
>
> Flynn picked himself up. "Which one of you sons of bitches did that?"
>
> "I did, sonny," said a huge gorilla of a man. "Want to make anything of it?"
>
> "Yes, I do," said Flynn. "Get off your horse."
>
> Nobody could stop it and the fight lasted a long time. At the end of it the gorilla lay flat on his back. After that everyone liked Errol much more.

According to Charles Higham, the "gorilla," after Flynn got through with him, had two black eyes and a broken leg.

During the shooting of *The Charge of the Light Brigade*, Flynn disappeared mid-production and sailed his yacht, the *Sirocco*, toward the West Indies, landing on the island of Cat Cay. Warner Bros. had to dispatch a studio representative on a seaplane from Miami to find Flynn and renegotiate his contract. The Warner Brothers knew Flynn had them by the short hairs; by the time he returned to Hollywood and *The Charge of the Light Brigade*, the despairing studio had doubled his salary. Apparently the strike wasn't entirely self-serving — Flynn was sickened by the killing and crippling of horses on location, and demanded it stop.

Flynn took little real joy from his wife Lili, who, fiercely jealous, intimidated and mocked him. In March of 1937, during a trip to Paris, Lili took Flynn to La Silhouette, a lesbian niterie, and made Flynn watch as she sensually danced with another woman. Enraged, Flynn walked the streets of Paris all night, later writing in *My Wicked, Wicked Ways* that he knew if he stayed with Lili, "I would have to kill her or get killed."

There were separations, but the torturous marriage continued.

Perceiving his overnight stardom and wealth as ridiculous, agonized by his Marelle memories, taunted by Lili, Errol Flynn found three life-saving escapes. One was his yacht, the *Sirocco*, which indulged his deep love of sailing and the sea. The second was a dog, Arno, whom he probably loved more sincerely than Lili or any of his whores.

The third was the band of "brothers" in drink — primarily John Barrymore.

As Flynn grew to know Barrymore, he quickly came to idolize him. He related to Mad Jack's love of the sea, his yacht, his animals; Flynn even got a pet monkey, "Chico," shades of Barrymore's lamented "Clementine." David Niven said he never understood Flynn's "hero worship" of Barrymore, who now, as Niven wrote, "seemed to go out of his way to shock and be coarse." Perhaps Flynn recognized the genius and perceived the torment. Via the Great Profile, Flynn would soon become a member of the gang destined to be known as the Bundy Drive Boys.

The Barrymore emulation was touching and finally tragic as Errol Flynn eventually aped the very Jekyll/Hyde decay that plagued his idol. The result, pitifully, was both emotional and physical. Not long before Flynn died, Olivia de Havilland felt a man kissing her neck at a party. She wheeled on the man and said, "How dare you!" Only after a moment did she recognize that the kisser to be Errol Flynn.

"He had changed so," said Olivia de Havilland. "His eyes were so sad. I had stared into them in enough movies to know his spirit was gone."

Errol Flynn claimed he first met John Barrymore when the latter was working on MGM's *Romeo and Juliet*.

Barrymore had come back to Hollywood after his pilgrimage to India, where he had spent most of his time in a sacred whorehouse. Metro Boy Wonder Irving Thalberg saw *Romeo and Juliet* as a valedictory to his wife, Norma Shearer. Leslie Howard was a wan Romeo, and it was Barrymore's job — as Mercutio — to provide some of Shakespeare's fire to the handsome but flaccid epic. His 1933 walkout on MGM was forgiven. To evoke the old Hollywood cliché, MGM had vowed to never let the son-of-a-bitch back on the lot, until they needed him.

Basil Rathbone, who won a Best Supporting Actor Academy nod as Tybalt, wrote in his 1962 memoir *In and Out of Character* of Mad Jack's antics the day director George Cukor tried to film Mercutio's "Queen Mab" speech. "There was that wild look in his eyes!" wrote Rathbone:

> ... the scene went smoothly enough until the line, "He heareth not, he stirreth not, he moveth not"; as he approached this line Barrymore took a deep breath, flexing his eyebrows and bulging his eyes. Then he said, "He heareth not, he stirreth not." Long pause, then with much relish, "He pisseth not!"
>
> George groaned, "Jack, please."
>
> "Strange how me heritage encumbereth my speech," was Jack's reply. "Dear Mr. Shakespeare, I beg you hear me yet awhile. I am but an improvident actor [pronounced actor-r-r] and yet I would beg you to consider an undeniable fact, I have improved upon your text. 'He moveth not' is not so pertinent to the occasion as 'he pisseth not.'"
>
> And so it went until nearly lunchtime. Thalberg was sent for and came onto the set. Very gently he pleaded with Jack to speak the line as it was written.
>
> "Very well," rejoined Jack, "just once I will say it that thou mayest see how it stinketh." And he did, and that's the only "take" they got from him that day and of course the one that appears in the picture. Jack was furious at the trick played upon him and vowed bloody vengeance on all who had so vilely betrayed him!

Thalberg ("a nice guy, but he could piss ice water," said MGM executive Eddie Mannix) eventually decided to replace Barrymore with William Powell, but Powell — a fan of the actor, and grateful to him for an early break in the business — refused. And so MGM, Louis B. Mayer and Irving Thalberg agreed to keep pisseth-not Mercutio on *Romeo and Juliet* under one condition:

To avoid any costly drunkenness, John Barrymore, every night of the shooting, had to stay in an asylum.

The asylum was named "Kelly's," conveniently close to MGM in Culver City. The home reeked of paraldehyde and housed screaming lunatics, as well as hopeless alcoholics. Barrymore, fearful of a possible permanent incarceration if he couldn't work, agreed to this temporary one. Nightly he allowed himself locked in with the screams and the stink, facing his most severe, almost lifelong nightmare. He ranted without his liquor, and one night in the throes of delirium tremens fought with Mr. Kelly so viciously that he tossed his "keeper" through a plate-glass window.

Gene Fowler came to the rescue, if by rather unorthodox means. As cohorts Ben Hecht and Charles MacArthur distracted a guard on the grounds with booze and patter, Fowler — aware Barrymore's room was one without bars on the window — tied a bottle to a bedsheet, allowing Mad Jack to pull up the brew to help him make it through the night.

Fowler probably thought he was being compassionate. Then again, a Bundy Drive Boy to the bone, he also believed 100% in a man's God-given right to destroy himself.

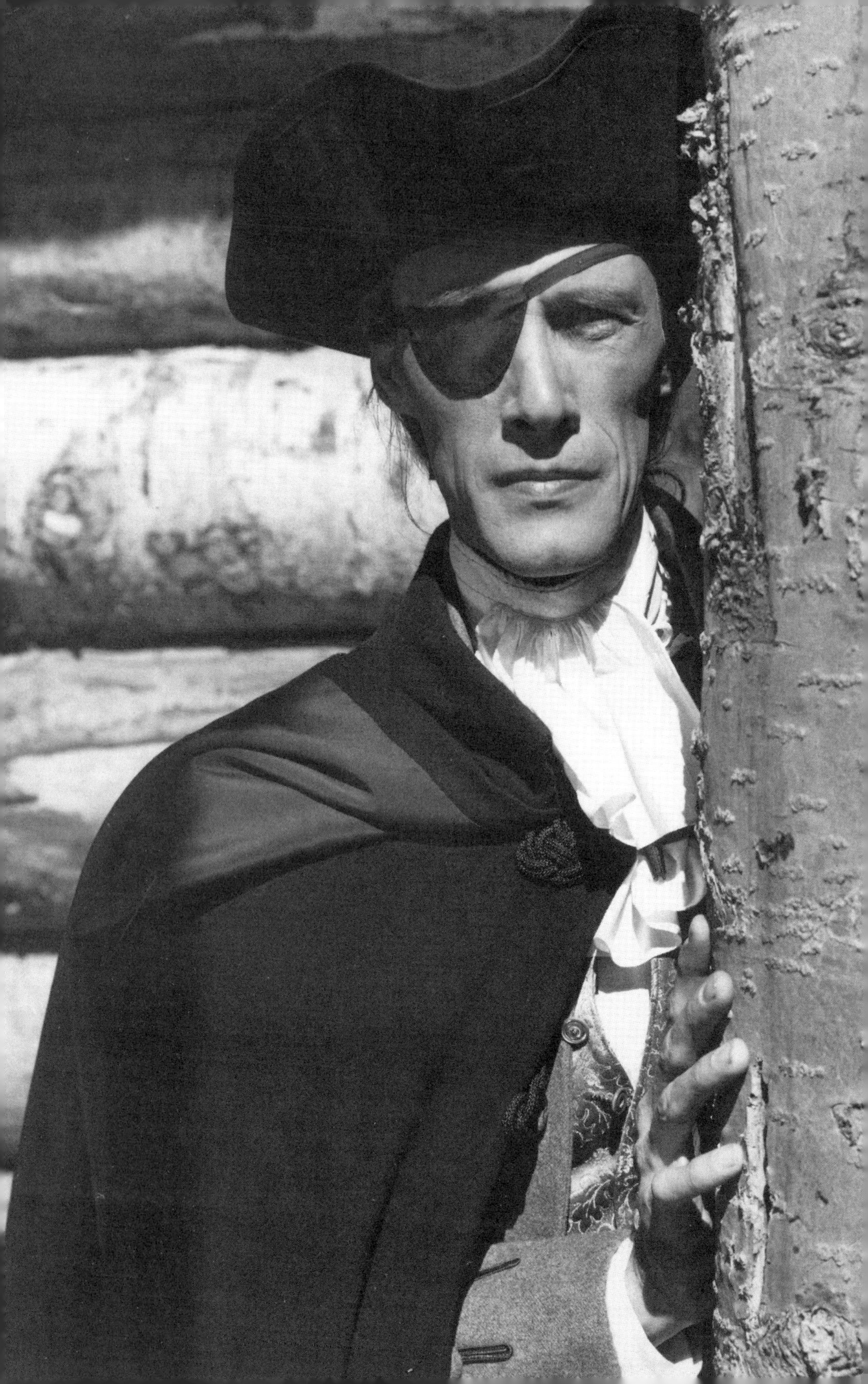

Chapter Ten

The Featured Players

> I remember a recurrent dream that scared the hell out of me: my Daddy, dressed up in a Dracula cape and a black hat, coming at me on a red tricycle with wings.
> —David Carradine

Hollywood's first impression of John Carradine was that he was a stark raving madman.

In the late 1920s and early 1930s, the gaunt, longhaired Carradine terrorized Hollywood Boulevard parading in rakishly-cocked Homburg and flowing cape, roaring out the great Shakespearean soliloquies. Legend claimed that Carradine scared away Peter the Hermit, a bearded old soul who had previously staked out the boulevard as his own runway for preaching apocalyptic repentance. The story goes that, after Peter glimpsed Carradine's demonic shade howling out Richard III —

> Deformed, unfinished, sent before my time into this breathing world half-scarce made up...!

The Hermit fled to the hills, surrendering his turf to the cadaverous usurper.

Visiting the Hollywood Bowl after midnight Carradine was wont to bellow classical verse to the 20,000 empty seats. Eventually the police chased him away and only years later did Carradine learn who had sicced them on him — John Ford, who later directed the actor in *Stagecoach* and *The Grapes of Wrath*.

John Carradine in *Drums Along the Mohawk*

"He lived up in the hills," said Carradine of Ford, "and said I was keeping him awake."

The mad Shakespearean eventually became one of Golden Age cinema's top character players, but not until after many grim memories. One of the worst was the night Carradine, near-starving, sat in his cloak and slouch hat outside a boulevard restaurant and looked woefully at the diners inside gorging themselves. A party by the window shrieked in laughter at the sight of him, and ordered food thrown out to the scarecrow on the sidewalk.

All the while they gleefully made bets as to when his stomach would burst.

Richmond Reed Carradine was born February 5, 1906 in New York City; his father was an Associated Press writer who died when he was three, and his mother was a physician. At an early age he saw Robert Mantell as Shylock and decided to become a classical actor. He passionately read Shakespeare and, blessed with a remarkable memory, had committed all the Bard's works to memory. In his prime, he insisted he could play any Shakespearean role with only 24 hours notice, and this incredible ability lasted him late into his life.

John Barrymore played Hamlet in New York when Carradine was 16 — Carradine professed to have seen Barrymore in the role six times and Barrymore became his idol. He made his own theatrical debut in New Orleans in 1925 in *Camille*, acted in stock company Shakespeare, and decided to take his chances in Hollywood.

His trek across the country was shades of John Decker. Carradine traveled as a quick sketch artist, pursuing important-looking folk and selling them a portrait for $2.50.

> I made as high as 10 to 15 dollars a day that way. Then I would move into the best hotel and order the finest dishes its restaurant afforded. By the end of the week, I would be accepted as an eccentric but devout genius and be invited to sing solos in the First Methodist Church.

Carradine became a "banana messenger" on a train bound for Los Angeles. His job demanded he run across the top of the train in the Texan desert, opening and closing ventilator hatches to keep the bananas at an even temperature. Considering Carradine had already selected his cloak and large black hat as his customary attire, he surely cut quite a figure as he scurried back and forth atop the train. Thus did he arrive in Hollywood in 1927.

After a brief stint as a scenic designer for Cecil B. DeMille, who canned him for not including Roman columns in his sketches, Carradine became an actor — usually on the street, sometimes on a local stage. He claimed to have played Richard III for the first time in 1929 at USC, and to prepare for the role, he decided it was time he met his beau ideal, John Barrymore. It was one of John Carradine's favorite stories: toiling up Tower Road to Bella Vista; finding a telephone at the back gate in a niche ("Everything in Hollywood is in a niche, like a saint," said Carradine); Nishi's Japanese voice answering and admitting him; Carradine walking under an arbor, and fencing with the veranda doorknob with his cane…

> Presently I saw something out of the corner of my eye and there was Barrymore, in a blue polka-dot dressing gown with his hands stuffed deep in his pockets and his head to one side like a bird — astonished at this apparition! For I was wearing the last of my stock wardrobe — a black braided jacket, striped morning trousers, spats (because I had no socks)… a wing collar, a York puffed tie, a Homburg hat and a cane. He took a step toward me, and I took a tentative step toward him…
>
> Finally I said, "Mr. Barrymore, I'm going to play Richard III." And Barrymore said, "Really? Let's have a drink!"

Barrymore dispatched Nishi to bring "two tall Tom Collins" and, in a dream come true, Carradine became a crony of his idol.

It was a ribald relationship. The story goes that Barrymore once arranged for Carradine to make a screen test, for which he was made up as a fantastic fop, with curly wig and lipstick, enjoying a banquet as he delivered a lengthy soliloquy. The speech was to end with Carradine luxuriantly wiping his mouth and exclaiming, in close-up, "Ah! Delicious! The best I've ever had!"

Barrymore, assuring Carradine the test was a star-maker, invited him and a bevy of Hollywood notables to its screening. The star himself introduced it, assuring the assemblage they'd see on the screen evidence of this young man's "remarkable and uncanny special talent." The room darkened, the scene began, and Carradine was shocked to see the speech cut down right to his final line and close-up—

"Ah! Delicious! The best I've ever had!"

—followed by a cut to Barrymore, from the waist down, pulling up his fly.

The late Henry Brandon, the towering character actor (best remembered as Barnaby in Laurel and Hardy's *Babes in Toyland*) recalled trading some badinage with Carradine, and confronting him with that account. "It's a base canard!" raved Carradine. "It's a tissue of lies!"

"The crazier he got denying it," laughed Brandon, "the more I knew it was true!"

John Carradine made his first film *Tol'able David*, in 1930. He played mainly bits in the early 1930s — such as a Christian martyr in DeMille's *The Sign of the Cross* (1932), and a hunter who crashes the peaceful idyll of Karloff's Monster and O.P. Heggie's saintly hermit in Whale's delirious zenith of Universal horror, *The Bride of Frankenstein* (1935).

It was *The Prisoner of Shark Island*, released in early 1936, which awarded John Carradine his fame. The actor played Sgt. Rankin, the Lucifer of a jailer who rules over the hellish Dry Tortugas, making life a Hades for his prize convict Dr. Samuel Mudd (Warner Baxter). With wild eyes, a satanic smile and a dash of Shakespearean bravado, John Carradine was the movie villain of the season.

"Hi'ya, Judas!" crows Carradine at the hapless Baxter.

Come the Hollywood premiere of *The Prisoner of Shark Island* at Grauman's Chinese Theatre, and Carradine realized how effective he was in the role. He took his new wife Ardanelle, and the departing crowd recognized him and booed him, causing his aghast bride to weep in mortification.

Overnight, John Carradine was a 20th Century-Fox contract player and a member of John Ford's stock company. Columnist Jimmie Fidler saluted Carradine's "rococo theatricalism," the fact that he attended premieres in his Duesenberg, with chauffeur and footman:

> An opera cape, top hat, ebony stick and glittering diamond studs set John apart in a town where a tuxedo is considered formal dress. At intermission, he stands gracefully in the lobby, smoking a long Russian cigarette and twirling his cane... It is the kind of exhibitionism that made Hollywood, in its colorful beginnings, the most talked-about town on Earth.

Now famous in his own right, Carradine could enjoy his frolics as a Bundy Drive Boy, gaining his entrée via Barrymore. As Errol Flynn told Charles Hamblett in his book *The Hollywood Cage*:

> Barrymore, John Carradine and I used to go three or four days without sleeping. We'd start out in some bistro at noon and a week later find ourselves in Mexico or in a yacht off Catalina with a dozen bottles on the floor and a gaggle of whores puking their guts up all over the place ... that's how we were then — so intoxicated with the sheer zing of existence, we were half-mad when we were technically sober...

In *Mary of Scotland*, (RKO, 1936), Carradine played Mary's confidante, David Rizzo, a role that provided him the chance to sing, as well as a moving death scene. Katharine Hepburn, who played the title role, failed to impress him.

The Decker painting that appalled Hepburn

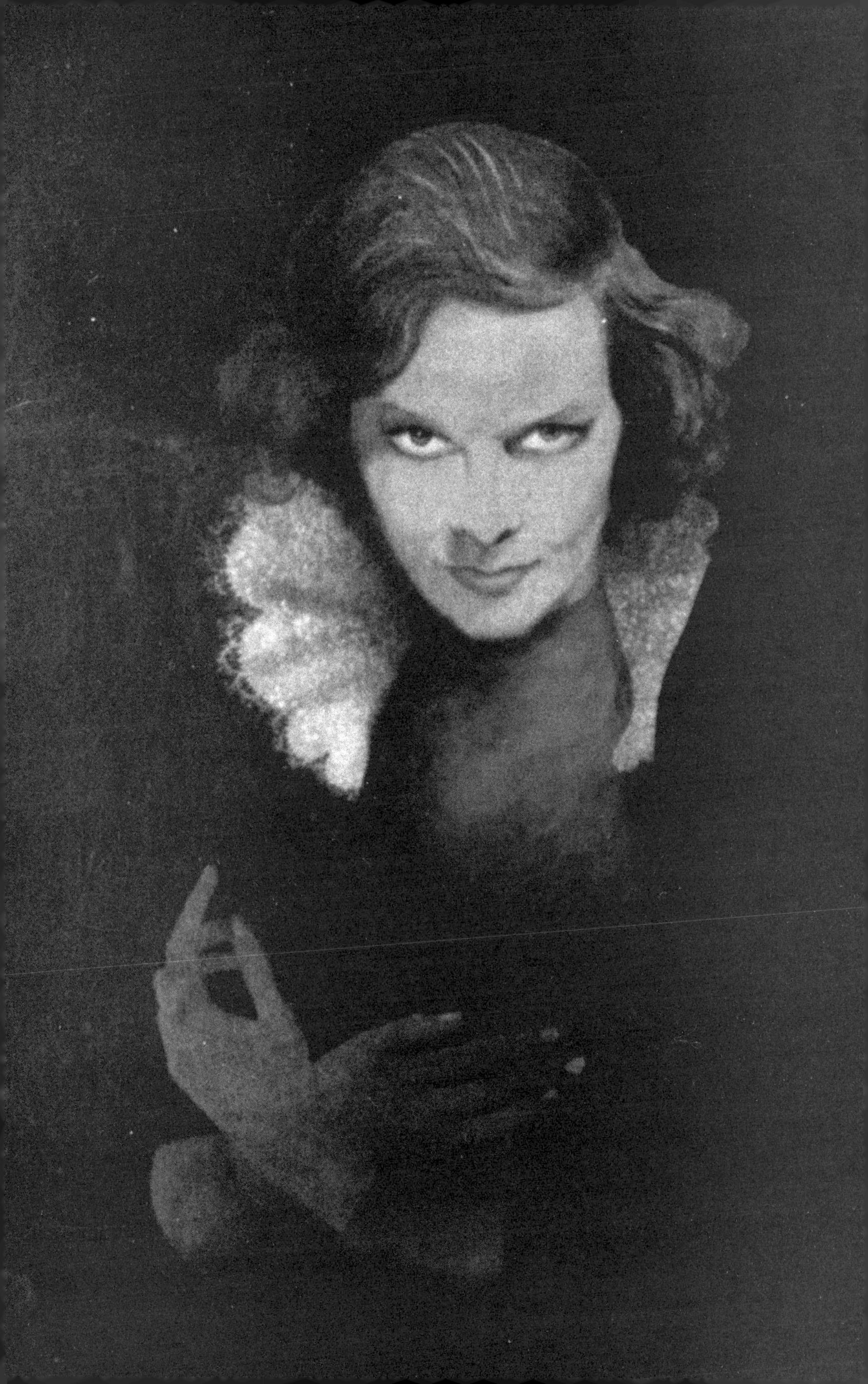

> Day after day Kate kept saying she really wanted to play both Mary and Queen Elizabeth (played by Florence Eldridge). We all got tired of hearing it. So one day I told Kate, "If you played both parts, how would you know which queen to upstage?" She walked off the set, and didn't speak to me for 20 years!

Meanwhile, John Decker painted Hepburn's portrait as Mary of Scotland. Once again, the "Poison-Caricaturist" had his wicked way and Kate emerged looking like a red-haired succubus. She was so appalled she vowed never to sit for another portrait and gave away the painting, which only emerged again in 2006 after years in an attic in the Hollywood Hills.

> If every producer were to drop dead today, show business still would go on. Seriously, if a bomb hit Hollywood it would only be a matter of time before someone was squatting amid the ruins telling stories.
> —Alan Mowbray

"Flamboyancy is neither word nor gesture," said Alan Mowbray, who always evoked a penguin pretending to be Oscar Wilde, or vice versa. "It's in the mind." Imposingly British, sardonically suave, he was a man of great wit, considerable talent and actually little ego — so hating the sight of his own face onscreen that he avoided his approximately 150 films and dozens of TV appearances.

Born August 18, 1896 in London, Mowbray later claimed he got to New York City by stoking a ship. He checked into the Webster Hotel and fled the bill two weeks later, exiting, as he recalled, wearing "two shirts, two compete sets of underwear, assorted extra garments stuck into his jacket pockets and razor, toothbrush, etc., cached elsewhere on his person." Life was so precarious that he slept on "a big, black smooth rock" in Central Park and ate leftover rolls at the Automat — "beating the bus boys to it," Mowbray later smiled, "with great skill."

He joined a Theatre Guild tour of Shaw's *The Apple Cart*, acted from 1923 to 1929 with New York stock companies and made his Broadway debut in *Sport of Kings*, which opened May 4, 1926 at the Lyceum Theatre. He loved to write and come August 15, 1929, *Dinner is Served* premiered on Broadway, written, directed and starring Alan Mowbray. *The New York Times* was appalled:

> When an actor writes a play for himself, as Alan Mowbray has done in *Dinner is Served*, now at the Cort Theatre, you expect him to do as well by himself as pos-

sible…. But Mr. Mowbray, being a glutton for punishment, has given himself a dull part in a dull comedy — nor has he spared his colleagues… speaking empty lines and walking through an endless succession of silly situations. Your heart might bleed for Mr. Mowbray, if he were not responsible for his own calamity.

Dinner is Served lasted four performances.

Mowbray and his wife Lorayne decided to try Hollywood. First he had to escape another bill, this one from New York's Algonquin Hotel, managed by the noted Frank Case. Mowbray told reporter Mel Heimer in 1954:

I left the Algonquin, where I had a lovely room — 1002 — owing $750. Later, when I had a bit of success in Hollywood, three or four years after that, I paid the bill — and, I believe, thus gave Case his first heart attack.

He played George Washington in Warners' *Alexander Hamilton* (George Arliss in the title role, 1931) and soon settled as one of the movie colony's busiest character actors, supporting such stars as James Cagney, Jean Harlow and John Barrymore — who became good friends with Mowbray and dubbed him "a worthy adversary." A rare star role came in Universal's bizarre fantasy *Night Life of the Gods* (1935), with Mowbray as an inventor who changes Greek statues into living beings at a New York museum; hilarity only intermittingly ensues.

Mowbray was both character actor and character. In January of 1933, he was arrested and charged with drunk driving after crashing his car into another at 5110 Los Feliz Boulevard. He pleaded guilty, paying a $200 fine and agreeing to his license being revoked for 90 days, but told the judge he was only doing so because he was busy working on a movie and simply wanted to "dispose of the matter." Yet Mowbray's most compelling work in the early 1930s wasn't on the screen, or in traffic court, but as a courageous founder of the Screen Actors Guild.

In the summer of 1933, a rebellious bunch of Hollywood actors, including Ralph Morgan, Boris Karloff and Alan Mowbray, had recognized the Academy of Motion Pictures Arts and Sciences as a dupe, all too ready to sell them down the river. On June 30, 1933, the Screen Actors Guild articles were filed. On July 10, Mowbray, who at the time had $60 in his checking account, wrote a check for $50 to retain Larry Beilenson as the SAG counsel. (According to Valerie Yaros, SAG historian, the Guild never reimbursed Mowbray for his expense.) Two days later, Mowbray became the first vice president of the SAG, with Ralph Morgan as president.

In October of 1933, 14 major actors, protesting a proposal for a salary control board, quit the Academy of Motion Picture Arts and Sciences. With the new influx of members to the SAG, both Ralph Morgan and Alan Mowbray voluntarily gave up their offices to make way for stars with big name power. Eddie Cantor became president, and Adolphe Menjou was first vice president, Fredric March became second vice president and Ann Harding was third vice president. Ralph Morgan became one of the directors and Alan Mowbray joined the Advisory committee.

Come the late 1930s, Alan Mowbray lived at 1019 Chevy Chase in Beverly Hills, and played in such popular films as *Mary of Scotland* and *My Man Godfrey* (1936). He was twice elected president of the Masquers Club, was a Fellow of the Royal Geographical Society and a popular lecturer, toastmaster and after-dinner speaker. He was a friend with many of the British actors, even the most aloof and mysterious ones; when Colin Clive, the monster maker of *Frankenstein* and *Bride of Frankenstein* died in 1937, Mowbray was one of the pallbearers.

He had enormous fun in his profession, even if he couldn't bear to witness his own work in it. And he made a fat salary, allowing him to own, at one time, 32 of John Decker's paintings.

> A man looks bigger in the bathtub than he does in the ocean.
> —Thomas Mitchell

A film critic once suggested that Thomas Mitchell, in every film role he ever played, was drunk, or at least pretended to be. He did a terrific, barnstorming drunk, no doubt, but the generalization is unfair to the man who, for moviegoers of the 1930s and 1940s, was a dynamic mix of legitimate character actor and high-spirited hell-raiser.

He had a potato face, the look of an over-age Irish delinquent, making him ideal for rowdy newspapermen (*Mr. Smith Goes to Washington*), Gypsy kings (*The Hunchback of Notre Dame*), gone-to-seed-and-madness aristocrats (*Gone With the Wind*) and drunken frontier doctors (*Stagecoach*). All of these came in 1939, and the last performance won him the Academy Award for Best Supporting Actor.

He was a first-generation American of Irish immigrants, born July 11, 1892 in Elizabeth, New Jersey. For a brief time he followed the family into journalism, but in 1913 became an actor, joining the company of Charles Coburn and training in Shakespeare. He made his Broadway debut in *Under Sentence* (Harris Theatre, October 3, 1916) and in 1918 appeared with John Barrymore in the play *Redemption*. As the future Bundy Drive Boy later told Gene Fowler in *Minutes of the Last Meeting*:

Alan Mowbray

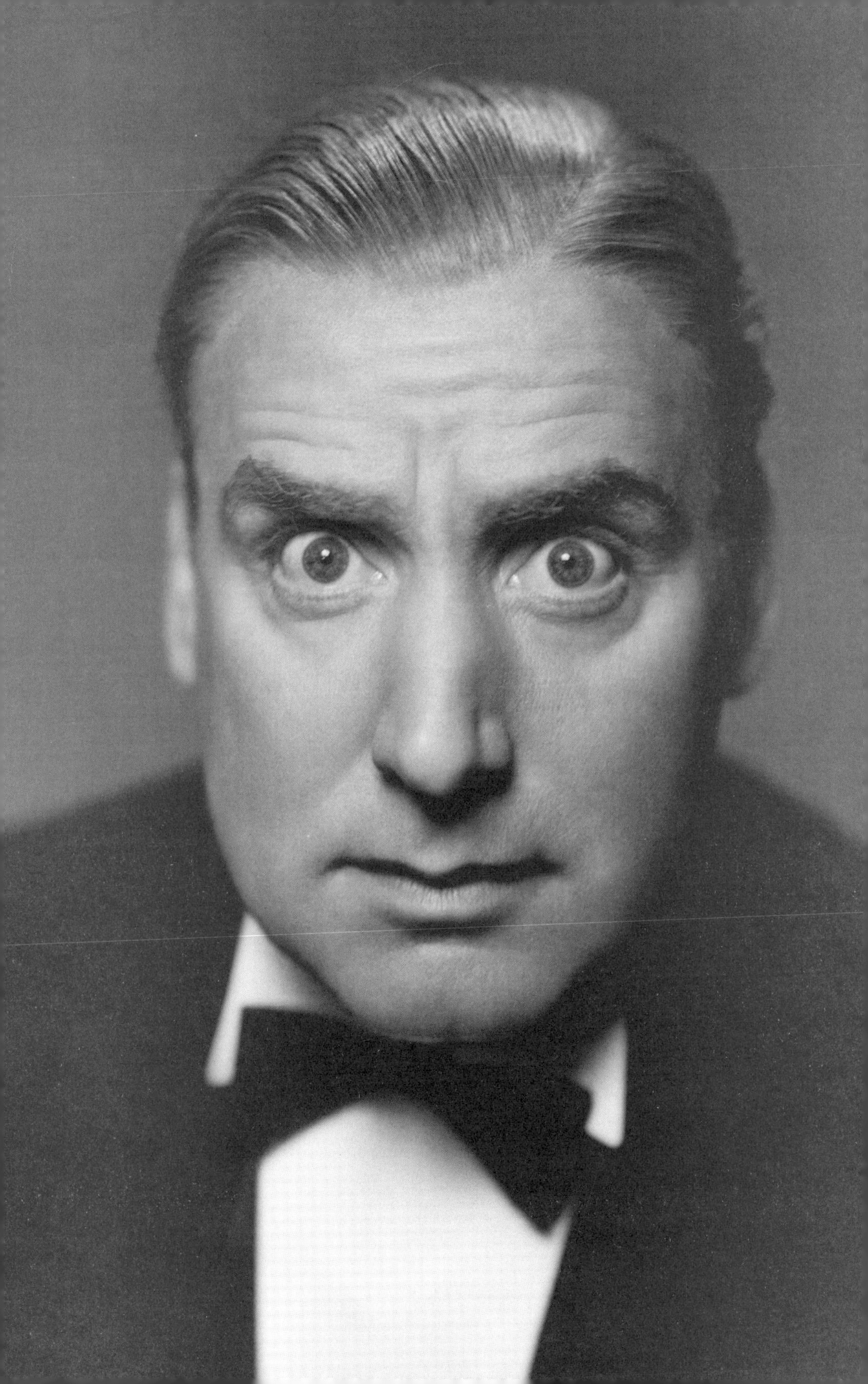

I didn't come on-stage until ten o'clock each evening. I had a long scene with Jack, a very important one for the understanding of the part he was playing. One night I was amazed when he began to cut his own lines and to speed up the scene with me. No matter how careless he may have been with his life, he was a martinet on-stage, and if anyone was in the least deficient in a scene with him, slow with the cue lines, or slovenly in delivery, he would blast that person as only he knew how to do. But tonight he left out great chunks of dialogue and kept whispering to me, "Are you all right, old man?" After the final curtain he came to my dressing room to ask again if I was feeling all right. I said of course I was, and what the hell? And he seemed greatly relieved as he said, "I thought I smelled booze on your breath as we began our scene." I told him I had had exactly one martini before going on, no more, no less. He smiled. "Oh, I was afraid you were drunk; and that's the only fault I can forgive in an actor. I merely wanted to take the strain off you."

Mitchell made his film debut in *Six Cylinder Love* (1923), which featured two of his future *Stagecoach* co-players — bald Donald Meek (also in his film bow) and florid Berton Churchill. Meanwhile, on Broadway, he did it all — produce, direct, write act. Among his credits: starring in and co-writing *Little Accident* (Morosco Theatre, October 9, 1928, 303 performances), starring in, directing and co-writing *Cloudy with Showers* (Morosco Theatre, September 1, 1931, 71 performances), directing and starring in *Honeymoon* (Little Theatre, December 23, 1932, 76 performances), directing Tallulah Bankhead in *Forsaking All Others* (Times Square Theatre, March 1, 1933, 110 performances), co-producing and directing *Twenty-Five Dollars an Hour* (Masque Theatre, May 10, 1933, 22 performances), directing and starring in *Fly Away Home* (48th Street Theatre, January 15, 1935, 204 performances), and directing the dialogue scenes of the musical review *At Home Abroad*, starring Beatrice Lillie, Eleanor Powell and Ethel Waters (Winter Garden Theatre and later Majestic Theatre, September 19, 1935, 198 performances). Between 1916 and 1935, he was involved one way or another with two dozen Broadway productions.

In 1936 Mitchell made his mark in Hollywood in such films as *Theodora Goes Wild*. He was impressive as banker/embezzler Henry Barnard in Frank Capra's *Lost Horizon* (1937) and as boozy Dr. Kersaint in John Ford's *The Hurricane* (copping a Best Supporting Actor Academy nomination).

Thomas Mitchell was a rip-roarer, and in life an art lover. The combo made him a natural to find his way to John Decker and the gang.

Roland Young as Uriah Heep in *David Copperfield* (1935)

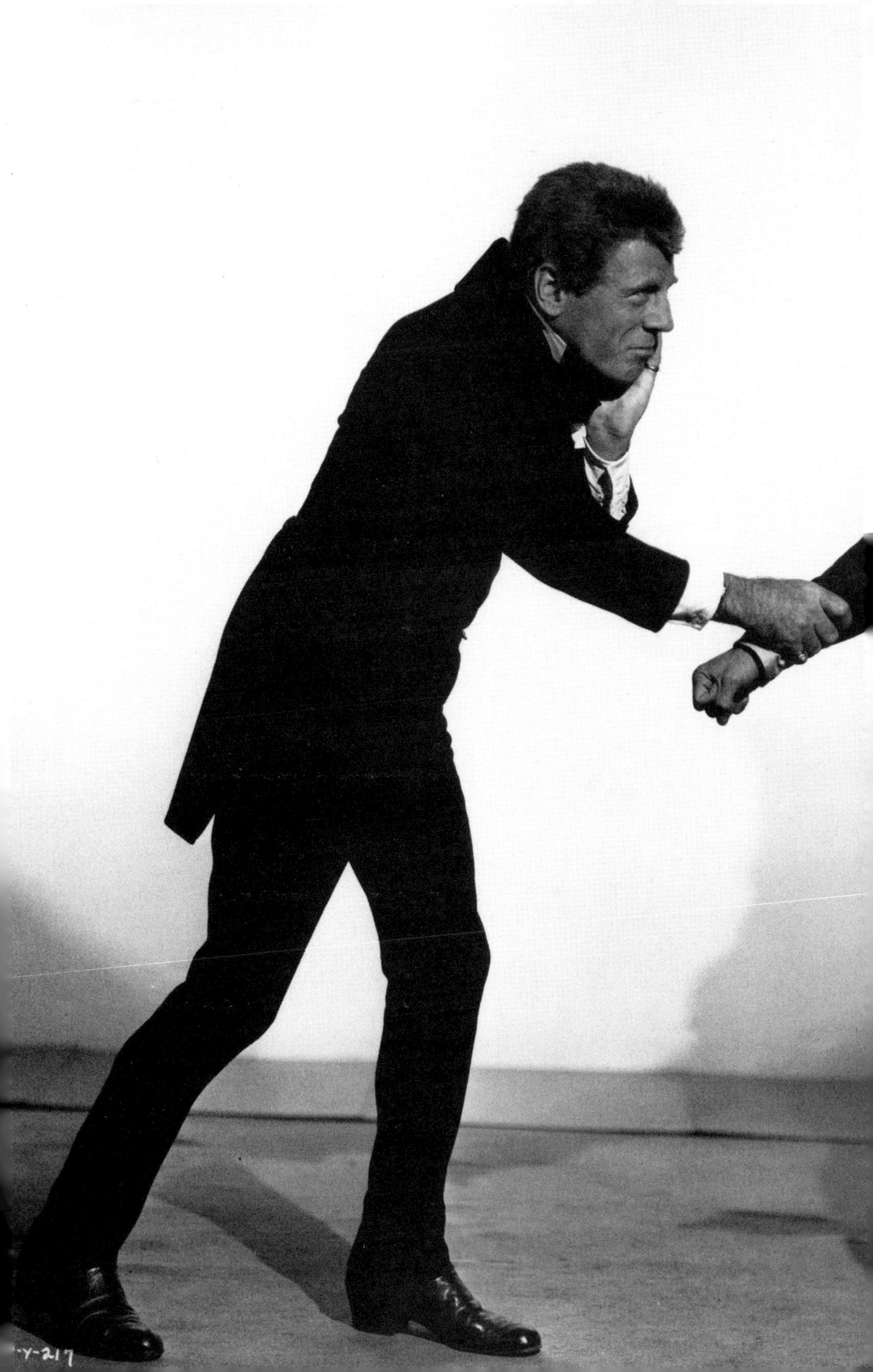
-Y-217

> While I consider a good expanse of black silk stocking quite alluringly shocking, I have frequently said to myself and others, girls with small brains wear ankle chains.
>
> —Roland Young

In 1922, John Barrymore had starred in the film *Sherlock Holmes*. His Dr. Watson was British actor Roland Young, and Barrymore remembered:

> When the modest, self-effacing Roland appeared on my horizon, I took a great liking to him; so much so that I began to feel sorry for him during our scenes together. For once in my life, I decided to be somewhat decent toward a colleague. I suggested a little stage-business now and then, so that such a charming, agreeable thespian might not be altogether lost in the shuffle. When I saw the completed film, I was flabbergasted, stunned, and almost became an atheist on the spot. That quiet, agreeable bastard had stolen not one, but every damned scene! This consummate artist and myself have been close friends for years, but I wouldn't think of trusting him on any stage. He is such a splendid gentleman in real life, but what a cunning, larcenous demon when on the boards!

Born in London November 11, 1887, Roland Young was a character player and scene stealer *par excellence*, best remembered for his unctuous Uriah Heep in *David Copperfield* (1935) and his portrayal of Cosmo Topper, capering with the ghosts of the Kirbys (Cary Grant and Constance Bennett) in *Topper* (1937), for which he received a Best Supporting Actor Academy nomination. Mustached and monocled, with the look of an elegant mouse, Young had enjoyed such Broadway hits as *Beggar on Horseback* (1924), *The Last of Mrs. Cheyney* (1925) and *The Queen's Husband* (1928) before settling in the film colony, where his charm, and ribald humor made him a charter member of the Bundy Drive Boys. As John Decker stated:

> Roland Young is another dear friend. One of my closest. I think the one thing that has forever fascinated me most about him is the way he talks without ever moving his upper lip. Moreover, he is a most mild soul. Yet, you always know what he is thinking, though in all his years, except once, I never heard him say a nasty thing or lose his temper.

That one lapse occurred at a party, when a dowager, in the midst of real intellects, spouted off for two hours on the subject of Art. Her opinions were worth nothing. Roland Young sat in a corner, buried in a newspaper. And after the dowager finished her second loud hour of blah, Roland Young suddenly rose, pecked his face into her, and blasted two words:

"Madame! Rubbish!" And he walked out!

Young enjoyed one of his finest roles (a starring one) in England, playing George McWhirter Fotheringay, the timid clerk who suddenly has the power to do anything he wishes in H.G. Wells' fantasy *The Man Who Could Work Miracles* (1936). Young himself was a talented caricaturist and a writer of verse — mainly "naughty" verse. During one of his plays, Young was supposed to scribble royal edicts. He in fact was writing racy poetry. His friends later persuaded him to publish the poems. The title: *Not for Children*.

I think I'm lucky. I was born with very little talent but great drive.
—Anthony Quinn

He was the youngest of the Bundy Drive Boys, and in a way, the most successful.

He wasn't nearly the actor John Barrymore was, but he won two Academy Awards, including 1964's *Zorba the Greek*. He wasn't an artist on the level of John Decker, but his paintings and sculpture won international exhibitions, commanded high prices and added to a personal fortune Decker never remotely approached. He wasn't the writer Gene Fowler was, yet he wrote his memoirs, twice. He was the last of them to die, tallying the most years of any of them, becoming the father of the last of his 13 children when he was 81 years old.

Anthony Quinn had more talent than he was comfortable admitting and a seething anger and ambition that perhaps was the major reason he became a notable man.

Born Anthony Rudolph Oaxaca Quinn on April 21, 1915, in Chihuahua, Mexico, his Irish/Mexican father and Mexican mother were involved in Pancho Villa's revolution, and when it failed the family crossed the border into El Paso, where Quinn's sister Stella was born. The Quinn family moved to Los Angeles, where Quinn's father found work taking care of the animals in the Selig studio zoo, eventually becoming an assistant prop man. It was the work of his zookeeper father for Hollywood that launched Anthony Quinn's dream of becoming an actor.

His father died when Anthony was nine. He grew up in a ghetto and worked jobs ranging from fruit and vegetable picker to saxophone player at the revival meetings of Aimee

Semple McPherson. He worked as a janitor at an acting school, where a sympathetic teacher gave him speech lessons, and in 1936 won his big break — lampooning John Barrymore.

The play was *Clean Beds*, produced by Mae West at the Hollytown Theatre in Hollywood. The role of an aging alcoholic actor, clearly based on Barrymore, was a plum and many actors auditioned for it —allegedly including John Decker, so tickled by the prospect of imitating his idol that he seriously considered resuming his acting career that so disastrously ended in New York in 1922. Quinn later wrote that Mae West tried to seduce him in her hotel suite, but "the paint on her face and the thick perfume" turned him off; nevertheless, she awarded him the role. With age makeup by actor Akim Tamiroff and a salary of $10 a week, Quinn scored a triumph, and as he was removing his makeup, there was a caller at his dressing room. As Quinn wrote in *One Man Tango*, there, "absolutely larger than life, was John Barrymore himself." The star seeing how young Quinn actually was, asked to see his father, whom he presumed had played him that night. "My father's dead, sir," said Quinn. Barrymore was puzzled:

"And who played me out there tonight?"

> "I did, sir." I could not tell if he wanted to rip into me or collect me in his arms. His glower could have meant anything.
>
> He looked me over carefully. "Christ, you're just a kid," he said softly. There was a long pause. I was dying to learn what would happen next. Then a grin creased Barrymore's face, and his stare softened. "You cocksucker!" he bellowed in his grand blast of a voice. "You shit!"
>
> This, I was to learn, coming from John Barrymore, was high praise indeed.

Barrymore invited him to Bella Vista, where he encouraged Quinn to train in England, and taught him the secret of acting — "Caress the word."

"I loved him enormously, from the first," wrote Quinn of Barrymore. The star's "saber like wit" and "flair for storytelling" enchanted Quinn, and he soon met John Decker:

> John Decker was a talented painter, with a special gift as a knock-off artist. Decker could do Picasso better than Picasso. He turned everything he painted into a kind of joke, almost always at someone else's expense, and his talents were a particular delight to Barrymore's crowd. At one time, half of Hollywood was decorated with Decker's deft imitations, and most of the stuffed shirts who bought his paintings had no idea they were not the real thing.
>
> How Decker loved selling forgeries to these snobs! He would bring the stories of his duping to Barrymore's table and leave us howling…

And so the Bundy Drive Boys gained their youngest member. Meanwhile, Quinn made his film debut: a 45-second bit in a Universal potboiler called *Parole* (1936). It was, however, as a Cheyenne in Paramount's *The Plainsman* (1936), starring Gary Cooper and Jean Arthur and produced and directed by the illustrious Cecil B. DeMille, that Quinn made his mark. Chanting a Cheyenne song, Quinn was to come across a campfire built by Gary Cooper. Quinn ad-libbed a bit of business — bolting behind a tree. DeMille fired him on the spot.

Quinn recalled his confrontation with the almighty C.B.:

> One hundred sets of eyes were on me. "Look," I said, "you fired me and it's all right, but I'm not an idiot and I am not a stupid Indian. I'm an actor. I know what I'm doing. I don't care about your fucking 75 dollars. You can shove the money up your ass. But I can't walk out of here without telling you that you've got the scene all wrong… You think an Indian doesn't know the difference between a white man's fire and an Indian's fire… What kind of an Indian would just stand there, waiting, without hiding to protect himself?"

The great man stared at the young actor, holding his breath, expecting the tirade of tirades. "The boy's right," said DeMille finally. "We'll change the setup."

Quinn left Paramount that day with DeMille's begrudging respect and an offer of a $250 per week contract. He admitted that emboldening him in his confrontation was the presence on the set of a beautiful young actress with "the most piercing eyes I have ever seen." She was Katherine DeMille, one of C.B.'s adopted children. With no aid or encouragement from her father, Katherine had begun as an extra, eventually playing the featured role of Princess Alice of France in her father's 1935 epic *The Crusades*. She was visiting the set of *The Plainsman* that day, and Quinn claimed he virtually fell in love with Katherine at first sight.

She was, as Quinn remembered late in his life and hers, "rarely as she appeared. There was a hidden girl: frightened, insecure, timorous." Yet he pursued her, and many claimed the Mexican-born aspiring actor was opportunistic as he romanced the daughter of one of Hollywood's most powerful men. On the night of October 2, 1937, 22-year-old Quinn wed 26-year-old Katherine at All Saints Episcopal Church in Hollywood. DeMille gave his daughter away—against rampant speculation that he would not—and Quinn admitted that no wedding invitations went to his own mother, sister or friends.

Yet it was the honeymoon, as Quinn wrote, that was truly "a nightmare." Quinn discovered his bride was not a virgin. He slapped her and ordered her to take a train to Reno. Then, haunted by "her sad, beautiful eyes," he got in his car, raced the train, caught up with it 50 miles from Reno, and found Katherine sobbing in a compartment. They reconciled.

Katherine DeMille limited her acting career, per her husband's request, and in 1939

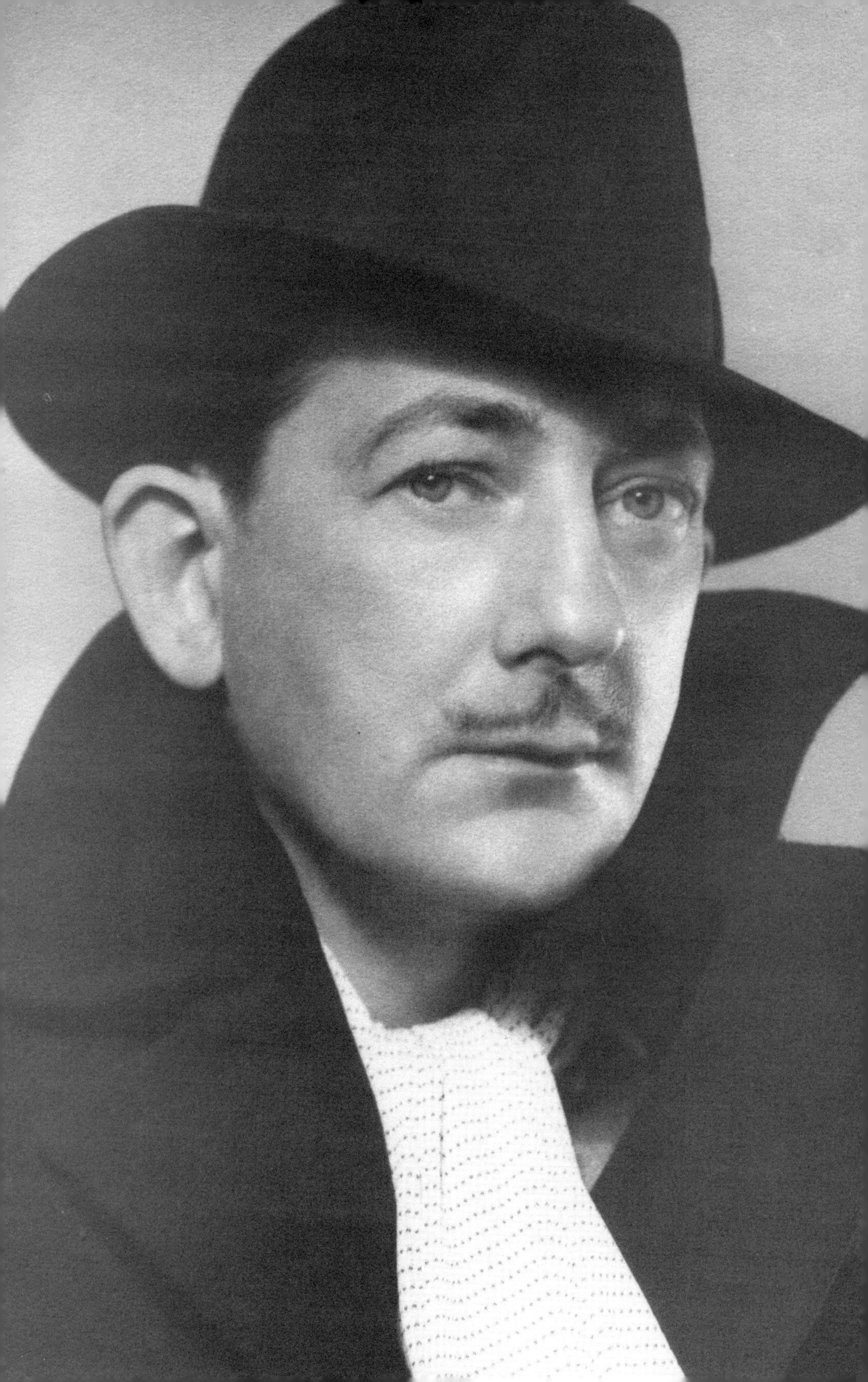

gave birth to their son Christopher, the first of their five children. But Quinn learned of her pre-marriage lovers (including Clark Gable and director Victor Fleming) and, late at night, his jealousy masochistically demanded she tell him details. Almost 60 years after his marriage and 35 years after Gable's death, Quinn, in his memoir *One Man Tango*, was still revisiting this torment. He claimed he had lived recently in Gable's old house, and would converse with his ghost:

> Gable... He haunted me throughout his life, and now he haunts me in death. His spirit permeates the house. He comes to me late at night, an apparition, when he cannot find peace. He is a drunken old fool. He knows what he has put me through. "Look at me," he says. "What is there to hate?"
>
> "I hate you for what you were," I answer. "Not for what you are."
>
> "And what was I? I was a pathetic actor, a burlesque. I had false teeth and big ears."
>
> "You were the king of Hollywood. You were a giant. You had it all."
>
> "Ah, that was just the columnists. I never thought of myself as the king of everything."
>
> "You were a king to Katherine. You were first with Katherine."
>
> He weeps, and I feel sorry for him....

Barrymore coached Quinn as an actor, reciting Walt Whitman's poem, "Two Strangers from Alabama," about two birds that, after their eggs hatch, are separated and never find each other again. By the time Barrymore masterfully finished reciting the poem, both he and Quinn were weeping. As Quinn wrote in his 1972 book *The Original Sin*:

> When he saw that, he laughed sardonically and said, "Well, kid, if you can read that poem in front of a mirror and while you're sitting on the toilet, you'll be an actor. Seated on your throne, naked, performing your maleficent duties, recite that poem. If you can forget that you're defecating and get lost in the beauty of the words, then you're an actor."

Barrymore also provided Quinn his opinion of women — "They're all twittering vaginas."

John Decker

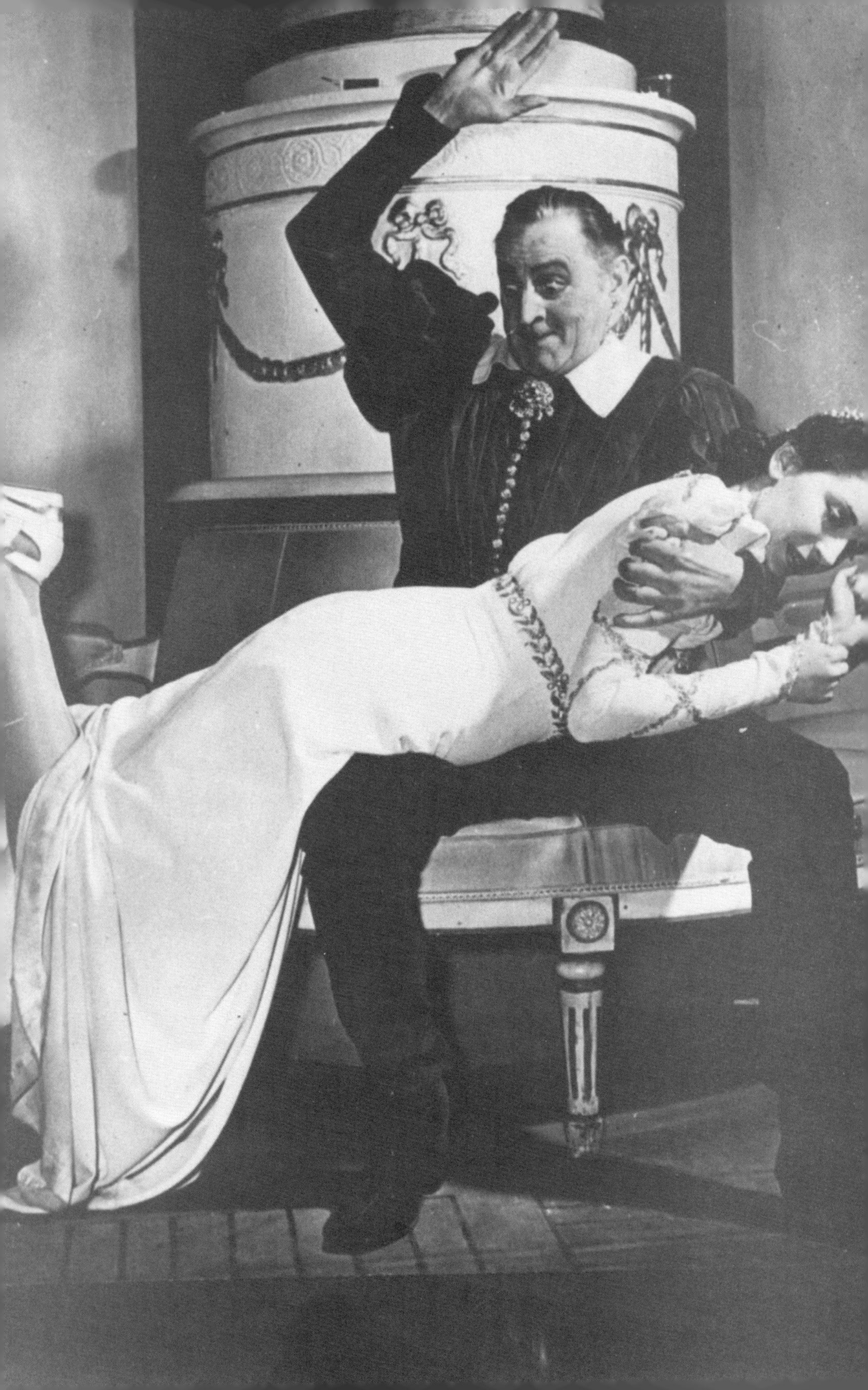

Chapter Eleven
The Last of the Twittering Vaginas

> She was the first of John's four wives to use the Barrymore name professionally, and the first Barrymore to undress onstage.
> —*The New York Times* obituary for Elaine Barrie Barrymore, March 4, 2003

For the Bundy Drive Boys, she was the vilest villainess of them all.

In Elaine Barrie Barrymore's own words. Gene Fowler would describe her in *Good Night, Sweet Prince* as "a combination of Lilith and the inventor of diphtheria." Lilith, so the legend goes, was the paramour of Satan, the mother of all incubi and succubi, and was painted by 19th-century artist John Collier as enjoying a giant snake entwining itself around her naked body.

Frankly, she looked the part. Sly, heavily made-up sloe eyes, tinted red hair, a voracious, heavily scarlet-lipsticked mouth, the toothy smile of a hungry shark — Elaine Barrie Barrymore evoked a 1930s vampire, part bloodsucker, part cocksucker. Her so-so figure received a coming-out party via her slinky star turn in *How to Undress in Front of Your Husband*, an infamous 1937 short subject she defiantly filmed during her stormy marriage to John, and much to the horror of the Barrymore family. Fiercely ambitious, assuredly seductive, she was one of John Barrymore's most spectacular torments, and certainly at times one of his great passions.

The "Ariel and Caliban" nicknames that Elaine and John Barrymore won from the press might have come from Shakespeare's *The Tempest* — Ariel the sprite, Caliban the

Elaine Barrie Barrymore gets punished in *My Dear Children*

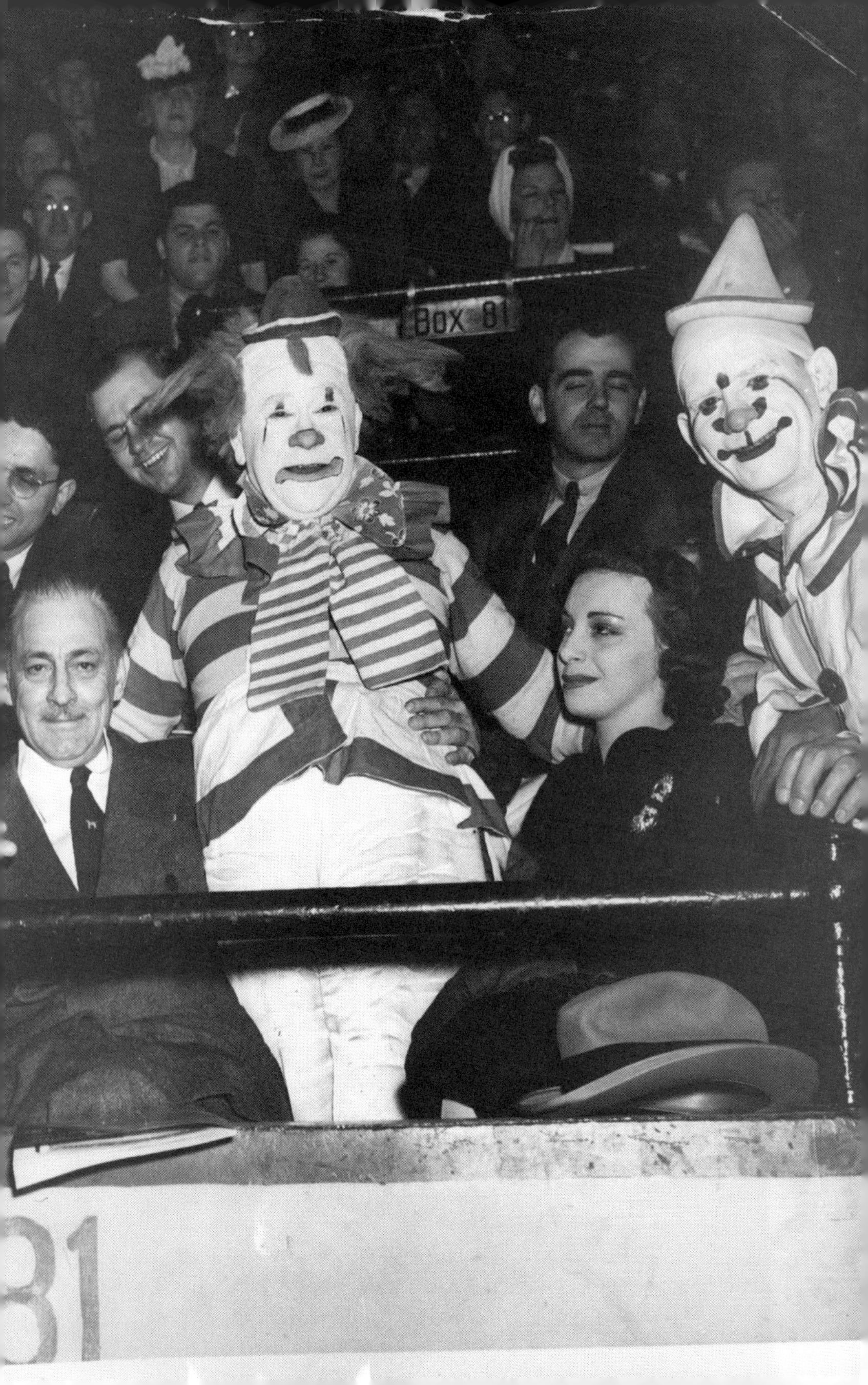
BOX 81
81

monster — but the act they tortuously played before the public was cheap burlesque, and the Bundy Drive Boys reviled her.

She hated them at least as viciously. In her 1964 memoir *All My Sins Remembered*, Elaine let fly at the Bundy gang. They were "senile delinquents," "parasites," "erudite morons." She was eloquent in her condemnation:

> Perpetuating the image of a sinking giant seemed to please the fancy of his friends who wept copiously and pushed him down a little further, like the mourners at a funeral who contort their faces in a grief meant to mask their elation at outliving the beloved. There was even a kind of revelry in John's fall from grace. When during our separation, he fell in with [the Bundy Drive Boys], he drank himself into a caricature, dancing to their tune, and laughing more cruelly than they at himself…

She did have "oomph," as the word went in the 1940s, and a flash of talent, and was at least partially on Barrymore's level. The first time he showed her Bella Vista, Elaine delighted in climbing up into the tower with him — Dolores was never interested and daughter Diana later thought the tower silly. Elaine also recognized the house (and loathed it) for what John, in his darker moods, had surely designed it to be: "the setting for Torquemada's grimmer pursuits."

Her legend is familiar to most Barrymore fans. She was Elaine Jacobs, a New York Jewish girl (whose race might have been another reason for her unpopularity in a nation which still had large pockets of anti-Semitism). She had seen Barrymore as *Svengali* at age 15 and fallen madly in love with him. When, as a student at Hunter College, she learned that Barrymore's marriage to Dolores had fallen apart, she confessed "turning faint with exultation."

In 1935, Barrymore, back from India, was in New York Hospital. Elaine paid a call on her idol. He shortly thereafter moved into the Jacobs family apartment. They cruised on *The Infanta* to Cuba, where John bought her a diamond ring so beautiful that Elaine, truly dramatic, felt the stone had "a soul." John's failure to claim it as they returned to the U.S. eventually cost him $8,000. The Hotcheners, Barrymore's advisors, tried to free him from Elaine and put him on a train for Hollywood. Elaine followed, Mrs. Jacobs in tow.

The Ariel and Caliban sideshow began.

For a time, Elaine had been with John during the calamitous shoot of MGM's *Romeo and Juliet* (1936). One night at dinner with Norma Shearer and Thalberg, Bar-

Jack and Elaine bring on the clowns

rymore called Elaine a whore. She and mother went back to New York; Barrymore, now addicted to the sado-maso relationship, fell apart without her — it possibly contributed to his first visit to Kelly's Asylum. Thalberg called Elaine in New York and enticed her back to Hollywood with an MGM contract — he needed her so John could play the villainous Baron de Varville in *Camille*, with Greta Garbo in the title role, Robert Taylor as Armand and Lionel Barrymore as Armand's judgmental old father. Elaine came back and found Barrymore, per MGM's orders, drying out again in Kelly's Rest Home in Culver City.

Elaine wrote of Mr. Kelly taking her to see her demon lover:

> We then walked into the corridor and into a Hogarth print. To me this simply wasn't a hospital, it was a madhouse and its inmates were wild animals. Now I knew what alcohol could do to people. Delirium tremens en masse was bedlam... Ogling, unkempt, pitiable creatures who were once men and women... The noises grew as we walked — simperings, groans and screams. As a door quickly opened and closed, I caught sight of an elderly woman, her hair in disarray, her cat's eyes staring in dumb reverie as she sat embracing herself. She was a grisly portrait of self-love and then our eyes met for a terrifying instant as she tried to shake loose of her straitjacket.

"The nightmare had no end," said Elaine, and she found John's small room with an iron-barred window. He had no tie — there was fear he'd hang himself with it. "Don't be revolted, Elaine, my Binky, my baby," she quoted John as saying, falling at her feet, claiming he'd die if she didn't want him, smothering her hand with kisses — at which time they heard "a shrill, cackling laugh," and realized some lunatic was playing Peeping Tom. Elaine ran outside to the car.

"Don't ever leave me!" she claimed John was screaming as she ran — "don't ever leave me!"

John Barrymore didn't get the role of the Baron de Varville in *Camille* — Henry Daniell played it, superbly — but he did get Elaine. They eloped by plane to Yuma in November of 1936, Elaine's parents in tow. Come New Year's Eve, and a violent battle at the Trocadero, they split. Elaine took a role in the play *The Return of Hannibal*, complete with a dance. It died in San Francisco, lasting one week. *Variety's* famous pan of Elaine: "She looks like Salome, acts like Salami."

Elaine's revenge: she starred in the short subject *How to Undress in Front of Your Husband*, parading about in her lingerie and high heels. New York State banned it and John,

Ethel and Lionel all sued to have the Barrymore name removed — unsuccessfully.

Reconciliations, fights, separations, more reconciliations. One of the separations occurred during John's 55th birthday (February 14, 1937) and the Bundy Drive gang sent a gift up to Bella Vista — a naked young lady wrapped in cellophane with a festive silver bow.

Not only did the Bundy Drive gang hate Elaine, so did the public, who for all their disgust at Barrymore's wasted genius, saw his new on-again-off-again Mrs. as a predator who sunk her blood-red fingernails into the ruins of a once-great man. She wasn't a gold-digger — the debt-strapped Barrymore had no more gold to dig; she was a ball-buster, who publicly boasted that she had to buy the marriage license when she eloped with her celebrated, flat-broke spouse. She quickly became a dirty national joke, with only sporadic defense from her husband, who cursed her in public, mocked her on the radio and, as David Niven remembered, was outspokenly vulgar in his reasons for marrying her:

> "You want to know what I see in my wife?" he roared. "Well, I'll tell you! You put it in, and it goes right through the main saloon and into the galley; then the cabin boy comes down a ladder and rings a bell... In other words, you stupid bastard, IT FITS."

Elaine had her own last laughs. "I know him better than any Barrymore," Elaine once crowed to John's daughter Diana, and in many ways she did. Their wedding night had been blissful, or so she wrote: "He made me unashamed of the natural. He made me glory in my sensuality." But she also had been with him at Kelly's. She had control, and indeed, come a 1937 reconciliation, Elaine demanded he not only allow her to pursue her career, but that he dress nicely, dye his hair (allowing a gray steak in the front), wear suits and ties, shave and all in all look his best — which now included the still-vain actor wearing a girdle.

He fought back wildly and viciously at times, yet Elaine usually succeeded in retrospectively twisting his rages to suit herself. She told Sandford Dody (who ghostwrote her memoir) of "that terrible night" in New York, presumably during their 1940 run together in Broadway's lamentable *My Dear Children*, when John tried to throw her from the terrace of their 20th-floor 79th Street apartment. Madly jealous, the actor had emerged from a 48-hour coma, believed his doctor was a pimp who ran a male brothel, and found a male nurse in the process of... well, as Elaine told it (and Dody recorded it in his own 1980 book, *Giving up the Ghost*):

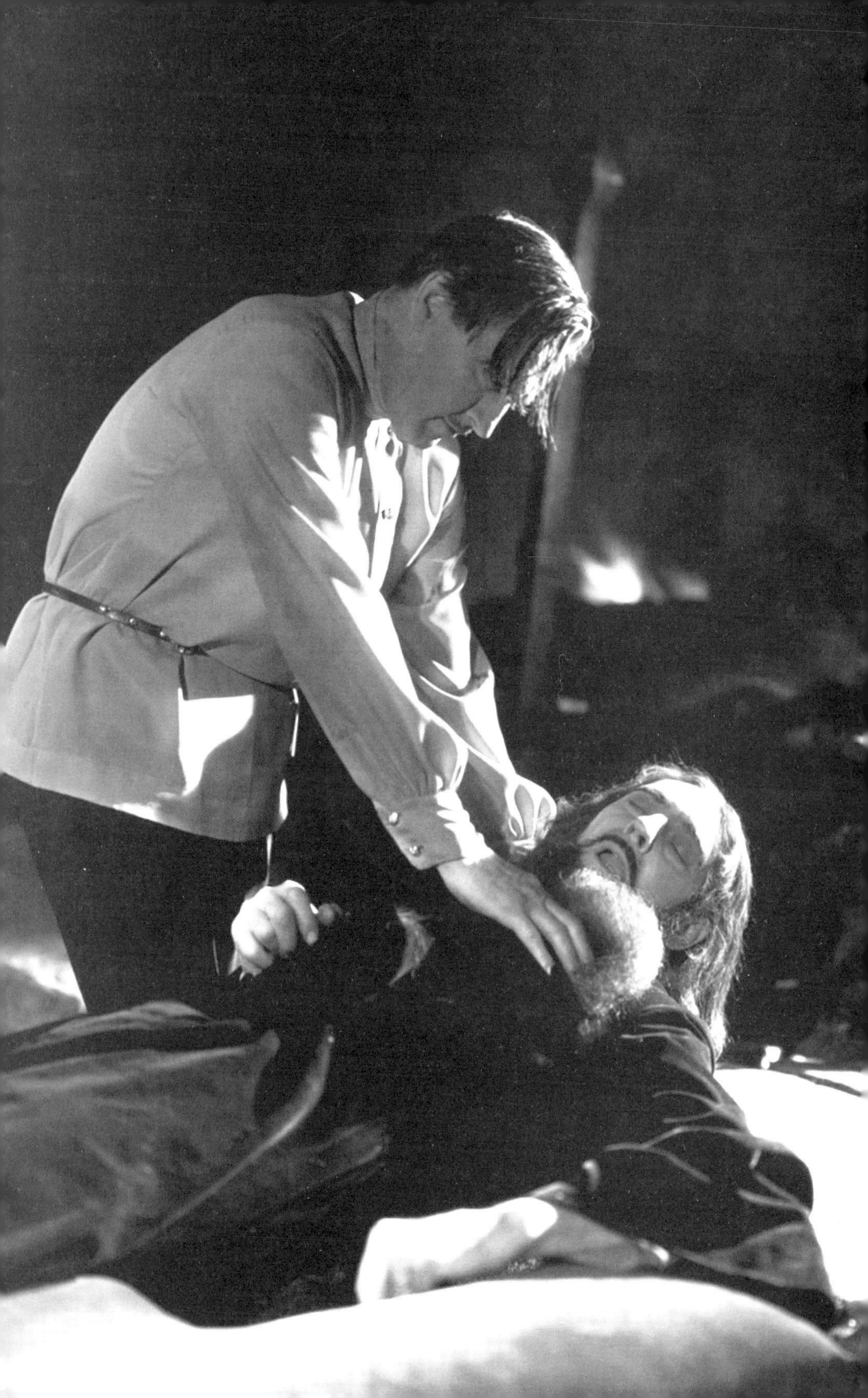

Now it is true that when John woke up, came out of his coma, the nurse was giving him a colonic — an olive-oil colonic — you may well raise your eyebrows, dear, but it does the trick. It brought him back. I'm quite an expert in these matters. It brought him back, all right, but John was outraged. The posture didn't suit him. And with rage he always had the strength of ten. That "big, blond stud," which John kept calling him, flew like a timid girl the moment his patient got violent. Flew — this dedicated man in white — leaving me with a homicidal maniac…

John kept circling me on tippy-toe. It was the most terrible sight, and he was smirking like a gargoyle and hissing invective. I remember thinking he looked like Ethel and Lionel and Satan as well. Even his eyes had turned color. Then he stopped circling and closed in. Twisting my arm, he dragged me out to the terrace through the French doors. The hedges, the privet hedges we had planted together, tore at me as I found myself half through them. He was now screaming about the parade of boys he saw me with after his death….

He was holding me over the edge and the street below rushed toward me and I felt sick.

"I will not allow you to make my grave a mattress!" he said. "Only if you die first can I have peace, slut. You've come as high as you could…Well, child of the asphalt," he now intoned, "You're going home at last. Back to the gutter!"

Elaine claimed she begged him to kill her, to give her peace. They ended up crying. "It usually ended that way," she said. Yet note the dramatic qualities of the story: John, humiliated from a symbolic anal rape, insanely jealous over her affections, and she the winsome heroine in the clutches of the mad actor — even *willing* to die, offering self-sacrifice.

She lorded over the man, enjoying her power as keeper of the ruins and even joining him on the radio series called *Streamline Shakespeare*. And yes, on July 11, 1937, they performed *The Tempest* — John Barrymore as Caliban, and Elaine Barrie Barrymore as Ariel.

Why did John Barrymore indulge her? One suspects that, in her vampy stylistics, capricious selfishness and self-serving seduction of a lonely and frightened lost soul, Elaine possibly reminded Barrymore of Mamie Floyd, his stepmother. Mamie sexually abused John in his childhood when he was 13, and Elaine was nailing him in his virtual second childhood when he was 53.

In his own earthy, masochistic, spectacularly self-destructive way, John Barrymore was fucking — and fucked by — one of his most merciless nightmares.

John throttles Lionel in *Rasputin and the Empress*

W.C. Fields was ill in these years, and made few screen appearances. However, his popularity stayed secure via his famous feuds with ventriloquist Edgar Bergen's top-hat-and-monocle-sporting dummy Charlie McCarthy on radio's *The Chase and Sanborn Hour*. The show also featured Dorothy Lamour and emcee Don Ameche, who sometimes refereed the insult battles, as on this May 30, 1937 broadcast:

> Ameche: Now Bill, don't be too angry with Charlie. He isn't feeling well today — he needs a doctor.
> W.C.: He needs a tree surgeon!

John Decker later claimed "the greatest unpublished W.C. Fields story" concerned "that hysteric occasion when his famous red nose exploded!"

> One weekend, Fields was down in the ocean, off Lower California, deep sea fishing. Since he was angling for big fish, and since he was drinking a bottle of Scotch, his helpers strapped him to a chair and then nailed the chair to the deck — so that if he fell asleep, a big bite wouldn't yank him overboard. It was a cool day, cloudy day, and after no nibbles and sufficient firewater, the comedian fell asleep per schedule. Ten minutes after he dozed off, the sun broke out hot and bright and searing. It roasted the boat, and there was Fields asleep on the deck. His helpers were afraid to wake him, afraid of his anger and wrath at being disturbed. So they allowed him to bake under the sizzling sun. In two hours, water blisters began to form on W.C. Fields' big beak, and then more blisters — and suddenly after four hours — they exploded on his nose! Some explosion! It knocked him out of his straps and flat on his back!
>
> "I was rushed to the hospital," Fields told me, "and they put my nose in splinters and tied it with bandages. I look back on that day with great embarrassment. You see, Decker, it was the only time in my life I blew up in public!"

As for Fields' nemesis Charlie McCarthy ("The woodpecker's pin-up boy," as W.C. called him), the impudent dummy arrived when Edgar Bergen commissioned Decker to paint Charlie's portrait in Old Masters style. Decker selected Franz Hals' *The Laughing Cavalier* as the showcase for Charlie, and told Irving Wallace:

> I shall never forget what occurred after I finished that portrait of Charlie McCarthy as The Laughing Cavalier. I took it up to Edgar Bergen's place to show it to him. I was halted at the entrance by Bergen's secretary. She asked what

I wanted. I held up the painting for her. She stared at it a moment, then said, "But it's ridiculous! You know Charlie doesn't wear that kind of costume!"

So that's why Bergen doesn't own the painting and why it's hanging in Billy Rose's Diamond Horseshoe in New York today!

Billy Rose, by the way, was a popular target for Decker's chicanery. The artist reveled in the story of how he once promised to get Rose a genuine Renoir, and naturally painted a forgery:

> Then, in a good mood, I had the copy slightly aged, wrapped it in old butcher paper, and wrote a semi-illiterate note with it which read, "Dear Mr. Rose, I understand you want a Renoir. I am a refugee from Europe. It is terrible in Europe. My uncle he gave me this original. You can have it for $524.49, which I need badly. My phone number is SR-90090. Signed Mrs. Schineskyvich."
>
> I sent this by special messenger over to Billy Rose's apartment. I got there before his messenger. I wanted to be in on the kill. Billy Rose was shaving when the doorbell rang. I brought in the package. He jumped over it. He jumps and hops after everything. He ripped it open, studied the painting, read the note and in a glow made one statement:
>
> "God, John, the price is right! And this is a Renoir!"
>
> Immediately he called the telephone number in the note.
>
> "Is Mrs. Schineskyvich in?" inquired Billy.
>
> "Who?"
>
> "Mrs. Schineskyvich. Is she in?" asked Billy impatiently.
>
> "This is Norma Shearer," came the answer.
>
> "If you're Norma Shearer, then I'm Billy Rose! Now will you put Mrs. —"
>
> The phone banged in Billy Rose's ear. He was in a lather, and not from shaving. And I was sprawled on the floor, convulsed. It was once I'd proved to Billy he didn't know a damn thing about art.
>
> But the anticlimax was even better. Billy Rose finally did get his hands on a genuine Renoir. He paid $25,000 for it and gave it to his handsome wife, Eleanor Holm, as a gift. He brought the Renoir into her room. Wanted to hang it on the wall. "You get that thing out of here!" ranted Eleanor. "You're not going to knock holes in my wall!"

John Barrymore had to work. MGM gave him a featured role in the Jeanette MacDonald and Nelson Eddy operetta *Maytime* (1937). As a Svengali-like impresario madly in love with MacDonald (he jealously shoots and kills Eddy come the climax), he actually had very little rapport with Metro's "Iron Butterfly" diva. Her futile attempt to upstage him met with a perfectly serious ultimatum.

"If you wave that loathsome chiffon rag you call a kerchief once more while I'm speaking," warned Jack, "I shall ram it down your gurgling throat!"

A happier time was had with Carole Lombard on *True Confession*, with Barrymore as a master of disguises, even performing a Chaplin impersonation. He was still a sight to see in his films, but the shadows were approaching, and he relied on blackboards from which he read his lines. Decker and friends fully believed Barrymore could remember if he wanted to — he no longer wanted to.

John Decker, meanwhile, continued to cherish his time with Barrymore:

> Barrymore's ability to turn a classical phrase was best illustrated on that afternoon when I went with him over to Gene Fowler's house. Fowler wanted to introduce Barrymore to his daughter Jane.
>
> Jane Fowler was thrilled. She said pertly, "Mr. Barrymore, to celebrate your meeting, let me mix you a drink."
>
> Barrymore beamed. "Fine, fine, fine."
>
> Alas, though, little Jane did not know the actor's taste. Naively, she mixed him a chocolate soda. She handed it to him. And without bothering to study its contents, Barrymore held the glass high, recited a toast and took a deep swallow. Just one swallow. Suddenly his eyes popped. He choked, shivered, sputtered and spat out the drink. He rose to his feet with a wild shriek.
>
> "Curses!" yelled Barrymore. "I have come to the house of Borgia!"

As for Gene Fowler, Decker had another favorite story:

> A spot of liquor does peculiar things to people. But to Gene Fowler it does the most peculiar thing of all — it makes him visit funeral parlors. Whenever Gene gets tight, he goes to the nearest funeral parlor and bargains for a plot of land in the parlor's cemetery. He argues with great passion. He wants to know details. How much land? What kind of grass? And so forth. In fact, I believe he owns a cemetery plot in every large city in these United Sates. Once, in San Francisco, a trifle plastered, Gene Fowler attempted to purchase a plot of land for four dead relatives to be buried standing up and facing the Pacific. "They're all sailors who died with their boots on," Fowler explained.
>
> There is one funeral parlor, in Los Angeles, which Fowler visited many

times. The director of it was his favorite character, a dour, sour little man who looked like Death itself. Gene Fowler had known this funeral director for five and twenty years and never once, not once, seen him smile. One afternoon, feeling gay, Fowler went into the parlor to visit with his gloomy friend.

The funeral director entered. And the left corner of his mouth was curled upward ever so slightly.

"My God!" exploded Fowler. "I bet you're smiling! Why are you smiling? What's happened?"

"Because this is a joyous moment in my life, Mr. Fowler," explained the funeral director. "There are five old maids living up the block. They are all Christian Scientists — and Diphtheria has finally broken out!"

Many believed John Barrymore was the inspiration for Norman Maine, the alcoholic, has-been suicide star, played by Fredric March in *A Star is Born* (1937). However, when Hecht and Gene Fowler did a rewrite on the original script by William Wellman (who directed the film) and Robert Carson, other influences were at play.

Wellman and Carson had tapped the sad fate of actor John Bowers, who on November 17, 1936, rented a sailboat, told a friend he was about to "sail into the sunset," and drowned. Hecht and Fowler, however, thought of MGM's catastrophic sound casualty John Gilbert. William MacAdams writes in his Ben Hecht biography:

> One evening in the fall of 1935 when Hecht and MacArthur were socializing with Gilbert and a few friends at his Malibu beach house, Gilbert had jumped up and announced he was going to kill himself by swimming out to sea. He rushed out of the house before anyone could stop him but was back an hour later, drenched. Opening his mouth to talk, he vomited instead, then collapsed on the floor. "Always the silent star," MacArthur quipped.

Gilbert had become lovers with Marlene Dietrich, and one night in early 1936 allowed the notoriously bisexual star to take him to a gay party in Hollywood. As he danced with Dietrich, his toupee either fell off or was yanked off — accounts vary — and as he tried to retrieve it from under La Dietrich's spiked heels, the lavender crowd shrieked and howled with laughter. It was the final humiliation — John Gilbert was found dead in his bed at his mansion on Tower Road (near Barrymore's Bella Vista) the next day, January 9, 1936, the victim of a heart attack. He was 38 years old.

Rather than tap this grotesque story, Hecht and Fowler respectfully gave the Norman Maine character a powerful, almost mystical suicide — simply walking into the Pacific at night. It was just what producer David Selznick wanted, and Dorothy Parker and Alan Campbell let it be as they performed a final rewrite. *A Star Is Born* won the 1937 Academy Award for Best Original Story, but the prize went to its original writers, William Wellman and Robert Carson.

Ben Hecht also scripted 1937's *Nothing Sacred*, a Selznick-produced Technicolor screwball comedy starring Carole Lombard and Fredric March, and opening with this Hechtian foreword:

> THIS IS NEW YORK
> Skyscraper Champion of
> The World...
> Where the Slickers and
> Know-It-Alls peddle gold bricks
> To each other...
> and where Truth, crushed
> to earth, rises again more
> phony than a glass eye...

The comedy, directed by William A. Wellman, concerns a Ben Hecht-like reporter (March) passing off one Hazel Flagg (Lombard), from Warsaw, Vermont, as dying from radiation poisoning. A send-up of the public's morbid fascination with Death, *Nothing Sacred* lives up to its title, a blazingly non-politically-correct movie that includes a black shoeshine man posing as a Pooh-Bah, a hilarious campy nightclub show (complete with a blonde-wigged Lady Godiva on a horse) and the marvelous moment when a little boy runs out of a Vermont yard and — for no reason at all — bites March on the back of his thigh.

In the fall of 1937, Warners began shooting *The Adventures of Robin Hood* on location — Chico, California standing in for Sherwood Forest. It remains one of Hollywood's few timeless, near-perfect films. Errol Flynn was captivating as Robin — swinging on a Sherwood vine, eluding a castle of villains, winning an archery tournament by splitting the arrow in a perfect bull's-eye (champion archer Howard Hill was on hand for that spectacle) and wooing Olivia de Havilland's lovely Maid Marian. Basil Rathbone was a wicked Sir Guy of Gisbourne, Claude Rains a splendid King John, and the lush Technicolor and Erich Wolfgang Korngold musical score all make *The Adventures of Robin Hood* a beautiful storybook of a movie.

The shoot, of course, was not so enchanting.

In Chico, Patric Knowles, who played Will Scarlet, taught Flynn (who had recently published his first book, *Beam Ends*, based on his early exploits) to pilot a plane, entirely against studio safety and insurance precautions. As Knowles recalled, "We had drunk a great deal," and as they flew back in the night, they remembered the little airstrip in Chico had no landing lights. The plane was running out of fuel and the two actors feared they were doomed. They battled over who would have the last cigarette and who'd try to land the plane, and Knowles finally saw the two water tanks he knew as landmarks, and the runway. As Knowles related in Charles Higham's *Errol Flynn: The Untold Story*:

> My heart turned over when I noticed a long line of automobile headlights. The people looking for us had placed their cars the whole length of the runway so we could see our way in. I handed Flynn the cigarette and said, "Now, Flynn you let me take this in because I've piloted this thing and I know what I'm doing." He said, "To hell with you. I'm going to hang on to the controls, too." He threw away the cigarette. We used the dual controls. We bumped our way up and down. It was a very bad landing…

Back in Hollywood, Knowles would face disciplinary action by the Screen Actors Guild for his joy flights. So would Flynn — for allegedly telling makeup man Ward Hamilton that he planned to complain about his wig, makeup and beard to delay shooting and wrangle another salary boost.

Also, after the company came back to Hollywood, Warners replaced director William Keighley (who was behind schedule, and whom Flynn greatly liked) with the hated, jodhpurs-wearing, whip-brandishing Mike Curtiz. Flynn was incensed. The first shooting day with Curtiz, on the castle banquet set, Flynn uproariously sabotaged a scene as he drank from a goblet and spat out the soda pop (that stood in for wine).

"You know what this is?" shouted Flynn. "It's panther piss!"

Curtiz screamed. Flynn threw the "panther piss" in Curtiz's face.

The Adventures of Robin Hood, all $2,033,000 of it (Warner Bros.' most expensive production to that time), premiered in April of 1938. It was one of the year's Best Picture Academy contenders, losing to Columbia's *You Can't Take It With You*. The swashbuckling classic survives as a testimony to the magic that Golden Age Hollywood could create with its full-blown resources — and Errol Flynn's Robin Hood is the cinema's greatest all-time costume hero.

The tribute, unfortunately, would have only found derision in the actor himself.

As David Niven remembered, Flynn and Lili had a separation about this time, and the two actors set up temporary bachelor quarters at 601 N. Linden Drive. The men nicknamed the house "Cirrhosis by the Sea," although the house (rented from Rosalind Russell) was in Beverly Hills. There Flynn and Niven experimentally chewed "kif," later more popularly known as marijuana. Flynn's early dope experiments eventually became far more serious.

Of course, David Niven enjoyed sailing with his screen-hero crony on weekend trips to Catalina, aboard Flynn's 65' *Sirocco*. There was always a squad of female "crew members" along, as Niven wrote in *The Moon's a Balloon*:

> Normally, the arrangement was that we provided the booze, and the girls, whoever they were, brought the food. There was one lady who had made a habit of showing up only with a loaf of bread and a douche bag.

In *Bring on the Empty Horses*, Niven wrote that "Flynn was never happier than when witnessing the discomfiture of his friends." He remembered mixing drinks below deck of the *Sirocco*, chopping up a large block of ice with an ice pick:

> *Sirocco* gave a violent lurch, and I found that I was unable to remove my left hand from the ice. Looking down, I noticed with a sort of semidetached interest that I had plunged the ice pick right through my middle finger.
>
> I yelled to Errol to come and to get ready with the first-aid kit. He was delighted at what he saw.
>
> "Hey, that's great, sport," he said. "Don't pull it out yet, we must show this to the girls!"
>
> Impaled on the ice block, I waited below while Flynn rounded up the "crew." Much to his delight, one of them fainted when she saw what had happened.

So Errol Flynn didn't always have the off-screen charm of Robin Hood — but who did?

W.C. Fields was haplessly starring in Paramount's *The Big Broadcast of 1938*, best remembered for Bob Hope singing (with Shirley Ross) "Thanks for the Memory." As W.C. took on Paramount, he also battled with Carlotta Monti.

"CARLOTTA MONTI PLANS $200,000 DAMAGE SUIT AGAINST W.C. FIELDS," headlined the October 15, 1937 *Los Angeles Evening Herald Express*:

> Just what really took place during that mysterious midnight episode at the Bel Air mansion of W.C. Fields, film and radio comedian, three weeks ago, may be disclosed in the courts.
>
> So said attorneys today in revealing that Carlotta Monti, beautiful actress/secretary of Fields, intends to file a $200,000 damage suit against the comedian.
>
> Miss Monti, Fields and Harold, the butler, were the three principals in the episode on Sept. 23, an episode that baffled Los Angeles radio police who made two futile trips to the Fields mansion.
>
> According to her attorney, Clifford A. Rohe, Miss Monti will tell her version of what took place in a complaint to be filed in Superior Court late today or tomorrow. She will allege, he said, that Fields broke a walking stick over her head, belabored her with a rubber hammer and used abusive language.
>
> "If Miss Monti makes such charges they will be false," Fields said today, "for the only thing that happened was that Miss Monti and the butler quarreled and I tried to pacify them so I could get some sleep. Anyway, she can go ahead and sue — I've been sued by experts and I know my way around."

W.C. eventually paid over $6,000 to make Carlotta go away, but she'd be back. Meanwhile, the comedian hoped to co-star in a film with John Barrymore, *Things Began to Happen*, at Paramount. W.C. even promised Barrymore top billing, and the two posed for publicity stills, one of which has Mad Jack coaching W.C. on transforming from Dr. Jekyll to Mr. Hyde!

Alas, the film was never made. John Barrymore carried on at Paramount in the studio's *Bulldogg Drummond* series, but his big 1938 film was MGM's long-awaited *Marie Antoinette*. Always interested in the mystic and spiritual, he had an idea of making a film based on Buddha, and even had talked to the famed guru Krishnamurti about playing the title role.

He was back with Elaine, who was still leeching and whining for a film career, and finally Jack went to bat for her and landed her a featured role in his next cinema opus.

Unfortunately, the film was *Hold That Co-ed*, a 20th Century-Fox football satire, with John as a top-hat-sporting governor who builds a million-dollar stadium.

To add insult to injury — and to the euphoric delight of the Bundy Drive Boys — Fox cut Elaine out of the picture.

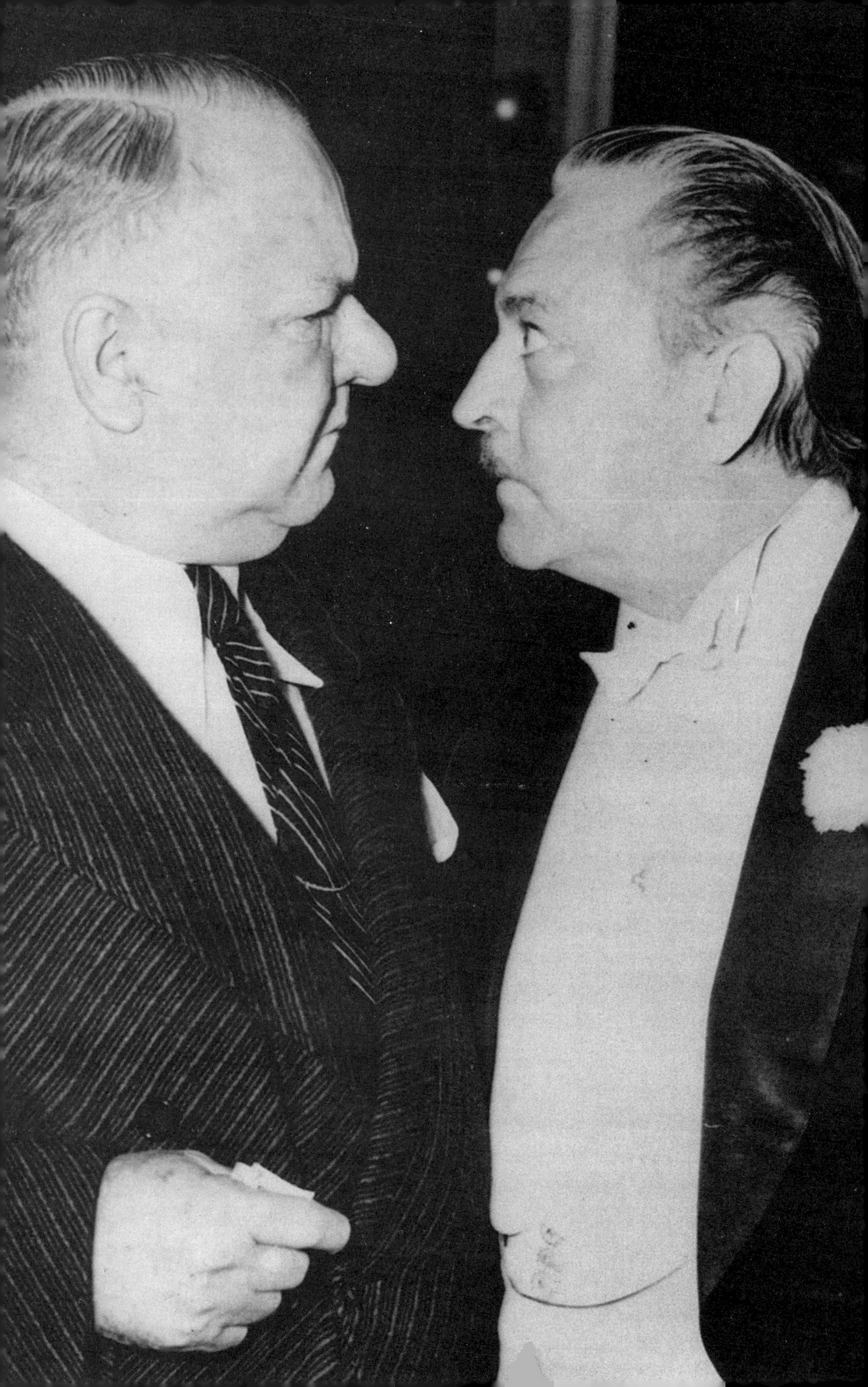

Chapter Twelve
The Greatest Year of the Movies, "The Spiritual Striptease of Gypsy Rose John," And John Decker's Biggest Caper

1939 was Hollywood's Greatest Year, distinguished by the release of a big parade of all-time classic films: *Gone With the Wind*, *The Wizard of Oz*, *Stagecoach*, *Mr. Smith Goes to Washington*, *Gunga Din*, *Wuthering Heights*, *Love Affair*, *Goodbye Mr. Chips*, *The Hunchback of Notre Dame*, *Of Mice and Men*, *Jesse James*, *Union Pacific*, *Dodge City*, *Son of Frankenstein*, *Dark Victory*, *The Roaring Twenties*, *Drums Along the Mohawk*, etc.

At the time, John Decker was living, as Gene Fowler remembered, "in a hillside studio that once had been a sanitarium for tuberculosis sufferers." He still survived primarily by painting Old Masters takeoffs and an occasional forgery.

John Barrymore would appear in two 1939 films. RKO's *The Great Man Votes* gave John a lead as Gregory Vance, a drunken schoolteacher with two children, and whose vote is crucial in an election. Director Garson Kanin recalled Barrymore's total reliance on blackboards, even to say the simple line, "Yes."

"I might say 'no'," Barrymore explained to Kanin, "and then where would you be?"

According to Kanin, Barrymore also violently erupted one day, cursing and hurling 12-year-old actress Virginia Weidler across the set because he thought she was scene-stealing from him. The other child actor, eight-year-old Peter Holden, spooked by Barrymore's rage, began laughing hysterically and had to be slapped by his mother.

Fields and Barrymore. Photo courtesy of Michael Morrison

Sadakichi Hartmann, Gene Fowler and John Decker visit Barrymore backstage at *My Dear Children*

Paramount's *Midnight* co-starred Jack with Claudette Colbert and Don Ameche, provided a nice featured role for Jack's old mistress Mary Astor, and is the one legitimate film in which Elaine appears (as "Simone"). The screenplay was by Billy Wilder and Charles Brackett, and in his 1977 book *Billy Wilder in Hollywood*, Maurice Zolotow records the popular saga of Jack wandering into the ladies' room on the *Midnight* set:

> He was pissing away when a lady opened the door. "This is for women!" she cried in outrage. "And so is this," Barrymore replied, shaking his tool at her.

Jack had debts, Elaine had dreams, and on March 24, 1939, *My Dear Children* opened at the McCarter Theatre, Princeton, New Jersey. The sorry excuse for a farce starred Jack as Allan Manville, gone-to-seed former Hamlet, complete with a painting of himself as the Melancholy Dane staring at the audience to remind them how the mighty had fallen. Holed up in a Swiss castle with his mistress (played by Tala

Birell), Manville receives a visit from his three daughters. The best of the daughter roles, Cordelia, was nabbed by Elaine Barrie Barrymore.

Come opening night in Princeton, Albert Einstein was in the audience. "Give those cues a little louder, sweetheart. We can't hear you," Barrymore ad-libbed to his offstage prompter. The audience roared, and as John Kobal writes in *Damned in Paradise*:

> Nobody laughed more heartily than Einstein. It was the first of innumerable ad libs which together with clowning, mugging, grunts, snorts, rumbles, yawns, bleats, belches, leers, sneers, smirks, ogles, roars, squeaks, eye-rolling, eyebrow twitching, strutting, mincing, pouncing, staggering, hop-skip-and-jumps, profanity, obscenity and general horseplay, would turn the vapid farce into a freakish smash hit unique in theatre annals.

There was a show-stopping scene in which Manville puts Cordelia over his knee and spanks her. But the Barrymores were battling for real. Elaine's latest dream of stardom went up in smoke as Barrymore vowed to kill her and demanded she be fired. As the company traveled to St. Louis via train, Otto Preminger, the hapless director, awoke in his train berth to find Elaine and mother Edna. Edna crowed that, if Elaine were fired, she'd tell the world that John Barrymore had raped her — several times.

"But who would believe you, Mrs. Jacobs?" sneered Preminger.

Elaine got canned. She stayed a while as a replacement learned her role. Come her last performance, Jack spanked Elaine so violently that her ass sprang welts. She retaliated by biting his wrist until it bled.

My Dear Children became a freak show sensation, running 33 weeks in Chicago as part of its pre-Broadway tour. It was Lloyd Lewis, Chicago historian, who so aptly described the debacle as John Barrymore's "spiritual striptease, with himself as a kind of Gypsy Rose John."

He was brilliant, even in his devastation. One night a siren of a passing fire engine wailed outside the theatre.

"My God, my wife!" ad-libbed Barrymore.

Immediately afterwards, a truck backfired.

"And she's got her mother with her!"

The star decayed during the long road trip. The management provided him three whores on call at all time; still he fondled his female co-stars. (Dorothy McGuire quit on the road.) As the play neared New York, Barrymore went on one night in Pittsburgh and vomited into the footlights.

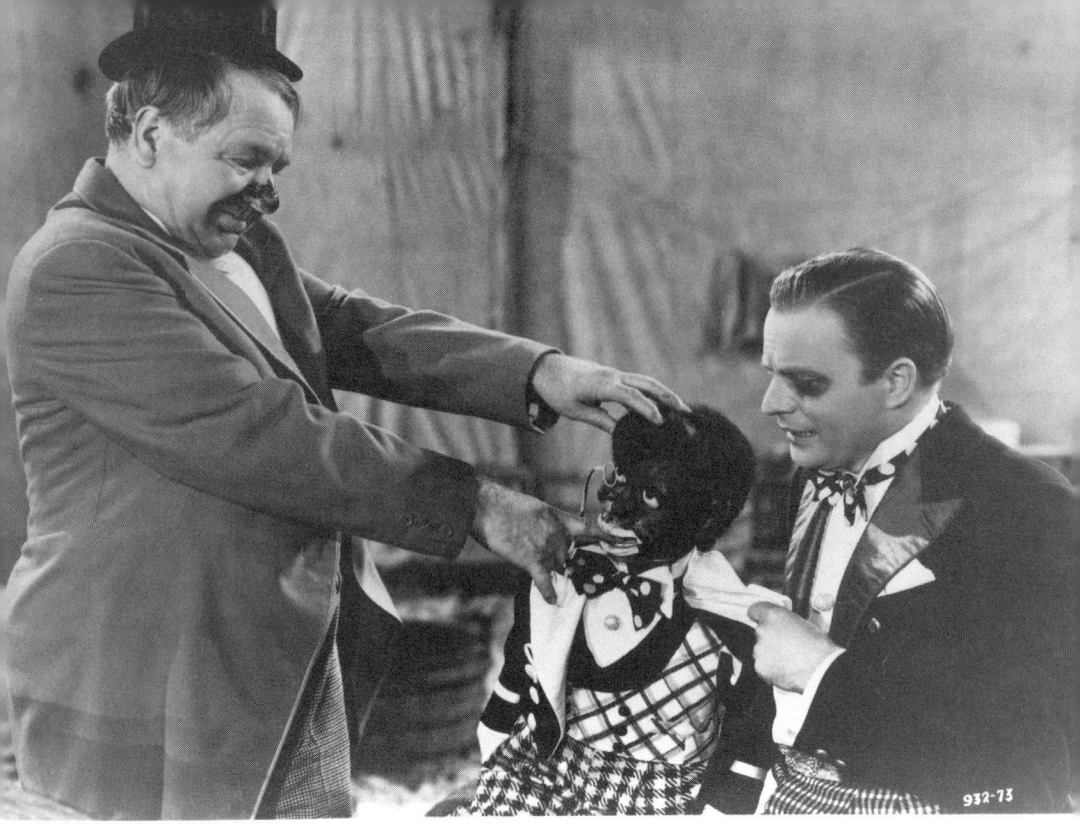

Fields gets bitten by Charlie McCarthy.

Barrymore was not present for the occasion when, at Gene Fowler's office at RKO, the writer unveiled John Decker's latest painting. Fowler had bought this original work, and as Decker told Irving Wallace:

> He unveiled it, amid mock fanfare, in his studio writing office. While two puzzled extras, attired handsomely as British sailors, hauled a Union Jack off the painting — revealing W.C. Fields as Victoria Regina — a third extra stood by and fired a one-gun salute, which almost killed director Leo McCarey in the next room.
>
> This oil of W.C. Fields as Queen Victoria was probably the most widely publicized I ever put to easel. Dave Chasen immediately ordered a copy for the lobby of his renowned Hollywood restaurant. Sir Cedric Hardwicke demanded a miniature copy, framed in white and gilt case, bearing the inscription, "W.C. Fields as Victoria Regina by Sir John Decker, R.A." You see, I was so pleased with the work I even knighted myself!

Fields, of course, was delighted — "Sabotage! Decker has kicked history in the groin!"

Although W.C. had been MGM's first choice to star as *The Wizard of Oz*, he opted to go to Universal for *You Can't Cheat an Honest Man*, co-starring Edgar Bergen and Charlie McCarthy. W.C. wrote the story, casting himself fortuitously as Larson E. Whipsnade, circus proprietor and con artist supreme. In the course of the comedy, Fields' Whipsnade also appears as "Buffalo Bella," bearded lady crack-shooter on horseback, and — in an apparent parody of Bergen — a ventriloquist sporting a big mustache and buckteeth to hide his moving mouth as he makes his grotesque dummy sing.

Fields and Bergen had been a sensation on radio's *Chase and Sanborn Hour* with their Olympian feuds. What radio audiences heard was mild compared to the badinage swapped for real on the Universal lot. Animosity between Fields and Bergen became so hot that the company actually split into two production units: George Marshall, the original director, continued with Bergen, his dummy and the featured players while Edward Cline took over the Fields scenes. The company met each morning to wing the script, with Fields and Bergen battling for one-upmanship. Constance Moore, who played Fields' lovely daughter in *You Can't Cheat an Honest Man*, told me about the mayhem of the shooting and the ultimate showdown between the two stars:

> It was so wonderful … Every morning at 9 o'clock, everybody was on the set, to plan the day's shooting. We met in a semi-circle, with our names on the chairs, and we'd have the old script, and the new script, and Bergen had his rewrites, and Fields had his rewrites! Bergen would use Charlie McCarthy — who, by the way, had his own chair — to confront Fields. And Fields would take great offense!
>
> So there would be this little creature, attacking Fields. Bergen was really a terrible ventriloquist — oh, he was so awful! — but the illusion was such, and things grew to such proportions, that Fields finally struck Charlie — the dummy — from the set!
>
> "Take that little bastard," Fields shouted, "and throw him out! Throw him out, chair and all! He's banned from this set!" And an assistant came, and off the set went Charlie!
>
> Bergen said, "Banned? He's banned?"
>
> "He's banned!" roared Fields. "Banned! And if you don't like it, you can drop dead as far as I'm concerned!"
>
> Fields had banned a little piece of wood from the set! Chair and all! It was so ridiculous! The dummy had to go to the prop room, and there he stayed until he was called into the scene. And now, without his dummy, Bergen never said a word — never a word — because he was obviously speaking through Charlie, his alter ego.

On October 4 of that same year, Fields wrote to Gene Fowler's daughter Jane at National Park College in Forest Glen, Maryland:

Dear Jane:

Some months ago, I met your drunken father in a beer parlor where I had gone to hear the results of the baseball game. He informed me that you had married. I was stunned. Knowing you as a very smart girl, I could not understand how you could let me slip through your fingers. I had bought you a mink coat and a string of black Romanoff pearls as an engagement present.

Last night I again met your Da-da and was he ga-ga! I checked up again with him and I find out it is your brother that is married. This is all too late for I have given the mink coat and the pearls and the cabochon ruby to a titled Ethiopian lady in appreciation for her assisting my chauffeur in washing the cars. I might add that I also had purchased for you some Royal Catherine of Aragon cigars and eighty pounds of Jolly Tar Chewing Tobacco.

When you next return to our Hollywood, what about a little swing-around — a day with the bangtails, lunch in the stand, dinner at Chasen's and after that, a rip through Chinatown or to see Buster Keaton and Chester Conklin in their latest movie, *Hollywood Cavalcade*.

Everyone knows now what your Mother went to Europe for. Her flimsy excuse that it was merely to get the autographs of Hitler, Goering, Stalin and Mussolini does not hold water. We know now why she screwed out of London just two days before the fireworks started… Now she is back in peaceful Hollywood, God help us.

An old fashioned hug, a hearty hand-clasp, and my warmest love,

From
Fieldsie Old Boy to you

Errol Flynn's '39 films — *Dodge City* and *The Private Lives of Elizabeth and Essex* — were both directed by the despised Michael Curtiz. Both also co-starred Olivia de Havilland, although in the latter, Bette Davis played the title role of Elizabeth and Errol was Essex. She had wanted Laurence Olivier for the part, and even later claimed she had tried to imagine Olivier in place of Flynn in their scenes together. Flynn, meanwhile, had little rapport with his imperious co-star Davis, who by now had collected two Academy Awards.

In *My Wicked, Wicked Ways*, Flynn told the story of Bette Davis, in a take, slapping him hard — and wearing heavy costume rings at the time. He retaliated by slapping the Queen of Warner Bros. on her ass so hard that she flew up in the air in her heavy Elizabethan costume and fell right on the floor in front of every actor and crewmember on the soundstage.

She never spoke to him again.

John Ford's *Stagecoach*, released by United Artists in March '39, was a milestone film for two of the Bundy Drive Boys. John Carradine enjoyed one of his richest roles as Hatfield, the mysterious Southern gambler in black cloak and white Stetson. It was Thomas Mitchell, however, who would reap the most benefit from this film by winning the 1939 Best Supporting Actor Academy Award for his alcoholic Doc Boone. It was, as Carradine said with justifiable pride, the "absolutely perfect" Western, with Claire Trevor's prostitute, John Wayne's Ringo Kid, Donald Meek's whisky drummer and the rest all battling their demons and the savages. The film made a star of John Wayne and Monument Valley, which became Ford's favorite location locale.

Stagecoach was Mitchell's second film for John Ford and Carradine's sixth. Carradine considered Ford a "sadist" who often terrified actors into giving good performances and the *Stagecoach* shoot was no exception. Sometimes Ford arbitrarily picked an actor from the cast to be his patsy — and on *Stagecoach* the patsy was Thomas Mitchell. Ford mercilessly taunted Mitchell until the day the actor retaliated, "That's all right, Mr. Ford. Just remember — I saw *Mary of Scotland*." Ford, sensitive about *Mary's* failure, stormed off the set and the bullying of Mitchell ceased.

The two Bundy Boys have great, antagonistic chemistry early in *Stagecoach*. In one scene, Carradine's Hatfield protests Mitchell's Northern Army-sympathizing Doc Boone smoking his cigar in proximity to the Southern aristocratic (and pregnant) passenger Lucy Mallory (Louise Platt):

> Carradine: Put out that cigar … A gentleman doesn't smoke in the presence of a lady.
> Mitchell: Three weeks ago I took a bullet out of a man who was shot by a "gentleman." The bullet was in his back!

Carradine's Hatfield comes to admire Mitchell's Boone after the "drunken swine" (as Carradine calls him) sobers up to deliver Lucy's baby. Both put up a hell of a fight in the great chase scene, as the Indians pursue the stagecoach and Carradine suffers a fatal bullet. "If you see Judge Greenfield," says the dying, fallen-from-grace gambler to Doc Boone and Lucy, "tell him his son…" — and John Carradine dies with his head on Thomas Mitchell's chest.

Although a Ford regular, Carradine's relationship with the tyrannical director was hardly a smooth one. As Nunnally Johnson (scripter of *The Prisoner of Shark Island* and *Jesse James*) recalled, "Carradine had an ego which was about three times John Ford's." Ford would scream and curse at Carradine, trying his vicious best to break him, but the actor stayed maddeningly calm in the face of the storm.

"You're all right, Jack," Carradine would smile, giving Ford a pat on the shoulder and walking away. Ford would sputter in profane frustration.

A peek at the salary list for *Stagecoach* (shot on a budget of $546,200) is revealing in its disparity between the money paid both the stars and the character players: Claire Trevor, $15,000 vs. John Wayne's $3,700; Thomas Mitchell, $12,000 vs. John Carradine's $3,666.

Thomas Mitchell, who had married second wife Rachel Hartzell the previous year, had fancy film credits in 1939, appearing in three of the ten movies nominated for that year's Best Picture Oscar. In addition to nominated film *Stagecoach*, he appeared in winning movie *Gone With the Wind* and nominated *Mr. Smith Goes to Washington*.

In *Gone With the Wind*, Mitchell played Gerald O'Hara, Scarlett's white-haired Irish immigrant father, a prosperous pre-Civil War plantation owner who goes mad during the film's Antebellum horrors. In addition to its Best Picture award, the film won nine other Academy Awards including Best Director (Victor Fleming), Best Screenplay (Sidney Howard), Best Actress (Vivien Leigh), and Best Supporting Actress (Hattie McDaniel) and grossed nearly 192 million dollars. Thomas Mitchell's Gerald O'Hara memorably delivered the pivotal line "Why, land is the only thing in the world worth workin' for, worth fightin' for, worth dyin' for, because it's the only thing that lasts," setting the stage for his daughter's obsession with Tara throughout the rest of the film. His later insanity is poignantly portrayed by Mitchell in the scene with Vivien Leigh's Scarlett where he refuses to acknowledge his wife's death. He shows his daughter the worthless Confederate bonds — all that's left of her inheritance.

> Scarlett: What are we going to do with no money and nothing to eat?
> O'Hara: We must ask your mother. That's it. We must ask Mrs. O'Hara.

John Carradine had a top year in 1939. He found one of his most infamous roles in *Jesse James*, 20th Century-Fox's Technicolor western epic, as Bob Ford — the cowardly traitor who, clutching his pistol in his trembling hands, climactically shoots Jesse (Tyrone Power) in the back.

Fox shot much of *Jesse James* on location in Pineville, Missouri. Power flew there with director Henry King in King's private plane, but a train transported the rest of the cast — Henry Fonda, Nancy Kelly, Randolph Scott, Henry Hull, Brian Donlevy, Carradine, et al. — to the Ozarks. Five thousand cheering, gawking folk awaited the train, and most of the company ran through the crowd to the safety of the studio cars.

Not John Carradine.

Looking like Lucifer in the mustache and goatee he'd grown for Bob Ford, perched on a site above the crowd, Carradine posed dramatically and proclaimed, "I am here for a sole purpose. To kill Jesse James!" He then launched into Shakespeare — causing many of the Ozark natives to believe he was reciting a foreign language — and braved his way into the mob to sign autographs.

Jesse James was a box office smash and passionate moviegoers never forgave Carradine for his perfidy. When the film opened in Joplin, Missouri, a man stood in the audience and shot Carradine on the screen. As the actor recalled,

> Another time I was out in front of a theatre where *Jesse James* was showing. A little kid said, "Did you shoot Jesse?" and I said, "Yes" and the son-of-a-bitch kicked me in the shin!

John Carradine's 1939 finale was *Drums Along the Mohawk*, John Ford's first Technicolor movie based on the Walter D. Edmonds historical bestseller. Claudette Colbert and Henry Fonda starred, and Carradine played the Tory villain, looking like a vampire pirate in his cape, eye patch and three-cornered hat. Once again, 20th Century-Fox sent the company on location, this time to Cedar Breaks National Monument, 11,000 feet up in the mountains of Utah. Every night there was a bonfire, and the actors would perform songs and skits. Carradine, naturally, recited Shakespeare, and the sight of him delivering the classics in firelight was a spectacle.

Anthony Quinn labored at Paramount in B-fare such as the 57-minute *King of Chinatown*. The studio's epic of '39 was Cecil B. DeMille's *Union Pacific*, starring Barbara Stawyck and Joel McCrea. The villain was a spit-curled Brian Donlevy, who heads west in a train filled with gamblers and whores; Anthony Quinn was one of the gamblers. "I found it embarrassing," said Quinn of his small role in his father-in-law's movie. A consolation for Quinn was his and Katherine's baby son, Christopher, whom they both loved dearly.

Ben Hecht and Charles MacArthur credits for 1939 included RKO's *Gunga Din*, a great adventure saga, and Goldwyn's *Wuthering Heights,* one of its greatest romances. Hecht and MacArthur humanized Brontë's doltish, selfish lovers Cathy (Merle Oberon) and Heathcliff (Laurence Olivier) so the story was actually tolerable and under William Wyler's direction, ultimately moving. As always, Hecht picked up fast cash doctoring scripts and making suggestions to producers and directors — including John Ford on *Stagecoach*. Ford said it was Hecht's idea to accent that Claire Trevor was playing a prostitute, and John Wayne an outlaw. The outcast quality was as much a texture of the rousing film as the stunning Monument Valley scenery.

He also spent two feverish weeks working with his old pal David Selznick ("Genghis Selznick," he called him) on the script for *Gone With the Wind*. Selznick wanted him to stay on for *GWTW*, and gave Hecht a firsthand look at the hysteria surrounding the epic one Sunday as Selznick acted out the saga for him, playing Scarlett and her father, while director Victor Fleming acted out Rhett Butler and Ashley Wilkes. Hecht skipped town and headed home to Nyack. Hecht received no onscreen credit for his work, and the 1939 Best Screenplay Oscar went to Sidney Howard, who'd written the original *GWTW* script and died in a tractor accident in '39. Howard's posthumous win defeated, among others, the screenplay of Hecht and MacArthur for *Wuthering Heights*.

The Bundy Drive Boys almost lost a member in late 1939. Gene Fowler and director Leo McCarey were driving back to Hollywood from Big Bear Lake, McCarey driving 95 miles an hour and singing away, when an elderly driver pulled out into the highway from an orange-grove trail. As Fowler wrote in *Minutes of the Last Meeting*:

I afterward learned that McCarey was hurled one hundred and twenty-six feet — by police measurement — into the freshly irrigated orange trees. The car, with me folded inside it, turned over three times. I stayed pinned upside down for a half an hour, my clothes and body drenched with raw gasoline. I suffered two split vertebrae, three cracked ribs, a skull injury, and wrenched knees. Otherwise I was as good as new.

An ambulance arrived in the darkness to take the unconscious McCarey to the nearest hospital at Covina. The ambulance doctor had been unable to find my pulse and understandably had sent for a mortician.

I briefly came to in a hearse. "Is anyone here?" I called out.

Both men recovered, with Fowler offering his agent 10% of his injuries. As he wrote 14 years later, "... even now, when I get out of bed, I sound like a castanet solo."

Meanwhile, John Decker had an idea for a movie. As he later explained:

I recall writing a movie scenario with a professional author [probably Gene Fowler] about a painter who forged Old Masters, foisted thirty million dollars' worth of them on an unsuspecting public, and when his conscience bothered him, decided to confess. But the painter wasn't permitted to confess. The police told him to forget about it. Because if the public ever learned about the wholesale forgeries, their confidence in art would forever be destroyed! Now that was just the idea of the script. The Hays office frowned on it — because in our story, the criminal was not brought to justice.

Word leaked out. And our idea appeared in the newspapers. One major studio liked our idea, copied it from the newspaper, and added a final twist more suitable to the screen. But the studio had no knowledge about copying Old Masters. So they sent one of their representatives to see me, with the audacity to ask me if I'd be willing to give them free technical advice on — the picture his studio had stolen from me! That's Hollywood!

As Decker remembered, he bellowed. "Go to Hell!" Yet his anger possibly fueled John Decker's fraud that still echoes in the sacrosanct halls of Harvard University's Fogg Museum.

A firsthand primary source account of the caper came from the late Will Fowler, in a videotaped interview Bill Nelson conducted in 1999. Nelson mentioned the rumors that Decker's forgeries still hang in major museums.

"What the hell are you telling me for?" laughed Fowler cheerfully. "I watched him paint a Rembrandt!"

> The Christ Head…. Thomas Mitchell wanted a Christ Head, and Decker said, "Well, you know, I think I know where I can put my hands on one." The L.A. Art Museum was just the worst museum in the entire world, and the curator there was named Valentini — he was a Dutchman, I think, whatever. So Decker told Tommy Mitchell, "I can get one for you for $2,000."
>
> This is back in 1940, almost 60 years ago, and the [San Fernando] Valley wasn't really developed then. We came out in the Valley, where there were antique houses, and they put their antiques on Ventura Boulevard — it only had one lane west of Sepulveda. We got one drawer out of an old dresser, the purpose being that we wanted the wood. So Decker said, "What size do you think we should do it?" — they measured art in millimeters. And my claim in history was that I said, "How about an 8 x 10?"— Like a movie star photograph! And this Christ Head is measured in inches.
>
> So Decker painted it, and then he aged it and then he took it and cracked the back. Then he gave it to Valentini, who was paid $600, and Valentini put it through customs in Amsterdam to give it a little history of its own. And then in Amsterdam they bent it back with criss-crossed pieces of wood, and each time it went through customs it got authenticated. Well… he sold it to Tommy Mitchell for $2,000 — and I watched Decker paint it, for Christ's sake!

There are, as will be noted, a few flaws in Fowler's account. The picture was painted in 1939 when "Valentini" (who was in fact Dr. W.R. Valentiner) was director of the Detroit Institute of Arts (he joined the L.A. Museum of Art in 1945). In fact, Valentiner had impeccable credits, but with one very sore Achilles heel. According to Alex Beam's feature "A Cloud Hangs over Rembrandt at the Fogg" in the *Boston Globe* (October 14, 2004, which included a color image of the painting), Valentiner had a hair trigger for authenticating Rembrandts — 700 of them in fact, about half of which turned out to be fakes. It's true that Valentiner was a crony of Decker's — indeed, after Decker's death, he wrote to Forest Lawn, campaigning to have Decker buried in the Court of Immortals (and receiving a resounding "No!"). Yet his validation of the Rembrandt was probably sincere, and Decker, aware of the man's overboard enthusiasm in validating Rembrandts, likely figured he was just the man he needed to make his forgery bear fruit.

At any rate, by June of 1939, *Bust of Christ* had arrived in New York City. According

Decker's Rembrandt forgery that still hangs in Harvard's Fogg Museum

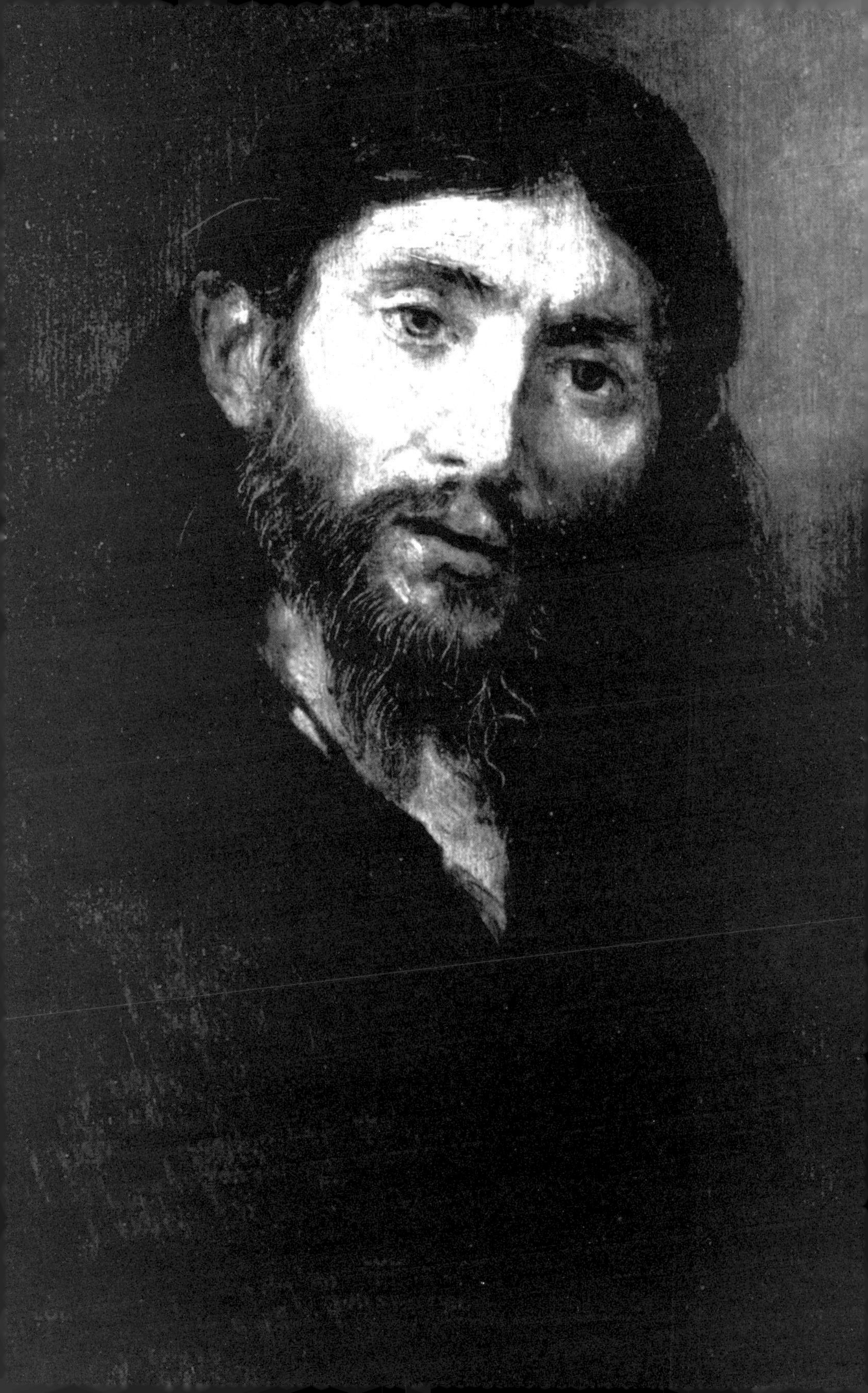

to Leslee Mayo, an expert on Decker forgeries, Thomas Mitchell had acquired a photo of the painting and assurances dated June 20, 1939 by Valentiner that it was a true Rembrandt. Valentiner's august authentication appeared in *The Art Digest* of March 15, 1940, under the headline REFUGEE REMBRANDT BOUGHT BY AN AMERICAN:

> The painting reproduced in this photo is, in my opinion, a remarkably expressive, original work by Rembrandt. It was painted in connection with the Christ of the Supper at Emmaus in the Louvre, about 1648, similar in type to the head of Christ in the Detroit Museum, and in the John G. Johnson Collection. These different representations of Christ belong to the most characteristic studies of Rembrandt at a period when he was especially interested in depicting the Passion of Christ. The painting is in a fine stage of preservation.

"A fine stage of preservation" indeed — considering the painting was very possibly not even a year old! The news spread and the legend grew. As *The Art Digest* noted, the painting was now in Thomas Mitchell's collection, and reported on its provenance:

> When the German Army last fall came crashing into Poland, an unnamed Polish prince, fleeing before the Blitzkrieg, gathered up some prized possessions among which was an unexhibited panel by Rembrandt that had long belonged in the noble's family. The prince brought his panel to New York and thence to the E. & A. Silberman Galleries....

Again, this is a howler — as noted, the painting was already in New York in June of '39, three months before the *Blitzkrieg*. *Time* magazine picked up on the story, with Mitchell claiming he'd paid the Silberman Galleries $45,000 for the *Bust of Christ*. (Was the $2,000 Mitchell paid Decker a finder's fee? Was Mitchell's $45,000 figure and name-dropping of the Silberman Galleries a creation of the actor to cover up his "underground" acquisition of a Rembrandt?)

Mitchell loaned his Rembrandt to Phyllis Decker for a showing after Decker's 1947 death, and the press played up its presence. After the showing, the painting went home to its proud owner, and Will Fowler told Bill Nelson:

> Years after Tommy died [in 1962], I went over to visit his widow. I still remember the address, 1013 North Roxbury Drive, just north of Sunset. She said, "Oh, you've come to see the Rembrandt!" I said, "Oh, yeah, sure!" And she had it above their huge fireplace — a big filigree with the Christ Head, and a light on it. I think the family eventually sold it for $180,000.

If so, the Mitchell family made a killing. Leslee Mayo learned that Seymour Silve, Fogg Museum director, saw *Bust of Christ* in the Paul Kantor Gallery in Beverly Hills in 1964 and had the painting authenticated by experts on the East coast and in Europe. A well-to-do donor named William A. Coolidge bought the painting for $35,000 (far less than Fowler claimed the Mitchell family received for it) and donated it as a gift to the Fogg Museum.

And what, after all these years, does the Fogg Museum officially have to say about all this?

In Alex Beam's *Boston Globe* 2004 story, Ivan Gaskell, curator at the Fogg, admits that the fairy tale of the Polish Prince, in his own words, "stinks." Nevertheless, based on a 1977 dendrochronological test (which Gaskell says is similar to "fingerprinting"), the Fogg dates the wood to Rembrandt's era and in fact claims it's the same wood Rembrandt used for *Portrait of a Young Jew*, which hangs in a Berlin museum. While Gaskell comes short of insisting the painting is by Rembrandt (in 1996, New York's Metropolitan Museum of Art hosted *Rembrandt/Not Rembrandt*, an indication of how many fakes are out there), he did tell Beam:

> There is nothing to suggest that this is anything other than a 17th-century painting on a 17th-century panel. This is my field of scholarly specialization. One must be open to the possibility that it's a forgery, but it's highly unlikely.

Who to believe? The Decker forgery saga surely has credibility, based on these points, as Leslee Mayo has expertly gathered:

- ★ Will Fowler's account, although incorrect in minor ways, described the painting accurately, including its size, crack, and criss-cross beams, matching the painting's description in the Fogg's records.
- ★ There is no record of this *Bust of Christ* having ever existed before it appeared in New York in 1939.
- ★ The "Polish Prince" story is surely nonsense and no other provenance has ever been established.
- ★ Dendrochronology checks the rings of trees, but Decker reportedly painted *Bust of Christ* on a flat wood that, as Ms. Mayo notes, "presumably was cut perpendicular to the rings."
- ★ W.R. Valentiner had a weakness for validating fake Rembrandts and was a buddy of John Decker.
- ★ Will Fowler was telling this story for years before his death, and long before the Fogg Museum officially responded to it.

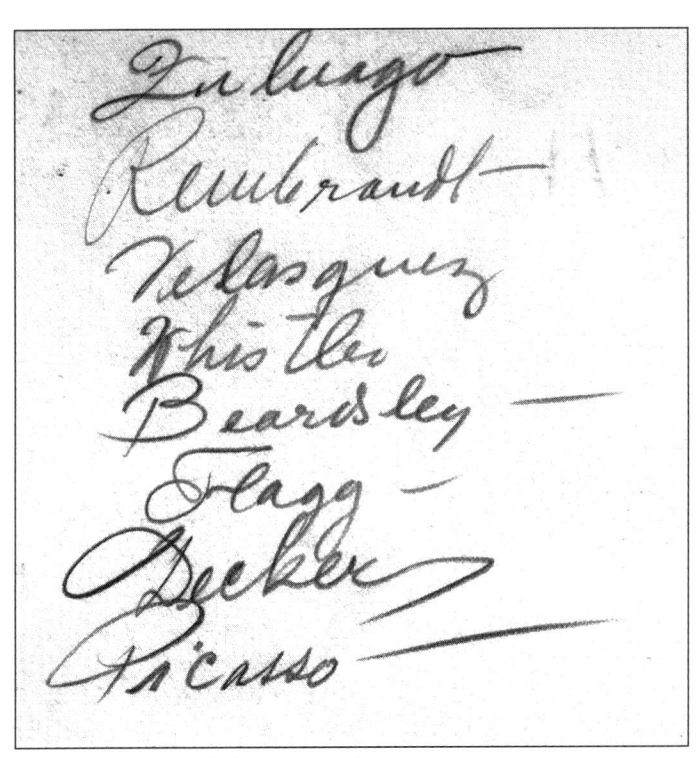

Decker's signatures of all the painters he forged

- ★ The posthumous tribute to John Decker at his studio had the *Bust of Christ* on the cover.
- ★ Decker's scrapbook has a professionally taken photograph of the *Bust of Christ*.
- ★ John Decker was a genius at aping the works of the Old Masters.

There's another key point that Leslee Mayo had not included: John Decker was, in Elaine Barrie Barrymore's words, "a bastard."

One of the real mysteries here is … *why?* Indeed, why did Decker play this fascinating but cruel prank on a man who was his friend? Thomas Mitchell loyally purchased Decker's work when the artist was in desperate straits, paid him handsomely to paint the fireplace tiles at his Oregon ranch, ignored his in-his-cups insults (Decker once called him, to his face, "a fat Borgian") and was unfailingly kind and generous to Decker—and after Decker's death, to his widow and his daughter, even taking in a destitute Phyllis for a time years later after a disastrous marriage.

True, Decker received $2,000 from Mitchell — almost five years' rent on the house/studio he moved into in 1940. However, the artist allegedly gave $600 of it to Valentiner, and the remaining $1,400 was nothing compared to the $45,000 Mitchell claimed he paid to the Silberman Galleries. Indeed, some believe that the hoax actually boomeranged, and if Mitchell told the truth, the Silberman Gallery realized over 20 times what Decker received.

Charles Heard, whose Decker paintings decorate his house, has long contemplated the intricacies of this mystery. His theory: Decker and Mitchell were partners in the elaborate hoax, with Mitchell tossing out the name of the Silberman Gallery and the $45,000 tag as "final touches in this elaborate scam."

> Think about this — Decker's fees for his paintings at that time in history had a mid-range of about $2,000. I think it's highly possible that Decker and Mitchell were in collusion to perpetrate an elaborate hoax on the art world. Mitchell would acquire an undiscovered Old Master treasure with global publicity. Decker would replenish the pirate's chest with a $2,000 fee and both would have an abundance of laughs over the caper.
>
> Manipulating the art publications and *Time* magazine into publishing the story and saying that Mitchell had paid $45,000 would have been the final touches in this elaborate scam.
>
> Decker, in all certainty, never had his hands on $45,000 at any time in his life… Mitchell would have had a great provenance and bragging rights on his Rembrandt painting and a load of inside chuckles for the rest of his life.

It all happened so long ago, and there are so many riddles remaining, that the mystery will probably never find a definitive resolution. Still, the question of Decker's overall motivation remains perhaps the most intriguing aspect of all.

Part III

1940-1947

To sing,
to laugh,
to dream,
to walk in my own way
and be alone…

—John Decker's favorite lines from
Cyrano de Bergerac

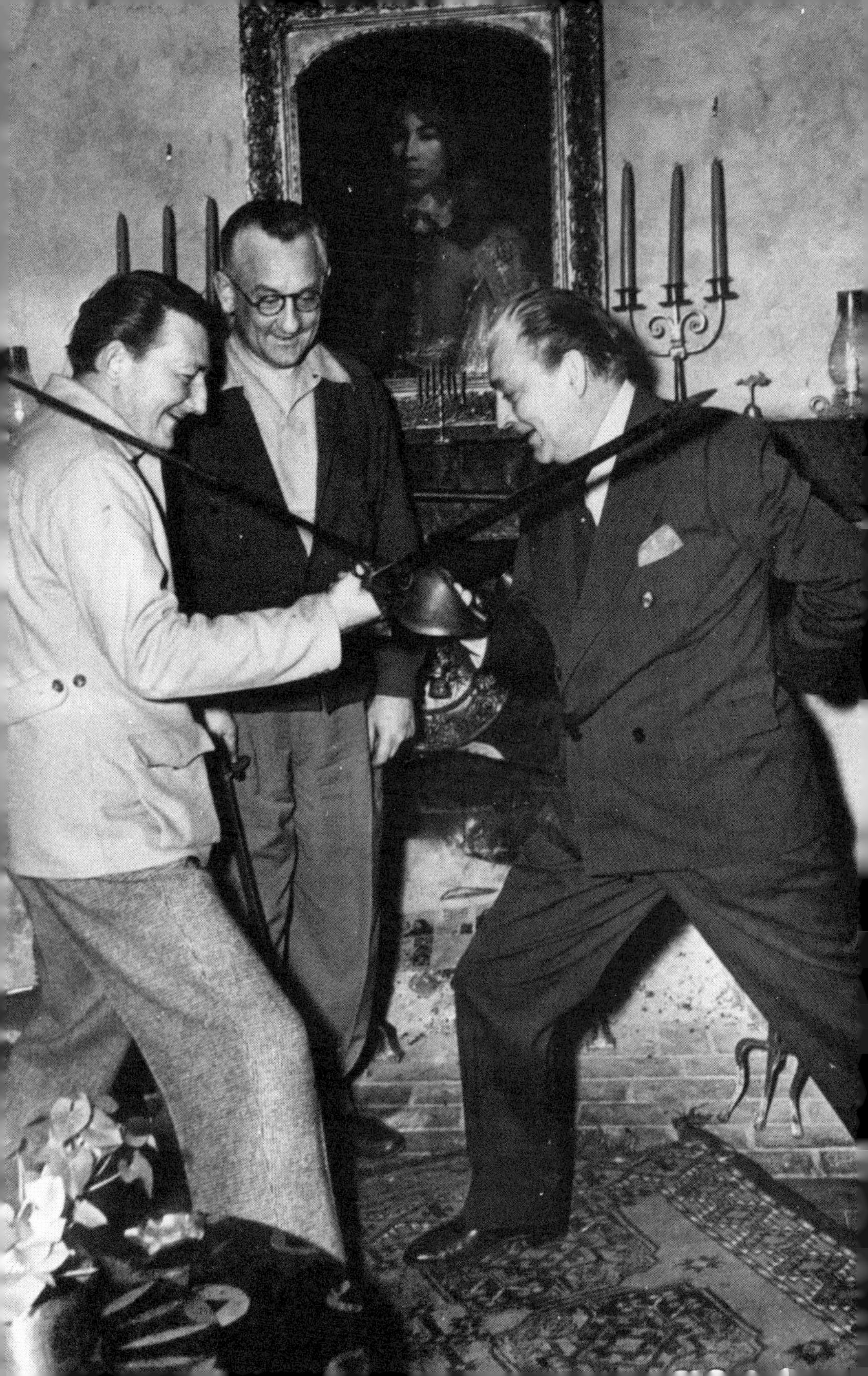

Chapter Thirteen
1940: Bundy Drive

The Brentwood colony of Los Angeles sits west of Bel Air, and east of Santa Monica and the Pacific Palisades. The area is pocked with bizarre Hollywood history. It was in Brentwood where Joan Crawford allegedly raised Christina in her horrific *Mommie Dearest* style, and where visitors could recognize the home of Erich ("Man You Love to Hate!") von Stroheim at Yuletide because it was the only house on its street with no Christmas decorations.

Tyrone Power, Shirley Temple, Henry Fonda, Jean Arthur, Fredric March, Joan Fontaine, Gregory Peck, Ilona Massey, Robert Preston — all these stars and many more lived at one time or other in Brentwood. A tourist today can see film zealots running about with maps, many below Sunset Boulevard, seeking 12305 Fifth Helena, the hallowed suicide (was it really?) house of Marilyn Monroe. Venture a bit farther south and one finds the murder site of O.J. Simpson's ex-wife Nicole and her friend Ron Goldman.

Bundy Drive runs north and south of Sunset. Its northerly sector is about a halfmile east of Bundy Drive South. Both are convenient routes to tragic sites. In 1940, it was pastoral, a run of ranches, farms and cottages. The blonde opera star Grace Moore had bought a home at 225 N. Bundy, calling the property a "dreamland," writing to a friend about the almonds, fruits and flowers abounding on the property. At 400 S. Bundy, Brian Donlevy, the scarfaced Sgt. Markoff of *Beau Geste* ("Does he drink tiger blood?" marveled one scribe of the tough-guy actor) had a farm, where he stripped

Decker, Fowler, Barrymore at 419 Bundy Drive

himself of toupee, girdle and lifts, and peacefully splashed in his pool, savored his wine cellar and wrote poetry.

In 1940, John Decker moved into 419 N. Bundy, a little English Tudor-style cottage, with gables and beams, a stone fireplace and living room balcony, leaded glass windows and towering trees and a small back yard. Its gables and leaded glass evoked a magical fairy tale house, but something about it — perhaps the towering, ancient chimney, the tall dark pine trees, or maybe the black shadows that thrived in its nooks, even in the California sunshine — gave the home an aura of oddly sinister charm.

The "mad artist" Decker (as he was soon hailed in the leafy neighborhood) quickly added the unicorn coat-of-arms to the door and his *Useless. Insignificant. Poetic* motto.

The Bundy Drive residents soon beheld the parade of stars arriving at 419 day and night. John Barrymore was back in Hollywood, bloody but unbowed after *My Dear Children*, which had finally opened in New York on January 31, 1940 at Broadway's Belasco Theatre and ran 117 performances. Elaine, who showed up opening night wrapped in gold lamé, red fox, her lips and nails painted scarlet for the kill, seduced Barrymore into sharing again her bed and the stage; when she resumed her role of Cordelia during the run, the New York audiences hissed and booed her.

Mad Jack would hold court on Bundy Drive, sitting in an antique chair once owned by Valentino, or reprise his Hamlet to Decker's Laertes as they fenced before the roaring fireplace. Errol Flynn, W.C. Fields and Thomas Mitchell all became regular callers — a passerby might see Robin Hood, The Bank Dick and Scarlett O'Hara's mad father all arriving at the unicorn-adorned door at the same time, and might have to pull an all-nighter to see them leave.

John Decker, in his maroon jacket and mascara-darkened mustache, loved playing host.

Gene Fowler called the Bundy Drive studio "an artists' Alamo, where political bores never intruded and where breast-beating hypocrites could find no listeners." Naturally, 419 soon became a "Den of Iniquity," the lights burning all night as the gang roistered, recited, sang, and, of course, drank the cases of booze the neighbors saw constantly loaded into the cottage. Aghast snoops saw it as an opium den in the country, a snakepit north of Sunset. The house truly seemed to have a personality, an energy, a dynamic all its own.

The men were at their most supercharged, and the house seemed to inspire their madness.

Decker at the Alta Loma gallery

It was at the Bundy Drive cottage where Decker, Flynn and Fowler devoted themselves one evening to bottles of absinthe. The spirit, widely banned internationally, had the sobriquet of "The Green Fairy" and an historically sinister reputation — Van Gogh allegedly drank absinthe before slicing off his ear. After the trio imbibed, they passed out, left their ears intact, and Decker recovered to paint the empty bottle. His painting *Absinthe* survives today in the Carmel, California home of actress Joan Fontaine.

Sometimes Flynn and Decker left Bundy for a new favored hobby — visits to the morgue by night. Decker might sketch a corpse that he found especially odd or intriguing. Ida Lupino, then a rising Warner Bros. star through such films as *They Drive by Night* (1940) and *High Sierra* (1941), was a close friend of Flynn, and through him met Decker. Ms. Lupino told Charles Higham of a birthday when a large wooden crate arrived at her house and she and her mother opened it. It was a series of increasingly smaller boxes — "like a Chinese puzzle," she remembered — and finally there was a small box with a note: "Happy Birthday, and don't let this happen to you. John Decker." Inside was "a perfectly wonderful painting" of a young Mexican beauty.

"There was only one strange thing about it," said Ida Lupino. "Her throat was cut."

Decker had sketched the Mexican girl's cadaver at the morgue. According to William Donati's *Ida Lupino*, the actress "was fascinated by stories of murder and enjoyed the thrill of being frightened," and "wondered how it felt to kill. " As such, she loved Decker's painting, but felt obliged to exhibit it in an upstairs corner. "Lots of people can't stand looking at the picture," said Lupino. "Seems to give them the willies. Personally, I like it, but I have to keep it in seclusion."

W.C. Fields, of course, came to call, bellowing, "That nitwit doctor! The nefarious quack claimed he found urine in my whiskey!" Fields arrived in his 1938 Cadillac with bar, from his new home at 2015 DeMille Drive in Los Feliz, across the street from the formidable C.B. DeMille. W.C. was annoyed at having such a pooh-bah for a neighbor, but the low rent ($250 per month) was irresistible, and he enjoyed shooting the birds that came to devour the fish in his lily pond. In 1940, an election year, Fields ran afoul of the FBI. According to Curt Gentry's *J. Edgar Hoover: The Man and his Secrets*, Hoover himself paid a call on W.C. for a bizarre reason:

> Fields… was so flustered by the FBI director's unexpected visit to his Los Feliz home that he kept calling him Herbert.
>
> Finally Hoover got around to the purpose of his visit. "I understand you have some interesting pictures, eh?"
>
> Fields did. His friend John Decker had painted three miniatures of Eleanor

W.C. at his Los Feliz residence

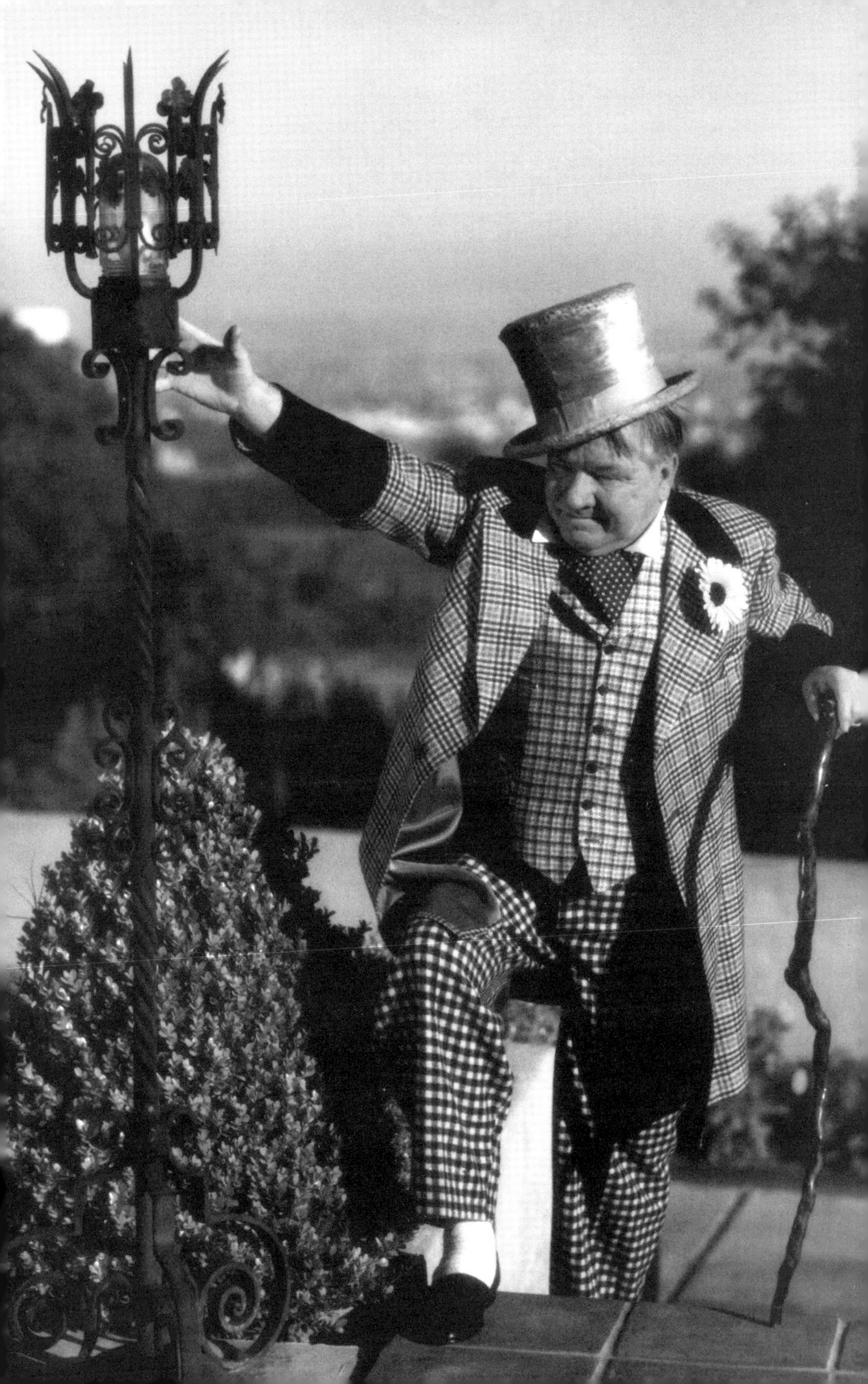

Roosevelt, whom Fields despised. Viewed upside down they depicted, in grossly exaggerated anatomical detail, a woman's sex organs. But fearing he was in danger of being arrested on a charge of possessing obscene materials, Fields affected a pose of uncomprehending innocence.

"No ladies' pictures?" his visitor persisted. "Maybe you can dig up a small one, or maybe even two studies of a certain lady in Washington?"

Fields pulled one out of his desk drawer and apprehensively handed it to the FBI director. To Fields' great relief, Hoover's laughter proved he was obviously no fan of the lady in question. When Hoover asked him if he would make him a present of the painting, Fields magnanimously gave him all three, in return for a jocular promise that he wouldn't display them unless "there's a change in the administration."

As Gentry added, "Although male visitors to Hoover's basement recreation room were invariably shown the cameos — the showing was a highlight of the FBI director's private tour — they are not listed in the itemized inventory of the late J. Edgar Hoover's estate. Rumor has it that a certain former assistant director now has them."

At 419 Bundy Drive, Fields hurled Olympian insults at Sadakichi Hartmann, who naturally found his way to the studio in his flowing camel's-hair coat and a virtual halo of dirt. Philip Paval, an artist who specialized as a silversmith and goldsmith, wrote in his 1968 memoir *Paval* that Sadakichi

> ... hated everything and everybody. He never kept himself clean and his foul pipe would stink to high heaven. One time he was sitting at John's bar and was too lazy to go. He emptied his kidneys right there with it running down his pants and forming a large pool under the stool, looking nonchalantly around as if nothing had happened. When someone said, "Hey what is that?" he said, "I spilled my drink." He did spill it all right, but after it had gone through his filter system...

John Carradine, wearing his slouch hat like a buccaneer, would come to call, proclaiming his greeting as Decker looked out the festive door's peep hatch, staying late into the night, roaring Shakespeare as if he were telling the entire neighborhood a classical bedtime story.

Gene Fowler was working at MGM on what proved to be his final script credit, MGM's *Billy the Kid*. His favorite work on *Billy the Kid* was a poem he wrote, *The Cowboy's Lament* — the saga of "God damn old Bessie Bond, the courtesan," that could never be used, of course, due to censorship and became, naturally, a Bundy Drive Boys favorite. To quote a verse:

Phyllis Decker

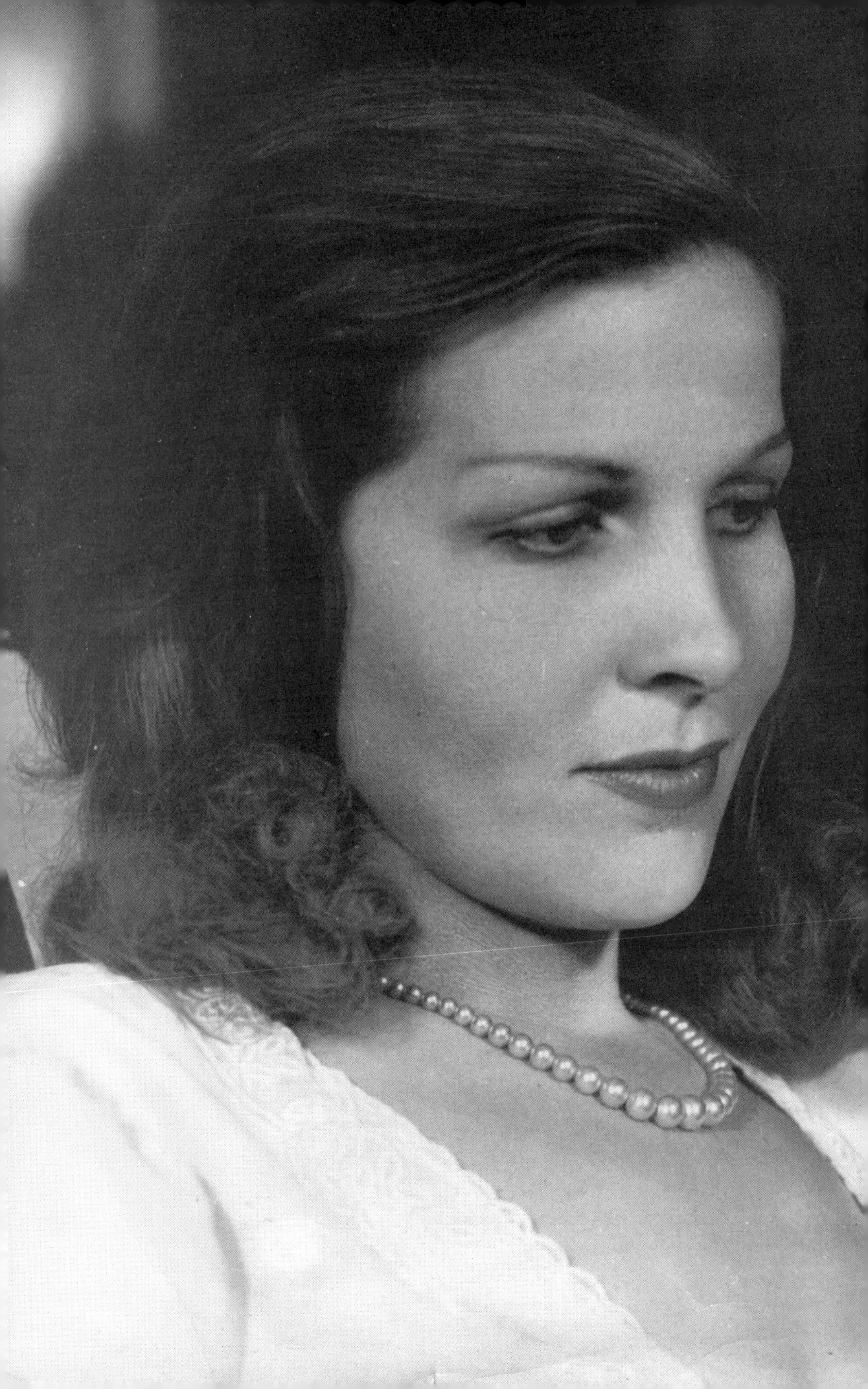

Oh! Bessie Bond, the shameless courtesan.
She's been the death of many a healthy man.
She demands the biggest fees, sir,
Then spreads the French disease, sir.
Oh! God damn old Bessie Bond, the courtesan!

Thomas Mitchell was a regular visitor, inviting the gang to come to his house and see the Rembrandt above his fireplace. Roland Young enjoyed the role of "Uncle Willie" in Katharine Hepburn's new film hit *The Philadelphia Story*. Ben Hecht had performed a sex change on his and Charles MacArthur's play *The Front Page* via the movie *His Girl Friday*, with Rosalind Russell as reporter Hildy Johnson and Cary Grant as editor Walter Burns. Bundy Drive provided a reunion for Hecht and a pal from Chicago, the visionary Polish-American artist Stanislaw Szukalski, who'd allegedly learned about anatomy by dissecting his own father.

Down the cellar, Decker kept his "treasure chest" — which contained the modest

John in the Bundy Drive backyard, Phyllis and Mary Lou, and Decker and Barrymore near Banning

sums he saved temporarily, eventually ramsacked time and again for booze, food and more sybaritic joys.

The house seemed a lasting inspiration to the Bundy Drive Boys' manic energy, and it was here that Decker took a stab at writing — the story, perhaps appropriately, entitled "Asylum." (Alternate title: "James Felton, Insane.") To quote a passage:

> The inside was, for some reason, intensely familiar to Felton. He never hesitated but ran frantically up the spiral staircase leading to the attic door. A dim light glowed from under the sill. Cautiously he opened the door. There in the dim flickering candlelight lay an immense black coffin. It was at last ten feet deep. A ladder leaned against it, and the lid lay crosswise on top of it. On a small dusty table fluttered a half-burnt candle. It was red, and the tallow had dripped from the table. But before reaching the floor, it had caught itself in a web that a spider had spun between the legs of the table, and it looked like a drop of blood suspended in mid-air. Felton eagerly seized the candle, scrambled up the

ladder, and gazed down into the coffin. There at the bottom lay Mona, silent, white, and beautiful. A great force like a magnet seemed to draw him into the coffin. Suddenly an unseen hand hurtled him into the coffin. A horrible hollow laugh rose above him. Felton looked up. He saw the hideous grinning face of Granville. In his hand he held a heavy hammer, and with frantic blows was nailing down the lid of the coffin…

That night they took Felton away to the asylum.

For all the high jinks and hell-raising, there was also a very definite aura of domesticity. For John Decker had moved to Bundy Drive with his new drop-dead alluring wife Phyllis, her little daughter Mary Lou, and their cocker spaniel Ginger.

> My mother was a very attractive lady, blonde, pretty. In fact, in the later 1940s, publicity agents asked her to go to functions and parties in Hollywood, and pose as Rita Hayworth, or Lizabeth Scott. But you can't believe what she could look like out in the garden at Bundy Drive! She'd be full of mud, and she'd always wear little bitty-short-shorts, and sometimes she'd have big heavy white socks on — because she'd put cream on her feet — and she'd go out in these big heavy white socks! And she'd wear white gloves, with cream inside them. No hat, because she was always trying to get tanned. She was a chain-smoker — everybody was in those days — but she'd be walking around with these cigarettes and the ashes would get longer and longer and she'd come in the house and flick them on the carpet and rub them in, saying, "Keeps the moths out!" I'd be so embarrassed when I'd bring my friends home!
>
> She was a quiet person in those days — I think she was a little intimidated. John was an intimidating personality!
>
> — Mary Lou Warn, John Decker's stepdaughter

When Phyllis McGlone married John Decker in 1940, he was 44, and she was 25. There had been a lot of living in those years, however, as Mary Lou Warn remembered in a 2006 interview:

> When my mother was 16 she met my father — a gambler, quite a bit older than she was, who had been born in Leone, because his father was the ambassador from Spain to Mexico. He was half-French and half-Spanish, and as far as my Irish grandfather (a railroad engineer from Toledo) was concerned,

Errol Flynn on the *Zaca*.

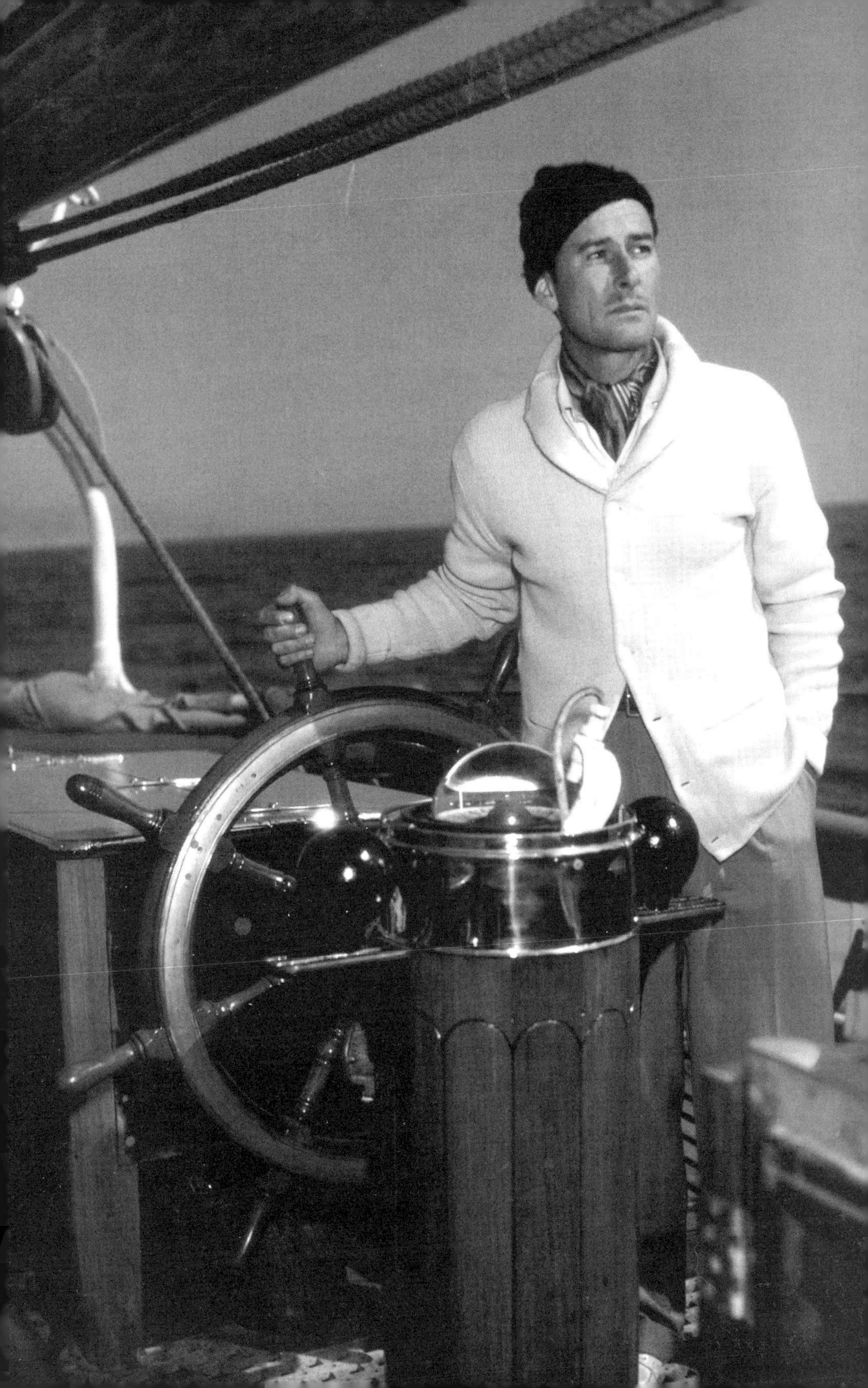

my mother might as well have married a black man in those days. After they got married and she was pregnant with me, my father went back to Mexico to his mother's funeral, and while he was gone, my grandfather declared him as an undesirable alien! My mother never saw him again, and I never saw my real father.

So after I was born in Toledo, mother headed to L.A. with me — I was always getting shuffled around [laughing] and probably slept in dresser drawers! During a stop-off on her way to Hollywood, she was at the Chez Paris in Chicago, as one of the "All-Blonde Chorus Girls," all beautiful blondes. In L.A. she married briefly a young man who managed a big downtown hotel — I probably was only about two at the time — and he died of appendicitis. Then Mother got a job at a nightclub, and through a friend named Audrey Higer, whose father owned the club, she met John.

I was in boarding school when she married John, her third husband, and they brought me out to Bundy Drive.

And how did Mary Lou, then in the second grade, regard her new stepfather?

Oh, he scared me! I was very meek, and I came from that old school of children who were to be seen and not heard. John treated me very well, but he wasn't demonstrative and he wasn't wild about children. He had to put up with my friends, and it was probably a little shocking to him to have little kids running through the house!

Although Decker's friends were probably at least as initially shocking to Mary Lou as her friends were to him, she soon became used to the men fated to be known as "The Bundy Drive Boys":

It was just very natural to me to come home and the house would be full of these characters. W.C. Fields would be in and out, and you could always tell when Roland Young was there — he had a big black limousine that always waited for him. I'd go to bed at night, up in my room off the balcony, and when I got up in the morning, they were still down there!

John Barrymore was at the house most of the time. He loved it — it was his second home, and he and John would just be drunk together all the time! John and Mother went a couple of times with Barrymore to Palm Springs, and they left me at his house, "Bella Vista," way up on the end of Tower Road. Barrymore lived then in only about three rooms of this huge mansion, and they'd leave me there with his Japanese gardener, Nishi, and Nishi's wife and several children. It was fascinating! Barrymore had been a hunter and collected things, and he had little Indian skulls. Nishi's kids told me that the hair would still grow on these heads and drop off, and I was just petrified! There was a pool there, but I don't think there was any water in it — Barrymore was pretty well gone then, and he had a dog he loved named Viola, a big Afghan, and for some reason he was afraid Viola would get into the pool and drown.

Sadakichi Hartmann was hanging around at Bundy Drive, and he smelled so bad! He chewed raw garlic constantly, and he wore filthy old clothes, and he'd piddle in his pants. I mean, I would go way out of the way to try to not even be in the same room with him! He was a very tall, lanky person with these hands — I'm sure today people would say they were magnificent hands, but he had these long fingers. I remember my mother saying later when I got into high school, "Oh, Sadakichi was such a brilliant man!" And I'd just say, "Egh!"

The Bundy Drive Boy I just adored was Anthony Quinn. My room at Bundy was off the balcony, and the stairs came right down into the living room. If I had to go to the bathroom, I'd come down, a sleepy little kid, and Anthony Quinn was there saying, "Oh, what a beautiful baby!" He loved children, and I just loved it when he was there because he'd pay attention to me and talk to me too! He would have been my favorite of all.

Mary Lou also came to know Errol Flynn, then the biggest of the stars who came to Bundy Drive:

Well, of course, Flynn was very charming, very personable, and he always took time to talk to my friends when they visited. I especially remember him later in my early high school years, after we had moved from Bundy to Alta Loma in West Hollywood. He would kid with us, and of course charmed all my girlfriends — everybody thought it was just wonderful to come to my house and see all the movie stars!

I had one particularly close girlfriend from Bundy Drive who had moved to Laguna, and later she came up to stay with me in West Hollywood, and Flynn took us out on his yacht. Wow! We'd be on the yacht in Santa Monica, with binoculars — and you'd see women in the water, trying to swim out to Flynn's yacht!

It was as a high school freshman that Mary Lou received her most vivid Errol Flynn memory:

> I was in 9th grade and in those days the girls were wearing these Viette brassieres — these pointed things that pointed straight out! I was a year younger than the other girls, and you had to wear a Viette brassiere, and I didn't have any chest — so I had a Viette brassiere stuffed with cotton. So I came home, and the boys were in the bar, and I was standing there chatting, and Flynn just reached over and tweaked this lumpy thing under my sweater! I was so absolutely humiliated!

One of Mary Lou's joys at Bundy was the zoo of pets Decker and Phyllis also enjoyed:

> John loved animals. When he and Mother got married, they had Ginger, a cocker spaniel, who moved to Bundy with us. I think it was my first Easter there that they bought me a little green chicken and a yellow duck, these two little teeny things. They were kept out in the back. Well, they grew, and then a neighbor's dog got the chicken, and then the duck would just quack, quack, quack early in the morning — and John always had a hangover! So the lady next door volunteered to chop up the duck, and we had roast duck for dinner one night. Everybody looked at it — and, of course, nobody could eat it!
>
> After that we had little bantam hens running about, and a rabbit, and then of course there was Gus. The story of Gus was that he had been Barrymore's dog — they were driving out Ventura Boulevard one day, which was country at that time, with great big poinsettia fields out there. Somebody had all these dachshund puppies in a child's playpen, selling them on a corner. So they stopped and Barrymore bought this little dachshund puppy, Gus. Well, Barrymore was always drunk or never home, and this poor little dog just wandered around, and Barrymore finally had his nurse/secretary, a nice young gay man, bring Gus down to us. So Barrymore (whose short-term memory was gone by this time) came to Bundy later, looked at Gus, and said, "Oh, I have a dog who looks just like that!" And we said, "That is your dog." Then Barrymore passed out, woke up later, heard my mother yell "Gus!" and said, "Oh, that's strange! My dog is named Gus, too!"
>
> So we had Gus, and a little black and tan dachshund to go with him, and they named her Tallulah Blankhead (not Bankhead!). And at one time, Errol Flynn caught a raccoon in a trap up at his home on Mulholland, and John brought

that down to the house. I remember keeping it in a big cage, but it was mean, its ankle was festered, and we couldn't get a veterinary to come out. The zoo finally came out and took it away.

All in all, these were happy days for Mary Lou.

I was so young, but as I say, they'd take me everywhere. I can remember going up to Fannie Brice's house several times. They'd just put me in the pool and I'd be very happy — I'd hang onto the side and kick and splash! John loved to cook — he made the English-type steak and kidney pies. I thought they were horrible, and they made the house smell so bad, but people seemed to think they were wonderful. He loved to cook and entertain, and when he had money, he just blew it on the best food and booze. And of course, John loved making headlines — he didn't care how!

1940 was a big year for most of the Bundy Drive Boys. Errol Flynn was starring in *The Sea Hawk*, a dashing performance in vivid contrast to his on-set behavior. On March 14, 1940, Warner Bros.' executive producer Hal Wallis fired off this memo to studio manager T.C. Wright:

For the past few days I have been getting a lot of reports via the grapevine about Errol Flynn. Also, Mike [Curtiz] has told me he loses hours every day on account of Flynn and is days behind because of him, that he doesn't know his lines, etc.
 I also understand that Flynn is late on the set practically every day, that he was called to work the other afternoon at 4:30, and at 9 o'clock said he was cold and that he was going home and proceeded to leave before the set was finished… Why do you as Studio Manager tolerate a condition of this kind?

Flynn's behavior wasn't much better on *The Santa Fe Trail* for Warners, again with the beautiful Olivia de Havilland, the despised Michael Curtiz, and as Custer, young Warner contractee Ronald Reagan. As the future U.S. President told film historian Tony Thomas:

Errol was a strange person, terribly unsure of himself and needlessly so. He was a beautiful piece of machinery, likeable, with great charm, and yet convinced he lacked ability as an actor. As a result, he was conscious every minute of scenes favoring other actors and their position on the screen in relation to himself. He was apparently unaware of his own striking personality.

W.C. Fields starred in Universal's *My Little Chickadee* tempestuously with Mae West, and their onscreen antics weren't as colorful as their offstage hostility. Ronald J. Fields remembered:

> I think it was an ego problem. If you think about it, she was the female W.C. Fields, so there was a clash right on that issue. Just as Mae West would be going into a scene, W.C. would say to an interviewer on the set, "Ah, there goes Mae West — a fine figure-eight of a woman, and so well-preserved." And he once said, "Mae West is a plumber's idea of Cleopatra." That would get to you!
>
> My first book on W.C. came out in 1973, and I was doing the talk shows, the radio shows. The first radio show I was going to be on was in L.A., and the producer asked me if I would mind sharing the mic with Mae West. He said, "I know this is going to take away a little bit from promoting your book," but I interrupted right there and said, "No, I'd love to meet her." So I get to the studio, and there's no Mae West. I asked the producer, "Are you expecting her soon?" and he said, "Well, to tell you the truth, Mr. Fields, when we asked if she'd go on with you, she said she didn't want to meet another Fields as long as she lived!"
>
> More fun was *The Bank Dick*, with W.C. as Egbert Souse, coping with a horrible family, nearly smashing a bratty daughter with a huge vase, and getting the bank inspector (Franklin Pangborn) drunk and nauseous (offering him pork chops fried in lard). Fields prepared the script under the nom de plume of "Mahatma Kane Jeeves," appalling the Breen Office, which responded with a barrage of censorship no-nos — no "nude figure of the girl, standing by the lake," no use of the word "stinko" or reference to "castor oil," etc., and climaxing with: "and, most vitally — nix the reference to the 'Black Pussy Café.' It would, however, be acceptable to say 'Black Pussycat.'"

It was shades of 1933's *International House* and W.C.'s "It's a pussy!" but he didn't get away with it this time. It was the Black Pussycat Café, where Fields had this timeless exchange with the bartender, played by Shemp Howard:

Sadakichi by Decker

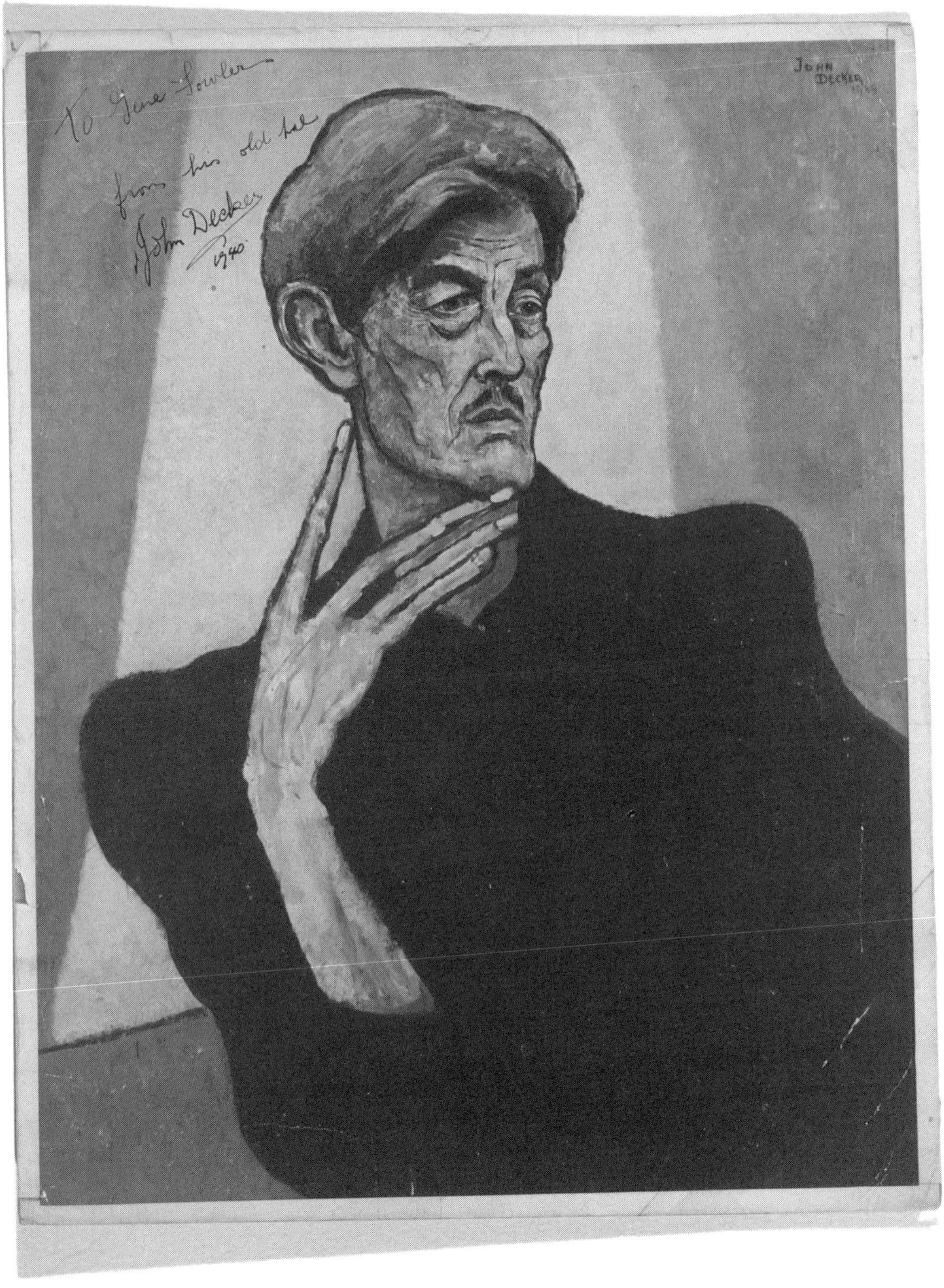
To Gene Fowler
from his old pal
John Decker
1940
JOHN
DECKER

Fields: Was I in here last night and did I spend a twenty dollar bill?
Howard: Yeah.
Fields: Oh boy! What a load that is off my mind! I thought I'd lost it!

Noting the 1940 election, Fields also wrote a book, *Fields for President*. In the book W.C. made special commemoration of August 18 ("the day I smoked my first marijuana cigarette") and wrote, "Remember, folks, cast a vote for Fields and watch for the silver lining. Cast several votes and watch for the police." Again, the humor was ahead of its time. An early 1970s reprint of *Fields for President* became a brisk seller.

It was also in 1940 that John Carradine enjoyed his role as Casy, the preacher martyr in John Ford's *The Grapes of Wrath*. He had ascended to top character actor rank, and 20th Century-Fox now paid him $1,000 per week. Carradine celebrated by buying a yacht, *The Bali*. Some of David Carradine's most vivid early memories of his father are as skipper of *The Bali*, which he preferred to sail in rough seas. As David wrote in *Endless Highway*:

> Once we were caught in a bad squall (actually a mini-hurricane) and Dad relived *Captains Courageous* for real. The wind ripped the sails off the masts and he ran before the storm on bare poles with seas as high as the masts. We all almost bought it. My strongest memory of that incident was when the storm first hit us broadside. The ship keeled over to starboard to the point that the gunwales were in the water. I was on the other side of the deck with Bruce and Mother, clinging to the sheets while the waves hit us broadside, almost drowning us each time. I was absolutely terrified and utterly thrilled. Dad was at the helm, windblown, pipe in his teeth, watching the swell for his next move, yelling orders to his crew. It was actually better than *Captains Courageous*.

Thomas Mitchell had meaty roles in *Our Town*, *The Long Voyage Home* and *Swiss Family Robinson* (for which John Decker did the promotional artwork). Alan Mowbray sliced delicious ham in the lead role of *The Villain Still Pursued Her* (which featured Carlotta Monti in a bit as a streetwalker). Anthony Quinn left Paramount and joined Warner Bros. where, as

Ann Sheridan's dance partner in *City for Conquest*, he met fellow cast member Elia Kazan. It was Kazan who later directed Quinn in the road company of *A Streetcar Named Desire* and in 1952's *Viva Zapata*, for which Quinn would win an Academy Award.

John Barrymore, meanwhile, starred in a travesty at 20th Century-Fox called *The Great Profile*. Decker, Fowler and Hartmann found their way to Fox, posing with Barrymore, who, in the film, was wearing a Hamlet costume — "God forgive everyone concerned!" wrote Fowler in *Good Night, Sweet Prince*.

"Can't you get me out of this?" Barrymore asked Fowler, referring to his agonizing marriage to Elaine.

It was also during the shooting of *The Great Profile* that Barrymore told the press of ten "extremely fine actors worth watching for pointers." They were Lionel, Spencer Tracy, George Sanders, Paul Muni, Henry Fonda, Roland Young, C. Aubrey Smith, George Raft, John Carradine and Maria Ouspenskaya. As Young and Carradine were Bundy Drive members, there was likely a celebratory party there that June night in honor of Barrymore's choices. Parties erupted there for lesser reasons.

The Great Profile is the film that won John Barrymore the honor of placing his hands, feet and profile into the celebrated cement of Sid Grauman's Chinese Theatre. On the night of September 5, 1940, Barrymore, in blue suit and flanked by *The Great Profile* co-star Mary Beth Hughes (whom Elaine described as "the blonde bitch playing my part"), made their way to the forecourt before a cheering crowd. Barrymore signed the slab "To Sid — A Great Showman — Jon Barrymore." He noted his error and the cement was smoothed as he corrected his misspelling.

The real trouble, however, came later. Grauman told the press that Barrymore, who was to enter his profile into the cement along with his hand and foot prints, would merely pose his profile near the cement — a plaster cast would provide the actual profile imprint later. However, as Barrymore posed, either a) He actually placed his profile in the cement in a fit of ad-libbed bravado or b) Grauman, in his own fit, suddenly shoved Barrymore's profile into the goo. News accounts of the evening support the latter, as Barrymore sputtered, cursed and tried to get cement out of his left eye and ear. Mary Beth Hughes ran to a nearby bar to get Barrymore a drink.

"I feel like the face on the barroom floor," said John Barrymore — perhaps his only printable quote about his immortality at Grauman's Chinese Theatre.

In *Good Night, Sweet Prince* and *Minutes of the Last Meeting*, Fowler recreates the first summer at Bundy Drive with almost idyllic grace and nostalgia. One charming vignette presents Decker, "who had on a hayseed hat and a paint-smeared shirt that hung outside his trousers and partly concealed a huge rent in the seat," watching plums drop off a tree in his back yard, as he prepared to paint the scene. Sadakichi had suffered a hemorrhage on his Indian reservation home, claiming he had survived a 60-hour seizure without water or any attention. He recovered at Decker's new home, reclining in a beach chair, listening to "The Dance of the Hours" on a portable radio, keeping time to the music with a fly swatter, claiming he was perhaps the only one in the world who could dance properly to it, and berating Fowler for not buying him a coffin.

John Barrymore was there, pretending to be aghast at Fowler's failure to provide a casket, hailing Sadakichi's slow death as "the work of a great professional." After Sadakichi wandered off, his friends looked for him and found the old man in the garage, seated behind a large gilt picture frame, as if to create a live portrait of himself.

At dinner, Sadakichi carved the beef, and responded to Barrymore's query as to the most beautiful words in the English language. "The words most beautiful to me are Sadakichi Hartmann," said Sadakichi Hartmann.

Then there was the late summer night that some of the gang decided to read aloud *Macbeth*. Sadakichi, of course, would star as Macbeth, Decker Lady Macbeth (W.C. Fields was Barrymore's choice, but he was home asleep), Barrymore was Macduff and Fleance, Roland Young was Banquo, Duncan and the Witches. Gene Fowler, cast by Barrymore in all the bit roles, protested that he'd rather be the audience. There was only one copy of the play at 419, so Karl Steuver, Barrymore's "keeper," embarked on what Fowler called "a midnight mission" to wake up neighbors and beseech copies of Shakespeare's allegedly cursed tragedy.

As Steuver banged on neighbors' doors, Decker amused the gang, dressing up in a top hat, a shawl Barrymore had worn in the silent film *Beau Brummel*, gluing fur to his chin, and playing Abraham Lincoln liberating the slaves. He followed up as Uriah Heep from *David Copperfield* (which must have especially amused Roland Young, who'd played that wormy role in MGM's 1935 film version) and, as a topper, put flour on his face, added wrinkles with crayon, and — *voila!* — became no less than Sadakichi Hartmann. Steuver, meanwhile, came back with two more copies.

"Perhaps you should play Lady Macbeth without the opera hat," Barrymore said to Decker, still in his Lincoln whiskers and flour-and-crayon face. "Unless, of course, you see her as the mannish type. And come to think of it, she was."

They prepared to bring the tragedy to life, Sadakichi performing a little dance. "Now," directed Decker, "let us turn to page 19."

Of course, page 19 in Decker's script was not the same page 19 in either Barrymore's script or Sadakichi's script. As Gene Fowler put it, "The Tower of Babel must have been exactly like this."

They stopped. Decker suddenly segued into a *non sequitur* tamper tantrum, demanding to know why Sadakichi never praised his "beautiful" art work. Sadakichi called him a caricaturist. Decker bellowed, Sadakichi cackled, Barrymore sang "Blow the Man Down," Decker's dogs barked furiously, the neighbors called the police…

Gene Fowler left with Roland Young in the latter's limo at 4 a.m. Dropping off Fowler at his home on Barrington, Young expressed it à la the Bard himself: "Decker, and not Macbeth, does murder sleep!"

On September 15, 1940, the *New York Times* published an interview with Gene Fowler, conducted in his Hollywood office. Fowler spoke of his recent near-death in the car accident, how he had looked over his life and reviewed what he should and shouldn't have done:

> And I decided that the great waste had been the time I had put in writing things that I didn't want to write. The time gained was that time that I'd spent writing to suit myself. And I like to write books. The last one, *Illusion in Java*, cost me 18 months of work, $25,000 in travel expenses and contracts for $90,000 worth of movie work that I turned down. It brought me in just two weeks' salary — $4,000.

Also in September, Decker, Gene Fowler and his son Will, concerned about Barrymore's increasing misery with Elaine, kidnapped him from the Bellagio Road house in Bel Air that the couple shared and took him back to Bella Vista. On September 23, Barrymore filed once again for divorce, claiming Elaine had caused him "grievous mental suffering and great bodily injury"— not specifying the nature of the latter. His lawyer also secured a court order to "protect" Barrymore from Elaine, restraining her from "harassing, annoying or interfering with the peace, quiet or personal freedom" of Barrymore and from "entering or attempting to enter the premises at No. 6 Tower Road."

On November 26, the divorce came through, dissolving the marriage of the 58-year-old Barrymore and 24-year-old Elaine. The fourth Mrs. Barrymore, described by the Associated Press as "smartly dressed and still wearing her wedding band and her 8 ½-carat diamond engagement ring," said in court that John had caused her a "great deal of anguish, sleeplessness and loss of weight." John, meanwhile, stayed safely in the office of his attorney.

John Barrymore had just launched a new career — as himself, mocking his image as a regular on Rudy Vallee's radio show. He was, in the words of the *New York Times*, "radio on a spree," and the steady salary held at bay his many besieging creditors.

Decker enjoyed telling the story of a "famed Russian sculptor" who visited him and Phyllis and Barrymore one evening at Bundy Drive. "We began drinking," relayed Decker:

> The Russian held up his drink and said, "Look how I drink. Yet, a couple years ago, I couldn't drink at all. It made a beast of me. I would get drunk and then I would beat and hit and slap my wife. Finally I went to a doctor. He operated on my ear and I've been fine ever since. I can drink gallons and never get wild. Barrymore, you should have an operation on your ear, too."
>
> We drank for ten more minutes in silence, and suddenly, after his seventh drink, the Russian let out a howl, bounded across the room and slugged his wife on the jaw with a right uppercut and beat her on the head. Then, at once, red-faced, he caught himself and turned apologetically to Barrymore.
>
> "You see," he gulped with fine restraint. "That's the way I used to be!"

Christmas Eve, 1940. Barrymore, John Decker and Gene Fowler paid a visit to W.C. Fields, who — even considering his hatred for Christmas — was in an epic foul mood. The director Gregory La Cava was there, and told the visitors that the Filipino houseboy of a neighboring woman had come to call. For a long time the woman had beseeched Fields to visit her, and the old misanthrope had steadfastly refused. The houseboy was so fervent this time that Fields actually went to the lady's house, only to suffer a shock. The lady's wish to meet W.C. Fields had been her *last* wish — she was

Barrymore on *The Rudy Vallee Show*

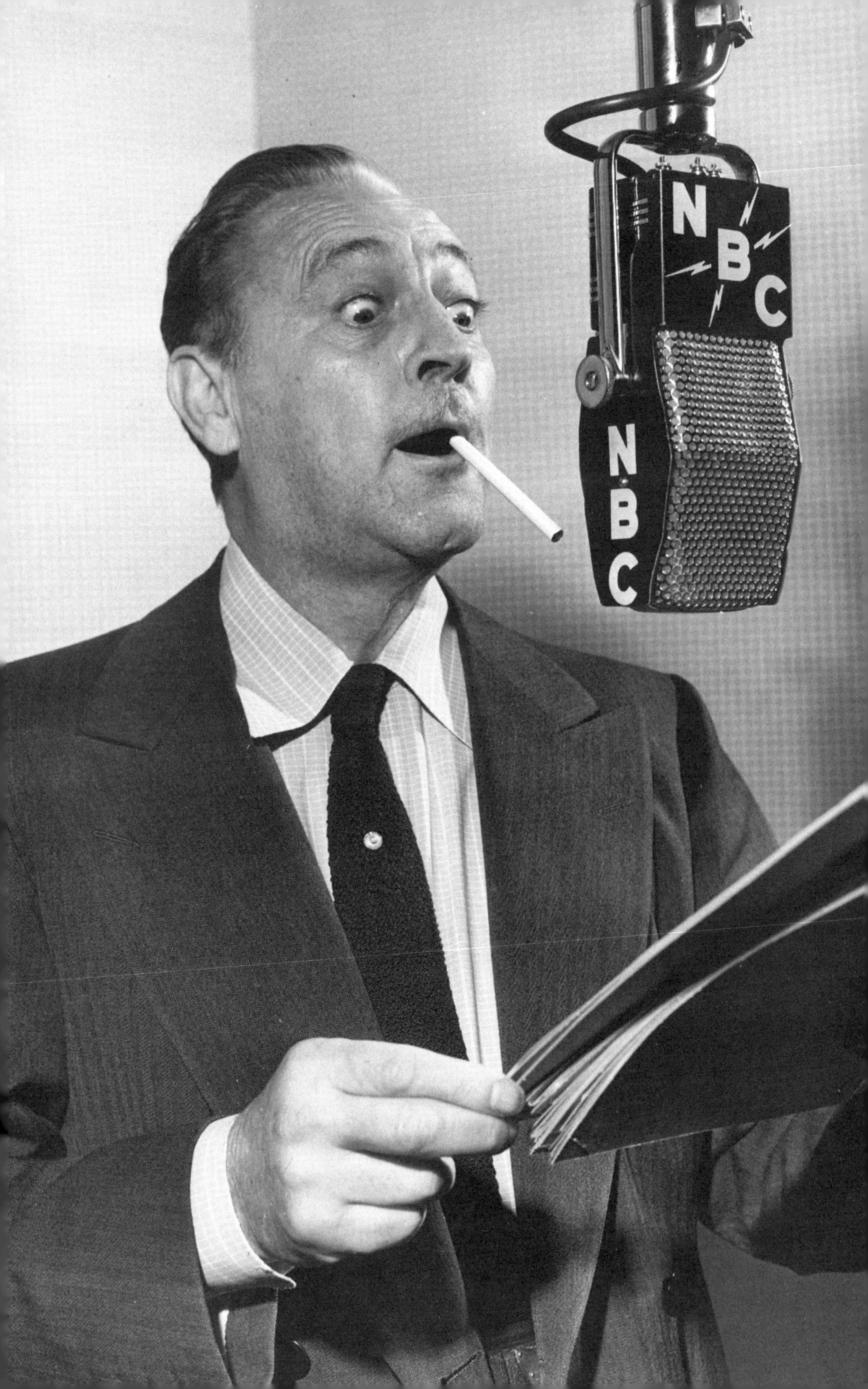
NBC
NBC

now dead, laid out in a coffin in her flower-filled parlor.

"I just don't like dead people!" ranted Fields.

"You don't even like live ones," said Gregory La Cava.

Decker and Barrymore took Fowler home, and returned to 419 N. Bundy to find that the congregated Yuletide celebrants had drained all the liquor. The host went out for more, and on the way home, a policeman pulled over Decker and saw the many bottles in the car. He took Decker into the station for a sobriety test. The doctor who checked him was a very short man.

"Do you think," asked the doctor, learning of Decker's profession, "that you would be able to paint a portrait of me in your present condition?"

"No," said John Decker. "I don't paint miniatures."

The fine was $300.

As always with the Bundy Drive Boys, the mask of comedy hung with the mask of tragedy.

As Anthony Quinn recalled, it was just after Barrymore's divorce that he had "one of the most beautiful moments I have ever experienced." The site was Bella Vista, and that night the gang sat in Barrymore's "dressing room" and talked of their favorite literary passages. "Everyone in that room had experienced success, except myself," wrote Quinn in *The Original Sin*, "and they all knew the emptiness of success without love." Decker recited Baudelaire. Roland Young delivered Shakespeare. Fields pantomimed.

"But it was all sad in a way," wrote Quinn, "because they were negating love."

Barrymore recited from T.S. Eliot:

No! I am not Prince Hamlet, nor was meant to be;
Am an attendant lord, one that will do
To swell a progress, start a scene or two…
At times, indeed, almost ridiculous —
Almost, at times, the Fool.

Quinn was shocked to see what Barrymore felt about himself. He had not yet recited, and the Bundy Boys began clapping in rhythm, goading him to perform. "Barrymore looked at me as if to say: Have the courage to stand up among these monsters," remembered Quinn, and he recited the Gettysburg Address for what he called "the most frightening audience I have ever faced."

"Oh shit," said Decker, while Fields, as Quinn put it, "made some derisive gesture as if I had just spoken about the Holy Trinity at a Jewish wedding." But Barrymore was crying.

"The only trouble is that the little shit believes it; he *believes* in those fucking words," said Barrymore. The room hushed.

"Well, kid, I hope they don't disillusion you," said the very disillusioned John Barrymore.

Anthony Quinn recalled that his wife Katherine didn't approve of his friendship with the Bundy Drive Boys — indeed, few of the wives of these men admired the gang. The drinking, the cynicism, the self-destructiveness — all were actually frightening in a colony which was already frightening in so many ways.

Jupiter and Saturn traveling together
April 1941

SADAKICHI HARTMANN
P. O. BOX 2
BANNING, CALIFORNIA

Dear Gene Fowler, either you are very sick or I have an idea that you are dead and that I was not informed of the flight - think of it my biographer's funeral and I not knowing anything about it. Well, anyway that relieves you from writing the biography !

If still alive, really do you not share my opinion that it is rather futile to write the biography of a pauper ? a pauper who has accomplished nothing what interests ordinary folks ????
    Anyway I feel like a pauper these days always get mad when I have no cigars - and the larder is empty too, no tea, no bread, butter in fact nothing but oatmeal and potatoes and not enough wood to cook them. And it rained like hell all the time.
    Life at my age is not worth living in such dis_comfort. If one is dead those things don matter, and if one is alive one is half dead anyway there is'nt so much difference.
    Well write to me at your leisure but dont wait too long - Decker has'nt committed suicide yet, expecting that too. I must say a cheerful letter this

Sadakichi Hartmann

Chapter Fourteen
1941: A Match for "All the Tribes of Hell"

Thus went Sadakichi's letter from Banning in the spring of 1941, a colorful and in some ways deeply tragic year for the Bundy Drive Boys.

As Gene Fowler admitted, John Decker was suicidal, vowing "to hang himself from one of the brown crossbeams of his studio." Instead, Decker poured his torment into a new painting: *The Royal Vagabond*, based on a still of John Barrymore in clown makeup from 1927's *The Beloved Rogue*. Barrymore, naturally, had made himself a rather creepy clown, but Decker embellished the grotesquerie. The satanic merrymaker with a tiny top hat and a cabbage head atop his scepter now smiled wickedly at the Bundy Drive studio, and rather than take his own life, Decker had created a new masterpiece.

The Bundy Drive Boys hailed *The Royal Vagabond* as Decker's latest triumph, and Phyllis—with a certain reluctance, based on her expression—agreed to pose for a photograph beside it. The surviving photo is striking, for the Barrymore clown seems to be eyeing and leering at the lovely blonde lady who shares the photo. "Everybody wanted to fuck Phyllis," recalls Phil Rhodes.

John Barrymore's films had descended a long way from the epic magnitude of *The Beloved Rogue*. January of '41 saw the release of Universal's *The Invisible Woman*, with John as a comic mad scientist, performing a grand lampoon of Lionel. Later in the year came Paramount's *World Premiere*, a pale shadow of *Twentieth Century*, with Barrymore as Duncan DeGrasse, head of Miracle Pictures ("If It's a Good Picture, It's a Miracle").

As David Carradine tells the story, it was during the filming of one of Barrymore's final films — he isn't sure which one — that the producers came up with a novel idea to keep him sober for shooting. They engaged a dazzling hooker, arranged for her to entertain Barrymore at a cabin in the Malibu mountains for the weekend, and directed her to provide him with all variety of sex — just keep him away from alcohol so he'd be able to work Monday morning. Friday night in the mountain cabin, Barrymore told the lady he was into bondage and asked if he might tie her up. Once he did, he got in the car, drove 30 miles back to Hollywood and hit the bars. Sunday night, a producer saw Barrymore at a watering hole — the actor's short-term memory had wiped away any recall of his obliging prostitute. The producer sped out to the cabin in Malibu, where he found the outfoxed hooker still tightly bound, and shrieking colorful profanities.

Anthony Quinn, fiercely ambitious, had moved to 2045 DeMille Drive in Los Feliz, near the homes of his father-in-law Cecil B. DeMille and Bundy Drive Boy crony W.C. Fields.

Anthony Quinn was at 20th Century-Fox, working on *Blood and Sand* as Tyrone Power's rival in the ring and boudoir. Quinn's wife Katherine had gone to a beauty salon and a dressmaker to prepare for a screen test. While they were away on this Ides of March, their two-and-a-half-year-old son Christopher escaped the attention of his nurse and wandered outside the house. The blond boy managed to toddle down the hill to the W.C. Fields estate where he saw a toy sailboat floating in the fish pond. Police later assumed the sailboat had attracted the delighted child, who played with it on the water until a breeze blew it beyond his reach. When Christopher tried to retrieve the boat, he lost his balance, fell into the pond, and drowned.

Realizing the child was missing, the nurse called the police. An hour search ensued until DeMille's gardener, Frank Richards, saw the white shirt of the boy in the pond. The Fire Department rescue squad, headed by Chief Ralph Watson, raced to the site and worked for two hours trying to revive the child.

The *Los Angeles Times*, reporting the tragedy the next day (with a photograph of the sailboat in the pond), noted that Katherine could not be reached at the time of the drowning. But Anthony Quinn was:

> The father... was not spared the crushing blow. For friends reached him by telephone at the studio and he rushed to the boy's side in time to see a doctor place his stethoscope in his pocket, shake his head and turn away.
> "He is dead."
> The words stunned Quinn, who stood speechless. Then the 180-pound actor fell on his knees, his body shaking violently as he sobbed.

"God, how I worshipped that boy!" Quinn wrote in his 1995 memoir, *One Man Tango*. He wrote he had never spoken of Christopher's death in over 50 years, even to therapists, but now in his book he recalled the horrible day:

> Some of the details I do not even remember. Others are etched into my every waking moment... When they came to get me I thought it a cruel hoax. No! To my own son? No! I lashed out, vowing to kill the fucking nanny we had hired to look after him. I would kill her with my own hands. I would see her deported, or fired, or left to suffer the way she had left us to suffer. I screamed for revenge.

Cecil DeMille had come to the scene, watching the resuscitation efforts with tears in his eyes. After the boy was pronounced dead, his grandfather, according to the *Los Angeles Times*, "reached under the blue blankets which were placed over the body and took the boy's head in his hands."

Quinn raged, and then he shut down. His denial was so complete that he didn't go to Christopher's funeral and admitted in *One Man Tango* that he had never been to the cemetery, Hollywood Forever, where Christopher Quinn is buried below a flat marker a few yards away from the lakeside mausoleum of Cecil B. DeMille and his wife. Quinn (who fathered many more children) wrote that, over the years, he had created an entire mythos for his late son — that Christopher was a San Francisco architect, married with children of his own.

Katherine — as Quinn wrote — was "never the same." Quinn's Bundy Drive friends offered their condolences, but Quinn would not accept them. Most devastated of all the friends was W.C. Fields, who had been away at the time of the accident but arrived home in time to witness the terrible scene of grief. According to James Curtis's *W.C. Fields: A Biography*, "the image of the boy's lifeless body haunted him." A very drunk Fields told his friend Eddie Dowling at Romanoff's, "Imagine a little kid. Imagine him drowning in my pool," and that Fields saw Christopher Quinn's death as some sort of cosmic punishment—"I kind of feel it's because of some of the things I've done."

"I want to get out of this cesspool!" a distraught Fields suddenly exclaimed in the midst of Romanoff's, and as Dowling remembered, "he gets up and he screeches and yells and carries on like mad, calling everybody names…"

W.C. Fields drained his fish pond and never refilled it. As Ronald J. Fields says:

> Magda Michael, my grandfather's secretary, remembered that he kept rose bushes. When he left DeMille Drive, the last thing W.C. did was cut off one of the roses and toss it into the empty pond.

If a residue of bitterness added itself to Anthony Quinn's characteristic rage after Christopher's death, he found comfort and amusement via his friends at Bundy Drive. John Barrymore's sardonic spirit was especially inspiring.

One of Quinn's favorite sagas involved the night he accompanied John Decker, Gene Fowler and Barrymore — shortly before the latter's 1942 death — to Earl Carroll's nightclub in Hollywood. Barrymore was almost denied admittance due to not wearing a tie, and borrowed one from the nightclub captain. As the foursome sipped champagne down front by the stage, a spotlight suddenly hit the table and the M.C., announcing a surprise, lured the ailing Barrymore to the stage.

"Mr. Barrymore," smiled the M.C., "the highest honor we can pay you is to let you dance a waltz with the most beautiful Earl Carroll girl."

The girl made her entrance — described by Quinn as "one of the ugliest, most clownish apparitions ever seen," complete with blacked-out teeth and fright wig. The audience howled with laughter.

Barrymore whispered something to his partner. She looked startled, stopped the clowning, straightened, and the waltz began. "She was transformed," recalled Quinn, and she danced elegantly, as if Barrymore in his old role of Svengali, had hypnotized her. As the "strange, macabre dance" continued, the audience sensed the magic — as Quinn remembered, "It was like watching something terribly personal happening before your eyes."

The waltz ended, Barrymore kissed the lady's hand, and she walked proudly into the wings. Barrymore moved to the microphone.

"And as for you, ladies and gentlemen," said John Barrymore, "you can all go fuck yourselves."

Following a brief stunned silence, the crowd — having witnessed a Barrymore miracle — stood and cheered the man who had cursed them.

Thomas Mitchell may very well have been enjoying his "Rembrandt" at his Hollywood home, but 1941 was a near-fatal year for him. On April 21, Mitchell, playing Daniel Webster in RKO's *The Devil and Daniel Webster*, was in a terrible accident as the buggy in which he was riding overturned. Mitchell suffered a concussion, and there was concern he might not survive. In time, Mitchell recovered, but not fast enough for RKO — the studio replaced him with Edward Arnold. (The sharp-eyed can still glimpse Mitchell in some of *The Devil and Daniel Webster's* long shots.)

Throughout 1941, John Barrymore continued as a regular on Rudy Vallee's radio show. Lionel, whose own financial situation was ever precarious despite his MGM contract, sometimes joined the hilarity as Vallee goaded on their insult volleys. From the May 1, 1941 broadcast:

> Vallee: Lionel, they call your brother the Great Profile. What do they call you?
> Lionel: Nearest responsible relative who owns property!

This particular show climaxed with a ghost from the past—John's Richard III, in a scene with Lionel as the Duke of Clarence. They played it sincerely and powerfully; John's cackling "Crookback" still sent a chill up the spine, and the audience gave the Barrymore brothers an ovation.

In May, 1941, John tested for the role of Sheridan Whiteside in the film of the Broadway hit *The Man Who Came to Dinner*. The screen test survives, showing John playing the acerbic Whiteside in a wheelchair, with different hairstyles and dialogue selections. Lee Patrick (who in 1941 played Bogart's girl Friday in *The Maltese Falcon*) appears in the test with Barrymore, who delivers his dialogue from the now always-present blackboards.

"I may vomit," announces Barrymore, intoning Whiteside's opening stage line (cut from the film) with all his sardonic charm. Bette Davis, set for the female lead, begged

Jack Warner to cast Barrymore. But the actor's reputation had preceded him, the blackboards were a nuisance, and risks too high. After testing such candidates as Fredric March, Charles Laughton and Laird Cregar, Warner signed Monty Woolley, who'd created the role of Sheridan Whiteside on Broadway.

A postscript on *The Man Who Came to Dinner* and the aforementioned Laird Cregar: the 6'3", 300-lb. Cregar had triumphed on the Los Angeles stage in *Oscar Wilde* in 1940, winning a 20th Century-Fox contract and scoring in such 1941 films as *Blood and Sand* and *I Wake Up Screaming*. Barrymore had seen *Oscar Wilde* and in the fall of 1941 attended an L.A. revival of *The Man Who Came to Dinner*, in which Cregar played Whiteside. Barrymore hadn't met Cregar personally, but he wrote the young actor a fan letter on his personal stationery, with his coat-of-arms crowned serpent:

> Laird — my Boy —
>
> I've said it to the Masquers, and there is no possible reason why I shouldn't repeat it to you — I may jest about the absurdities of life, but Acting is a sacred subject to me and I say this in deadly earnestness:
>
> You are one of the truly great young actors our stage has produced in the last ten years.
>
> I have watched with vast enjoyment your work in Oscar Wilde — and The Man Who Came to Dinner and saw with delight and humility — the quality that makes great actors.
>
> Believe me
> Most sincerely
> John Barrymore

Laird Cregar was overjoyed. He decided to host a dinner party for Barrymore, hiring a caterer, inviting guests and engaging his mother to be hostess. Come the night of the party, Barrymore failed to show up. The food was ready. The waiting and hungry guests were drinking too heavily. Cregar was in a panic. Then, very late, John Barrymore at last arrived — completely plastered. The host was too awed to speak, and Mrs. Cregar took matters into her own hands.

"Oh, Mr. Barrymore!" she exclaimed, soon turning the attention to her son and escorting Barrymore across the room to meet him. "My son Laird so appreciated your letter. His studio is so impressed with his work — they all think he's going to be a major star. I know you two have never actually met, so let me introduce you both. Mr. Barrymore, this is my son, Laird Cregar. What do you think?"

The 5'9" drunken Barrymore looked up and up at the towering, 300-pound giant smiling before him, and shook his head in wonderment.

"Madame," said Barrymore, "that must have been some fuck!"

The joke had its dark side. Cregar was so upset by the evening that he could be heard sobbing in his dressing room at the studio the next day. Best remembered as Jack the Ripper in *The Lodger* (1944), the young actor — an unhappy homosexual, fearful of becoming typecast as a hulking villain and plagued by his own demons — underwent a merciless diet that reduced him by 100 pounds and resulted in a fatal heart attack December 9, 1944. He was only 31 years old.

Gene Fowler, having racked up another writing credit via MGM's 1941 picture *Billy the Kid*, was 51 years old and at a crossroads. He took no joy in his screenwriting and wanted to write books. He considered a trip to Tahiti and meanwhile, sought the advice of John Barrymore.

"I am doing the work of a whore," said Barrymore sadly, citing his radio and cinema work, his salaries going to his creditors. He continued:

> There is nothing as sad in all the world as an old prostitute. I think that every artist somewhere along the line should know what it is to be one, a young one, but reform. Please, my friend, don't keep on working in pictures, where you most certainly don't find any real satisfaction. Get out now!

Gene Fowler sailed to Tahiti and never again labored as a screenwriter. (MGM's 1949 Wallace Beery vehicle *Big Jack* was a revamp of a project he'd fashioned in the early 1930s for W.C. Fields.)

After Fowler returned to L.A. in late June of 1941, he visited Bundy Drive to check up on his friends. Decker now had a pet parrot that roosted on his shoulder. It gave him the look of a pirate, and the bird was worthy of one, as Mary Lou remembers:

> The parrot hated mother [Phyllis] — it absolutely hated her, because it sat in its cage on a big coffee table and every morning mother drank her coffee, smoked her cigarettes and played solitaire. And the bird hated all that! At first nobody could get close to the cage to feed it — I'd have to try to push the food in with a broom handle.

Eventually the rapacious parrot took a peck at his master's eye, but missed, only to bite Decker's already broken nose — ripping away a morsel and warping his proboscis even more. Always the animal lover, Decker forgave the transgression.

Come Fowler's return, Decker prepared a celebratory meal of veal. "We have killed a fatted calf. Something appropriate to welcome home the prodigal son." Unfortunately, due to his diabetes, Decker couldn't savor a bite of the meal. Sadakichi Hartmann lambasted Fowler for forsaking his biography to enjoy "a pleasure cruise," while W.C. Fields opined that Fowler wasting his time on a book on Sadakichi would be akin to "digging your own grave with a quill."

"Hah!" cackled Sadakichi.

"Hah yourself!" volleyed W.C. "In fact, a double hah! And also drat!"

Errol Flynn had an eventful 1941. On May 31, his son Sean was born in Beverly Hills. As "Tiger Lil" gave birth, Flynn was sailing his yacht the *Sirocco*, "deliberately distancing himself from the happy event," wrote Errol and Sean Flynn biographer Jeffrey Meyers in his book *Inherited Risk*.

Fatherhood did nothing to tame the "magnificent specimen of the rampant male," as David Niven later described Errol Flynn. 1941's *Dive Bomber* would be his final film with Michael Curtiz. Flynn recalled why:

> I grabbed Mike by the throat and began strangling him. Two men tried to pry me off. They succeeded before I killed him. That was the end of our relationship. I deemed it wiser not to work with this highly artistic gentleman who aroused my worst instincts.

Raoul Walsh, mustached, eye-patched (a jackrabbit had crashed through his windshield one night in the desert, causing the loss of his right eye), and fated to become one of Flynn's most loyal pals, took over *They Died with Their Boots On*, starring Flynn as Custer. The cast also included Olivia de Havilland (as Mrs. Custer in her final film with Flynn) and Anthony Quinn as Crazy Horse.

The throttling of Curtiz certainly wasn't Flynn's only brawl of the year. In July of 1941, Flynn's beloved dog Arno died. His master had taken him on the *Sirocco*, where Arno delighted in leaping and snapping at the flying fish. In one of those leaps and snaps, Arno fell overboard and drowned.

Columnist Jimmie Fidler, meanwhile, had maneuvered himself onto Flynn's bad side, testifying before a Senate committee that Warners should never have made *Dive Bomber* (Fidler was an isolationist and resented British attempts to draw the U.S. into WWII). But the last straw came as Fidler denounced Flynn for not retrieving his dead, washed-up-to-shore Arno. Actually, Flynn couldn't bear to see his dead drowned dog, but in Fidler's words, the star "didn't even bother… that's how much he cared for him."

It was dangerous to accuse a Bundy Drive Boy of not caring for his pet.

Saturday night, September 22, 1941: Errol Flynn entered the Mocambo and saw Jimmie Fidler. The columnist, as Flynn recalled, tried to hide under his chair but Flynn caught him and KO'd him with one punch. The spectacle included Lupe Velez as a screaming cheerleader, exhorting Flynn "Geev it to heem, big boy!" and Fidler's wife, defending her husband by stabbing Flynn in the ear with a fork. Flynn later joked that Mrs. Fidler used the wrong fork — "a dreadful solecism."

FIDLER-FLYNN FRACAS TO BE AIRED BY JUDGE, headlined the September 30, 1941 *Evening Herald-Express*, reporting:

> The session was called by Judge Cecil D. Holland of Beverly Hills Justice Court, to whom Fidler complained that Flynn had punched him in the face. Flynn, who declared Mrs. Fidler punctured his ear with a fork during the hostilities, denied he punched Fidler and said he only slapped him; that a slap is more of an insult in Ireland, where his forebears come from.

John Barrymore's consolation prize for losing a role in *The Man Who Came to Dinner* was RKO's *Playmates*. The top-billed star: Kay Kyser, "the old Professor" of radio's Kollege of Musical Knowledge. Barrymore's role: John Barrymore.

Playmates is surely his most whorish 94 minutes.

The scenario: Barrymore, strapped by debt, agrees to coach Kyser in Shakespeare to land a contract and avoid bankruptcy, jail or both. Lupe Velez played Barrymore's fiery ex-wife Carmen (sort of a south-of-the-border Elaine Barrie), Patsy Kelly acted his wisecracking agent Lulu, and the whole farrago climaxed with a "swing" version of *Romeo and Juliet*, as Velez chases Barrymore (in Shakespearean doublet and tights), yanking off his costume wig.

Barrymore cackles, shrieks, spits out coffee, clowns with "Ethelbert" (his padded tights, clearly based on the "symmetricals" he wore in the 1920s), gives an autograph to a pretty girl who thinks he's Adolphe Menjou, fights a sword duel with Kyser and performs a nightclub dance with old May Robson. There's even a Kay Kyser nightmare vignette, almost phantasmagoric, that must be seen to be believed — Kyser a matador, fighting a bull (two men in a suit) with a Barrymore head (complete with horns), as all the while Velez cheers and tosses roses.

Yet *Playmates'* most amazing moment comes as Barrymore first coaches Kyser (who laments that he himself reads Shakespeare "like a Ubangi"). Barrymore sits down, murmurs "It's been a long time," and doesn't require the blackboards as he begins:

To be, or not to be,
That is the question...

He recites the soliloquy beautifully — and the tears are pouring down his face. Barrymore of course could cry on cue ("It's not acting, it's crying!" he'd quip), but the tears appear all too real here. The sight of this fallen, weeping man, amidst all the silly cornpone and slapstick, is mesmerizingly tragic. Apparently even the irreverent Barrymore, at this stage of his life, couldn't shake the shadow of Shakespeare's lines about heartache and the fear of death, nor the horror of his own downfall.

He finally breaks off in a jarringly edited moment. "These tears taste like vodka," Barrymore joked after the camera stopped, trying to spare himself and the others embarrassment. Still, he'd given director David Butler and the company far more than they bargained for, and Barrymore's Hamlet recitation and tears bequeath a tragic and disturbing moment.

Steve Beasley, producer of the DVD documentary *Kay Kyser, The Ol' Professor of Swing!* shared a few anecdotes about *Playmates*:

> During a lunch break on the RKO lot, Kyser happened to walk past Barrymore's dressing room, where Barrymore was taking a nap on his couch with the door open. Kay could see there was a hole in the bottom of Barrymore's shoe, so he gently slipped it off, took it to the lot shoe repair, had it fixed and slipped it back on Barrymore's foot and never told Barrymore a thing about it.
>
> Also, one of Kyser's musicians told me that they were looking for Barrymore one afternoon to shoot a scene, and couldn't find him. Someone located Barrymore sitting in a cab on Gower Street, down the block from the studio, drinking with the cab door open.

Playmates was John Barrymore's final film.

Decker had been painting the murals — sketches of stars around the bar — for the gala premiere of the new Hollywood cabaret of John Murray Anderson, and his new stage show *Silver Screen*, "a musical glamorama of the movies," at the New Wilshire Bowl. It was Anderson who had engaged Decker to create the sets for *The Greenwich Village Follies of 1922*. Barrymore had been tagging along to ogle the chorus girls, and Decker feared another misadventure. Whenever Barrymore eyed a chorine too closely, Decker drew a mercilessly nasty caricature of the lady and showed it to Barrymore, who'd moan, "Hmm. I see what you mean."

As Phyllis Decker expressed it, "The girl was saved."

The Bundy Drive Boys appeared at the Anderson club opening in September, 1941. The star-studded evening was colorful — Barrymore proposed playfully to Mae West, and the two traded ribald zingers. W.C. Fields suggested they have a similar evening out "say in about 90 years," and Decker, Barrymore and Fowler returned to Bundy Drive — where, as Fowler recalled, Decker desperately poured out the story of his German birth. He was terrified that his ancestry would result again in incarceration these war days and the nightmares of the Isle of Man came back more horribly than ever.

On October 10, 1941, Universal released *Never Give a Sucker an Even Break*, W.C. Fields' trouble-plagued star vehicle. The film (its title lifted from *Poppy*) features Fields as the "Great Man," with the ideal fantasy daughter in Universal starlet Gloria Jean. As Ms. Jean told Gregory Lewis in *Films in Review* (November, 1973):

> After working with Mr. Fields, I always remembered the color of his nose. It was like a multicolored popsicle. It's said he didn't like children, but he tried to get along with me. I do recall I annoyed him when I tried to offer him something to eat. He liked what was in his glass better! All in all, working with him was a great experience.

The framework found W.C. trying to sell a story to "Esoteric Studios" producer Franklin Pangborn. Playing Pangborn's secretary, Carlotta Monti spews her wrath at some anonymous male:

> Carlotta: You big hoddy-doddy! You smoke cigars all day and drink whiskey half the night! Someday you'll drown in a vat of whiskey!
> W.C.: Drown in a vat of whiskey... Death, where is thy sting?

As Danny Peary writes of *Never Give a Sucker an Even Break*:

> It's the film where the surrealistic nature of Fields' comedy is most evident. Fields plays himself... he leaps from an airplane to retrieve his whiskey bottle and falls thousands of feet before landing safely on rich Margaret Dumont's mountaintop estate, where she lives with her pretty young daughter (to whom he teaches "Post Office"), a gorilla, and Great Danes with fangs....

"He didn't get that nose from playing ping-pong," says the grand Madame Dumont, the Marx Brothers' famous stooge, of W.C. in *Never Give a Sucker an Even Break*. The film suffered pre-shoot censorship trouble (W.C. tells the audience a scene in an ice cream parlor was supposed to take place in a saloon), as well as a major cut — the death of Gorgeous, the trapeze artist (played by the sad-eyed Anne Nagel). Once again, W.C. had hoped for a depth in the film that the studio wasn't prepared to allow. Still, *Never Give a Sucker an Even Break* is erratic but personal to its star — and it was the last film in which W.C. Fields starred. His remaining films would offer him only specialty acts. The *Christian Science Monitor* cared little for *Never Give a Sucker an Even Break* and the star fired off this letter to the *Monitor*, dated February 7, 1942:

> Dear Editor:
> On January the 28th in the Year of our Lord 1942, The Christian Science Monitor printed:
> "Never Give a Sucker an Even Break: W.C. Fields acting out a story with results that are by turns ludicrous, tedious and distasteful. There is the usual atmosphere of befuddled alcoholism."
> If the chosen people decide that The Christian Science Monitor is expressing the thoughts of the majority of the people in the United States, it is possible they would bar me from their studios and bar my pictures from their theatres, which would force me into the newspaper business. And if I used your tactics I might say:
> "The Christian Science Monitor: Day in and day out the same old bromides. They no longer look for love or beauty but see so many sordid things that Mary Baker Eddy did not see in this beautiful world she discovered after trying her hand at mesmerism, hypnotism, and spiritualism before landing on the lucrative Christian Science racket."
> When I play in a picture in which I take a few nips to get a laugh (I have never played a drunkard in my life) I hope that it might bring to mind the anec-

dote of Jesus turning water into wine.

And wouldn't it be terrible if I quoted some reliable statistics which prove that more people are driven insane through religious hysteria than by drinking alcohol.

Yours very truly.
A subscriber,
W.C. Fields

Late in 1941, Errol Flynn began building his famous "Mulholland Farm," 7740 Mulholland Drive, with its spectacular view of the San Fernando Valley and a master bed with a mirror in the ceiling. According to Charles Higham, "The house bristled with sexual jokes. On Flynn's instructions, John Decker designed an obscene mural for the fish tanks which ran high along the walls of the first-floor den: the painted fish behind the real ones boasted enormous pendulous testicles."

Flynn hosted cockfights at Mulholland Farm. There were plenty of other animals, too — dogs, cats, lambs, horses, and Flynn's monkey Chico. The door was always open to John Barrymore, who loved the zoo.

It was in November of 1941 that John Barrymore, apparently desperately lonely, took a desperately lonely final stab at a reunion with Elaine. She had sent him flowers during his latest hospital stay, and now he desired a reconciliation.

He restored Elaine's picture to a silver frame, prepared a formal dinner, ordered wine and flowers. Still almost touchingly vain despite his self-mockery, he cleaned up, and put on his girdle and formal dress. Finally, he barred the gates of Tower Road from the Bundy Drive Boys who, as he accurately predicted, had planned to crash the lovefest.

Fowler, Decker and various members waited at the brothel of 300-lb. prostitute Jane Jones, where Nishi telephoned them half-hour bulletins.

Elaine never showed.

Come midnight, Nishi called that Barrymore was violently raging: "The Monster" had gone mad. He ripped Elaine's picture from the frame, threw the flowers into the fire and drank all the wine himself. The last call from Nishi came at 2 a.m. as the Monster still roared about Bella Vista — "King Lear was declaiming on the Heath," as Gene Fowler put it.

The rage lasted for some days and nights and climaxed with a violent desecration. Barrymore had illustrated his second wife Michael Strange's 1921 book of poems, *Res-*

urrecting Life. The color frontispiece showed Barrymore's painting of a divine female, naked and beatific, rising toward a golden, flower-circled chalice, ascending above fallen males caught in the tendrils of horrific monsters. He had saved the original painting at Bella Vista, and if it was Barrymore's tribute to the superiority of womanhood, he now thought better of it. As Gene Fowler watched, Barrymore bitterly painted over the ascending woman, obliterating her and replacing her with a rapacious, nightmarish, predatory male bird, beak sharp and wings outstretched.

For the Bundy Drive Boys, 1941 climaxed on Friday night, November 21, 1941, as the Frank Peris Gallery hosted John Decker's new art show. As Bill Wickersham wrote in his "Hollywood Parade" column:

> Among the celebrated Hollywoodites rarely seen at social events, Lionel Barrymore and Joel McCrea are second only to Garbo. But, indicating John Decker's popularity and the great admiration with which the film colony regards his artistry, both actors attended the cocktail party and private preview of the Decker exhibition at the Frank Peris Gallery.
>
> In fact, the event provided a veritable field day for autograph seekers and, aside from the superb exhibit, it became one of the gayest parties of the month for the illustrious guests.

Phyllis was there, as was Hedy Lamar, Charles Boyer, Gloria Vanderbilt, Charles Laughton, Fannie Brice, Lionel Atwill, Reginald Gardiner and almost the whole Bundy gang: John Barrymore, W.C. Fields, Thomas Mitchell, John Carradine, Gene Fowler, Ben Hecht, Roland Young, Sadakichi Hartmann, and Alan Mowbray — his wife Lorayne "looking as colorful as a Decker canvas herself" (wrote Wickersham) in a Kelly green suit and hat with "dashing red gloves." Mowbray told a reporter: "Pshaw, this isn't a representative Decker exhibit. Why, there are only 20 paintings and I have 24 Deckers hanging in my house alone!"

Entertaining at the party: John Carradine performed for the guests— à la John Barrymore — Gene Fowler poems such as "The Cowboy's Lament:"

> O! Bessie Bond, the vicious courtesan,
> 'Twas she who wrecked the noble Ku Klux Klan.
> Each knight who flipped her garter
> Became a crippled martyr —
> Oh! God-Damn old Bessie Bond, the courtesan!

And, of course, "The Testament of a Dying Ham":

> To the poseurs who simulate talent —
> The nances, the Lesbian corps,
> The cultists, the faddists, the blustering sadists,
> The slime of the celluloid shore...

Carradine's Barrymore impression was a remarkable show, and as Bill Wickersham reported, "His most delighted listeners were John and Lionel Barrymore."

There was, of course, mockery of Hollywood in Carradine's mad mimicry, Fowler's sardonic verse and Decker's brilliant art — but if the guests realized it, they didn't mind. It was a raucous, wonderful night. Flowing liquor. Beautiful, laughing women. Famous, admiring men. Striking art. A smiling, triumphant artist.

John Decker had fully and officially arrived in Hollywood — just in time for World War II.

December 7, 1941: Pearl Harbor. Most of the Bundy Drive gang, of course, were too old to be soldiers.

Errol Flynn, the prime specimen, was also 4-F, due to an early bout with malaria and a touch of tuberculosis — a considerable embarrassment to Warner Bros. and to Flynn himself. John Carradine, 35 at the time, very much wanted to fight, but was rejected (according to son David) due to his teeth. "I'm not planning to *bite* the Japs!" protested Carradine, who sailed his yacht *Bali* as part of the coastal patrol.

The youngest Bundy Drive Boy — Anthony Quinn, 26 at the time of Pearl Harbor — was not a U.S. citizen (he became one in 1947) and hence was exempt from the draft.

Home Defense called for any man under 60 to sign up, and the Santa Monica registration site had a surprise one day when in came 59-year-old John Barrymore (wracked by alcoholism and a repertory company of ailments), 51-year-old Gene Fowler (who had cardiac trouble and still walked with a stick two years after his near-death car accident), 45-year-old John Decker (gaunt from his diabetes) and 61-year-old W.C. Fields (prepared to lie about his age). W.C. was especially picturesque — looking "like the wrath of John Barleycorn," as Fowler put it — complete with a wad of cornplaster on his bulbous nose after it had blistered and exploded during a fishing trip to Catalina. The "sweet-faced young woman" who handled registration eyed this incredibly motley crew.

"Gentlemen, who sent you?" she asked. "The enemy?"

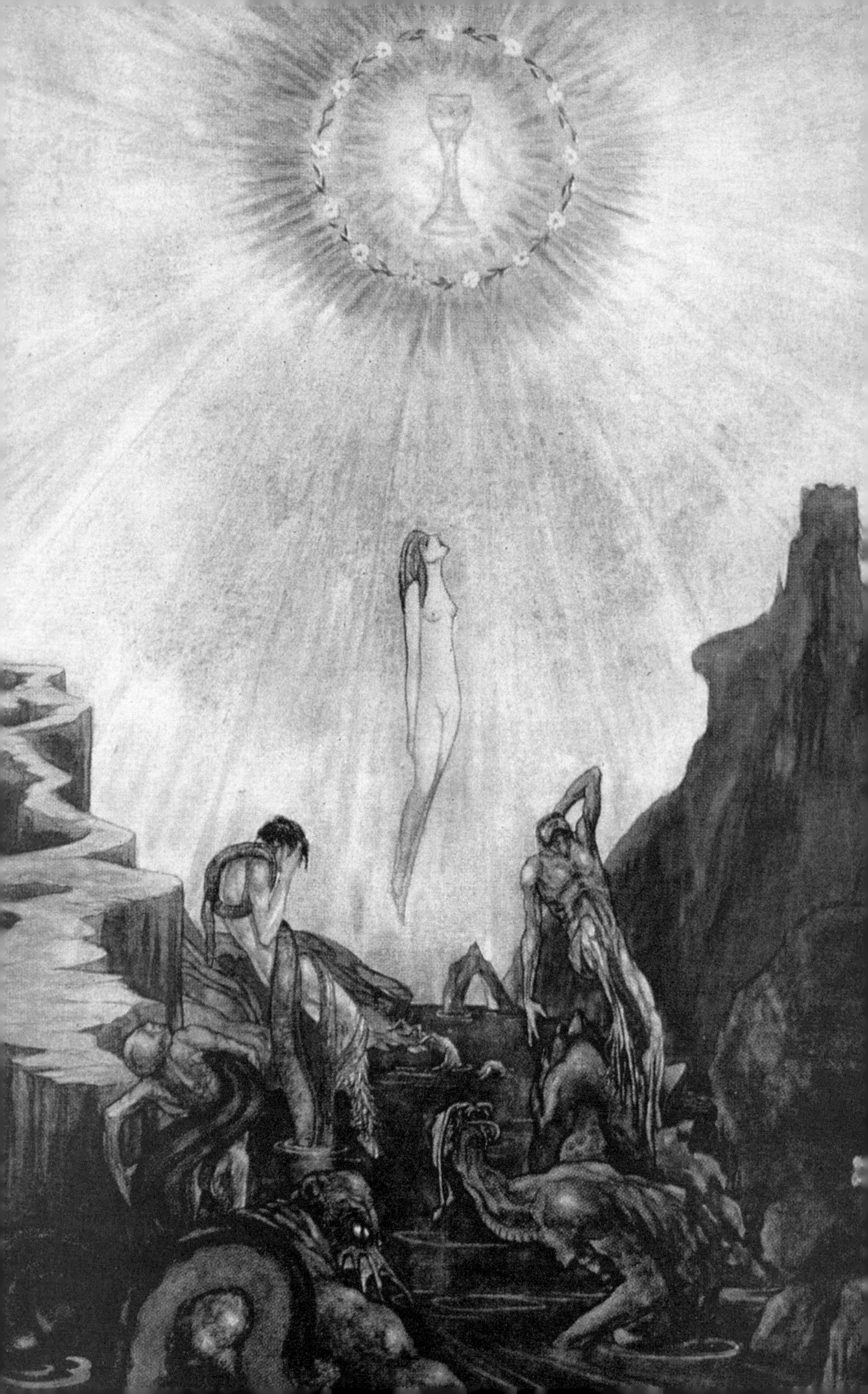

Chapter Fifteen
The Death of John Barrymore

> I direct my executors to take all necessary steps and for this purpose to employ such doctors or other skilled persons as they may think proper and to pay any bills incurred by anyone otherwise interested in any way whatsoever and to cooperate fully with any such person who may wish to do so for the purpose of ascertaining that I am in fact dead and not in any other state having the semblance of death, in order so far as possible to avoid all risk of my being buried alive...
> —From the Last Will and Testament of John Barrymore, December 30, 1941

John Decker's deathbed sketch of John Barrymore is perhaps his most famous work, and likely his most heartfelt. Magnificent and nightmarish, it evokes a fallen god, or ravaged demon. The sketch (originally done on brown wrapping paper) captures, naturally, Barrymore's left profile, but Decker also does magical things with the one mad, visible eye, almost rolled up into the head, the shadows so black as to seem the garish makeup of a whore, and seemingly glaring defiantly at the heavens.

Yet perhaps the most startling thing about the deathbed sketch is Barrymore's right hand, resting below his chest. The actor had despised his stubby, ungraceful hands, and Decker makes a monster of the hand, as if it's some awful deep sea creature... or a spider, grossly parasitic, horribly vigilant on the dying man's torso and impatient to

Barrymore painting praising the spiritual ascendancy of women
that he later destroyed in an Elaine-inspired fit

gobble up the corpse. One remembers the vignette in the 1920 *Dr. Jekyll and Mr. Hyde* in which a giant spider crawls up into Jekyll's bed, evaporates into him, and causes Jekyll to awake as Hyde. Barrymore's hand in the Death Bed sketch chillingly reminds one of that spectral spider, no longer playing a symbolic Hyde, but Death itself.

By 1942, "Mad Jack," AKA "The Monster," was free-falling into either the snake pit or the grave.

His film career was over, his personal life was in ruins and his Hollywood reputation that of a fun-house mirror grotesque. The cinema colony now noted him less for his Hamlet, more for his prodigious pissing in public. His fear of ending his days and nights in an asylum à la his goat-suckled father was now merciless.

It was the compassionate Gene Fowler who tried to allay his friend's deepest fear. Fowler pointed out, cynically but truthfully, that a crazy man with no money was likely heading for the psycho ward, but a crazy man earning $2,000 a week, as Barrymore continued to do via his raucous weekly humiliations on *The Rudy Vallee Show*, was safe. His creditors simply couldn't afford to surrender him. Of course, Fowler, with his love for Barrymore, tried to persuade him that, whatever the situation, he personally would never allow his friend to suffer what had always promised to be the climax of his lifelong torment.

Yet the fear wouldn't go away. It had been haunting him for too many years. The self-destruction continued. As Barrymore told John Carradine, he wasn't a good enough Catholic to go to Mass every Sunday, but he was too good a Catholic to commit suicide — at least instant suicide.

For a man whose greatest acting achievement and most agonizing personal torment lie rooted in incest — a new tragedy, masquerading as a blessing, came to enflame his final days and nights.

Diana Barrymore, with less self-ravaging genes, might have been a major star. Everything was slightly off in her packaging. She almost had a great "look"— the face and mane of a classical actress — but the jaw was too thick, the hair usually pinned up. She had an attractive figure — her slightly full hips and plump legs were typical of the ladies of the early 1940s, yet she photographed portly. She had talent, but the underplayed style of 1942 movies doused her fire, making her seem merely haughty and affected. The lady herself was immediately aware the camera wasn't in love with her at the preview of her first film, *Eagle Squadron*.

"… under Stanley Cortez's lighting magic," she remembered in her famed 1957 memoir *Too Much, Too Soon*, "my crooked nose remained crooked but a railing emerged as a work of art."

She had come to Hollywood for Universal Studios in January of 1942, following her success in Broadway's *The Land is Bright*. Bramwell Fletcher, "Little Billee" in 1931's *Svengali*, had proposed to her the day before she left for the West Coast, and Diana accepted. John was at the railroad station to greet her as she disembarked holding her puppy Moko.

"Are you going to be good?" Diana whispered into her father's ear as the press took pictures.

"Of course not," said Barrymore.

"Good," smiled Diana. "Neither am I."

During her first day in the movie colony, Diana drove with her famous father and Karl Steuver up to Bella Vista, which she described as "a castle out of a fairyland hanging from the crest of a precipitous mountain." It disturbed her, however, that Barrymore and Steuver were the only inhabitants of the "castle, aside from John's beloved afghan Viola. Diana was moved that Barrymore had been up all night preparing her room, filling it with fresh flowers. He'd also refilled the pool. She had not moved in (at least not yet); her mother, Michael Strange, perhaps sensing the debacle that would indeed eventually come, had forbidden her to stay with her father.

That evening, Diana met her first "Bundy Boy." Father and daughter dined at Romanoff's, and John Carradine came to the table, kissing Diana's cheek, she recalled, "with almost Victorian politeness." Diana wanted to meet her Uncle Lionel, and Carradine, in what Diana called his "ancient Packard," drove them out to the ranch in Chatsworth. Lionel received them upstairs in bed. They drank champagne, and John requested that Carradine recite "The Testament of a Dying Ham" for Lionel. Carradine "shot a glance at me," remembered Diana, "decided I didn't shock easily, and immediately launched into a long, ribald and enormously witty poem."

> To the wenches who trumped up a passion
> And held a first lien on my cot,
> To the simpering starlets and gleet-ridden harlots
> Whose sables were masking their rot…

Many in Hollywood considered Diana Barrymore "a simpering starlet," with only a flash of her father's talent and just enough of his madness to be a nuisance. She was in place for the fireworks and burlesque antics of John Barrymore's Last Act, a color-

The famous deathbed sketch by John Decker

ful featured player in the tragedy, with both father and daughter, despite an originally benign reunion, sadly inspiring the worst in each other.

In fact, there's some evidence that the sexual aberration that would drive them apart was reciprocal. Perhaps more memorable than any of her eminently forgettable movies was a candid shot taken of father and daughter together at this time. A voluptuous Diana, her hair loose, mouth sensual, perversely sits on her father's lap, arm around his shoulder, her cheek against his forehead, with a seeming sense of naughty awareness. Barrymore, his "fried egg" right profile to the camera, his face just above her breasts, sits sadly but smolderingly, the aged, debauched star — tormented most of his life by incestuous memories and urges — seemingly scenting a new temptation.

The reunion would end, as many had predicted, sadly and sordidly.

In 1942, Barrymore visited Errol Flynn's "Mulholland Farm," and stayed for a time. He also came and sojourned at John Carradine's house, 5433 Ben Avenue, on the outskirts of North Hollywood. Other times he crashed at Bundy Drive. It was truly Mad Jack's travelin' freak show now, and at each stop, he had the habit of pissing out the windows.

"He'll soil your best carpets and send women screaming out of the room!" lamented the usually unshockable Decker, who recalled a night at a hamburger stand where Barrymore, feeling passion for the waitress ("a blowsy bitch with a wart on her nose," quoth Decker), crawled after her over the counter, shrieking, "My last Duchess! Hoist your dresses, Madam, and let me see Epping Forest again!" As Decker put it, "We had to run for it."

Ben Hecht was in Hollywood again, working profitably on such 20th Century-Fox scripts as *Tales of Manhattan* and *The Black Swan*. He found Barrymore restlessly napping on the couch at 419 N. Bundy and shouting for the host. "Goddam your arsehole of a couch, Decker!" roared the awakened Barrymore. "This shambles of a couch is not fit for a pair of midgets to fuck on! Out of what swill barrel do you furnish your disgusting habitat?"

He fell back to sleep and Hecht proposed to Decker the idea of a spectacular Barrymore birthday party.

"In some sewer, I hope?" asked Decker.

The site was Hecht's expensive rented home, and the only way to get the major Hollywood names there was to be mysterious about the party's purpose. When word leaked about just who the guest of honor was, prior to his arrival, there was much grousing. "They'll crucify him!" warned Dr. Samuel Hirshfeld, the actor's physician. Decker, uncharacteristically cowed by the potential disaster of the night, had the job of delivering Barrymore to the party, and arrived "red and squinting with tension." Barrymore, in a tuxedo, appeared perfectly composed.

The night proceeded quietly, until Louis B. Mayer threw down the gauntlet. He taunted Barrymore about his bad behavior at MGM, noting that it surely had caught up with him. One wishes Barrymore had launched into a verse from "The Testament of a Dying Ham":

> To the mountebank clan of producers,
> Who hang their dull stars in the skies,
> Who rifle the pockets and gouge the eye-sockets,
> But never look higher than thighs…

Instead, rather than responding directly to the almighty Louis B., Barrymore talked of his pilgrimage to India — "Have you never in your life yearned to meet a saint?" he asked Mayer — and proceeded to reminisce about a Calcutta whorehouse, the *Kama Sutra* ("which

Diana and Daddy

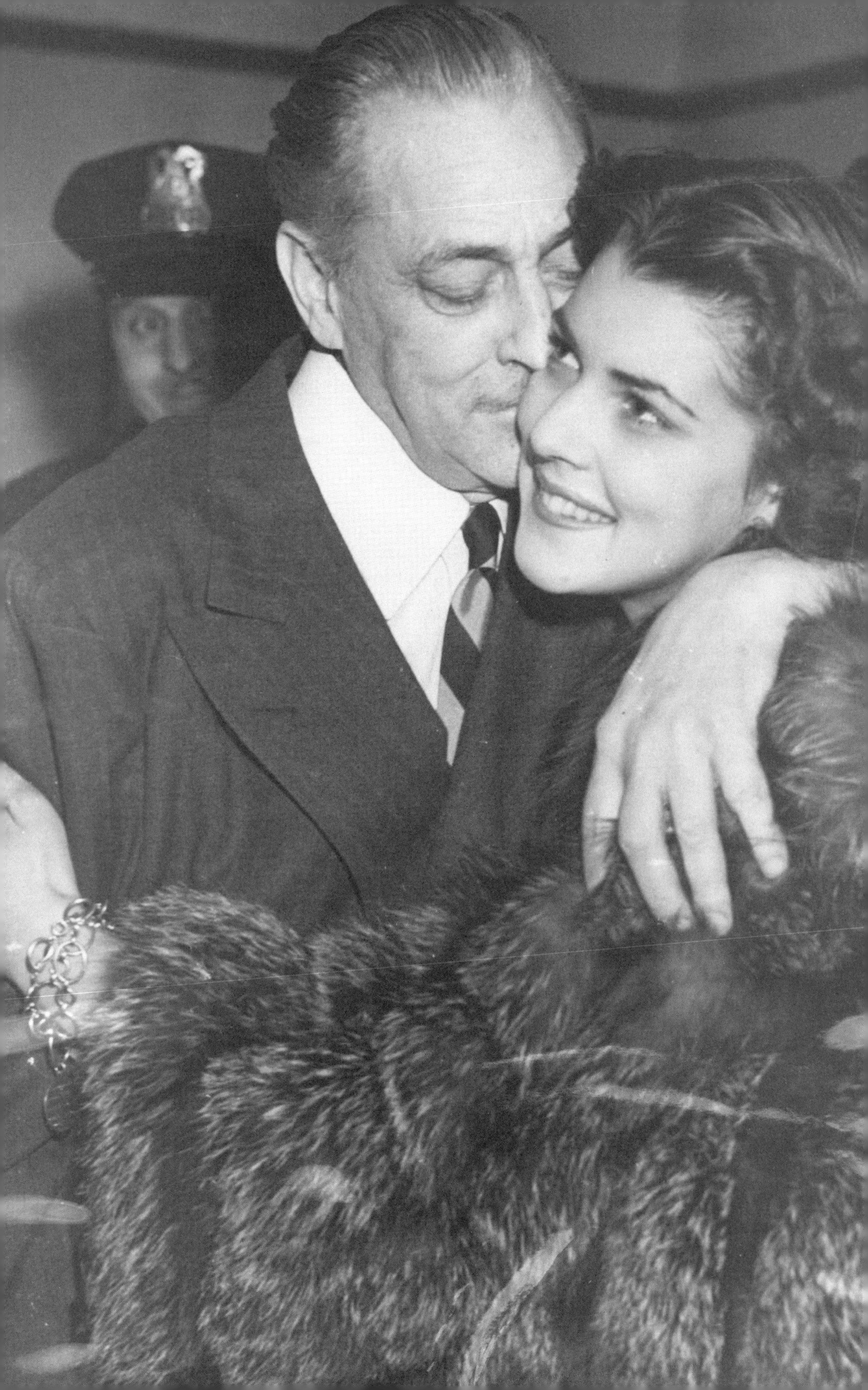

teaches that there are 39 different postures for the worship of DingleDangle — the God of Love"), and how he had opened in London as Hamlet drunk and besotted from an afternoon tryst, and, between soliloquies, vomited in the wings. All in all, the evening was a strikingly touching mix of spirituality and sordidness, intellect and irreverence that characterized John Barrymore. Mr. Hyde peeked out again, as Barrymore even took a shot at Decker:

> Yes, I was a triumph in London. I have never kept a scrapbook of my questionable activities as a man of grease paint. But there's one set of dramatic notices I have saved. I still have them, unless my good friend Decker here has sold them to keep himself in liquor.

As Ben Hecht wrote, "He glared at poor Decker, who was sharing his few desperately earned dollars with his idol." If it had been meant as joke, neither Decker, nor the assemblage, was laughing.

Barrymore spoke of "the foolishness of fame — and the lunacy of life in general — 'a song sung by an idiot running down the wind.'" Then he suddenly shut his eyes, and after a cold, unnerving silence, turned to Decker.

"You better take me off, Johnny," whispered Barrymore. "I've gone up in my lines."

John Decker and Ben Hecht helped him to his feet and escorted him from the room, one on each side, like guards. As Hecht wrote, "A few minutes later, the birthday cake with which I had refused to interrupt Barrymore's storytelling was brought in. Its many candles blazed like a triumphant row of footlights."

March 3, 1942 was Diana's 21st birthday. She had forgotten it, busy at Universal, but Barrymore remembered, inviting her to Bella Vista for dinner and celebration. Instead, he had Karl Steuver stop at Decker's. As Diana recalled in *Too Much, Too Soon:*

> John Decker, the artist, was one of Daddy's great friends; he looked like an aged, incredibly decrepit Adolphe Menjou. When we arrived at his house, I walked in to find a tree and a blown-up photograph of me and under it a cake with 21 candles! Daddy was like a little boy, so delighted with his surprise. "Well, Treepee?" he asked. "How do you like your cake?"
>
> "Oh Daddy," I said and cried. It was the first birthday my father had ever spent with me.

Barrymore was still a regular on Rudy Vallee's radio show, and father and daughter performed the balcony scene from *Romeo and Juliet* together. Lionel joined them March 5, 1942 for a scene from *Julius Caesar* — Jack as Brutus, Lionel as Caesar, Diana as Calpurnia. Diana encouraged her father to star with her in Emlyn Williams' *The Light of Heart* — he as a ravaged has-been matinee idol forced to play Santa Claus in a department store, she as his crippled daughter. Diana wanted to do it as a play, Barrymore as a film. There was no interest. "Treepee, you are going on to great things," said Barrymore. "I am already dead."

"I cried myself to sleep that night," remembered Diana, "the first time in Hollywood."

Learning Diana was engaged to Bramwell Fletcher, Barrymore personally invited him to come to Los Angeles, and put him up at Tower Road. Embarking on a camping trip to Mount Baldy, he even offered his bedroom to his daughter and her lover. As Diana remembered, 16 hours later, there came a pre-dawn pounding at the bedroom door, and Barrymore roaring, "You monsters! What are you doing in there? Get out!" When they unlocked the door, Barrymore said, "I forgot — I thought there were two other people in there."

"For all I knew, he had," said Diana. "You could never be sure with daddy."

On April 7, 1942, W.C. Fields wrote to Elise Cavanna, his loose-limbed partner in *The Dentist* sketch and short:

Dear Elise:
Pardon this long silence on my part. It was not due to remissness but I have been busy writing and performing in a sequence of *The Tales of Manhattan*. Then I got an infected great toe which the doctor says was due to kicking those Jews in the can over at Fox…

Tales of Manhattan, concerning a coat as a "hook" of various stories, starred Charles Boyer, Rita Hayworth, Henry Fonda, Charles Laughton, and Edward G. Robinson (who always wanted to be a Bundy Drive Boy, but was never admitted, according to Errol Flynn, because he took himself too seriously). Thomas Mitchell and Roland Young were in the film too, but come its release, *Tales of Manhattan* did not include W.C. Fields. 20th Century-Fox cut his skit (with Margaret Dumont and Phil Silvers) from the release print — possibly due to time consideration, possibly due to his battles with director Julien Duvivier, maybe both. The Fields sequence was restored a half-century later to the video release.

The day after Fields wrote his letter, April 8, Errol Flynn and Lili Damita finally divorced. "Tiger Lil," after seven years of ravaging Flynn's manhood and self-confidence, sashayed away with a bloodsucking financial settlement. Flynn carried on, starring in 1942 in *Desperate Journey* and *Gentleman Jim*, flashing his same old fuck-you smile. It gallantly and sensitively concealed the fact that the screen's great cavalier had been so hurt and reduced by his first wife and by his own mother.

There came the night at Tower Road that John Barrymore, as Diana helped him into his bed, asked his daughter to telephone a whore to come to the house. Diana protested. They fought.

"Don't be so goddamn finishing school, Miss!" snarled Barrymore.

Diana made the call. The whore came — "blonde and pretty," as Diana recalled. She had been there before and knew the way upstairs. Diana left and slammed the door. "How *could* he do that!" she ranted in *Too Much, Too Soon*. "How *could* he ask his own daughter! How could he!"

They were, as Diana put it, "strangers again." Then, two weeks later, Diana received an after-midnight call from John Decker.

"Your father's here. He's asking for you."

Diana had no affection for Decker. She drove to Bundy Drive, where a "bleakly silent" Decker stood at the fireplace. Paper, drawings and liquor bottles littered the table, where "two heavily made-up blondes," whom Diana regarded as "common as cat-meat," sat purring.

Barrymore, in a drunken stupor, sat on the sofa.

"You're supposed to be his friend," Diana scolded Decker. "You know he's not to have sex or liquor. Why do you get girls for him?"

"Well, as I live and breathe," wheezed Barrymore mockingly as Diana took his arm. "If it isn't Miss Newport."

He walked, Diana recalled, like a man going to his grave, and she got him in her car to drive him home. They drove silently in the after-midnight darkness up Tower Road, ascending to the ruins of Bella Vista. Diana had once considered it "a fairy tale castle," but now virtually everything about it was dark and sinister. The accursed totem pole loomed in the night (on a recent visit, Decker had noted a raven roosting in its top head). The now-mocking stained glass window of an angelic John and Dolores, the unkept aviary with its stuffed animals and crocodile… everything about the site seemed nightmarish. The pool, which Barrymore had filled for Diana, was empty again, and a single spotlight was shining on it.

In *Too Much, Too Soon*, Diana related that she suggested to "Daddy" that they not see each other for a while. He invited her in to "check up" — "Maybe your old Daddy's hidden a young lady to diddle with."

"You bore me," she said, close to tears.

"You bore me as much as I bore you," said the father to his daughter. "Good night."

This was only the public version. Diana later told Gene Fowler that, on that horrible night up at Bella Vista, John Barrymore tried to lure Diana to go to bed with him.

Presumably she didn't.

The final collapse of alcoholic, incontinent, impecunious John Barrymore came on Tuesday evening, May 19, 1942, at a rehearsal for the Rudy Vallee show. There are at least two versions. Gene Fowler wrote in *Good Night, Sweet Prince* that Barrymore, ill and wandering lost in the NBC Studios after the rehearsal, by chance landed in the dressing room of John Carradine. Fowler reported that Carradine had opened the night before in *The Vagabond King* as King Louis XI, that he had asked Barrymore's advice on playing the role, that he brought the newspapers with the reviews to the studio, and that Carradine himself had just completed a guest spot on Edgar Bergen and Charlie McCarthy's *The Chase and Sanborn Hour*.

"You could get away with anything, you lean, cadaverous bastard!" Carradine remembered Barrymore telling him. "You could play…" And he broke off, gasping.

There are several problems with this account that ace newspaperman Gene Fowler should have checked. Carradine had opened in *The Vagabond King* at the Los Angeles Philharmonic May 11, not May 18; also, the night of Barrymore's collapse was a Tuesday and *The Chase and Sanborn Hour* aired on Sundays, and a review of the May 19, 1942 radio programming shows no special episode of Bergen and McCarthy on that date. John Decker later protested to Fowler that he shouldn't have written that Barrymore had fallen in Carradine's dressing room because Carradine was too unimportant, and his dressing room was an unworthy site for the ultimately fatal collapse of a titan such as Barrymore. Neither Fowler nor Decker apparently suspected that John Carradine, whose flair for fanciful tales would confound many a film historian, had made up the story — along with Barrymore's salute to his acting ability.

More believable is the account that Barrymore, hamming it up at rehearsal, had just recited Romeo's "Arise, fair sun, and kill the envious moon" when he collapsed into Rudy Vallee's arms. "I guess this is one time I miss my cue," said Jack, tears running down his face. Dr. Hugo Kersten, always on call at NBC just in case Barrymore collapsed at the studio, drove the star to Hollywood Hospital, where John Barrymore was admitted. He had $.60 in his pocket.

The death watch began.

Lionel camped across the hall, moaning "Why in God's name can't I do something for him?" He filled in for Jack on the May 21st *Rudy Valle Sealtest Show*. ("He should have told Sealtest and Vallee to go to hell," wrote Barrymore biographer Margot Peters.) John Decker and Gene Fowler were at the hospital day and night. Thomas Mitchell and Alan Mowbray kept vigil; Anthony Quinn visited, having bought Jack a Chinese carved ivory boat he knew his friend had wanted ("You little shit, how did you know?" asked Jack, weeping). W.C. Fields sent a wire: "YOU CAN'T DO THIS TO ME."

Dolores called. Diana came to the hospital, where only once did her delirious father seem to recognize her, saying "Treepee." And Elaine Barrie came back, telephoning daily and sending flowers — although Lionel blockaded her from actually laying eyes on her ex-husband.

Phil Rhodes, 65 years after Barrymore's death, still marvels at the "positive energy" the man radiated. There was a remarkable spirituality within him, always at war with the self-destructiveness, and now, on his deathbed, he received the Last Rites of his Catholic faith. The sacrament, administered by old family friend Rev. John O'Donnell, supposedly came at the urging of Lionel. Still, it's significant that Jack accepted it, and that he rallied later enough to joke with his priest.

"Father," moaned Jack, "I have carnal thoughts."

"About who?" marveled Fr. O'Donnell.

"Her!" said Jack, indicating his old, plain nurse — who blushed.

Thursday, May 28, was Barrymore's tenth day in the hospital. He asked for Gene Fowler — "Will you hold my hand while I sleep?" asked the dying man. He lapsed in

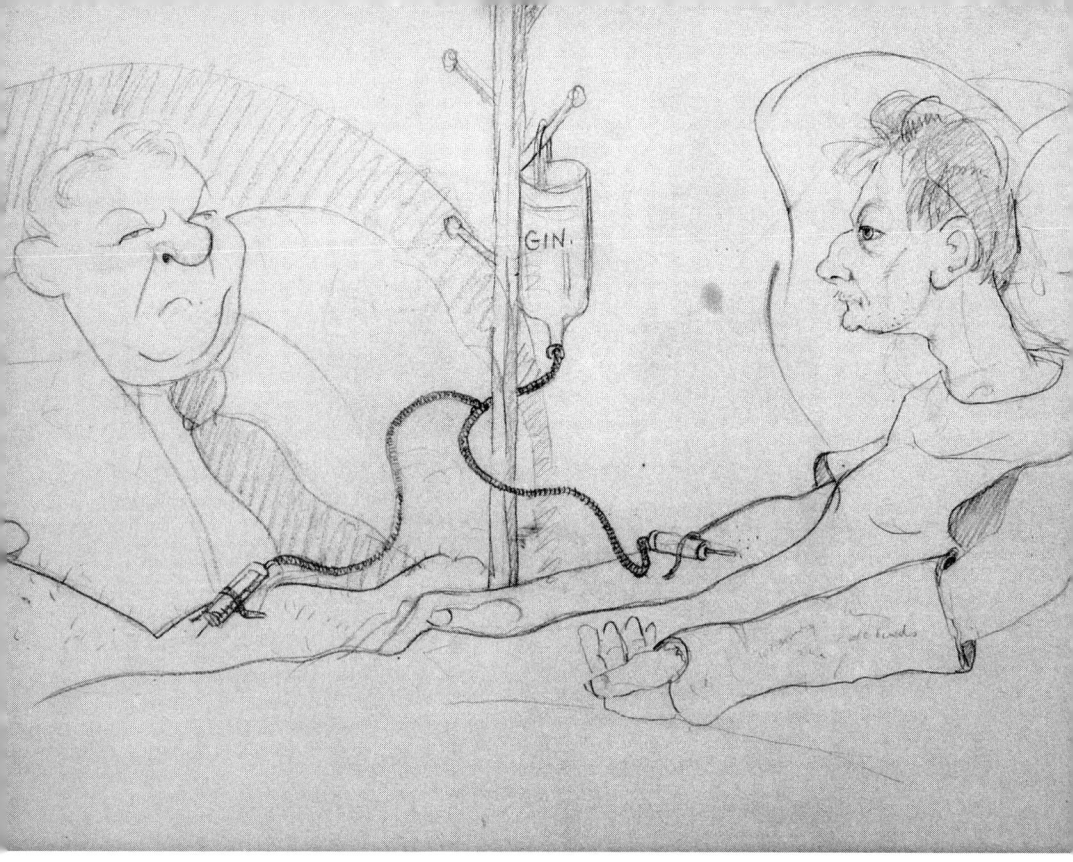

Fields and Barrymore IV the Bombay, by Decker

and out of consciousness, spoke incoherently, talked of his children, and murmured "Mummum, Mummum" over and over — the love for his grandmother, without whom he had never felt safe, still fervent. Then, as Fowler wrote in *Good Night, Sweet Prince*:

> "Lean over me," he said quite clearly. "I want to ask you something."
> I was unprepared for other than some last request by a dying man. I should have foreseen that this mighty fellow would not surrender with a sentimental, prosaic statement. The cocked-up eyebrow should have warned me that mischief never sickened in his soul.
> "Tell me," he asked, "is it true you are the illegitimate son of Buffalo Bill?"

Come his final agonies, John Barrymore was indeed "The Monster." He so ripped at his eczema-inflamed skin that nurses put white mittens on his hands – "It was as though he had put on the boxing gloves to meet the dark foe," wrote Fowler. He fought so manically, with such mad spirit that the nurses had to restrain him. His breathing, as Fowler wrote, "came like the sound made by a knife-blade being ground on a stone wheel." Fowler couldn't look at him any more. He sat across the hall, hearing Barrymore deliriously crying out, and at one point Lionel hobbled into the room.

"What did you say, Jake?" asked Lionel.

"You heard me, Mike," said Barrymore, presumably his last coherent words.

His real-life death scene, as it had been in *Richard III* and *Hamlet*, was epic. At nine o'clock on the night of Friday, May 29, John Decker entered the room and caught the majesty and horror in his famous deathbed sketch.

"Mummum," he cried, time and again.

At 10:20 p.m., John Barrymore died. The causes of death were acute myocarditis, due to chronic nephritis, due to cirrhosis of the liver. He had lasted, quite amazingly, 60 years, three months and 15 days.

In John Barrymore's *Dr. Jekyll and Mr. Hyde*, the moving fade-out showed the diabolic Hyde morphing in death into an angelic Jekyll. In his own life and death, John Barrymore's corpse underwent the Jekyll and Hyde redemptive magic.

Diana Barrymore, on the night of her father's death, was at Hollywood's Pantages Theatre and the premiere of *Eagle Squadron*. A motorcycle escort delivered her to Hollywood Hospital after word had reached her that the end was near, but she arrived too late to see her father alive. Fowler, Decker and her Uncle Lionel had all left their vigil, and Diana accepted the doctor's invitation to see her estranged father in death. She remembered in *Too Much, Too Soon* that she went into the room "by myself and closed the door and looked down at my dead father":

> Mother had once said, "When he was young, your father was the most beautiful man that ever lived. He looked like a young archangel, divinely beautiful."
>
> I began to cry. I was looking at the man she had described. Perhaps I wouldn't have cried then had he looked old and withered. But he looked young! Lying there, his hands crossed on his breast as they had been placed by the priest who gave him the last rites, he looked like the young Hamlet, the young, dead Hamlet... All my life I had seen my father's photographs, and now it seemed I saw him as he must have looked in the roles he made immortal. For death had done something subtle and wonderful to him: his chins were gone, his jowls were gone, everything of age and dissipation was gone... He lay in death like a beautiful young man!

Thank God, I thought, Death took him that way, not as the old, broken shell of a man he used to say he was. He used to tell me, "I'm an old gadzooks — I'm nothing any more." And I used to say to him "Oh, no, Daddy, don't think that way!" But he had no confidence, no anything, about his own soul, his own heart, his own destiny. But when he was dead, he was beautiful!

Diana became hysterical. Screaming, she had to be dragged from the room.

When Gene Fowler realized Barrymore would very likely die this time, he planned to set the hands of an old cuckoo clock that Barrymore had liked, and that had been broken for two years, at the time that his friend died. He wrote in his foreword to *Good Night, Sweet Prince* that, as he moved to set the hands of the clock that morning at the tributary time, it wasn't necessary: "The hands of the clock," he wrote, "had stood for more than two years at ten-twenty."

Dr. Hugo Kersten had been Barrymore's final physician, and Dr. V.L. Andrews performed the autopsy. Dr. Andrews concluded his findings jocularly; he wrote that the case was an equation of "WINE WOMEN SONG," noting "A recent comment which I heard was to the effect that this particular individual was not buried after his death, he was just poured back into a bottle." The doctor also added some mathematical statistics, based on 40 years of drinking (very conservative in Barrymore's case):

> 40 years of drinking with an average minimum of 10 two ounce drinks daily.
> One year — 7,300 oz — 249 qts. — 80 gal.
> 40 years of life — 292,000 oz — 10,000 qts. — 3,200 gals. or 640 barrels.

The Pierce Brothers Chapel, 720 W. Washington Boulevard, would prepare the body and host the wake. The death of Barrymore spawned one of the great apocryphal tales of Hollywood lore — the kidnapping of his corpse by Raoul Walsh and the Bundy Drive Boys, who claimed to have taken the cadaver to Errol Flynn's Mulholland Farm house for one last drink. Flynn himself included the saga (and apparently originated it) in his memoir, *My Wicked, Wicked Ways*. Yet there was no abduction. The only abnormality was that, during the viewing, Gene Fowler and his son Will kept an all-night vigil, and Jane Jones, the aforementioned 300-lb. hooker, paid a middle-of-the night call. As Margot Peters wrote of Jane Jones in *The House of Barrymore*:

> She asked to spend ten minutes before the bier, where she knelt with difficulty and prayed. Jack was a great patron of prostitutes. He would have appreciated one praying over him.

The morning after Barrymore died, Gene Fowler received a phone call from Sadakichi Hartmann who began arguing that Holbein had been left-handed. He said nothing about Barrymore's passing. Fowler hung up on him. Later, in his usual compassionate way, Fowler regretted his rudeness, believing that Sadakichi's "cynical show of indifference at the death of a friend had meant to conceal a real sense of personal loss."

Maybe.

The John Barrymore funeral was, of course, a Hollywood spectacle.

"Camera-armed spectators stalk film stars at John Barrymore's funeral," headlined one L.A. paper. The locale was the Catholic Calvary Cemetery in Whittier, east of Los Angeles. The Rev. John O'Donnell, who had administered the Last Rites to Barrymore, led the casket into the chapel, and the pallbearers included Bundy Drive habitués John Decker, W.C. Fields, and Gene Fowler, as well as E. J. Mannix, C. J. Briden and Stanley Campbell. Fields served under protest. Fowler came to his home the morning of the funeral, found Fields in a virtual crib with slatted sides to keep him from falling out during the night; "lying there in his nightclothes," recalled Fowler, "he resembled nothing so much as a wicked baby."

"The time to carry a pal," said Fields, "is when he's still alive." Nevertheless, he reluctantly agreed, but only if he could drive there in his chauffeured 16-cylinder Cadillac, fully stocked with his "necessary tonics."

A number of Bundy Drive Boys were "honorary pallbearers": Ben Hecht, Thomas Mitchell, Alan Mowbray and Roland Young. Also marching as honorary pallbearers were playwright Edward Sheldon, Charles MacArthur, Herbert Marshall, George M. Cohan, newspaper editor Herbert Bayward Swope, and writer/director Arthur Hopkins, as well as Diana's fiancé, Bramwell Fletcher.

There were either 1,000 to 2,000 people at the funeral (newspaper accounts varied). Diana, all in black, never resembled her father as strongly as she does in news photos from the funeral; the mourning daughter attended with her Uncle Lionel, who — ever stoic — abandoned his crutches to stand with Diana. "Well, it's a nice day for Jack," said Lionel as he emerged from the car — the first time he had spoken to Diana during the trip to Calvary Cemetery.

There was Elaine — the fourth Mrs. John Barrymore and the only ex-wife to attend the funeral. "Ariel" attended with her mother Edna, who had insisted Jack had preferred her in bed to Elaine; considering his Freudian hang-up, perhaps he had. Both women wore (in the purple prose of the *Los Angeles Examiner)*, "unrelieved black." They were among the last to arrive, and as Elaine walked up the chapel steps, clinging to Edna's arm, a strangely appropriate accident happened: her dress rose up on the right side, almost above her knee, as if heralding one last peep show for the star of *How to Undress in Front of Your Husband.*

The members of the public battled for camera vantage points and, as the hysteria soared, some of the Circus Maximus crowd broke through the rope barriers, forcing security to subdue them. Inside the chapel, which could seat only 75 guests, a Bundy Drive Boy was providing his own show, as producer/writer Nunnally Johnson remembered:

> The first thing I saw when I walked in was old John Carradine sitting there, rocking back and forth and keening so you could hear him all over the church.

Anthony Quinn was in the chapel, as was Helen Costello, Dolores' sister, and her father Maurice Costello (whom Jack had called "my favorite ex-father-in-law"). Louis B. Mayer attended, and Cecil B. DeMille, but Jack would surely have been happier to note the presence of Mark Nishimura, his Japanese gardener, who had been sent with his family to the internment camp at Manzanar. The *Los Angeles Times* reported that Lionel Barrymore had arranged "Nishi's" temporary release to attend the rites.

Although John Barrymore was a death-bed Catholic, there was no Requiem Mass, but simply a prayer service. Two towering crosses of white flowers loomed on the altar, and three tall candles burned on either side of Barrymore's silver-plated copper casket, which was covered by a fern blanket with a huge spray of orchids. The Rev. O'Donnell intoned the ancient prayers:

> Eternal rest grant unto him, O Lord. Let perpetual light shine upon him.

There was no eulogy, but had there been, it was ironically Elaine Barrie Barrymore who captured John Barrymore with the most insight and forgiveness: "You couldn't really hate him because he was such an abomination to himself."

The burial site was in the Calvary's Main Mausoleum, block 352, but before the body was sealed into the bottom-row crypt, W.C. Fields had reached the end of his stamina. "Let's blow," he whispered in Gene Fowler's ear. Their departure from Calvary Cemetery was not without incident. Some children, recognizing Fields, darted under the restraining ropes and pursued him for his autograph.

"Get away from me, you little bastards!" shouted Fields. "For two cents, I'd kick in your teeth! Back to reform school, you little nose-pickers!"

En route back to the movie colony, Fields and Fowler saw Earl Carroll in one of the funeral limousines. They invited him to join them and Carroll obliged. He accepted a martini from Fields, and then noted the glasses. The label on them read "Earl Carroll's" — Fields had pilfered them from the impresario's nightclub.

The mourners all left Calvary Cemetery with their own private emotions.

Lionel, on his way back with Diana, stunned her when he made the comment, "Yes, Miss Barrie knew him better." His remark, which Diana found "cryptic" and "rebuking," seemingly inferred that a monstrously ambitious young shrew had known John Barrymore better than his own daughter. Margot Peters believes that Lionel (who eventually carved "Good Night, Sweet Prince" on his brother's crypt) was talking about himself, regretful that he hadn't been the brother he should have been.

John Barrymore was the first Bundy Drive Boy to perish in their "terminal passion play" via his own horrific Calvary. John Decker wished he had been crucified on either side of his friend Jack, like the two thieves. After the funeral, W.C. Fields and Gene Fowler arrived at Bundy Drive, where Fowler wanted to pick up the deathbed sketch. He would display it near the Richard III sword that Barrymore had given him and the broken cuckoo clock reading 10:20. A surprise awaited them. On a large canvas of Sadakichi Hartmann, Decker had added Golgotha — showing John Barrymore, in loincloth, crucified between two naked women.

One was Elaine, and the other was her mother.

Barrymore's bequests were primarily spiritual and artistic—financially he was bankrupt. On August 24, 1942, there was a Federal court auction of John Barrymore's "effects." S.H. Curtis bought the letter written by Abraham Lincoln to Louise Drew, Jack's aunt, for $325. Frank Peris, agent for the San Diego Museum of Fine Arts, obtained the famed John Singer Sargent crayon portrait of Barrymore for $250.

Edgar Bergen bought most of the paintings by Barrymore, as well as the actor's silent film collection and two of his shrunken heads. As for the Bundy Drive Boys, Anthony Quinn paid $250 for Barrymore's burnished Richard III armor, John Carradine $225 for a silver service, and John Decker bought a number of Barrymore's drawings. Lionel Barrymore bid $160 for the Paul Manship bust of his brother. This still didn't settle all the outstanding debts, and personal clothing and items would go on the block the following year.

1942 was a tragic year, with the world at war and all its ensuing horrors. It had been an especially ominous, scandalous year for the Bundy Drive Boys, and for a time there seemed a curse was on them following Barrymore's death:

- ★ November 2, 1942 saw Errol Flynn reporting to court for a preliminary hearing on his alleged attack on two teenage girls.
- ★ Sadakichi Hartmann, in the California desert, was ostracized from the Banning community due to his German/Japanese ancestry, including prejudice from the Indians who lived on the reservation. (He was now insisting, incidentally, that he was Indian.)
- ★ Gene Fowler, beginning his book on Barrymore, suffered extreme heart trouble.
- ★ Diana Barrymore began an affair with her leading man Brian Donlevy on the set of Universal's *Nightmare,* nine weeks after her marriage to Bramwell Fletcher.
- ★ Elaine Barrymore couldn't find an acting job.

The death of John Barrymore was the tragic centerpiece of a harrowing year. As for the Bundy Drive Boys, the Barrymore idolatry only increased after his demise. No figure affected them so powerfully and profoundly; as many Christians offer up their suffering in the spirit of Christ at Calvary, so did the "Boys" later embrace their own failings, as if partaking in some sacrament in honor of Saint Jack. Little wonder Errol Flynn created the legend of Barrymore's stolen cadaver — it was the closest he could credibly come to providing John Barrymore an Easter Sunday resurrection.

Barrymore disciples during his life, they would be his zealots in death, and self-destruction was a major rubric of their worship.

In his will, Barrymore had requested, "I desire that my body shall be cremated and placed in the family vault at Philadelphia, Pennsylvania." Lionel, as a will executor and with his Catholic sensibilities, had vetoed cremation and opted for burial. In 1954 Lionel died, having stoically labored to the last at MGM, and was buried in the crypt above John at Calvary's Main mausoleum, and beside his wife Irene Fenwick.

Dolores Costello, remembered by her first husband as "too beautiful for words but not for arguments," died March 1, 1979, almost 37 years after the death of John. She had lived on an avocado ranch in Fallbrook, California, where a flood had destroyed much of the Barrymore memorabilia she'd taken from Bella Vista. However, some treasures remained, and she passed them on to John Drew Barrymore.

Wild-eyed, bearded, looking every bit the Hollywood warlock, John Drew Barry-

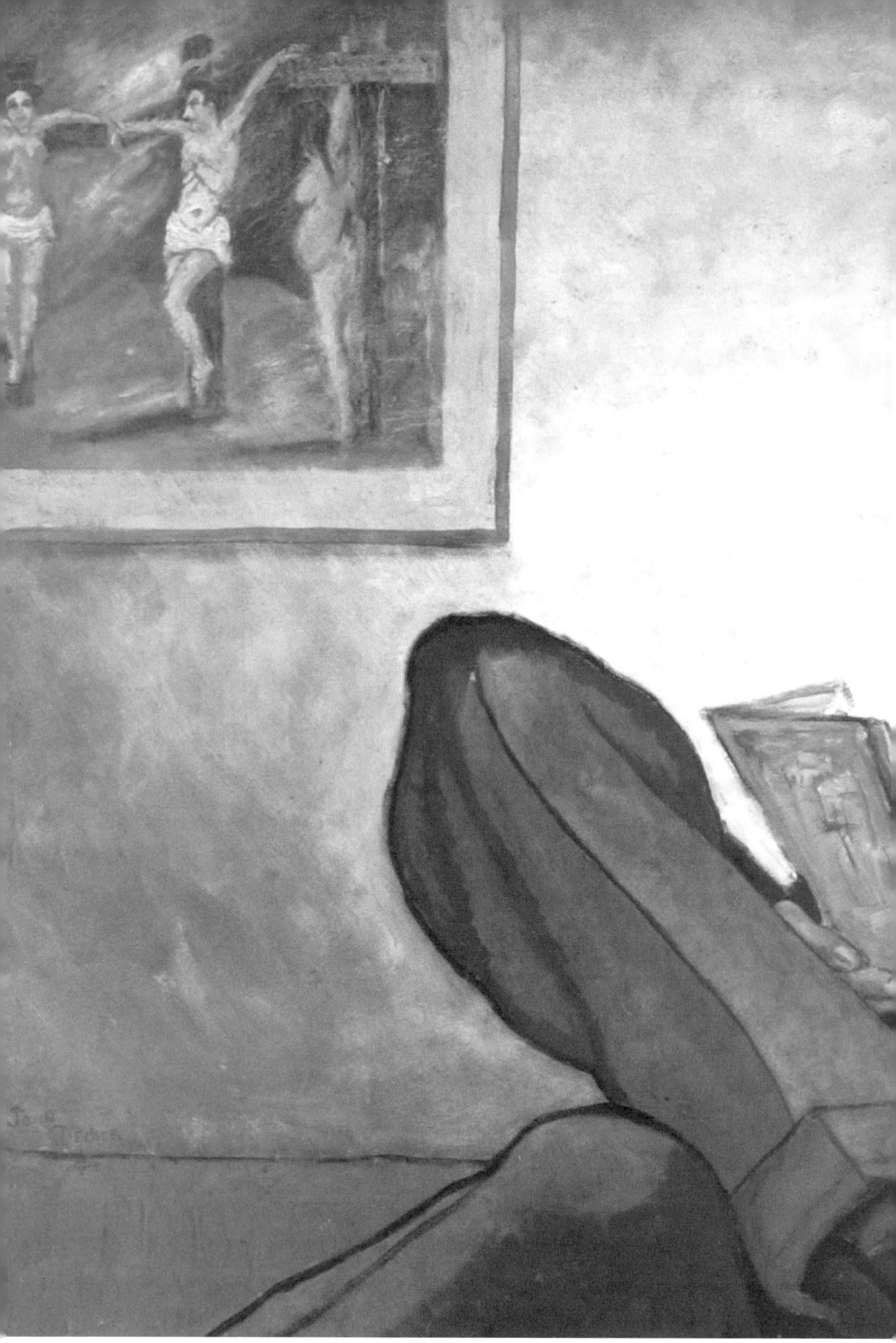

Decker painting of Sadakichi and the crucified Jack Barrymore. surrounded by whores

more, AKA "Johnny" Barrymore (and whom we'll refer to as John II) had long ago seen his own career explode in a cloud of alcoholism, spousal abuse and drug busts. "Johnny had a problem," says Phil Rhodes. "He thought he was rejected by his father. But his father didn't come around because he was afraid Dolores would have put him in an asylum."

John Blyth Barrymore, son of John Drew and actress Cara Williams and stepbrother of Drew, who now calls himself John Barrymore III and whom his father called Jake, posted an amazing "true story" on the Barrymore family website titled "Invasion of the Body Snatchers." John III wrote that he and his father began enjoying "a greatly improved standard of living" as they pirated Barrymore treasures from Dolores' estate. The Georgian Knights' candelabra, the 13th-century hand-executed *Book of Hours*, the Louis XV furniture, the religious icons… passed on to John II, who began to sell much of it. "After several years of abject poverty," wrote John III, "we were now comfortably ensconced in adjacent one-bedroom apartments at 8440 Sunset Boulevard — now the site of the trendy Hotel Mondrian."

One "Barrymorebelia" buyer was named "Red Dog" — "a notorious Hollywood reprobate," as John III described him. Red Dog loved rare books and reading them aloud to anyone who'd listen. It was Red Dog's spirited delivery of Robert Service's poem *The Cremation of Sam McGee* that got John II weeping, and committed to granting his father's final request.

"Jake," said John II to John III, "we've got to get my daddy up."

The caper began. John II got John III to join the crusade, and his lawyer Bruce Pedy. The exhumation demanded dispensation from the Catholic Church (which now allowed cremation) and the Health Department, and signatures from all living heirs. Pedy handled the church document, and John III admitted to forging the family signatures in lieu of dealing "with my insane Barrymore relatives."

So John Drew Barrymore, John Blyth Barrymore, Bruce Pedy and (as John III wrote) "a one-eyed Carpathian pirate named John Desko" all came to call at Calvary Cemetery. Dolores was buried there now, outside in Section D with her parents; her marker, along with her name and years, bears the inscription "Mum-Mum."

At the mausoleum, John II and company waited while Calvary's Mexican gravediggers had their lunch. They all ascended to the Main Mausoleum's second floor, opened the crypt, and removed the marble plaque upon which Lionel had personally carved "Good Night, Sweet Prince." (The marble plaque with its quote still remains at Calvary.) The smell from the opened grave was overpowering. The stinking solid bronze casket, despite its glass lining, had presumably cracked and the corpse was still decomposing after 38 years. The leakage had sealed the casket to the marble slab and the gravediggers couldn't budge it.

"Out of the way!" shouted a drunk John II.

It had always been a Barrymore custom to give a red apple on an opening night performance. This was after all, as John III noted, "an opening," and John II had brought apples, which he now handed to the gravediggers. Then he personally grabbed the coffin, placed his feet against the wall of the tomb and "yanked." The coffin surrendered, the gang hefted it onto a hand truck and wheeled it out to a waiting brown Ford van. "The body fluids were leaking out all the way," wrote John III.

John II and his mourners made a beeline to Odd Fellows Cemetery, locale of the closest crematory, and selected a book-shaped urn. Before the immolation, John II decided he wanted to take a look at the father of whom he had so little memory. The Odd Fellows pleaded with him not to do so, but John II gave them apples, remained insistent, and they finally obliged, although John III passed up the viewing — "the smell had been more than enough for me." He went outside. John Drew left the crematory pale and crying.

"Thank God I'm drunk," wept John II to his son. "I'll never remember it."

Although John III hadn't seen the cadaver, Bruce Pedy had, and John III included the nightmarish description in his "Invasion of the Body Snatchers":

It seemed that even in so horrific a state, John Barrymore was still the Great Profile.

LOS ANGELES

LIBERTY UNDER THE LAW — TRUE INDUSTRIAL FREEDOM

SATURDAY MORNING, OCTOBER 17, 1942.

Errol Flynn Accused of Attack on Girl, 17, at Bel-Air Party

Charge Pressed After Grand Jury Fails to Return Indictment

Dashing, debonair Errol Flynn, actor, yesterday was accused in a District Attorney's complaint of criminally assaulting a 17-year-old girl during a gay Bel-Air dinner party last Sept. 27.

Named in the same complaint were three film studio employees—Armand Knapp, 18; Morrie Black, 22, and Joseph Geraldi, 20. All are charged with mistreating pretty Betty Hansen, a Lincoln (Neb.) girl who came to Hollywood seeking glamour.

FOUR ARRAIGNED

Flynn and the others were arraigned late yesterday before Municipal Judge Oda Faulconer, released under $1000 bail each and ordered to appear for preliminary hearing next Friday.

Miss Hansen appeared last Thursday before the county grand jury with Agnes Toupes, brunette beauty known as "Chichi," and Lynne Boyer, blond singer, who assertedly were at the house party with her.

'EVIDENCE IGNORED'

The jury failed to press charges against Flynn and his codefendants. Dist. Atty. John F. Dockweiler, in issuing the complaint at the insistence of police juvenile officers, commented:

"The grand jury apparently ignored the evidence in the case."

Miss Hansen, taken into custody by juvenile officers Oct. 9 when she was reported missing from the home of her sister, Mrs. Patricia Marsden, told the grand jury she accompanied Knapp to the home of Fred McEvoy, British sportsman.

She was promised an introduction to Flynn and thought the swashbuckling actor might be able to obtain film work for her, the witness said.

'DID LITTLE DANCE'

At the luxurious estate the guests played for a while in the swimming pool, then had dinner, according to testimony. Miss Toupes said she later "did a little dance" and recalled that she did not see Flynn or Miss Hansen in the room at the time.

It was at this moment, testimony before the jury indicated.

Turn to Page 3, Column 3

Cadets Will Be 'Lombardiers'

SURRENDERS—Errol Flynn lights cigarette after surrender on charge of attacking 17-year-old girl at a party.

Henderson Hints Coast to Get More Gasoline

Special Attention Paid to Special Needs of West, O.P.A. Head Tells Senate Group

Presaging a possible increase in the amount of gasoline to be allotted western motorists, O.P.A. Director Leon Henderson yesterday told a Senate appropriation subcommittee in Washington that the people of the West will find "that special attention has been paid their special needs" when nation-wide gasoline rationing goes into effect Nov. 22.

This was in answer to an ever-increasing clamor by Pacific Coast transportation experts that the giant war plants would be crippled by the drastic rationing regulations first proposed.

Studies in the West have been made, Henderson explained, to determine whether the rationing system used in the East "is elastic enough, under the direction of local boards, to accommodate the needs."

Paul Barksdale d'Orr, State rationer, yesterday announced that all experts in gasoline, tire and automobile rationing are scheduled to attend a three-day conference in San Francisco next Thursday, Friday and Saturday for detailed instructions.

The experts will be given their printed instructions from Washington, and then other experts who have attended conferences in Chicago and Washington will interpret the instructions and explain to the others the methods to be followed in speeding up the program.

HERE'S PROCEDURE

Attending the conference will be d'Orr, C. W. Dessart, gasoline rationing executive in the Los Angeles area who has just attended a conference in Chicago.

Russ Yield More Ground in Stalingrad

Fight With Backs to Volga as Nazis Pour Thousands Into Attack

MOSCOW, Oct. 17 (Saturday.) (AP) — The Stalingrad garrison "withdrew from one of the city's settlements" yesterday under the pressure of thousands of "numerically superior" German shock troops who were supported by hundreds of tanks and planes in their furious new effort to split the Red army defenders.

A midnight communique, announcing the third Russian withdrawal in two days, emphasized the peril to the Volga River city, now in its 54th day of siege, and the retreat apparently meant the Russians had abandoned the factory district of Northern Stalingrad.

DESTROY 43 TANKS

"In the Stalingrad area," the bulletin said, "our troops are repulsing furious attacks by numerically superior enemy forces. According to preliminary data during the day, we destroyed 43 German tanks and annihilated about a regiment of enemy infantry.

"After stubborn fighting our units withdrew from one of the city's settlements."

NORTHWEST OF CITY

The Russians said there was only "fighting of local significance" northwest of the city where a Red army offensive against the Nazi flank has been under way for weeks in an effort to ease the pressure on Stalingrad.

Two companies of Nazi infantry and 200 Rumanians were killed in that sector and Red army artillery was reported to have destroyed 5 tanks, 4 mortars, 16 machine guns, 2 antitank guns and 28 enemy blockhouses.

OTHER AREAS

Indecisive but heavy fighting continued also in the Mozdok sector of the mid-Caucasus where the Russians said they killed approximately 400 Germans and destroyed five tanks and an ammunition dump.

On the only other fronts mentioned the communique said enemy troops were slain on the front west of Moscow "by artillery reconnaissance units and snipers," and the Germans also suffered "many dead" in unsuccessful attack on northwestern or Leningrad front.

ACCUSER—Betty Hansen, 17, accuser of Errol Flynn, hides face on Policewoman Dorothy Pulas' shoulder.

Flynn Accused of Attacking Girl, 17, at Party in Bel-Air

Continued from First Page

that Flynn took Miss Hansen to an upstairs bedroom.

McEvoy, also a witness before the jury, was reported to have told the panel that Flynn "might have been" upstairs during the party. Miss Hansen assertedly was mistreated by Flynn's co-defendants sometime after the party at McEvoy's home.

When the jury failed to act in the case, Lieut. R. W. Bowling of the police juvenile bureau informed Dockweiler that he had been instructed by Chief of Police C. B. Horrall to press the charges. The complaint against Flynn was signed by Mrs. Marsden.

Flynn, at his arraignment, denied the charges and said he had only played tennis at McEvoy's estate the night of the party and had left early.

Flynn's last appearance be-

fore the grand jury was two months ago when the panel investigated the injury of a butler he had "borrowed" from Heiress Barbara Hutton. No legal action was taken.

The actor, represented in the present case by Attorney Robert Ford, was divorced by Lili Damita last April 1. They were married in Yuma in 1935 and have a 17-month-old son.

Mrs. Patricia Marsden — Fred McEvoy

WHERE

CHICKEN TAIX

EVERY SUNDAY
3 to 8:30 P.M.

FRENCH R
321 COMMERCIAL ST.

Chapter Sixteen

*1943:
In Like Flynn,
Courtroom Melodramas,
Jane Russell's Brassiere,
Ghosts from the Past,
Dream-Turned-Nightmare
"Am I Supposed to Eat This — or Did I?"*

The year was so wild, so raucous, that it seemed a Bundy Drive Boys pagan celebration to commemorate John Barrymore's death.

Three of the gang had court trials, one of them among the most famous (and sordid) in U.S. judicial history. One achieved his most glorious dream-come-true, only to pay for it, personally and professionally, for the rest of his life. And for one of the men, perhaps the most painful anguish of his life awaited him, and one for which Barrymore himself might have been personally sympathetic.

January 9, 1943: The year in Hollywood began with a bang — Errol Flynn's statutory rape trial began.

The two underage girls were 16-year-old brunette Peggy Satterlee ("night club performer," noted the *Los Angeles Examiner*) and 17-year-old blonde Betty Hansen ("movie struck Nebraska waitress"). Flynn, according to Peggy's lawyers, had "criminally ravished" her (twice) on his yacht the *Sirocco*. As for Betty, Errol allegedly "lured her to an upstairs bedroom and raped her" (once) at the mansion of "wealthy sportsman" Fred McEvoy, 345 St. Pierre Road, Bel Air.

It appeared clear that the L.A. District attorney's office was on a crusading rampage at this time — Flynn, Lionel Atwill and Charlie Chaplin all faced sensational sex trials during the WWII years. It also appears the D.A. was desperate for witnesses against Flynn: Peggy Satterlee was a necrophile and Betty Hansen was already in legal trouble for having performed an act of oral sex.

The famed Jerry Geisler was Flynn's defense lawyer. If convicted, Errol Flynn faced up to 50 years in prison.

January 14: Betty Hansen, who wanted to be an actress, and dramatically glared at Flynn from the witness box, showed up dressed in schoolgirl attire. Asked about being disrobed by Errol Flynn, she admitted, "I didn't have no objections" — the courtroom spectators roared with laughter at her grammar and coyness. Betty insisted, however, that she thought Flynn was only putting her to bed because she didn't feel well. She also said she'd only sat in his lap because she had felt ill (and, in fact, had vomited) and he'd suggested she sit down. Wanna-be actress Betty also provided her personal critique of Errol Flynn the actor.

"Not so good," she replied, when Geisler asked if she had liked his acting. "He don't act like a gentleman, I will tell you!"

The spectators laughed long and loud again, and Geisler had Betty's canard stricken from the record.

January 15: It was circus day in court. The *Los Angeles Evening Herald-Express* would report: "A melodramatic attempt of Lynn Boyer, golden-haired party girl witness, to jump from a window on the eighth floor of the Hall of Justice today abruptly interrupted the Errol Flynn attack trial." The report cited her "screaming, hysterical tantrum" and her howl "I'll jump … I'll jump!" as she ran for the open window. Judge Leslie Still called a brief recess. "Although she has beautiful golden hair," wrote the *Evening Herald-Express* of Lynn, "she has appeared daily in a black wig and has also worn dark glasses. She has removed the wig each day after entering the courtroom."

Meanwhile, two jurors were charged with perjury, Lynn Boyer cried on the stand and tore her handkerchief to shreds, and the highlight of January 15 came when Jerry Geisler cross-examined Betty Hansen:

"Didn't you testify before the county grand jury that you committed an act of perversion?"
"Yes."
Do you know that this constitutes a crime in California?"
"Yes."
"And you hope not to be prosecuted for this act?"
"Yes, I do."

Geisler had set up Peggy for the kill — she had a scandalous past, had played up to Flynn to try to get into the movies, and was testifying against the star to escape other possible prosecution. For all her "I-hate-you!" glares at Flynn, Betty gave testimony that only added to his legend and lore, including that he kept his shoes on during sex:

Geisler: Miss Hansen, the act itself lasted how long, please?
Hansen: About fifty minutes.
Geisler: About fifty minutes?
Hansen: Yes, that's right.
Geisler: And during that entire time, he was on top of you?
Hansen: That is right.

Betty seemed determined to publicize her own star attributes. Geisler asked if she remembered what Flynn said to her while "having the act with you":

Hansen: I do. He said I have a nice pair of breasts.
Geisler: Anything else?
Hansen: Yes. And I had a nice fanny.

January 19: Betty was virtually a warm-up act for Peggy LaRue Satterlee, who now had her first day on the stand. The *L.A. Examiner* described her as "Sitting primly in the witness chair, clad in a powder-blue tailored suit with a small pair of silver wings pinned to the pocket, her dark hair pompadoured and tied in long curls," and noted she spoke "in a demure, little-girl voice, that most of the time was so low that jurors cupped their hands behind their ears to hear her..." She described the two attacks on the *Sirocco*: one as she lay in her bed in slip and panties and Flynn came in wearing pajamas:

"I told him not to. I didn't know what to do. I pushed him away."

The second attack came later after Flynn allegedly told Peggy "how much prettier the moon was when seen though a porthole." They went to Flynn's cabin, where "the second attack" took place.

"Did you resist?"

"Some. I knocked down a curtain beside the bed."

"Did you say anything?"

"I wanted him to leave me alone."

Peggy claimed she told her mother she'd been raped, and she, mother and sister went to the Hall of Justice. She saw a doctor for an examination. She testified she later telephoned Flynn from a hospital.

"He left word for me to call, and I called him back. He asked me if I loved him. I said that naturally I hated him. I said my mother was going to prosecute him."

"Did he make any reply?" asked the D.A.

"I don't remember."

"What was the last thing you said to him?"

"I said, *He Died With his Boots On*. That was the name of one of his pictures. Then I hung up the phone."

Once again, Geisler went for the throat: he managed to get Peggy to admit she'd been intimate with an "unnamed man" and had an abortion (then a felony in California) before ever sailing on the *Sirocco*. Like Betty, Peggy was shamelessly cutting a desperate deal with the D.A. to escape her own prosecution.

Geisler tricked the prosecution into calling Owen Cathcart-Jones, a 42-year-old Canadian flyer, who had known Peggy and would (so the prosecution thought) testify as to Peggy's fine moral character. In fact, Geisler had received an anonymous tip that Peggy and Cathcart-Jones had visited an L.A. funeral parlor one night where Peggy "had frolicked about, pulling sheets from the naked bodies and peering at them."

> Geisler: Well, you also were with her down to a mortuary down here in Los Angeles, were you not?
> Cathcart-Jones: Yes.
> Geisler: And she was kind of playing hide-and-seek around the corpses, wasn't she? Do you remember that night?

Cathcart-Jones: Yes.

Geisler: Do you remember she showed you — opened up and showed you — the body of an elderly lady?

Cathcart-Jones: Yes.

Geisler: And pulled the sheet down in the mortuary on a Filipino who had been crippled across the center?

Cathcart-Jones: I remember that.

Geisler: And then went back to where they inject the veins of corpses and there opened and looked down at an elderly man lying there, and her head was pushed down against the man's face. Do you remember that?

Cathcart-Jones: Yes, I remember that.

By now, the courtroom spectators were gasping and screaming. "Keep them quiet out there, Mr. Bailiff!" ordered the Judge.

Yet another show-stopper came on the stand when Geisler showed Peggy a picture of herself from the previous fall, appearing at the preliminary hearing in pigtails. Peggy, in a spine-tingling moment, loudly and startlingly cackled at the picture and turned her face from the jury.

Geisler's depiction was now complete: Peggy Satterlee, in addition to her previous intimacy and abortion, was a necrophile witch.

The jury visited Flynn's *Sirocco* and studied the phases of the moon, thereby casting doubt on Peggy's porthole story — the moon made no appearance the night in question. The story was sordid escapism to the U.S. at large, coping with the anguish of war news.

January 27: Errol Flynn, in dark suit and sans mustache, took the stand. He denied it all: he never called Peggy Satterlee "J.B." (jail bait) or "S.Q.Q." ("San Quentin Quail"), did not spike Peggy's milk with rum, did not put his arm around her, did not rape her at Fourth of July Cove, never asked her to look at the moon through his cabin's porthole, and never raped her en route back to the mainland. Nor had he ever gone upstairs in Fred McEvoy's Bel Air mansion and raped Betty Hansen.

Flynn was smooth in the witness box, a masterful actor. He was, in fact, terrified, and later admitted keeping a plane and pilot on call to flee the country if the jury returned a verdict of Guilty.

February 2: Deputy District Attorney Arthur Cochran took a full day to sum up the evidence, noted that the jury would decide whether the punishment was a year in the county jail or one to 50 years in San Quentin. "Send this man to San Quentin where he belongs!" demanded Cochran.

February 3: It was Geisler's turn. As for Cochran's claim that the Defense "would tear the girl witnesses limb from limb and throw them out the window in an attempt to smear their characters," Geisler was cool: "I say to you," he addressed the jury, "it's not the Defense that has tried to smear the character of these girls. Unfortunately, the girls smeared themselves long before I ever heard of them or they ever heard of me."

February 6: The jury, after 24 hours of deliberation, returned its verdict. Geisler, himself nervous, squeezed Flynn's knee as the sentence passed down: Not Guilty. The courtroom cheered. A juror told the press they only took so long to convince the public that deliberation had actually taken place.

"Oh well, nobody got hurt," blithely said Betty Hansen's mother, who insisted Betty was "a clean little Christian girl." Peggy Satterlee bitterly claimed of Flynn, "I hate him more than anyone else in the world." She went back to Applegate, CA, where her own father was soon convicted of molesting two underage girls.

Very few people believed Flynn never had his way with his two accusers. Indeed, the jury even ignored (or forgave) what was very likely perjury on Flynn's part. The fact was that Flynn had no need to rape them — they were apparently all too willing — and the trial became a dynamic against hypocrisy and self-righteousness.

Errol Flynn, incorrigible, had meanwhile been keeping 18-year-old Blanca Rosa Welter — later known as movie star Linda Christian (and a Mrs. Tyrone Power) — at Mulholland Farm. He was also attracted during the trial to the tall, red-haired teenage girl working the cigar counter in the courthouse. Her name was Nora Eddington, fated to be Flynn's second wife. And, as Nora told Charles Higham in *Errol Flynn: The Untold Story*, come the spring of '43, and Flynn did indeed commit rape — and she was the victim:

> I didn't know what was happening. I was terrified. Suddenly he was thrusting into me. It was like a knife. I felt I was being killed. I screamed and screamed. He went on and on. I couldn't push him out. There was blood everywhere. It was on the sheets, on the wall...

Flynn would marry Nora that August, and they lived in separate quarters. If one believes Higham's book, the actor was also doing espionage as a Nazi spy. The accusation reaped headlines but few believers when the book was published in 1980.

February 15, 1943: *The Film Daily* reviewed *The Outlaw*, featuring Thomas Mitchell as Pat Garrett. Howard Hughes produced and directed this infamous sex saga/Western, as well as creating "the cantilever bra" for *The Outlaw's* female star discovery, 36D-26-36 Jane Russell (who claims she never actually wore the bra — "I just told Howard I did").

"How Would You Like to Tussle with Russell?" teased *The Outlaw's* promotional copy. To make the sexually bizarre Western ever stranger, Tommy Mitchell's Pat Garrett and Walter Huston's Doc Holliday appear to be undeniably gay — two aging, Out-West-style homosexuals, both pining for Billy the Kid (Jack Beutel). The interpretation seems too overt to be denied, and was probably another inside joke reason for this promo for *The Outlaw*: "SENSATION Too Startling to Describe!"

Much to Hughes' delight, *The Outlaw* faced wildly publicized censorship battles, didn't have wide release until 1946 and after being banned in New York State finally opened there September 11, 1947. Business everywhere, primarily due to Ms. Russell's pneumatic talents, was record-breaking.

April Fool's Day, 1943: W.C. Fields began his own court case, sued by Harry Yadkoe, a New Jersey hardware store owner. Yadkoe claimed he sent Fields some comedy material, including a snake story that Fields allegedly used in *You Can't Cheat an Honest Man*. Yadkoe demanded $20,000 in damages.

Fields ("his nose bigger and redder than ever," noted the *L.A. Daily News)*, came to court throughout the trial with a keg, such as a St. Bernard would carry in the Alps, and claimed the "contents of the keg were to be used as a stimulant should the verdict of the action go against him." The trial found W.C. in fine form, seemingly enjoying himself and apparently confident of victory. On April 7, he told Yadkoe's lawyer "I fell on my head the other night," and later elucidated:

> I was taking a steam bath and a rubdown and was lying on the table. The steam sort of soothed me and I dozed off. All of a sudden I fell right on my noggin. The maid rushed upstairs thinking I had committed suicide over this case. I was a sight, black and blue all over.

On April 9, the verdict came back: Fields was told to pay $8,000 to Harry Yadkoe. He was also appalled and angry. "It is outrageous and ridiculous," he snarled, promising an appeal. Jubilant at the verdict, Yadkoe jumped to his feet, made an attempt to shake Fields' hand and was rejected as Fields took a draught from his keg.

"I've been seeing snakes all night," Fields told the *Evening Herald-Express* on the morning of April 10:

> I thought the writer was just some poor guy when I got the letter. I thought I'd be kind and answer it. But I had a feeling I was going to get the works. Never do a kind deed — it's likely to turn around and bite you in — look!… Avaunt, grim monster! Snakes — snakes — SNAKES!

On the night of June 28, 1943, the final artifacts of John Barrymore — his personal clothing — went up for auction. Most of the major relics had gone on the block the previous August, and now the *Los Angeles Times* reported the sale of such items as Barrymore's flamboyant silk pajamas with coronet, his battered black Homburg hat ("that WAS John Barrymore," quoth the *Times*), a pair of green wool socks, and:

> Even the pink girdle which once supported the sagging paunch of the Great Profile was sold. Edward Molen, a business man with a stomach he thought would fit the garment, paid $4.50 for the elastic belt.
>
> "Just a memento," said Molen as he walked through the crowd of 300 curious with the girdle under his arm.

There was more, including Barrymore's pearl-gray fedora. The *Times* reported that John Decker was present, watching "in a retrospective mood," as was Errol Flynn "with a dark-haired girl on his arm."

"And when the shelves were cleaned," concluded the *Times*, "there was nothing left of John Barrymore in this world, nothing but a memory."

July 2, 1943: John Decker starred in his own newspaper headline court case — with a co-star who likely had a devastating impact emotionally on him for the remainder of his life.

Thomas Mitchell and Walter Huston in *The Outlaw*

To Decker's surprise, his first wife, Mrs. Helen Decker, who had left him July 15, 1928, and whom he had not seen since the summer of 1929, had suddenly shown up in Hollywood. In tow was their 20-year-old daughter, Gloria, who claimed she read a magazine feature about Alan Mowbray and his paintings by John Decker:

> We were living in New York and I told mother I would like to see and know my father. Shortly after that we came to California.

Result: John Decker suddenly had two spouses. In fact, he possibly had *three* — there's no evidence he ever divorced wife #2, who had mysteriously disappeared and whom no reporter was apparently aware of during the news coverage of this "Enoch Arden" situation. As Decker explained it:

1940 — 1947   275

In 1928 we were living here and one night when I came home from work I found my wife and daughter gone. That night I phoned all our mutual friends but found no trace of them. The second day after she left I met a friend who told me my wife and child were living on La Brea Avenue. I went to see her and asked her to come back but she said she wanted to live alone.

In less than a week after I located her she left town and I heard nothing from her. Several months later I learned she was in New York and I went there to ask her to come back. Again she refused and I returned to Los Angeles.

My letters were returned and I heard nothing more from her until my daughter contacted me.

Mary Lou Warn, Decker's stepdaughter, offers a different version of the events that led to this headline story:

Helen, John's first wife, had been hit by a truck while crossing a street in downtown New York. I remember she talked in a whisper — she had lost her voice and had sued the trucking company and she got, I suppose for those days, a lot of money. So she took Gloria and just left John. John went to California, and I don't recall any details that Helen and Gloria had ever been in California with him.

So Helen had gone through the money from the truck accident, and she and Gloria started reading about how successful John was, so they decided to pack up and go to California and see good old John, because they figured he probably had a lot of money now. Which he didn't—he just had a wife! So it was an interesting little fiasco.

The *Los Angeles Times* reported Decker's big day in court, before Superior Judge Jess E. Stephens:

"I took advantage of the legal procedure which states that a person who disappears for more than seven years, leaving no trace, is legally dead," the artist testified.

He said he made every effort to find his first wife before he remarried.

"Was that before you arrived as a painter?" Judge Stephens asked.

"An artist never arrives until after he is dead," retorted Decker.

Gloria Decker Smouse — in a large picture bonnet — took the witness stand, cooed her story, and persuaded Judge Stephens to grant the interlocutory divorce de-

Portrait of Decker
signed to Will Fowler

To Bill
from one ?
to anoth[er]
John ...

cree. The Judge, probably amused by Decker, got into the spirit of the trial by explaining it might constitute "cruel and unusual punishment under the Constitution to make a man go through life with two wives."

However, the true fireworks of the trial weren't in the words — they were in the pictures.

Newspaper photos of father and daughter are intensely startling: Baby-faced, brunette Gloria, in her big movie-star hat, seemingly making goo-goo eyes at a father who looks alternately lustful and lovesick.

There came the day that Mary Lou came home early from school:

> Gloria was very young, and I was just so infatuated with the fact that, all of a sudden, I had a sister! I was an only child, and everybody else had brothers and sisters, and I thought Gloria was wonderful.
>
> Right after Gloria and her mother arrived from New York, I came home early from school one day — I was in about the fourth or fifth grade. Mother was out for the afternoon. In our Bundy Drive house the bedroom was downstairs off the bathroom and when I came home I saw John and Gloria in bed together. It was kind of "Wow!" and I dashed out and upstairs to my room, and nothing was ever said about it again.
>
> I heard that John had promised Gloria a car — God knows what he was going to buy her a car with, he never had any money. But that might have been what was luring her.

It was not a one-afternoon stand. The 48-year-old Decker and his 20-year-old daughter began visiting a hotel to continue their affair. Phyllis presumably never knew — indeed, she and Gloria became good friends. After Decker's death, they even opened an art gallery together in the Del Mar Hotel, which was short-lived ("Mother was not a business person," says Mary Lou).

Decker gave Gloria a self-portrait that hung in Gloria's home in Laurel Canyon until she destroyed it before her death.

As for Barrymore incest, Phil Rhodes tells this story:

> My wife and I lived for a time in the 1950s with Johnny Barrymore, Jack's son, up in Laurel Canyon, near Errol Flynn's house. Johnny had no rent money and we were helping him. Diana was in town. Dolores' daughter Dede (Johnny's sister) had a baby and Dolores wanted Johnny to be godfather and Diana to be godmother. Johnny hated Diana — "I won't be godfather if she's godmother!" But everybody thought it would sober up Diana, so Johnny agreed, but said,

"I'm doing it under duress!"

Later one night up at the house, I heard the window open in Johnny's bedroom and Johnny yelled, "Diana! What the fuck are you doing here?" There was a long silence — quite long — and then I heard Diana sigh, "Oh, Johnny... Daddy would have loved this!"

In 1943, a new member entered the Bundy Drive fold — Vincent Price. The future King of Hollywood Horror had scored on Broadway as the villain of *Angel Street*, and 20th Century-Fox had signed him to a film contract, commencing with *The Song of Bernadette*. "Being a religious film," wrote Price in his 1959 book, *I Like What I Know*, "the studio approached it with typical lugubrious reverence. It took nine months to make, and the boredom of waiting for a call from the studio began to pall."

So Price and actor friend George Macready opened their own art shop, "The Little Gallery," in Beverly Hills. As Price recalled, the shop was "between a bookstore and a very popular bar," and they had figured correctly "that we'd catch a mixed clientele of erudites and inebriates." As such, Price soon met, as he expressed it, "the delightful, tragic, and genuinely Bohemian John Decker."

One of Price's favorite buyers was Barbara Hutton, the famed heiress and the second wife of Cary Grant. As Price wrote:

We had an exhibition of [Decker's] paintings, the best and least eclectic he ever did, and we sold many of them. "Ghost Town," which Thomas Mitchell bought, is to my mind his best work. Miss Hutton loved the pictures — and Decker — but just couldn't find the one that said hello to her. In the gallery one day she told Decker of her love for Venice. He allowed as how there was one picture he just didn't have time to finish for the show, but he thought it would be finished the next day and that she might like it. She promised to come back.

By noon the next day Decker was back and so was Barbara, and more importantly, so was the painting — a three-foot-long, two-foot-high painting of... Venice. Palaces, gondolas, the Canal shimmered from the canvas with the authentic light of Venice. Sold to Barbara Hutton... one painting of Venice by John Decker ... as wet as the Grand Canal, having been done from start to finish in 12 hours' time.

Decker now received coverage from the two major news magazines in the U.S. two weeks in a row. On September 13, 1943, *Time* ran a profile, "Hollywood Headsman," with a picture of Decker and a shot of the Fields Queen Victoria painting. The following week, September 20, 1943, *Newsweek* published "Double Decker," with a picture of the Harpo Marx Blue Boy painting and a shot of Decker with a painting of Barrymore as Hamlet framed on his wall.

Decker had based this Barrymore painting on a photograph from *Hamlet*, in which John exposed his "bad" side right profile. Adding dark shadow, Decker provided an especially haunting depiction of his tormented friend, and the actual painting eventually ended up for sale in Vincent Price's "The Little Gallery." As Price wrote in *I Like What I Know*, the greatest of all Barrymore fans, Tallulah Bankhead, bought it.

> In celebration Decker gave a bang-up party for Tallulah. There were 50 guests, and, more surprisingly, there were four huge roasts of beef and lamb. No one could have that many ration tickets, but on inquiry as to how he got the meat [during War ration days], Decker led us all into his studio and unveiled an enormous canvas of a rather handsome, overblown blonde, entitled "My Butcher's Wife."

Sunday night, October 24, 1943: "John Carradine and his Shakespeare Players" opened in *Hamlet* at the Geary Theatre in San Francisco. Carradine — producer, director, star and owner of the company — naturally played the melancholy Dane, and would follow at the Geary as Shylock in *The Merchant of Venice*, and as *Othello*.

"If this goes over," Carradine vowed to the press, "I'm through with Hollywood forever!"

It was, as *Time* magazine reported, "the city's biggest Shakespeare premiere of modern times," and the opening night house included one empty seat, reserved by Carradine for the ghost of John Barrymore.

The dream had come true, but at a cutthroat price. To finance his company, Carradine had mortgaged his North Hollywood house and sold his yacht. He'd acted in films such as Monogram's *Voodoo Man*, playing a bongo-playing geek who fetches female zombies for Bela Lugosi. Carradine had been acting in *Voodoo Man* at Monogram by day while by night fulfilling a pre-San Francisco tryout of his Shakespeare

John Carradine

and Company in a . . . .

Shakespearean Repertoire

company at the Pasadena Playhouse. The quick-money movie jobs, taken to pay for his repertory company, permanently scarred his cinema reputation.

He also fell in love. The lady was Sonia Sorel, a blonde beauty who'd play Ophelia, Portia and Desdemona in the Carradine company. Dean Goodman, an actor in the troupe (and later a San Francisco film critic) wrote in his book *Maria, Marlene, and Me*, "Carradine was determined to bed this lady or die trying." His marriage to Ardanelle, who was at the mortgaged home with their two sons, was doomed.

"John Carradine and his Shakespeare Players" began a tour of the Pacific coast. Playing the great classical roles, madly in love, John Carradine was at his rococo best, as Dean Goodman wrote:

> John was a character, to say the least. Fancying himself as an actor-manager of the old school, he dressed accordingly — in a wide-brimmed black fedora with a long flowing black cape. He also sported a walking stick which he flourished extravagantly at every opportunity. He was hardly inconspicuous as he walked down the street... Those of us in his company regarded John and his shenanigans with amusement. He was a lot of fun, and we enjoyed being part of his traveling circus.

The company played Seattle and Portland and, in December of 1943, the Biltmore Theatre in Los Angeles. All the while, Carradine was a show in himself, on and off the stage. Dean Goodman wrote:

> I recall one incident which illustrates John's bawdiness, his ribald sense of humor and a flamboyance which sometimes bordered on bad taste. He, Sonia and I were having lunch at a restaurant in Portland. When the waitress brought his entrée, John took one look at the plate in front of him and grunted, with a curl of his lip, "Am I supposed to eat this — or did I?"

The divine madness was there, but the bookings weren't. Carradine's envisioned coast-to-coast tour and Broadway opening never happened as the troupe went bust and the final curtain fell on his lifelong dream.

John Carradine would pay for it, personally and professionally, for the rest of his life.

Sonia Sorel and John Carradine

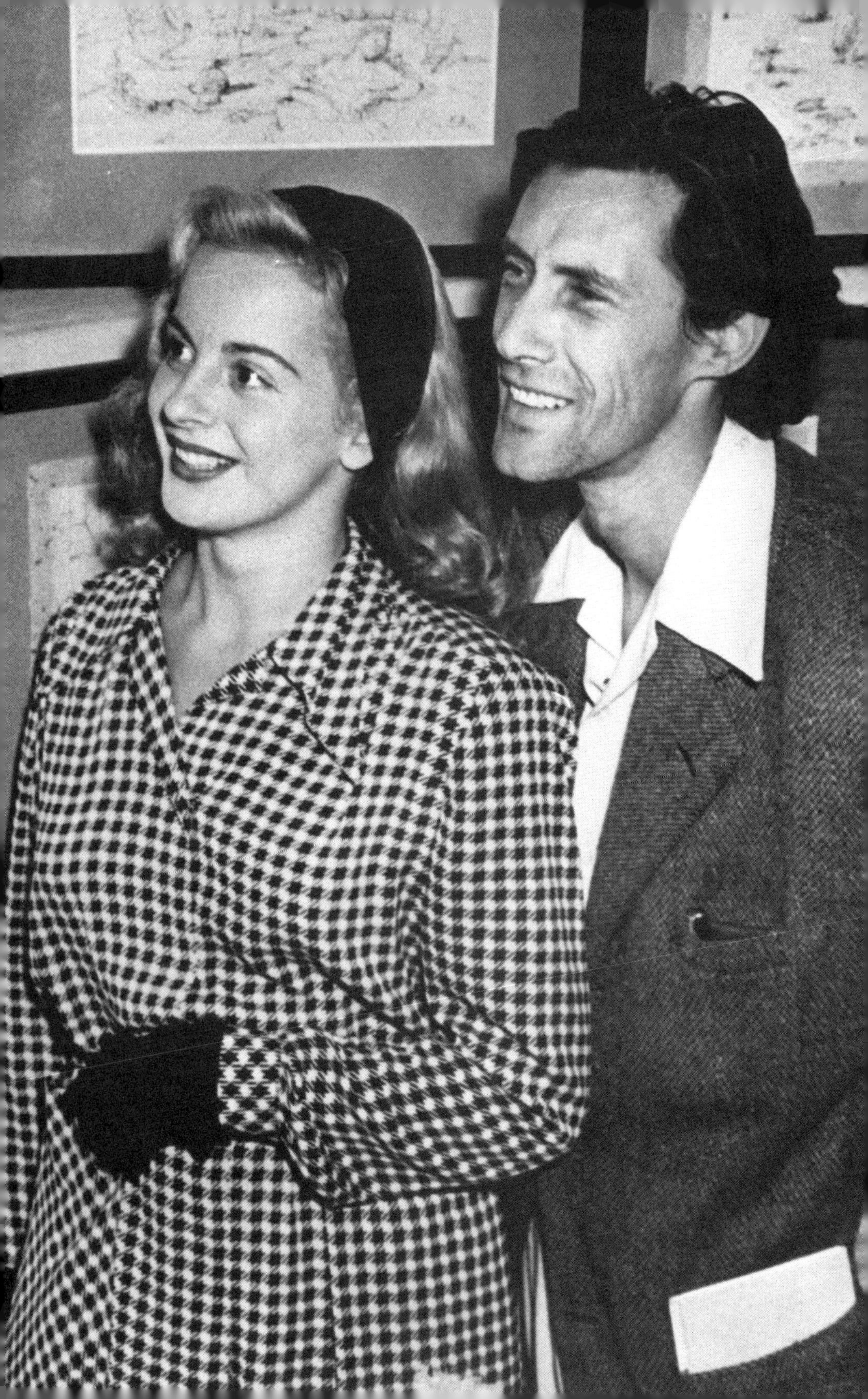

John Barrymore's ghost wasn't only invoked by John Carradine's repertory company. On December 22, 1943, the *Los Angeles Times* headlined "Barrymore's Pet Dog Follows Actor in Death." There was a picture of Gus the dachshund, profile to profile with John Decker. The story reported that Barrymore had given Gus to Decker after the dog had been lost on the Bella Vista estate, and related:

> Decker believes the dog was as much the actor as his master. In fact, he thinks the animal's untimely death may have been suicide — resulting from the frustration of his dramatic talents.
>
> Each year, it seems, a local production company borrowed the dachshund for a light opera presentation in which the dog was carried under the arm of a woman alighting from a cab. Gus ate it up. He followed the gyrations of the orchestra leader with his head, emulating all the contortions. The audience was convulsed.
>
> This year, when the producer appeared at Decker's home, where Gus was idling before the fireplace, the entrepreneur mentioned casually that they had found another dog for the role.
>
> "Gus got up and ambled out of the house," said Decker. "A few minutes later a neighbor told us he had been run over by a car. He had never run in front of or after a car before."

Decker buried Gus under a tree in his yard.

As 1943 ended, the Bundy Drive Boys achieved a special distinction: Viking Press published Gene Fowler's *Good Night, Sweet Prince,* which introduced the gang to the readership of the bestselling John Barrymore biography.

The cover illustration, appropriately, was the John Decker Barrymore-as-Hamlet painting that had sold to Tallulah Bankhead. Fowler's love for Barrymore was evident throughout, yet he delicately presented the demons, limited the sordidness of the final fall, and made John Barrymore a tragic hero. Ben Hecht read the book New Year's Eve of 1943, and wrote to Fowler January 4, 1944:

> You made me feel once again the one epic quality in Jack I always admired. Having elected to destroy himself and set the eagle nibbling on his own gizzard, he never cried out — never complained against God or man... The

> book is much more than the biography of an actor — It is the most moving saga of a stormy, twisted and brave soul I've ever read...

Hecht, guessing that Fowler was suffering post-publication depression (he was), noted "… it is a mood unworthy of your achievement. You should be sitting in the Taj Mahal and planting gardenias in your navel."

Ardanelle Carradine was also reading *Good Night, Sweet Prince* on New Year's Eve, 1943, as John told her he was madly in love with Sonia and was leaving Ardanelle and their sons to be with her.

Allen McNeill, Will Fowler, John Decker, Sadakichi Hartmann and Gene Fowler at 419 Bundy Drive

Chapter Seventeen
1944:
"A Superbly Weird Imagination," Farewell to Bundy Drive, "Jesus" Walks the Pool, W.C.'s Last Popinjay and the Passing of "Chrysanthemum"

> A true artist cannot be ordered about. He goes his crotchety way, and does as he damn pleases AT ANY COST...
> —Sadakichi Hartmann, from *White Chrysanthemums*

On a cold rainy day in January of 1944, Sadakichi Hartmann sat at the Bundy Drive studio, devoured a ham sandwich, and made his prognostication on the longevity of his fellow Bundy Drive Boys: W.C. Fields would die in two years, John Decker in three years, and Gene Fowler in four years. As for Sadakichi himself, the prophet gave himself less than a year.

As fate had it, Sadakichi nailed three of four predictions.

1944 would prove the turning point of World War II; Hollywood was booming and vital turning points were in play, too, for the Bundy Drive Boys.

Gene Fowler's *Good Night, Sweet Prince* had become a national bestseller. There were detractors. Threatening a lawsuit, Elaine Barrie Barrymore claiming the book's depiction of her ruined her career as an actress and caused her mother to try to jump out a window. Ethel Barrymore, who would win the 1944 Best Supporting actress Academy Award for *None But the Lonely Heart*, said, "I admire Gene Fowler, and I like his story of John very, very much."

The adulation did little to exhilarate the moody Fowler. Early in 1944, he wrote to W. C. Fields:

Dear Uncle Willie,

Thank you for your note. I am passing through a period of slight melancholia, and my recourse to the bottle only heightens it.

I hope to see you soon and join you in your old Crow's Nest so that we can sit and look out at the world and despise it thoroughly.

Meanwhile, the best to you,

Gene Fowler

January 30, 1944: Sadakichi Hartmann put on his old camel's hair overcoat, headed to a bar in Banning and was almost hit by a car. The penitent driver gave him a lift — which eventually took him all the way to Bundy Drive, just in time to disrupt plans for Phyllis' birthday. It was there he made his predictions of longevity of the various Bundy Drive pals. Fowler, given four years, had agreed to finance Sadakichi's planned trip east if the prophet gave him 10 more years.

"I'll even make it 12," said Sadakichi, weighing the offer.

"This is blackmail," said Fowler, "but it's a deal."

During his Bundy Drive stay, Sadakichi had observed Decker's recent paintings. Now in his letter, Sadakichi saluted Decker as "a full-fledged artist," said his new output was "so far away and beyond the shystermagoria of your 'Old Masters'" and continued:

What has suddenly come over and into you? Your sickness, isolation, loneliness, abstention from drinking? The departure of Barrymore must have something to do with this transformation. What I admire first of all is the vigorous groping for a new technique — fluency of expression and a devil-may-care nonchalance toward the medium. What I like best is the row of houses in the ghost town; the distortion and strange combination of anatomical structures; and what you call "clowns," those gruesome bastard derelicts that I would not like to meet in life... They are so uncouth that they are the great and uncanny inventions of a superbly weird imagination.

Yes, John Decker, you are a great painter — if you can keep it up.

John Decker considered the missive his greatest honor. And it came at a fitting time. Decker was about to give up Bundy Drive (Fowler had been paying the rent) and move to a new home and studio at 1215 Alta Loma Drive, on the Sunset Strip, just behind the Mocambo nightclub. It would be known as the Decker-Flynn Galleries, and now Errol (who had acquired a Gauguin under Decker's tutelage) took up the subsidy of the living expenses of John Decker and family.

As for Sadakichi, he was about to vacate his shack in Banning and depart on his trip east, his final Odyssey. John Decker would never see Sadakichi Hartmann again.

March 18, 1944: John Decker won a prominent art prize — the John Barton Payne Medal for his painting *Circus Strong Man* in the Virginia Museum of Fine Arts' exhibition of contemporary American painting. The round, bronze medal gave him great pride — although not as great as Sadakichi's letter.

April 7, 1944: *Uncertain Glory*, Errol Flynn's only release of the year, opened at Broadway's Strand. The saga: French criminal Errol, *en route* to the guillotine, escapes due to a British bombing. Pursued by detective Paul Lukas (1943's Best Actor Oscar winner for *Watch on the Rhine*), he scores a heroic victory for French patriotism. Archer Winsten in his *New York Post* review got off the best critical crack: he wrote that Flynn rescued Faye Emerson in the film "almost before you can say 'Geisler.'" Directed by Raoul Walsh, *Uncertain Glory* featured a strong performance from Flynn, but was not a box office hit.

April 23, 1944: It was Shakespeare's 380th birthday. John Carradine's dream had been to premiere his "John Carradine and his Shakespeare Players" on Broadway this very night. Alas, the company had gone bust, and come the feast day of the Bard, Carradine was set to report to Universal City, California to play Count Dracula in *House of Frankenstein*.

It was "a monster rally," with mad doctor Boris Karloff resurrecting Carradine's

Carradine in *House of Dracula*

bloodsucker, along with the Wolf Man (Lon Chaney) and Frankenstein's Monster (Glenn Strange), all the while assisted by a homicidal hunchback (J. Carrol Naish). The censors were at least as concerned about Elena Verdugo showing a flash of her black panties in her Gypsy dance as they were with the film's eight violent deaths.

Carradine, in flowing cape and stylishly cocked top hat, naturally gave Dracula his own mad flair — quite different from Bela Lugosi's:

> My attitude would be definitely Shakespearean, with a nod to Richard III. Dracula is a tragic figure — a monarch of the undead, in some respects like Lear, his kingdom gone, forced to live among inferiors, an outcast. I added my own ideas to personalize the role — I wore the top hat at an angle because this man could afford to be debonair. I used my eyes like weapons since Dracula could, of course, bend one's will to his own…

It sure wasn't Shakespeare on Broadway, but *House of Frankenstein* gave Carradine one of his great all-time cinema death scenes — screaming as his vampire falls and decays under the rays of the dawn. It became his most famous horror role and, ironically, is the reason many fans remember John Carradine.

At the time, Carradine was "living in sin" with Sonia Sorel at the Garden of Allah, 8152 Sunset Boulevard, the colony of haciendas built around a pool shaped like the Black Sea. It had once been the home of Alla Nazimova, the legendary Silent Screen star, who now lived at her former showplace in a single apartment. The liquor flowed freely, John and Sonia had many fights, and Sheilah Graham's *The Garden of Allah* provided the baroque imagery of Sonia chasing her lover around the pool, waving a wickedly spiked high heel as a weapon as Carradine "recited Shakespeare to the adjacent hills." As Ms. Graham continued:

> Carradine could be serious, but mostly he was eccentric. He had a bust made of himself and took it to the swimming pool while he swam. The bust was made of bronze and he believed it would get a nice patina in the sun.
>
> Then there was the night that Carradine decided he was Jesus and tried to walk across the swimming pool. [Playwright] Marc Connelly, always a gambler, was betting on John to make it. He lost his bet.

Carradine, who desperately wanted to fight in the War but was rejected, managed one heroic act. Edgar Ulmer, who directed Carradine (and Sonia) in PRC's *Bluebeard* in 1944, visited the couple one day at the Garden, along with his wife Shirley and little daughter Arianne. As the adults chatted by the pool, Arianne, in the pool in her water wings, sank. It was Carradine who noticed her plight and dived in to save her.

April 24, 1944: EGG BOPS ERROL FLYNN IN BATTLE OF BEAUTIES headlined the *Los Angeles Evening Herald-Express*. It seems Errol was enjoying a Mocambo catfight between Miss Toby Tuttle ("23-year-old entertainer") and Miss Virginia Hill ("wealthy southern girl whose parties have made more or less a splash in Hollywood"). Toby admitted throwing the egg — she felt Flynn should have done something to break up the fight — "so I grabbed an egg from the tray of a passing waiter and let fly at him." Flynn's pal Freddie McEvoy helped him get the egg out of his hair and, as the *Evening Herald-Express* put it, "The two then left the battlefield to the ladies."

April 25, 1944: Universal's morale-booster *Follow the Boys* had a big Broadway opening at Loew's Criterion Theatre. It featured such acts as Orson Welles sawing Marlene Dietrich in half, Jeanette MacDonald singing "Beyond the Blue Horizon," Sophie Tucker, Dinah Shore, Arthur Rubinstein, four orchestras, virtually the entire contract roster of Universal Studios in guest appearances, etc., including, as the *New York Times* noted, "W.C. Fields doing his delicious pool table act." It was a patriotic show for armed services morale, and as the *New York Herald Tribune* reported:

> When you see W.C. Fields running through his elliptical billiard cue routine before a group of inductees, for example, there is no question that *Follow the Boys* is in a great tradition of showmanship.

W.C. made two more 1944 film appearances. On June 6, D-Day itself, United Artists' *Song of the Open Road* opened at Broadway's Loew's Criterion, and the *New York Herald Tribune* gave thanks that it was "almost pure escapist entertainment." Fourteen-year-old radio personality Jane Powell was the star, and the show included a W.C. Fields vs. Charlie McCarthy donnybrook. In truth, the old hearty fighting form was failing; Fields was making more and more visits to the Las Encinas Sanitarium in Pasadena, plagued by cirrhosis of the liver. On July 6, United Artists' *Sensations of 1945* premiered at Loew's State Theatre. Eleanor Powell was the star, and W. C. Fields was one of the "sensations," along with Sophie Tucker, the acrobatic Cristianis, the Pallenberg Bears, Cab Calloway and Woody Herman and their orchestras, the Flying Copelands, et al. As the *New York Sun* put it:

> At the end W.C. Fields appears in a singularly unfunny scene, Sophie Tucker sings loudly and Miss Powell dances with a high school horse as partner. This dance is the best part of the picture.

W.C.'s partner in the skit is Louise Currie, a blonde actress perhaps best remembered as the heroine who lashes Bela Lugosi with a whip in *The Ape Man* (1943). Ms. Currie oomphs on a railway set as the great man tries to get her into a train compartment. Drunks show up and fight as W.C. offers a running commentary ("Oh! That's terrible — I must try that on my wife"). He was, in truth, very ill. Ms. Currie remembers that W.C.'s memory (and eyesight) were so bad that he had to use huge blackboards — à la the declining John Barrymore — to read them, and that multiple takes were necessary. The skit concludes:

> W.C. Fields: Yeah, aren't drunks repulsive? Come, my little popinjay.

The repulsive drunks joke was, ironically, W.C.'s last line in a movie, and *Sensations of 1945* was W.C. Fields' final film.

FAN FARE

PRIZE CONTEST!

Can You Describe Errol Flynn IN ONE SENTEN[CE]

Using Just 20 Words

HOW proficient are you in the use of adjectives? In order to describe Errol Flynn most effectively at least three descriptive adjectives should be used. For instance, here's a sample sentence of 20 words containing three adjectives which we think fit his type and personality:

One of the most *debonair* and *adventurous* Hollywood actors is *attractive* Errol Flynn whose hobby is travelling in strange places.

There are dozens of adjectives equally descriptive of Errol Flynn. All you have to do is think up three which you think describe him most aptly and incorporate them into a well-rounded sentence of your own, using not more and not less than 20 words. Write your sentence on the coupon below.

There will be four prizes awarded to the writers of the four best sentences, in our opinion. These prizes consist of four beautiful gold wrist watches made by the Longines-Wittnauer Company. They are watches which everyone of you would be proud to own.

PRIZES TO BE A[WARDED]

FIRST PRIZE
Lady's wrist watch, value[d]

SECOND PRIZE
Man's wrist watch, valued

THIRD PRIZE
Lady's wrist watch, value[d]

FOURTH PRIZE
Man's wrist watch, value[d]

CONDITIO[NS]

1. Sentences must not be [ ] not less than 20 words. [ ] more adjectives must b[e]

2. Contest closes Midnigh[t]

3. In the event of a tie,

USE THIS COUPON TO SEND IN YOUR ENTRIES
(Write Plainly)

July 9, 1944: The *Los Angeles Times* noted the Decker-Flynn Galleries was hosting a show of 50 Decker canvases:

> His portraits of clowns have a room to themselves. The larger gallery features a portrait of Earl Carroll, looking saintly under a spotlight in his theater, one of Decker's wife against a background of Paris, and a beautiful "Grand Canal, Venice," loaned by Mrs. Cary Grant (Barbara Hutton).
>
> A large twilight picture entitled "Pigs in Clover" was painted looking out the gallery's side window. It shows the junky back end of a Sunset "Strip" nightclub. In the windows guests are eating.

The nightclub that the *Times* was careful not to name was, of course, the Mocambo — which sat right in front of the new Decker-Flynn Galleries. Charlie Morrison, the Mocambo's owner, learned about the painting that showed the rear of his glamour Strip niterie littered with bottles and garbage and, rather than raise hell, proceeded to correct the conditions. Decker thought Morrison such a good sport that he gave him the painting "Pigs in Clover," and Morrison, delighted, presented Decker with a free pass for drinks, food and entertainment at the Mocambo — all he had to do was tip the servers.

It was drinks on the house 24/7 for John Decker. Christmas had surely come early.

October 17, 1944: W.C. Fields wrote a letter to Fowler, which proved neither time nor tide was reducing his Olympian wrath:

> You will note by the gentleman who lived to be 104 that the panacea of all ills is tobacco and "demon rum." Longevity can only be reached by the use of these stimulants….
>
> Did you read that son-of-a-bitch Truman's speech and did you glom his store teeth. What a deceitful bastard he must be…

October 31, 1944: Harrison Carroll reported in the *Los Angeles Evening Herald-Express* what he described as "Positively the funniest of the one punch brawls," with the hero Anthony Quinn. At the Beverly Hills art gallery of Vincent Price, a big lout greeted Quinn with, "Hello, Mr. DeMille." When Quinn ignored him, the antagonist asked, "So, since you've married into a big family, you won't talk?" — and gave Quinn a shove. As Carroll wrote:

Tony let him have it and the screwball hit the floor, where he sat rubbing his cheek and muttering, "Well, well, well."

"I hated to do it," says Quinn, "but I still have a little of the common touch even if I did marry into a distinguished family."

Quinn played in four 1944 releases, including the Technicolor *Buffalo Bill*, as Chief Yellow Hand. (*Buffalo Bill* also featured Thomas Mitchell, going strong in 1944 in five major releases.) Quinn was still a character actor — stardom appeared to be far away.

Meanwhile, Quinn joined Errol Flynn and Gene Tierney on a bond tour. In his book *My Days with Errol Flynn*, Buster Wiles (Flynn crony and stunt man) wrote:

> Flynn was scheduled to do a Red Cross radio broadcast in the Chase Hotel, and we schemed an elaborate gag with Tony Quinn as the victim. We had sent a script to Tony and asked if he would kindly participate in the show.
>
> The radio personnel were all in on the joke, playing it straight as Flynn and Tony began rehearsing their material. The director gave notice that the live broadcast was about to begin. Once underway, Flynn suddenly blurted out some very foul language, then in a shocked voice, he exclaimed, "Why, Tony! Why did you say that?"
>
> Tony turned white and tried to continue. More foul language from Flynn. The director stormed from the control booth, indignantly yelling at Quinn.
>
> Errol in a shocked tone, said, "Tony, you shouldn't talk like that."
>
> "But… but I didn't," responded poor Tony.
>
> "Yes, you did!" shot back the director, "I heard you!"
>
> Flynn just shook his head. "Shame on you, Tony."
>
> Another guy ran up, saying, "We're getting telephone calls from around the country, wanting to know why Anthony Quinn cursed on the radio!"
>
> "I'm ruined," said a distraught Quinn. "I won't even be able to do a B–picture now…"

In his book *One Man Tango*, Quinn offers a different version of the story, claiming Flynn referred to C.B. DeMille on the broadcast as "that sonofabitch," called Gene Tierney "a real fucking sweetheart," etc., owning up to his remarks but making Quinn guilty by association. Quinn wrote that he returned to his hotel and received calls from Hedda Hopper, Louella Parsons, father-in-law DeMille, and wife Katherine, until Flynn himself called.

"Gotcha, Tony!" said Flynn — who then, as Quinn expressed it, "laughed like a madman."

There had been no actual broadcast, and the callers from Hollywood had all been in on the joke.

November 21, 1944: Sadakichi Hartmann, age 77 years, 11 months and 13 days, died at about 11 p.m. at the home of his daughter, Mrs. Dorothea Gilliland in St. Petersburg, Florida, the cause of death: coronary thrombosis. The *L.A. Times* noted that Sadakichi "had arrived there only two days before from his celebrated shack on the outskirts of Banning." The obituary called him "The self-crowned 'King of Bohemia,'" "an incredible figure on the American scene for more than threescore years" and a "quaint genius" who "was a legend from Greenwich Village to Telegraph Hill."

His final years had been, due to his German and Japanese ancestry, one of fear and persecution. In their introduction to *White Chrysanthemums*, Harry Lawton and George Knox wrote:

> The Riverside County Sheriff's Department staked out Hartmann's shack. When his daughter, Wistaria, or his son-in-law drove into town, they often found themselves followed by a patrol car. Indian families at Morongo also banded with the townspeople in the common cause of hatred towards Hartmann. When Sadakichi walked the desert at night, drawing up charts of the constellations, it was rumored that he was making one of his periodical climbs to the top of Mount San Jacinto to signal Japanese bombers off the coast with a lantern.

Sadakichi and Gene Fowler had been squabbling via letters during 1944, both sides still angry about the aborted biography. Fowler had been promising Sadakichi an overcoat since March. Sadakichi also wanted brandy and still was waging his years-long campaign for Fowler to buy him a coffin, according to Will Fowler, who quotes Sadakichi in *The Second Handshake*:

> Sarah Bernhardt used to sleep in one, and I, the great Sadakichi Hartmann, shall be marked down in history more indelibly than that shrieking female. Thank you. Hah!

A letter from Gene Fowler, dated November 2, 1944, survives in the Sadakichi Hartmann Collection, University of California, Riverside — it came accompanied by the long-promised coat. Perhaps sensing the end was near, Fowler praised Sadakichi in the accompanying letter and expressed how he deeply valued his friendship. Apparently Sadakichi wore the coat on his final trip across the country.

According to *White Chrysanthemums*, Sadakichi's final resting place is "a pauper's grave surrounded by ancient magnolias heavy with Spanish moss." In his feature, "John Decker's Hollywood" in *Esquire* (December, 1945), Ben Hecht provided a none-too-respectful eulogy for Sadakichi, via analysis of Decker's painting of the subject:

> Sadakichi Hartmann was exactly what the Decker brush says he was — a truculent poseur, a battered and dyspeptic ego. Decker's Hartmann is a mocking valentine to this most pretentious of his Hollywood friends. Sadakichi was part German and part Jap. He was also part faker and part bore. There was enough left over to sneer at his betters and write an occasional line of wild poetry. But chiefly Sadakichi lived and died as an angry light under a bushel. Decker went under the bushel with Hartmann to paint him. He painted a great man, macabre and ridiculous as a poem by Baudelaire.
>
> The painting is owned by Burgess Meredith, whose bride, Paulette Goddard, gets the hiccoughs every time she looks at it.

Sadakichi received a far more affectionate tribute in Gene Fowler's 1954 book *Minutes of the Last Meeting*. The popular book inspired Wistaria Hartmann to exhume her father's manuscripts, release his angry spirit, and sue Gene Fowler.

More on that later.

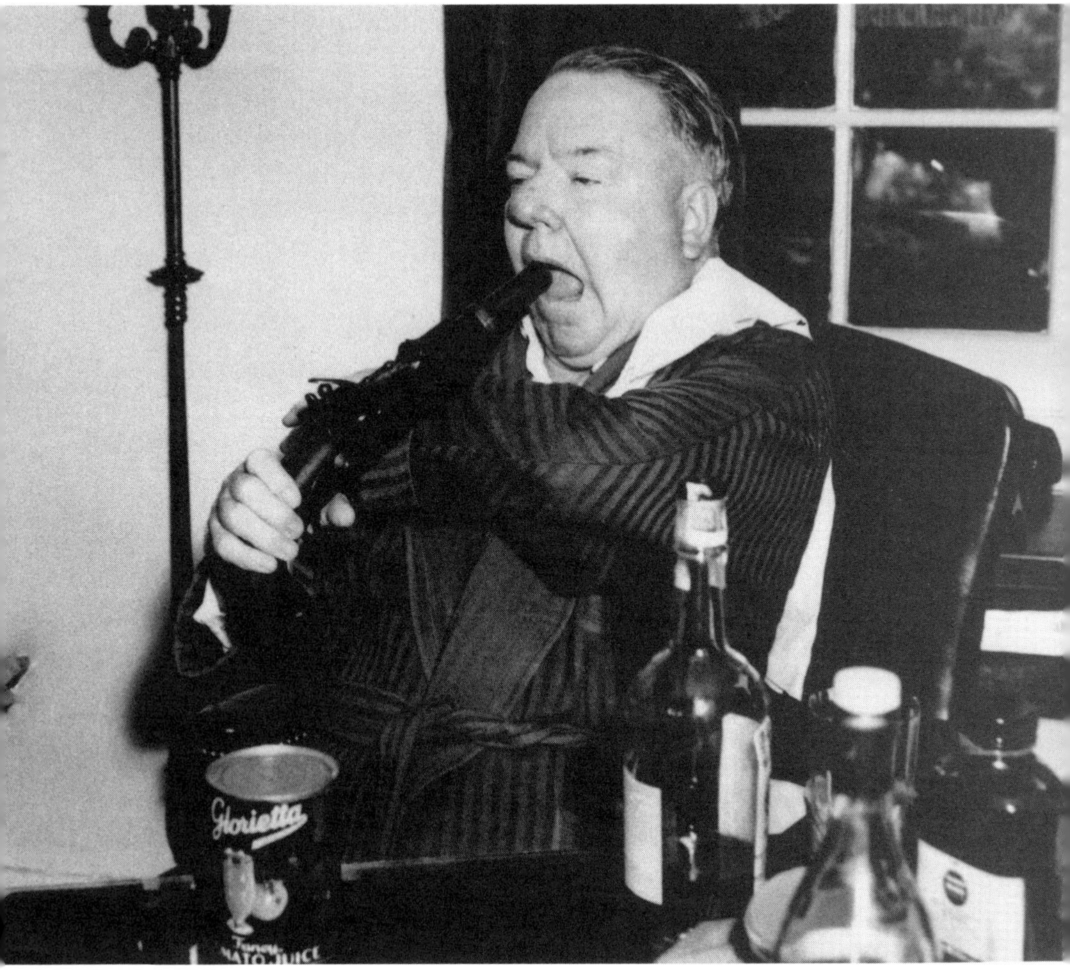
Glorietta

Chapter Eighteen

*1945:
End of a War,
The Paintings of Scarlet Street
And "The Five Million Virgin Cunts
from Heaven"*

Decker's studio-gallery in Hollywood is full of his potential sitters. It is unlike any painter's studio I have ever known. In it famous and fabulously wealthy people sit constantly eating and drinking at Decker's expense.

Movie stars, society leaders, literary Pooh-Bahs and rogues of every hue and accent occupy the couches and sprawl in the corners. It is the only spot in Hollywood where you will never hear movie or money talk. The Decker bar at one end of the studio is a sort of confessional to which the Famous bring their insecurities and humilities. Decker of the broken nose, Byronic collar, hangover eyes, rhapsodic chuckle and slyly delicate hands is himself as strange a figure as ever paced an atelier. He looks like a composite of all his celebrities on canvas — a feline fellow full of grace and disintegration, elegant and unconvincing as a con man and turning thirty years of anarchy and derision on his come-lately disciples.

A contempt for the shams around him lies under (and sometimes over) his swashbuckler humors. And the celebrities who haunt his one-man Bohemia for free eats and drinks, sit and stare for hours at the things they have forgotten and that keep banging out of the Decker canvases — the mysteries of lonely

places and the enchantment of the unimportant out of which Art is made.
— Ben Hecht, "John Decker's Hollywood," *Esquire,* December, 1945

Germany surrenders May 8, 1945. Following two atomic bomb blasts, Japan surrenders August, 1945. World War II was over, and a blast of postwar euphoria explodes in the United States, especially in Hollywood.

None of the Bundy Drive Boys had actually fought in the war. As it approached its end and its conclusion, the surviving members were still at war with their demons, experiencing both victory and defeat.

Errol Flynn became the father of daughter Deirdre January 10, 1945; he also rode the rumors of a divorce from new wife/mother Nora and, in April, engaged in an epic fight with John Huston (supposedly over Flynn's remarks made about Olivia de Havilland) that provided Flynn broken ribs, Huston a broken nose and put both in the hospital. Sensitive about accusations of winning the war on a Hollywood back lot, Flynn endured his most relentless pounding for Warners' 1945 *Objective Burma,* which brought Flynn an especially hot roasting by the British press.

John Carradine married Sonia Sorel March 25, and they cut the wedding cake with Hamlet's sword. Ex-wife Ardanelle pursued her ex-spouse for alimony contempt and, come the summer, had John arrested — the actor, in slouch hat, dramatically posing for the press from behind bars. He got out in time to reprise John Barrymore's unworthy vehicle *My Dear Children* with Sonia at Coney Island, and came back to Hollywood to play Dracula again in Universal's *House of Dracula,* once again sharing the screen with Lon Chaney's Wolf Man and Glenn Strange's Monster, as well as a female hunchback (Jane Adams sporting a plaster-of-Paris hump).

Thomas Mitchell was still racking up credits, including *Adventure,* which MGM sold with the famous teaser, "Gable's Back and Garson's Got Him." Roland Young had one of his best film roles as Detective Blore in *And Then There Were None,* based on Agatha Christie's *Ten Little Indians.*

Anthony Quinn co-starred with John Wayne in *Back to Bataan.* Ben Hecht scripted the Alfred Hitchcock hit *Spellbound,* produced by David O. Selznick, starring Gregory Peck and Ingrid Bergman, and featuring a dream sequence filled with paintings by Salvador Dali.

A sadly ailing W.C. was failing, but still his feisty self. James Curtis writes of a hot day in the summer of 1945 when Gene Fowler, his daughter Jane (then 24 years old) and clarinet virtuoso/bandleader Artie Shaw all visited W.C. at Los Feliz. Curtis quotes Shaw as saying,

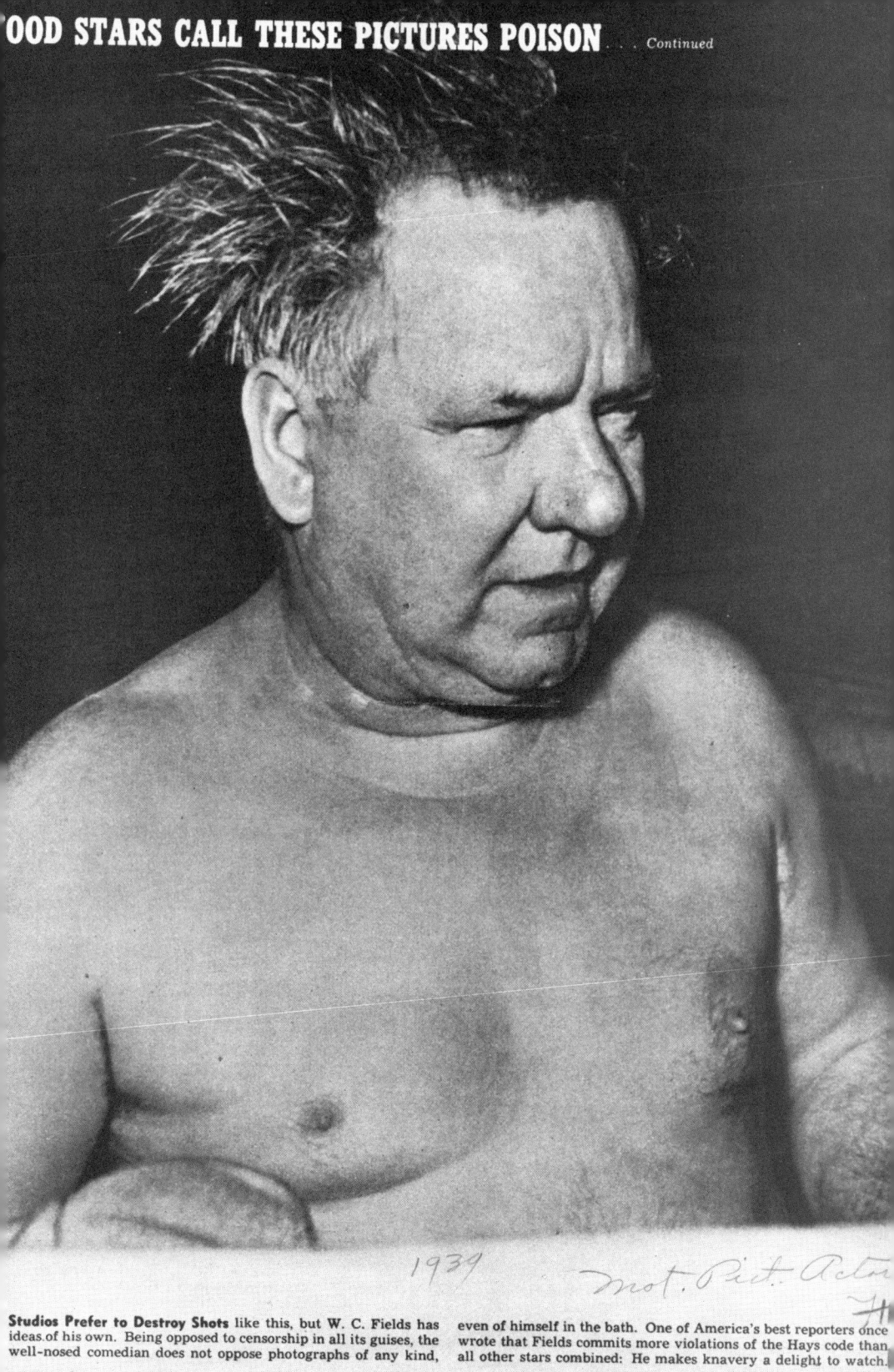

OOD STARS CALL THESE PICTURES POISON... Continued

Studios Prefer to Destroy Shots like this, but W. C. Fields has ideas of his own. Being opposed to censorship in all its guises, the well-nosed comedian does not oppose photographs of any kind, even of himself in the bath. One of America's best reporters once wrote that Fields commits more violations of the Hays code than all other stars combined: He makes knavery a delight to watch.

Fields was seated at a table in what appeared to be the living room, going over some household reports. He was wearing a straw hat — a boater — and it appeared as if he was wearing shorts but no shirt. When he saw Jane, he immediately stood — he was a very courtly man — and it was then that we realized he was absolutely stark naked. Fields acted as if it was perfectly natural to receive friends that way. Jane burst out laughing, and the conversation ensued as if nothing happened.

That fall, the 65-year-old W.C. Fields gave up his Los Feliz house and entered Las Encinas Sanitarium in Pasadena.

A pencil-written letter survives in one of the Decker scrapbooks — it's undated, but the allusion to his being "near fifty" dates it to circa 1945. In handwriting that becomes increasingly distorted, a clearly drunken Decker scrawls page after page, eight in all, some of it on his "Decker and Flynn Galleries" letterhead, pouring out his misery to Phyllis, bemoaning his sexual impotence and avowing his love for her:

My dear Phyllis and wife—
It seems very difficult to think and also get over the thoughts one has — and more difficult to be great… in my opinion you are much greater than I am… I swear to you… nobody else could interest me outside of you! I love you very much and just as I don't answer letters and important things I don't seem to tell you about such things enough — I know I am at fault — but God knows I do not go out or react to anybody but you… I do love you so much and if you ever left me, that would be the end of everything… I am not potent or [sic] I have been to a doctor for that purpose. I only find alcohol stimulating. I shall go and find out about that — I am near fifty and shall try to find something that does things for me to be able to satisfy your desires for me… my lack of potency does not refer to an old bag such as Gene Fowler's wife — because you are as alluring as I met you — it is me that finds no Glamour in female of any sort young sophisticated or cunt of any sort… I don't know why people laugh when people become impotent at fifty… if five million virgin cunts droped [sic] from heaven you still would be my only love — I've done so many things to hurt you and you've done the same but you and I are the same sort of people — please don't destroy you and me!!!
Yes — I am selffish [sic] but I will only live for a few years….

The rest of the letter is written under such obvious distress that it is difficult to decipher. Decker seemingly refers to his daughter Gloria, and possibly their allegedly incestuous situation, losing control with words such as "…son-of-a-bitch ex fuck swine… I hate her gutts (sic)…" He writes "I dug my own grave," concludes "I am so sick and tired about blackmail," and finishes off with "I love you and nobody else in the world."

He signs the letter to his wife in full, "John Decker."

Was Gloria blackmailing Decker? Had her trip to Los Angeles been for the purpose of seducing her own father, and making him pay? Was his surrender to her charms (or their mutual seduction) been the "grave" he had dug? Did Phyllis know about the alleged incest? Was the entire *l'affaire Gloria* threatening Decker's sanity?

DECKER and FLYNN Galleries

Significant Paintings

1215 ALTA LOMA ROAD
LOS ANGELES 46, CALIFORNIA

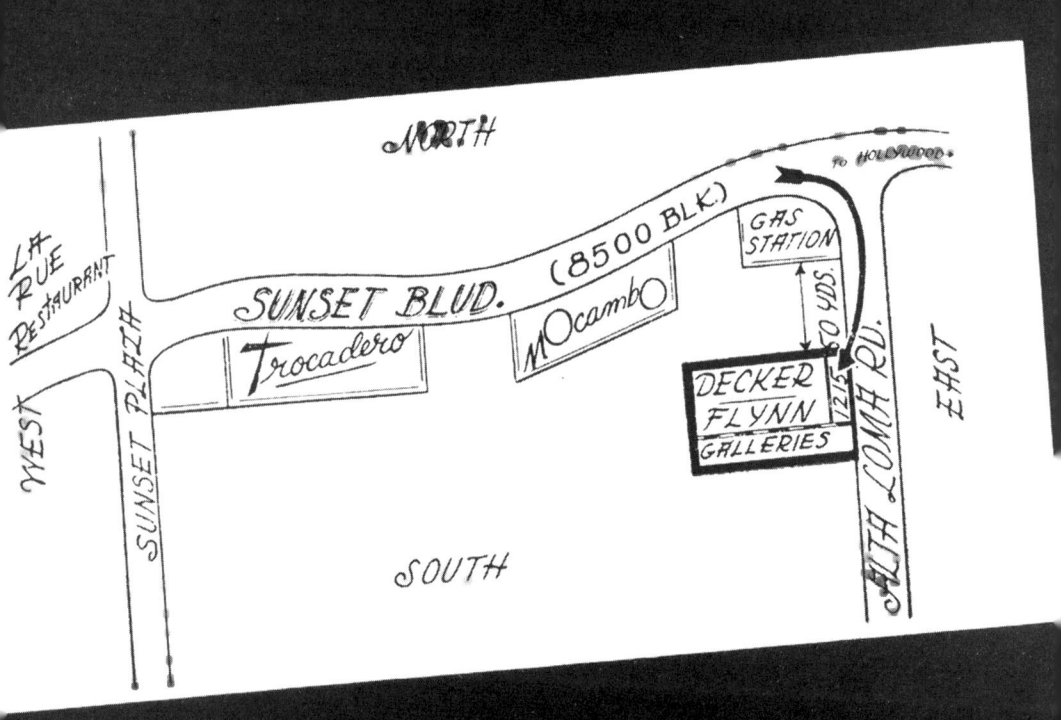

Telephone BRadshaw 2-1460

Map:

- NORTH / SOUTH / EAST / WEST
- To HOLLYWOOD
- SUNSET BLVD. (8500 BLK.)
- LA RUE Restaurant
- SUNSET PLAZA
- Trocadero
- Mocambo
- GAS STATION
- DECKER FLYNN GALLERIES — 1215, 50 YDS.
- ALTA LOMA RD.

Chapter Nineteen

*1946:
Mona,
Peeing in the Wind,
A Female Captain Bligh,
And the Passing of the Great Charlatan*

> I demand a creature of another sex, but as hideous as myself… It is true, we shall be monsters, cut off from all the world; but on that account we shall be more attached to one another… O! my creator, make me happy…!
>
> — *Frankenstein* by Mary Shelley (1818)

It was perhaps right and proper that John Decker — after a garish court battle with "ghost wife" Ellen, his Freudian escapade with his alluring, long-lost daughter Gloria, and amidst a mid-life crisis with Phyllis — would create his own woman.

Of course, the miracle was doomed, and Decker's God-emulating role became less of a Pygmalion, and more of a Dr. Frankenstein. At any rate, the artist's stab at black magic spawned one of his most aberrant misadventures, climaxing in what L.A. papers proclaimed Hollywood's "Battle of the Century" and providing John Decker some of his most spectacular publicity.

It was the saga of… Mona.

She was beautiful. She was a heartbreaker.

She was a mannequin.

Gene Fowler remembered that Decker and Errol Flynn discovered Mona while shopping in downtown Los Angeles for furnishings for the Alta Loma studio. She was sporting only a strawberry blonde wig, and as Mona posed seductively in the store window, she enchanted her two famous admirers, enjoying an instant conquest. Notoriety was immediate as Flynn and Decker drove Mona to Alta Loma in Flynn's convertible — fellow motorists believed that Flynn and pal, in their wicked, wicked ways, were taking a naked strawberry blonde for a joyride.

While Decker didn't create the original mannequin, he instilled the personality. Mona, in all her glory (and the eyes of her admirers), was a diva, a voluptuary, a fetishist's dream girl. In his column "Bits and Pieces" (November 1945), Alan Mowbray, despite his jocular tone, could barely disguise his own personal infatuation with Decker's "blessed event":

Decker at his Alta Loma gallery/house with a probable Modigliani forgery

Mona, there's a real girl. Somewhat of a shock when you first see her, because she is completely uninhibited, brazenly displaying her charms to all and sundry.

The night I first met her, she was leaning nonchalantly against the bar in a corner of the studio, wearing a John Frederics hat, a pair of very expensive stockings of black net held up by a pair of very saucy and ornate French garters, and a mink coat draped becomingly, but loosely and revealingly, over her shoulders.

Like most beautiful girls, she is a little on the dumb side... in fact she is a dummy, but I warn you not to take your maiden aunt into the Decker studio, because Mona looks all too real, and all too naked, in the careful high light in which she resides.

Decker apparently had a longtime fantasy of just such a "Mona." In his story "Asylum Soliloquy," Decker had written a virtual horror tale in which the narrator searches for a woman named Mona who had driven his friend into an asylum. To quote a passage:

> I was restless. I had just finished reading a morbid book entitled *Alruane* by Hanns Heinz Ewers, a story about a girl who had been born through a strange unnatural way to the parents: the father a lust-murderer; the mother a frigid whore. It had been the experiment of a mad scientist. The girl had been born without human feeling or emotions of love and destroyed all men who came in contact with her. There was Mona again…

As the ever-resilient Phyllis learned to live with Mona, the mannequin's perverse allure captivated not only Decker but other Bundy Drive Boys as well. "Mona became an important part of the scene at the new studio," wrote Gene Fowler in *Minutes of the Last Meeting*. "Indeed, she was the cause of a fistfight between two gentlemen who grew overzealous about having the next dance with her."

"Decker is giving a shower for her," wrote the ever-ardent Alan Mowbray (who one suspects wanted to rumba with Mona), "and in the very near future she will be one of the best-dressed women in town."

And there came the night of Thursday, January 17, 1946.

It wasn't promoted as a "shower" for Mona — it appears Decker saw the big night as rather a coming-out party. Diana Barrymore later remembered that Decker had promised "to unveil a new statue," but none of the Los Angeles papers that covered the debacle to come would report this *raison d'être* for the party. They would report the presence of Mona.

The guest list at Alta Loma was impressive. Besides Decker familiars such as Errol Flynn (and wife Nora), Ben Hecht, Anthony Quinn, and Alan Mowbray, there was Paulette Goddard and husband Burgess Meredith, David O. Selznick and Jennifer Jones, Ida Lupino, Merle Oberon, Harpo Marx, Constance Collier, Raoul Walsh, Lon Chaney Jr., Diana Barrymore, Jack La Rue and Lawrence Tierney. It was a volatile assemblage. Flynn, of course, was a lightning rod for fistfights. Chaney, Universal's Wolf Man, was fond of drunken brawls. But the real dynamo of the guests was Tierney, who played the title role in 1946's *Dillinger* for RKO Studios and was one of the most violent, profane, out-of-control personalities in postwar Hollywood.

The festivities began. Mona was apparently veiled until the Cinderella fairy-tale moment that Decker would remove the veil and — *voila!* — introduce her to Hollywood society. How they would react to his show window dummy was anybody's guess, but Decker was surely ready to relish any shock and welcome any adulation.

However, the unveiling never happened, at least not how Decker intended it, and the result was a disaster.

"HOLLYWOOD BRAWL" headlined the *Los Angeles Evening Herald-Express*, (January 18, 1946) which reported:

> It's been a long — long — time —
> Since Hollywood has had as interesting and mysterious a brawl as climaxed at a glamorous party before dawn today in the home of John Decker, noted artist and bosom pal of the late John Barrymore…
> Among the Hollywood stars reported as principals in the slugfest, which started over indignities done "Mona," a mannequin who was smashed to pieces, were Jack La Rue, film "heavy" player Lawrence Tierney, who played Dillinger "in the films," actress Diana Barrymore, and actor Anthony Quinn.

There were at least two versions of the fracas that night at Alta Loma:

- ★ Sammy Colt, Ethel Barrymore's son (and Diana's cousin), accidentally knocked over Mona, so Lawrence Tierney punched Colt in the face. When Jack La Rue came to Colt's defense, Tierney punched La Rue in the face.
- ★ Tierney claimed that guest Bill Kent ("stepson of the owner of a noted Sunset Strip nightclub," noted the *Evening Herald Express*) razzed him, claiming "that anyone who liked Errol Flynn was no good anyway." Anthony Quinn tried to intervene, but Tierney and Kent battled outside the studio. When Jack La Rue tried to play peacemaker, Tierney claimed that "I pushed him away and he fell and hit his head." (In fact, La Rue ended up at West Hollywood Emergency Hospital with cuts about the head, nose and lower lip.)

In her memoir *Too Much, Too Soon*, Diana Barrymore provided a vivid account of the melee, professing Tierney the villain, supporting the charge that he'd punched both Sammy Colt and Jack La Rue:

> When I saw blood on Sammy and Jack, I exploded. I rushed up to Tierney — he'd ripped off his shirt and stood like a belligerent Tarzan — "You dreary, dreadful actor!" I cried. "If you want to fight, hit me! You're punching everyone else, so why don't you hit a woman?" I slapped him with all my might, half-a-dozen times. I was wearing two rings and they must have hurt.
> A woman egged me on, screaming, "Hit him, Diana! That's the girl! Tell him where to get off!"

By the way, the *Evening Herald Express* claimed Diana had slapped Tierney *eight* times. In the night and the atmosphere, accurate counting was surely a challenge.

Diana Barrymore also wrote of the true horror of the party, at least for its host: the notorious battle followed Mona's symbolic deflowering and decapitation:

> A great deal of drinking went on; guests came and left. Several abortive fistfights broke out. The statue (sic) was knocked over before it could be unveiled. It crashed to the floor; the head broke off and rolled away. Decker uttered an anguished cry, swooped down and picked up the headless figure, and hugged it to him…

Surely the sight of Mona, broken, battered, her bald, unwigged head severed from her torso, broke the heart of her creator. As most of the famous guests fled in the night, trying to escape the nasty publicity, Alan Mowbray stood in for the grieving host, loyally taking on the role of spokesman, informing the press that all had been well before the despoiling of Mona.

"Until then it was a lovely party," insisted Mowbray.

John Decker naturally talked with the press, although he claimed he had no account of the battle to offer, for he'd been inside "cleaning up the pieces" of the shattered Mona.

"I don't pay any attention to them anymore," John Decker said of the donnybrook. "Somebody's always fighting at my parties."

The reporter asked if any drinking had taken place.

"Certainly there was drinking," replied Decker. "What the hell kind of parties do you think I give?"

The *Bride of Decker* horror show had its baroque climax. Mona's desecration was a lasting shock for Decker — he could never bring himself to restore her to her former glory. John Decker had only a year and a half to live, and as he sensed his approaching mortality, illusion was still necessary, but perhaps harder to sustain.

In February of 1946, Errol Flynn published his second book, *Showdown*, the well-written saga of an Irish soldier of fortune who leads a Hollywood film crew into cannibal-infested New Guinea. He dedicates the book to John Decker.

Spring: John Decker enjoys a new distinction as 12 of his paintings from the film *Scarlet Street* are displayed at New York's Museum of Modern Art. Decker placed the value of the paintings at $35,000.

Soon after, Decker and Errol Flynn visit San Francisco, where 64 of Decker's paintings are hung at a one-man show at the DeYoung Museum. While in Babylon by the Bay, Decker recognizes a genuine Modigliani in an antique shop window, convinces the proprietor the painting was a fraud, buys it for $400, and sends a telegram to Thomas Mitchell (still savoring his "Rembrandt"), claiming he found a true Modigliani and sells it to Mitchell for $2,000. As before, Decker crows to everyone but Mitchell about his latest flim-flam. Ever-forgiving Gene Fowler claims Mitchell "had no cause for complaint," because he later sells the Modigliani for $15,000.

June 8: *Los Angeles Times* reports that Decker hobnobs at the home of multi-millionaire Atwater Kent. Then, on June 23, the *Times* offers the headline, "John Decker Exhibits His Best Art Yet":

> In recent years John Decker, who is peculiarly Hollywood's own painter, had been creeping out of the theatrical murk that once tinged his work into the upper air where painting can be viewed on its merits. His new exhibit, which opened last week at the Francis Taylor Galleries, Beverly Hills, to July 13, is the best he had yet presented.
>
> Here are huge still lifes of glassware — "The Cognac Drinker," "The Absinthe Drinker" — of astonishing depth, clarity and brilliance. The human significance that carries a picture beyond its esthetic values is present, too, but it is translated into fine form, color, line and textures.
>
> There are city scenes with a curious timelessness — the peculiar beauty of old brick shining from a church, the spell of a lighted street at night. Tiny pictures of lemons and strawberries are gems that attract the eye and fascinate the mind. And, one of the show's finest, there is the tiny picture of a herring. Decker's brown-reds are something to note and remember.
>
> His power to convey the drama that is life, unweakened by sentimentality, is seen in the three death mask paintings, one being of Beethoven. One large painting, charged with pathos, is that of a gravestone upon which is written, "Ici repos Vincent Van Gogh." A real tribute from one artist to another.

With his triumphant art show, John Decker was faring better in 1946 than some of his fellow Bundy Drive pals.

John Carradine was performing a wild John Barrymore take-off, complete with cocked slouch hat and loud nose-snorting, in *Down Missouri Way*, a musical from Poverty Row's PRC Studios. He explodes in *Twentieth Century*-style battles with his leading-lady-from-hell (Renee Godfrey):

> Carradine: My dear Gloria, the true artiste can rise above her role, if she but possesses the divine madness!!
> Godfrey: Madness, my eye! I wasn't born yesterday!
> Carradine: How true! But with the proper makeup, I think we can effectively conceal that from the camera!

Down Missouri Way bore the strange distinction of having its world premiere in the Missouri State Prison auditorium in Jefferson City. Shortly after its shoot, Carradine and wife Sonia flee L.A. — ex-wife Ardanelle was about to have him jailed again for alimony contempt. The Carradines settle in New York, where they made their Broadway debuts in *The Duchess of Malfi* (October 15, 1946). Life wasn't ideal. As Sonia remembered: "We moved to the Ritz Towers in New York. We had a lot of hopes then. But they didn't last long. Broadway producers knew that John couldn't go back to Hollywood. It put him in a bad bargaining position."

Anthony Quinn was experiencing career and financial troubles. "The war years may have been a boon for the industry," he wrote in his book *One Man Tango*, "but they were a bust for me." When offered a supporting role in Paramount's Western *California* starring Barbara Stanwyck and Ray Milland, Quinn demanded $15,000 for a week's work. As he proudly noted in *One Man Tango*, he got it.

Ben Hecht had scripted Alfred Hitchcock's *Notorious*, rating another Academy nomination. Alan Mowbray won the role of Shakespearean actor Granville Thorndyke in John Ford's *My Darling Clementine*, and recited Hamlet's great soliloquy, possibly Mowbray's finest moment in films. Thomas Mitchell, too, played one of his best-remembered roles: the eccentric, pitiful, bespectacled Uncle Billy, who has a pet bird on his shoulder (and who loses the money) in Frank Capra's *It's a Wonderful Life*.

Errol Flynn had a new yacht, the 120' *Zaca*. David Niven wrote about coming home from the War and Flynn showing him Mulholland Farm and the *Zaca*, which he called his new "wife":

"And let me show you the house flag," he said as he unfurled a symbolic crowing rooster. "A rampant cock, sport, get it? That's what I am to the world today — goddammit — a phallic symbol."

He didn't smile as he said it.

August 8: "Flynn's Scientist-Father Ready for Fish Study" headlined the *Los Angeles Times*. Dr. T. Thomson-Flynn, "internationally known authority on marine life," was a zoologist, as well as dean of Queen College's School of Science in Belfast, Ireland. He would join his famous son on Flynn's new yacht the *Zaca*, sailing the seas of lower California and Mexico. As Dr. Thomson-Flynn told the *Times*:

> Eventually the big fish follow the smaller ones to the area, and a run is on. If we can learn what controls the density and movements of plankton, we will be able to accurately forecast a run of commercial fish.

Flynn made a reported $76,000 worth of renovations on the *Zaca* for this voyage, and gathered a crew for the adventure including Errol's wife Nora (who was several months pregnant), champion archer and underwater photographer Howard Hill, Prof. Carl L. Hubbs of Scripps Institute of Oceanography, sportsman photographer Teddy Stauffer (then planning a *National Geographic* feature), motion picture cameraman Jerry Courmoya, Flynn stand-in and secretary/manager Jim Fleming ... and John Decker.

Decker's presence, according to the *Times*, was "to sketch specimens encountered." One suspects Flynn also enlisted Decker and fellow hell-raiser Jim Fleming to ensure against the sea expedition being too dry. They set sail from Balboa August 12, 1946, and John Decker — a splendid white captain's cap cocked back over his hair — was delighted to join the crew.

In 1952, six years after the voyage, five years after Decker's death and four years after Flynn's divorce from Nora, Warner Bros. released a documentary short subject, *The Cruise of the Zaca*. The documentary has some great color photography and fun moments, as when a fully-clothed Flynn falls from a seaplane's pontoons while filming and splashes into the ocean. Decker appears in a number of shots, and Flynn speaks of his "old pal" with affection and admiration:

> Decker's crayons and brushes were always moving... His reproductions were lifelike and technically almost perfect...

The Cruise of the Zaca gives absolutely no indication of the madness that truly transpired during its fitful voyage. For a time, all sailed merrily, the *Zaca* crew enjoying the beauty of the sea. In his book *Forever Is a Hell of a Long Time*, Teddy Stauffer, later known as "Mr. Acapulco," wrote:

> John Decker turned into an unusually funny man on this trip and provided many laughs day and night. He made every attempt possible to act and look like John Barrymore, a close pal of his, and these imitations were something to behold...
>
> Decker, our pseudo-Barrymore, provided us a few yuks as he struggled to prove his seaworthiness, but he needed his entire box of matches to light one cigarette, and, even in moderate seas, he would turn green, hurry to the fridge where he kept his pills, taking several which he chased with straight gin. So poor John continued on, constantly seasick, drunk, vomiting, or slugging gin down his gullet.
>
> He often offered to help out sailing the *Zaca*. Any Gordian knot he tied came untied or could only be opened with a sail maker's awl or a knife. He couldn't hold a course and was always ten to fifteen degrees off. He couldn't help weigh anchor or set a sail, much less start the auxiliary engines or run a line.
>
> And drunk or sober, he always peed in the wind.

As Stauffer remembered, Decker fooled experts Professors Flynn and Hubbs by presenting a dead fish, which, at first examination, seemed a remarkable discovery:

> This was little wonder for John had dried a common sea perch, cut its fins into exotic designs, and painted it all colors of the rainbow. As he was a famed artist, the result was spectacular. The paint dried, and then John wet the fish, innocently announcing that he had just "scooped it in" from the sea.
>
> Errol's dad practically died of mortification that evening at dinner when the story was told. The rest of us split our sides.

Yet a battle of wills rapidly developed between Decker and Nora. Decker was hell-bent on making the cruise — to paraphrase David Niven's old remark — "Cirrhosis on the Sea." Nora, distinguished father-in-law aboard and herself cautiously pregnant, was equally fervent in safeguarding against any such nautical high jinks. As Decker later lamented to Will Fowler:

> Just as soon as Nora got her sea legs, she took over command of the boat and started shoving everybody around... This was the first time she started playing the role of Mrs. Errol Flynn and it has gone to her head... It's too bad this little mosquito came between Errol and myself. Hers was a constant pin-pricking process calculated to wear me down.

Decker, in Nora's eyes, was a prick. As Teddy Stauffer wrote:

> Decker continued his antics, wandering around the ship with brush and paint. He painted a huge face on the side of the cabin's wall around a scrub brush, a perfect caricature of Groucho Marx. He tidied up the tips of all the broom handles, painting them to resemble long, flesh-colored phalluses, and on the wall inside the dining lounge he did a full-length painting of Nora, who was quite pregnant, and every day he increased her pregnancy by several inches until the work of art became so ludicrous that Flynn made him paint it out.

At one point, Dr. Hubbs discovered a small fish (with camouflaged eyes at its tail, an evolutionary trick to confound predators) and named the discovery after Nora. One might have sensed insult in her name being attached to a fish with eyes in its ass, but Nora was thrilled.

Meanwhile, Decker also emulated John Barrymore's hygiene, or lack thereof. As Charles Higham wrote in his Errol Flynn book, the entire crew had become "disgusted by Decker's smell":

> A hasty conference was held and Errol decided to have him keelhauled: thrown overboard in a net and dragged behind the vessel until he was thoroughly washed, a variation of a technique used by Captain Bligh of the Bounty. Swearing and screaming and throwing his arms around, the unfortunate artist was picked up by his arms and legs and with three hefty swings tossed into the sea. When he was dragged out several minutes later a long brown puddle at his feet indicated how long it had been since he last took a bath.

Nora Flynn laughed at Decker's keelhauling. A showdown — or actual mutiny — was in the air.

The plot thickened as crew member Wallace Beery (no relation to the MGM star) pursued a shark in a Sorocco lagoon, panicked as the shark stared him down and retreated. Climbing onto the *Zaca*, he accidentally shot himself in the foot with a double-pronged harpoon, and pinned his foot to the deck. The men unpinned the screaming Beery and performed emergency surgery. Decker encouraged Flynn to sail 1,000 miles to Acapulco to secure proper medical care for Beery. Nora, still incensed by Decker's grotesque pregnancy painting, phallic broom handles, fake fish, peeing in the wind, etc., claimed Decker wanted to reach Acapulco only to go drinking and whoring. By the time Errol agreed to head for Acapulco, a hurricane was forming, the crew had mutinied, and Nora — aware that Decker was diabetic — was frighteningly vindictive.

"So the bitch locked all my insulin in the refrigerator and hoped I would lapse into a diabetic coma!" Decker told Will Fowler.

Nora had her own side of the story, of course; one of the mutineers had cut off the water supply, and Errol had told her to lock the refrigerator to save ice in case the hurricane blew the ship off course.

At any rate, Decker's mocking of Nora as "a female Captain Bligh" had a violent impact on Flynn — for the nickname surely reminded him of his horrible mother, whose family owned Captain Bligh's sword. Based on Flynn's consequent actions, he hated Decker for giving Nora the nickname and hated Nora for earning the nickname.

Under its "rampant cock" flag, the *Zaca* sailed into the hurricane, and as the sea and storm raged day and night, so did the onboard melodrama. Decker attacked Nora and gave her a black eye. She received no protection from her husband — Nora had told Prof. Flynn that Errol was taking drugs and begged his help, so enraging Flynn ("a monster under the influence of the drug," wrote Higham) that he kicked his pregnant wife in the stomach and knocked his father down a companionway, worsening the man's bad leg. Nora then attempted suicide by sleeping pills. When Flynn finally came out of his dope fit and realized what he'd done, *he* attempted suicide and, as Prof. Hubbs remembered, "wanted to throw himself into the wild sea."

John Decker eventually smashed the lock on the refrigerator, rescuing his insulin and grabbing some bottles of booze besides. The *Zaca* somehow survived the hurricane and the demons of its crew and docked at Acapulco. Prof. Hubbs summed up the cruise of the *Zaca* thusly:

> Drunkenness, two men with broken ribs, wife beating followed by a frustrated suicide, mutiny, virtual running out of water (with tanks of water closed off somehow), engine stoppage, a very close escape from shipwreck here at Acapulco, something wrong with almost everything mechanical about the ship were among the highlights.

In Acapulco, Decker jumped ship. The redoubtable Jim Fleming reportedly left with him, as did Professor Flynn. Decker ended up paying to fly home to Los Angeles, joining Prof. Flynn in an open cockpit plane. En route, Decker found a new joy — peeing out of the cockpit.

Nora Flynn arrived in Los Angeles October 28, 1946, via considerably more elegant means — a Pan American Airways transport. Decker's laments had preceded her, and the *L.A. Times* covered her return:

> Nora Eddington Flynn, tall, tanned and tactful, didn't look much like a "female Capt. Bligh" when she swept her small daughter Deirdre into her arms yesterday on arriving here from Mexico City…
>
> Wife of Film Actor Errol Flynn, Nora recently was characterized by Artist John Decker as the arbitrary skipper of Flynn's yacht *Zaca*, during a cruise to Acapulco, Mex., where the painter said he jumped ship "because she wouldn't even let me flick cigarette ashes on the deck."
>
> "Did John say mean things about me?" she asked with wide-eyed, well-registered innocence in parrying a reporter's question. "Why, I'm surprised. Really, I am!"
>
> Did she really play "Capt. Bligh" to cause Decker's "Mutiny on the *Zaca*"?
>
> "Why, I'm surprised you'd ask such a thing!" she smiled sweetly.
>
> Flynn, she said, will sail the yacht from Acapulco to Tahiti and then fly home "about the last of February" when Nora is expecting a second youngster.

Errol Flynn accepted an offer in Acapulco to rent the *Zaca* to the company of *Lady from Shanghai*, directed by Orson Welles, and starring Welles and his then-spouse Rita Hayworth. The Decker vs. Nora clash signaled the end of his friendship with Errol Flynn.

During Decker's Zaca trip, his rapacious pet parrot had escaped its cage and terrorized Phyllis and Mary Lou, who remembers:

> One night the bird opened up the cage and got out into the room, a combination den/dining room/kitchen. We had to close the doors to the den because the parrot was out, and we were scared to death!

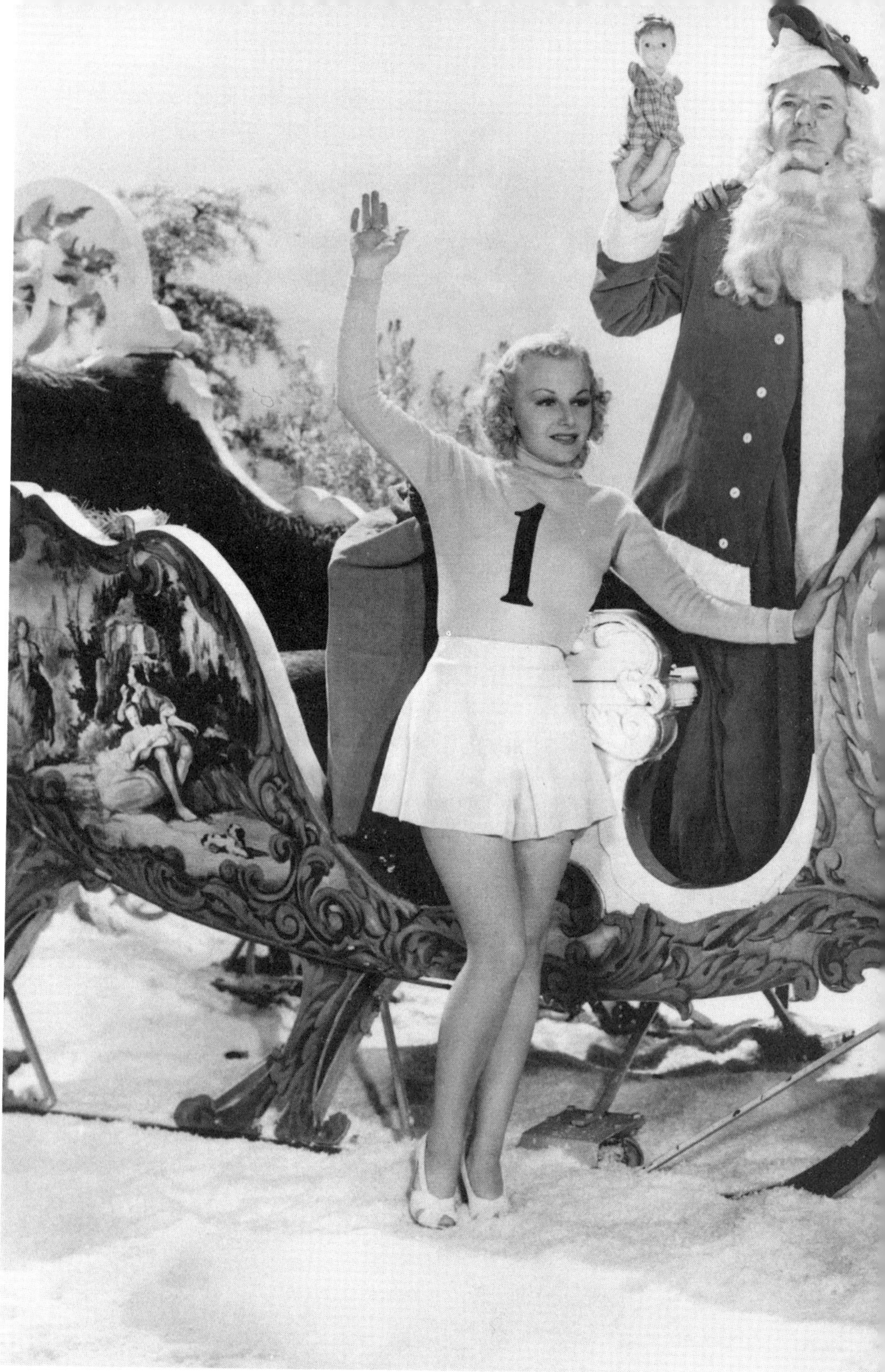
1

Publicity still of the man who hated Christmas

Decker believed the bird must be ill, and he concocted a cure: he'd give the parrot one of his insulin shots.

He buried the parrot in the garden.

As Philip Paval (a goldsmith and silversmith artist, who spent much time with Decker at this point) remembers, Flynn came over for the parrot's funeral. However, after the *Zaca* debacle, the Decker-Flynn friendship was dying. On January 29, 1947, John Decker presented a new art show, "Moods of Tropical Mexico Painted on a Recent Trip on Errol Flynn's yacht *Zaca*," in Los Angeles. When the Flynns tossed a big party upon Errol's return to Los Angeles after his Acapulco sojourn, Decker was pointedly uninvited. Paval recalled that he and Decker crashed the party, with unhappy results:

> When Errol saw us, he grabbed John by the collar; John said, "Hit me and I'll sue you for everything you're worth." I went out to the garden, got myself a drink and talked to some nice chicks in swimsuits. When I went back into the living room John said, "Let's get out of this damn dump away from this stupid jerk." I did not see the Flynns again until Decker's funeral.

Flynn considered evicting Decker from the Alta Loma studio. As the friendship was dying, so was a friend.

> I direct my executors immediately upon the certificate of my death being signed to have my body placed in an inexpensive coffin and taken to a cemetery and cremated, and since I do not wish to cause my friends undue inconvenience or expense I direct my executors not to have any funeral or other ceremony or to permit anyone to view my remains, except as is necessary to furnish satisfactory proof of my death.
> —from W.C. Fields' will, signed April 28, 1943

By the close of 1946, W.C. Fields had spent 14 months, the last several drinking only ginger ale, at Las Encinas Sanitarium in Pasadena. The end came as "The Man in the Bright Nightgown" (as W.C. referred to death) paid his call 12:03 p.m. on Christmas Day, 1946. Fields, a hater of Christmas since age eight, was 66 years old.

The death certificate lists the cause of death as "Cirrhosis of the Liver" (duration, five years), due to "chronic alcoholism" (duration unknown).

Carlotta Monti later claimed that she had comforted the old man to the very end, and that the dying words of W.C. Fields were, "Chinaman... Goddamn the whole frigging world and everyone in it but you, Carlotta." Ronald J. Fields is convinced by his own research that Carlotta wasn't there — she was, he claims, with a lover that Christmas day in Santa Barbara. Only W.C.'s secretary Magda Michael and a nurse were present at the time of W.C.'s death.

"He brought his forefinger to his lips to signify quiet," wrote Ron Fields, "winked, then closed his eyes; and 'the Man in the Bright Nightgown' took him away."

It was a cold, rainy Christmas, and restaurateur Dave Chasen and casting director Billy Grady had gone to Las Encinas to visit W.C. with a case of whisky and some delicacies. Gene Fowler was planning to come later. As Chasen and Grady arrived at the patio gateway, two men left W.C.'s cottage, carrying W.C.'s corpse in a basket. "The rain of the gray Christmas," wrote Fowler, "beat down upon the men and upon the basket."

On December 26, Gene Fowler naturally held a wake, appropriately at Chasen's, where the mourners sat near the John Decker portrait of W.C. as Queen Victoria. Ben Hecht was there, as well as directors Eddie Sutherland and Gregory La Cava, sports writer Grantland Rice and Gene's son, reporter Will Fowler. Gene Fowler telephoned a full-page tribute to the *Hollywood Reporter*:

> The most prejudiced and honest and beloved figure of our so-called "colony" went away on a day that he pretended to abhor — Christmas. We loved him, and — peculiarly enough — he loved us. To the most authentic humorist since Mark Twain, to the greatest heart that has beaten since the middle ages — W.C. Fields, our friend.

Gregory La Cava was a bit less florid about it all. "Bill never really wanted to hurt anybody," said La Cava. "He just felt an obligation."

W.C. Fields, who wanted no funeral, got three of them, all running consecutively on January 2, 1947. The formidable Hattie Fields and her lawyer son Claude — who were living together in Beverly Hills, and both of whom had inspired so much of W.C.'s comic misanthropy — had suddenly shown up, with an agenda and a vengeance. Funeral no. 1 was a private service at Forest Lawn's Church of the Recessional. Among the 50 mourners were John Decker, Gene Fowler, Ben Hecht, Leo McCarey, Jack Dempsey, Eddie Cline and Earl Carroll. Edgar Bergen gave the eulogy, somehow managing without benefit of Charlie McCarthy:

It seems wrong not to pray for a man who gave such happiness to the world, but that was the way he wanted it. Bill knew life, and knew that laughter was the way to live it. He knew that happiness depended on disposition, not position.

We simply say farewell…

Also among the mourners — and getting her picture in the *Los Angeles Times* — was Carlotta Monti, in black bonnet and widow weeds, bringing along her father, sister, nieces, and Mae Taylor, "a Hollywood spiritualist," noted the *Times*, "through whom Carlotta said she spoke with Fields after his death." As Will Fowler put it, Carlotta "represented a modern *pieta*, now that she had finally lost her intimidating sugar daddy." Carlotta claimed Fields' ghost had commanded her to attend "the three-ring circus" and to "get a front seat."

For Funeral no. 2, the Fields family moved to Forest Lawn's Great Mausoleum, final resting place of the remains of Jean Harlow, Carole Lombard, et al., for a Catholic ceremony. Ignoring Fields' dictate for cremation, the Fields family escorted the flower-covered casket to the crypt — commanding that Carlotta and company stay away, across the mausoleum. The *Times* reported:

> When the family departed Carlotta tried to go to the crypt. A cemetery attendant stopped her. On orders of Mr. Fields' son, she was not to be admitted until the crypt was sealed. She waited, and while she waited she announced that a wristwatch she was wearing — a gift from Mr. Fields — had stopped the moment the actor's body had entered the tomb.

After the sealing of the crypt, the black-clad Carlotta and her coterie visited the grave, and there came Funeral no. 3, Mae Taylor officiating. There was a heart of white chrysanthemums and scarlet roses on an easel by the crypt, and Carlotta took three roses before departing the Great Mausoleum.

All the while, a former vaudevillian, claiming he was part of "Duffy and Sweeney" and had known Fields in those bygone days and nights, roamed about the funeral site and asked to pay his respects at Fields' crypt. The Forest Lawn attendant refused to show him where it was.

"Well, I guess it was all right that I just came here anyway," said the teary-eyed old man, and he left.

It is true W.C. Fields' will included this bequest:

Upon the death of my said brother, Walter Dukenfield and my said sister, Adel C. Smith and the said Carlotta Monti (Montejo), I direct that my executors procure the organization of a membership or other approved corporation under the name of the W.C. FIELDS COLLEGE for orphan white boys and girls, where no religion of any sort is to be preached. Harmony is the purpose of this thought. It is my desire the college will be built in California in Los Angeles County.

Fields was eventually cremated, as he had requested, several years after his entombment. The marker reads:

W.C. Fields
1880–1946

The ashes rest in the Columbarium of Nativity (another irony for the man who hated Christmas), Hall of Inspiration, Holly Terrace, at Forest Lawn Glendale's Great Mausoleum. But the years-later cremation was just part of the battle that began waging six months after his funeral. Fields had named a long list of personal beneficiaries, including Carlotta ($25 per week until $25,000 had been paid, plus his 16-cylinder Cadillac Limousine), Magda Michael ($2,500), and various family members, including Hattie and Claude ($20,000 to be divided between them). But Hattie, knowing she was the inspiration for every sourpuss harridan who ever terrorized his comedies, was out for blood and money. She filed for a hearty chunk of the Fields estate (originally estimated at over $700,000).

The case would go on for eight years, until Hattie — then 75 — scored victory, winning legal distinction for her contribution to California law regarding spousal inheritance.

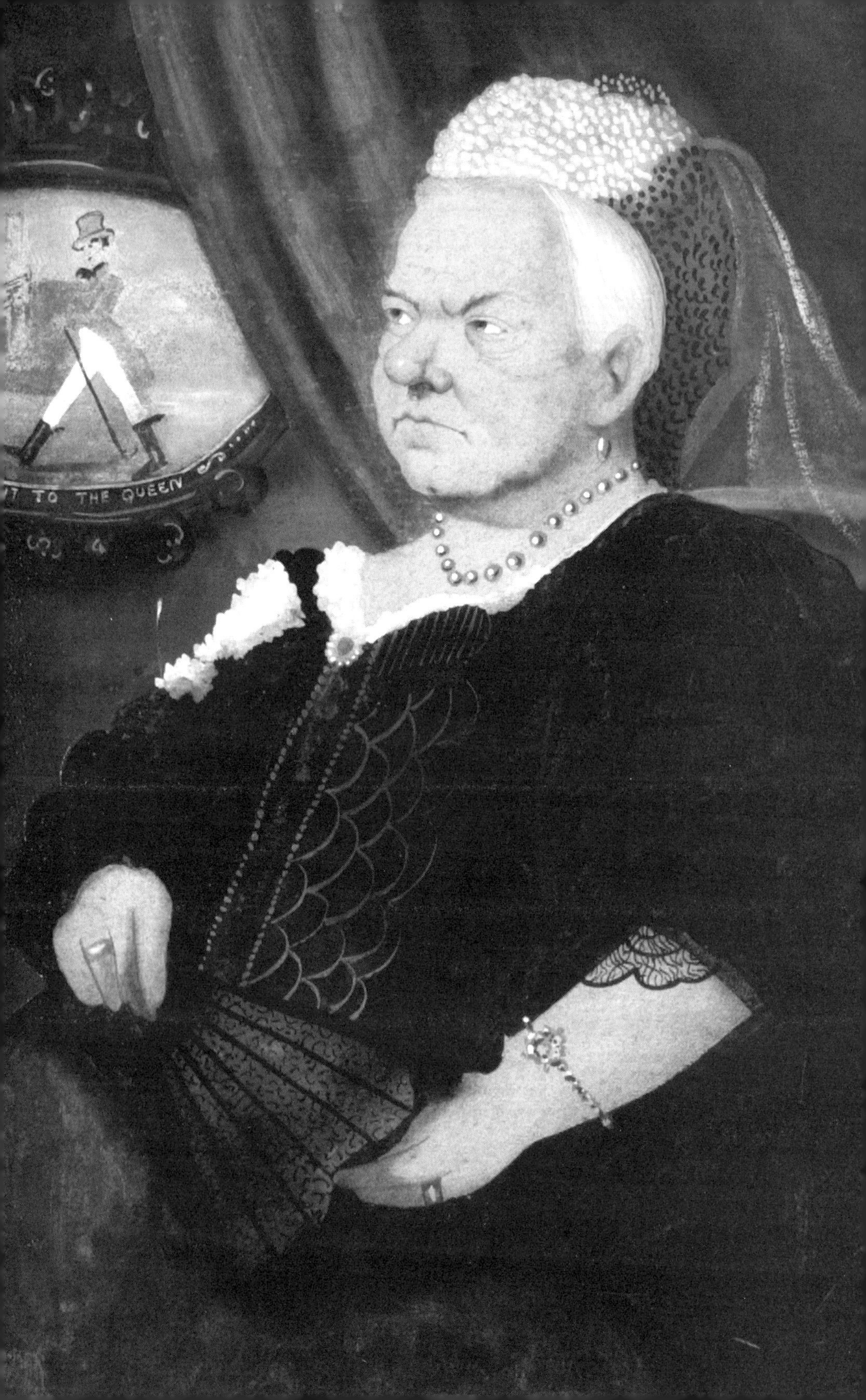
TO THE QUEEN

Chapter Twenty
1947: Raphael's Angels

> What is real in me are the illusions which I create.
> —John Decker, 1947

The old gang was disintegrating.

Barrymore, Fields and Hartmann were dead. John Carradine had fled to New York to escape jail for alimony contempt. Gene Fowler was scheduling time in Manhattan to write the biography of Mayor Jimmy Walker. Ben Hecht also was away from Hollywood and at home in Nyack. Anthony Quinn was so desperate about his career that he produced his own star vehicle movie, *Black Gold*, and persuaded his wife Katherine, who'd not worked in a while, to co-star with him. Thomas Mitchell, Alan Mowbray, Roland Young and the now-loyal Paval were about all that was left, along with recent member Vincent Price, whose humor, intellect and great knowledge of art made him a vital young presence.

Yet life simply wasn't the same. There were still splashes of the old madness and chicanery, such as the day Philip Paval came to Alta Loma and found Decker groping about in the toilet bowl:

"Oh Christ, I lost my uppers!" lamented Decker.

Paval contacted a dentist, Dr. Vernon Swall, and made a quick deal; Decker would provide the dentist a painting if the dentist made him a new set of teeth. Decker tried to bilk Dr. Swall and his wife by offering them a print of Stanley Barbee's *Clown with a*

Uncle Claude as Queen Victoria, courtesy of Decker

Watch. Paval blew the whistle on him and the couple returned to Alta Loma, selecting, as Paval recalled "a still life with eggs."

He enjoyed his family. As Mary Lou Warn remembers:

> John was very good to me. I started maturing young — I was attractive at 14, the Hollywood High type, the California Girl — tall and tan. Once there was an Earl Carroll party, and mother didn't want to go (I think she'd get partied out). So John took me. It was a big, big party — Earl Carroll had hired divers who jumped into a swimming pool with waterfalls! We didn't stay long, but it was written up in a column the next day — "John Decker was seen with a very attractive young girl at Earl Carroll's party!"

Yet for Decker, life was rather hollow without his pals, despite the loving and loyal Phyllis and Mary Lou. He was ill — diabetes and cirrhosis of the liver — and at age 51, it seemed unlikely he'd be able to battle his old demons as long as John Barrymore had survived his own.

Meanwhile, there was, perhaps, one final forgery caper.

William Goetz was the son-in-law of Louis B. Mayer, having married Mayer's imperious daughter Edie. He became head of Universal-International Pictures in 1946, pledged to produce primarily films of artistic merit, and likely would have run the studio into bankruptcy had it not been, ironically, for the 1948 release of *Abbott and Costello Meet Frankenstein* (which Goetz abhorred). At any rate, Goetz won far more note for his lavish art collection than his producer acumen, and in 1947 acquired what he believed to be a Van Gogh, *Study by Candlelight.* According to Leslee Mayo, Goetz bought the painting from art dealer Reeves Lewenthal, who was cryptic about its provenance — "It is a business secret," he said. J.B. de la Faille authenticated *Study by Candlelight*, but others cried "Fake" — including Van Gogh's nephew, who'd never even seen it. "Goetz threatened to sue him," notes Ms. Mayo, "and this began THE art story of 1949–1950."

The Metropolitan Museum of Modern Art, a Van Gogh committee in Amsterdam and the U.S. Treasury Department all investigated — and failed to agree. The experts have never agreed over the decades and their discord over the picture's validity has consigned *Study by Candlelight*, as Leslee Mayo says, to a "state of artistic limbo." Christie's auctioned the Goetz family art collection in 1988, but cautiously declined to offer *Study by Candlelight*. The year that the picture appeared on the L.A. scene, its mysterious provenance, and the fact that if it *is* fake it's *still* fine enough to fool many Old Masters experts, all point to….guess who.

Anthony Quinn and John Decker

Will Fowler also claimed *Study by Candlelight* to have been a forgery by John Decker. As noted, Will was an avowed believer in "poetic license," and the mystery lingers.

Decker now became fascinated with the death masks in his studio. They were the masks of Beethoven, Sir Walter Scott, and — most precious to Decker — the Madonna of the Seine. In *Minutes of the Last Meeting*, Gene Fowler quoted Philip Paval on the Madonna:

> Oh yes. She was very real. She was a young and beautiful girl, and she drowned herself, oh, maybe a century ago; and when she was taken from the water she had a beautiful soft smile on her face, just like the Mona Lisa, and that's why they called her the Madonna of the Seine. She was a Paris girl. Nobody ever knew just who she was; but she was beautiful, and sad, and virginal. And they made a death mask, and it became a must when you went to school in Paris; to learn how to draw you had to make a sketch of the Madonna of the Seine…

It was the Madonna of the Seine who now haunted this hell-raising artist, who seemed to find a strange comfort in the death mask, which he'd touch up time and time again. Gene Fowler, noting the obsession, asked Decker her story. Yet raconteur John Decker — perhaps sensing his own time was very short and reflecting on his own tragedies — never would take the time away from the mask to tell his friend the Madonna's own sad tale.

Decker also found time to pursue a different obsession. He kept recording lines from *Cyrano de Bergerac* on his tape recorder, which struck him as deeply personal:

To sing, to laugh, to dream, to walk in my own way, and to be alone…

In the spring of 1947, Warner Bros. released *The Two Mrs. Carrolls*, starring Humphrey Bogart, Barbara Stanwyck and Alexis Smith. The melodrama cast Bogie as a mad artist who, before trying to kill his wife Stanwyck, paints her as "The Angel of Death." Naturally, Decker relished his job of creating the Angel of Death for Warners, even if it seemed that such an angel would soon have a date with him. It was his final contribution to a film.

Decker and Philip Paval had a joint art show at the Pasadena Museum. It was a mutual triumph. The *Pasadena Star News* reported:

Visitors found Mr. Decker's works to be in the mood of the present day and his technique direct enough to elicit spontaneous enjoyment by the casual observer. Much of the artist's own emotion radiates from his paintings as noted in his painting of the late John Barrymore, his personal friend.

Decker was too ill to attend the joint show opening at the County Museum and Paval attended the dinner with the owner and Francis Taylor (Elizabeth's father and an art gallery owner). Paval came home and received a call from Phyllis, asking him to come to Alta Loma — Decker had suffered a stomach hemorrhage. They had great trouble getting the stretcher down the studio steps and the ambulance took the critically ill man to Cedars of Lebanon Hospital.

Naturally, the scene at Cedars became black comedy. "Phil, I'll never get out of this goddamn place alive!" roared Decker to Paval, who found Decker on a stretcher in a hallway — the hospital had originally refused him a room because of his lack of money and insurance. When they finally provided him a room, it was a double, and his terminally ill roomie was in pitiful shape. Philip Paval recalled,

> Very macabre. The guy was lying there. He was dying. And he had some kind of — he must have had cancer — because it's so vivid in my mind, and he had a drain in his back, and it went pop! pop! You could hear the damn thing.
> "Jesus!" wailed the old dying man. "I won't be here another minute!"
> "Get me out of here!" howled Decker. "I can't depend on this man's promise. He might live a whole hour!"

Paval stayed the first night, during which time Decker once again quoted *Cyrano de Bergerac*: "It is much finer to fight when it is no use."

Fannie Brice, who'd provide a wing to Cedars, pledged the finances for Decker's care. Treatment began, Cedars providing morphine, blood transfusions and a suite with a private sitting room. Phyllis was there constantly. Fannie Brice brought homemade broth. Gene Fowler, meanwhile, had suffered a severe heart seizure in New York. He demanded to come home to Los Angeles, but was too ill to visit Decker, or even receive his telephone call.

For four weeks, John Decker was in Cedars of Lebanon Hospital, reciting Cyrano, terrorizing nurses, hurling bedpans, terrified that his creditors would seize his paintings. As Gene Fowler wrote to Ben Hecht:

He had three nurses whom he abused roundly, and there were frequent resignations on the part of the shocked Florence Nightingales. Numerous suggestions made to them by the dying man as to where they could place the bedpans and what they could do to themselves in general (and in particular) caused complaints such as to rouse the facility to threats of expulsion.

Surgeons removed Decker's stomach. "Who wants to live without a stomach?" he gloomily asked Philip Paval, who had made him a ring with a miniature death mask of Beethoven. Now Decker never removed it.

Anthony Quinn constantly donated blood. And on Decker's final day, an old Bundy Drive neighbor, Harriet DeLaix, a graduate nurse, visited him at Cedars. She noted the ring, and remembered that, despite the surviving handsomeness, "John himself looked like a death mask."

His eyes closed, Decker beckoned Ms. DeLaix to his bedside and held her hand with the one not receiving a transfusion. She had brought from Bundy Drive a mock strawberry plant, with yellow flowers. Decker opened his eyes and looked at the plant.

"The blossoms," said John Decker, "are the same color that Raphael used for the hair of his angels."

Saturday, 8 p.m. June 7, 1947, John Decker died. The cause of death was the gastric hemorrhage, due to cirrhosis of the liver. Phyllis, Alan Mowbray and his wife Lorayne were at his bedside. The artist whom Ben Hecht had called "a one-man Renaissance" and "the broken-nosed Cinderella" had lived 51 years, six months and 29 days.

John Carradine had a favorite John Decker story — whenever his creditors were about to pounce, Decker would insert his own death notice in the L.A. papers. "Then," recalled Carradine, "if any of them missed seeing the notice and continued to send bills, Decker would return the bills with a copy of the death notice. That would usually persuade even the most relentless creditor to abandon the chase and let poor John Decker 'rest in peace.'"

This was the real RIP. Decker's estate was nil and his creditors were out of luck.

The funeral, of course, was a combination art show, boozefest, charity drive, horror show and robbery.

Honoring Decker's wish, Phyllis arranged with the Utter-McKinley Mortuary, 8814 Sunset Boulevard, to conduct the wake at 1215 Alta Loma. The studio bar would become an altar, festooned with candelabra and flowers. Decker paintings would hang in tribute, and the tableau was to evoke Van Gogh's bier. Mary Lou, who had been hav-

Phyllis Decker in mourning

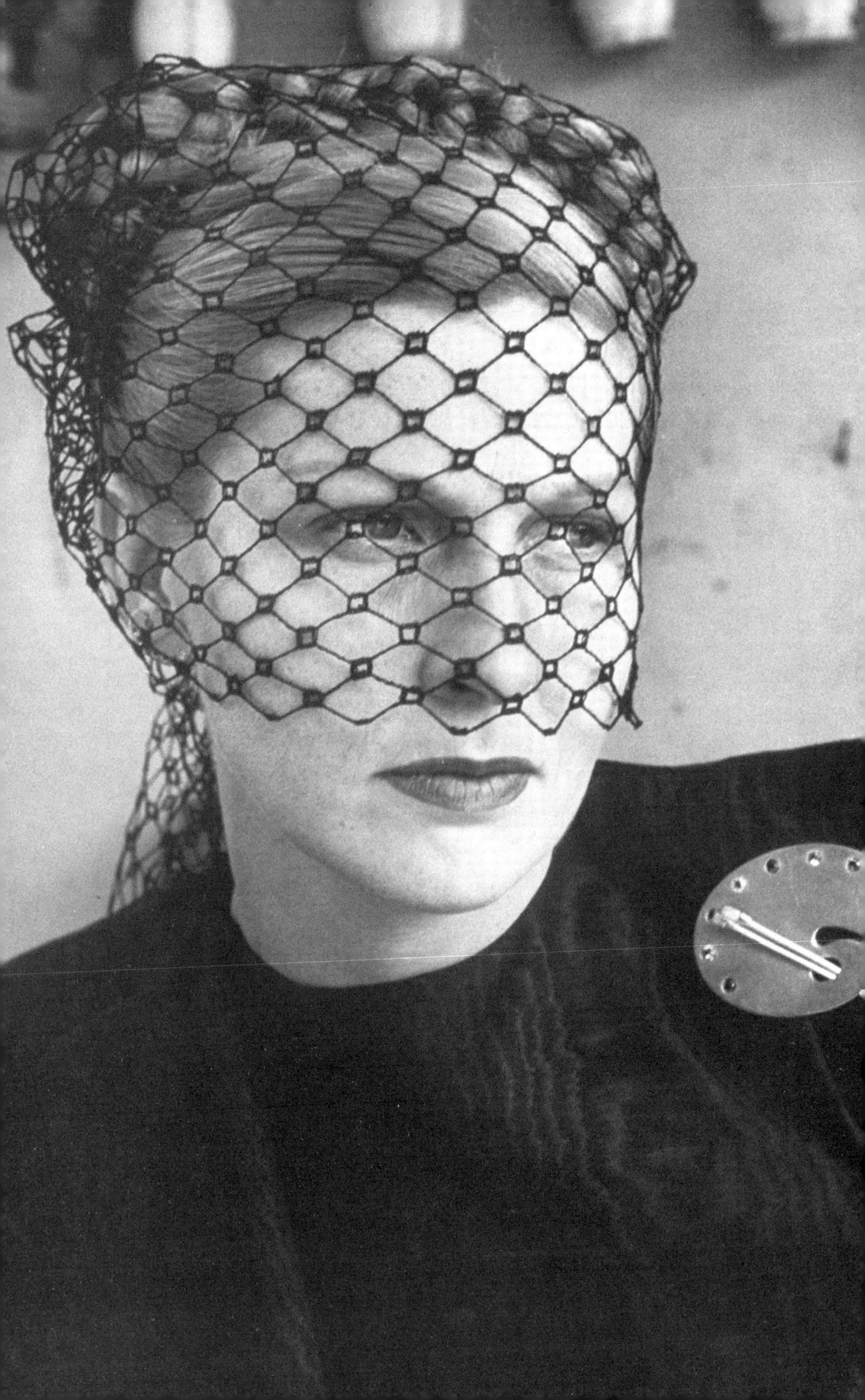

ing "battles" with her mother and had gone to live with an aunt in Toledo, returned to Los Angeles for her stepfather's wake.

A special funereal feature: Decker's John Barrymore death-bed sketch would rest atop the lower half of the casket.

Tuesday, June 10, 1947, 1:30 p.m. — the funeral began. Utter-McKinley had delivered corpse and casket to Alta Loma, where the black-widow-weeds Phyllis — who'd sent orders to the undertakers to be sure to darken Decker's mustache — was distressed to see it still too red. She darkened it herself with her mascara as Decker's portrait of her, *Wife with Pearls*, hung on display beside Decker's portrait of Barrymore, *The Royal Vagabond*.

The studio filled up with the Who's Who mourners. Pallbearers were Alan Mowbray, Dr. Frank Nolan, Anthony Quinn, Vincent Price, Norman Kerry (the Silent screen actor who'd played the romantic hero of the 1925 *The Phantom of the Opera*, and Decker's pal), and Philip Paval. Gene Fowler was too ill to be a pallbearer, or to even attend the service. Errol Flynn (pointedly not asked to be a pallbearer) and the dreaded Nora were there, despite the recent feud; Flynn had played hooky from a day's shooting of Warner's Western *Silver River* and, as an L.A. newspaper reported, "kept a movie cast of 400 waiting so he might pay a last tribute." Thomas Mitchell (then acting with Flynn in *Silver River*) was present. So were Ida Lupino, Red Skelton and his wife, producer Buddy De Sylva, writer Dudley Nichols (who'd worked on the screenplay of *Scarlet Street*), Peter Lawford, Mocambo manager Charlie Morrison, millionaire Atwater Kent, actor Arthur Lake and his wife, artist Henry Clive… all in all, there were approximately 200 in attendance, the studio so crowded that the mourners overflowed out onto the patio.

There were popping flashbulbs, wreathes of roses, gladioli and dahlias, loud weeping, considerable drinking and baroque surprises. In his 1991 book *Reporters*, Will Fowler recalled Phyllis' sister Blanche hugging him and weeping of the deceased, "He was such a great piece of ass!" Presumably she wasn't so effusive that the widow heard her.

What everybody *did* hear were the comforting words of the Rev. S. Mark Hogue, pastor of the Westwood Congregational Church. He kept it simple and noted, to knowing smiles and weeping, that Decker was together again with John Barrymore and W.C. Fields. The most memorable moment came, as previously noted, when the flowers decorating the Barrymore death-bed sketch frame fell as the Rev. Hogue intoned "Let us pray."

Come the finale of the service, and the assemblage heard Decker's recording of lines from *Cyrano de Bergerac*, which he had made six weeks before his death:

> To sing, to laugh, to dream, to walk in my own way and be alone….
> I am too proud to be a parasite and, if my nature wants the germ that

grows towering to heaven like the mountain pine, or like the oak, sheltering multitudes — I stand, not high, it may be, but alone!

It was Cyrano's "No thank you" soliloquy, and John Decker's defiant last words.

The hearse traveled south to Inglewood Cemetery, followed by a large limousine carrying the pallbearers. Philip Paval remembered one of them remarking, "Where are the sirens? John would have loved that." As Paval described the cremation:

> We arrived at the cemetery chapel and carried the casket into a small anteroom where there was an iron grate like a fireplace. It was a fireplace all right; the gate slowly opened and there was the oven. One of the attendants came and lifted the lid of the casket (as we were witnesses to the cremation, we had to make sure it was John) and said, "Gentlemen, this is John Decker." Alan Mowbray spoke up and said, "Well, if this isn't John Decker, he took a hell of a beating for the last six weeks." The iron grate opened and the casket was rolled into the furnace; the gate closed again and we could hear the flames starting. The attendant came and asked if we would care to watch the cremation, which is permitted. So we all went back and looked through the hole in the gate facing the room. Their business must have been good as there were many aluminum boxes stacked in one corner. Through a small hole in the roof we could see smoke coming up the chimney. I looked through the round circle in the gate and saw John raising himself; Dr. Noland said that the heat does that.

It was a morbid spectacle, and Anthony Quinn was rattled as they left Inglewood Cemetery: "I don't like cremations. I would rather be buried in the good earth with a tree growing up from my grave."

The show went on and on. The pallbearers returned to Alta Loma, where Charlie Morrison sent lavish food and drink from the Mocambo, complete with a waiter. Phyllis accepted a few drinks and finally went to sleep, while the more devoted mourners, as Paval recalled, "held a regular old-fashioned wake" that "lasted for days." They told their favorite Decker sagas and played his recordings time and again.

Naturally, there was a blasphemy of sorts. A mourner managed to steal one of Decker's paintings, *The French Scene*, which he'd painted in 1944. The painting showed a priest and children in a public park, and Decker was so proud of it he'd refused to sell it. Gordon Levoy, Decker's attorney, assured the guilty party no questions would be asked if he/she returned it via insured mail within a week. Various Decker disciples have alleged that the culprit was Alan Mowbray, but this seems out of character. Shortly after the funeral, Mowbray hosted a big party for Phyllis and, to raise money for the insolvent widow, raffled off one of Decker's paintings and raised $1,500. Thomas Mitchell won and promptly returned the painting so it could be raffled again. In Paval's opinion, "Alan Mowbray proved himself a very fine friend for that generous gesture."

All the while, Will Fowler was involved trying to get contributions in money to pay for the funeral and blood to repay Cedars for the many blood transfusions. There'd be little money or blood forthcoming.

There was basically no estate. Decker's handwritten will dated August 7, 1946 left everything to Phyllis. The October 18, 1947 *Los Angeles Times* noted that "Decker's holdings consist only of furnishings, books and paintings worth less than $1,000." Fortunately a legal loophole noted that one's work as an artist could not be considered part of one's estate — otherwise creditors would have ransacked the studio. Phyllis had petitioned that she and Decker owned 1215 Alta Loma in joint tenancy, and hence the home/studio was not included in the estate.

Phyllis, mourning her husband, was determined, despite her insolvency, to provide him a final memorial. She aimed for the loftiest locally available: the "Circle of Immortality" of the Memorial Court of Honor at Forest Lawn Memorial Park, Glendale. She had William A. Valentiner, Director Consultant of the Los Angeles County Museum (and Decker's old accomplice in the aforementioned Rembrandt *Bust of Christ* fraud), make her pitch to Forest Lawn. On July 24, 1947, Dr. Hubert Eaton — Chairman of Forest Lawn, and its founder — personally sent Phyllis a copy of the letter he'd sent to Valentiner:

> I am afraid someone does not understand. Money cannot buy anything within the Memorial Court of Honor. No one can recommend any person for "Immortality" within the Memorial Court of Honor. The Council of Regents of the Memorial Court of Honor is the only group having the power to select "Immortals." The Regents operate solely through their "Committee on Research of Famous Persons" which is constantly at work. In fifteen years only two persons have been selected as "Immortals."
>
> Beneath the Last Supper Window and the marble floor of the Memorial Court of Honor are crypts which money cannot buy. They are reserved as gifts of honored interment for famous Americans who have contributed outstanding service to humanity. The illustrious dead of England are entombed in Westminster Abbey. In the United States, military and government dignitaries are interred in Arlington Cemetery. There has long been a need for

a place of honor dedicated to the nation's lay great, and it was to service this need, that the majestic memorial Court of Honor was created by Forest Lawn. The Press of the United States has reputedly referred to it as the "New World Westminster Abbey."

Eaton's letter noted that the Memorial Court of Honor was only for those who had fame "of a lasting quality" and had achieved something "for humanity at large." Eaton noted that Mount Rushmore sculptor Gutzon Borglum was in the Memorial Court, as was "I Love You Truly" songwriter Carrie Jacobs-Bond. The letter's inference was that John Decker surely was not in their league. Eaton wrote that he'd pass on Valentiner's suggestion to the Secretary of the Council, who'd refer it to the Committee on Research. "You, of course, realize that no Regent will ever admit that any particular name has ever been voted upon," concluded the letter.

Of course, John Decker's ashes never got anywhere near Forest Lawn, Circle of Immortality or otherwise. Philip Paval put out the word that Decker required a proper final resting place, and Edward G. Robinson — long ago rejected as a prospective Bundy Drive Boy — was among those who contributed to a fund for that purpose. Phyllis, however, became unhappy with the idea and the money was returned.

The story goes that the ashes somehow ended up on a shelf at Westwood Cemetery, which later became the trendy final destination for Marilyn Monroe, Donna Reed, Natalie Wood, Darryl F. Zanuck and his wife, and many more. Phyllis apparently never paid for a niche and eventually received a bill for the ashes' rental. The late Will Fowler claimed that he had interceded for Phyllis, learning that Bob Yeager had purchased Westwood, and reported that Phyllis soon received a letter from Yeager — informing her that Decker's ashes had been scattered in the rose garden and marking the account "Paid in Full." He allegedly added on the statement, "Anything for a friend."

There are many legends in Hollywood. This, as will be noted later, is apparently one of them.

Phyllis Decker hoped to keep the John Decker Gallery — which Errol Flynn apparently deeded over to her — a going concern at Alta Loma. She presented a show of his works March 26, 1948, and wrote in the program:

> John Decker lived as he painted — vigorously and brilliantly. He would have held no brief for the perpetuation of a "shrine" for any personal commemoration. In presenting this first posthumous exhibition of John's work, I do so in that same spirit and without conventional solemnity.

However, money troubles and zoning issues eventually forced Phyllis to close the gallery and sell the property to Paulette Goddard. There was also the concept of a film tribute, under the aegis of none other than Jim Fleming, Errol Flynn's rowdy sidekick. Shooting began with Thomas Mitchell and Philip Paval participating, but troubles abounded that would have delighted Decker (the cameraman shot some footage with the lens shut, fuses exploded and shut down the power, etc.). The project collapsed.

Jim Fleming never completed his movie but he got a consolation prize: in 1949, he married Phyllis.

In 1942, after John Barrymore's death, Ben Hecht had written:

> They're dying off, all my exuberant and artistic friends who were the landmarks of a mirage known as Happy Days. They came bounding into the Century like a herd of unicorns… they were a part of the last high old time when news was made by madcaps rather than madmen, and they were sustained through hunger, calumny and hangovers by the conviction that they were improving the world. Now whenever one of them falls, brought down not so much by the barrage of years as by disillusion and a drop too much of alcohol, I mourn doubly. I mourn the passing of another of the moonstruck gentry, and of the era that specialized in hatching their dwindling tribe. Every time one of these battered old iconoclasts waves good-bye, that era grows dimmer and all its carnival fades a little more.

It was truly the proverbial end of an era. John Barrymore's 1942 death had wracked the Bundy Drive Boys, as had Hartmann's in 1944 and Fields in 1946; now, with John Decker gone, the saga was over and the gang disbanded, even though various prominent members still had years to go.

The death hit all the men hard. Thomas Mitchell returned for a time to New York; so did Anthony Quinn. Errol Flynn mourned in character. Notes by Jack L. Warner, prepared for a talk with MCA agent Lew Wasserman and included in *Inside Warner Bros. (1935–1951)* as "undated, circa June 1947," report troubles on the Western *Silver River*:

> So there will be no further misunderstanding, our company is reserving the right to keep track of the things that transpire during each day the picture [*Silver River*] is in production.
>
> If Flynn is late, if liquor is being used so that from the middle of the after-

noon on it is impossible for the director to make any more scenes with Flynn, if liquor is brought on the set or into the Studio — we must hold Flynn legally and financially responsible for any delay in the making of this picture.

We may go so far as to abrogate the entire contract and sue him for damages…

As Rudy Behlmer, *Inside Warner Bros.'* editor, notes after this inclusion, "Apparently, from all evidence, the practice continued — or at any rate resumed a short while later."

"The death of Decker has of course saddened me greatly," the ailing Gene Fowler wrote to Ben Hecht, "because there are not many of his kind walking the earth now. I am beginning to feel like a survivor, alone and without my toys."

★

Part IV

The Aftermath

In the poet's eye, Time is a circus, always packing up and moving away. And he asks us to remember how happy its music made us.

—*Ben Hecht*

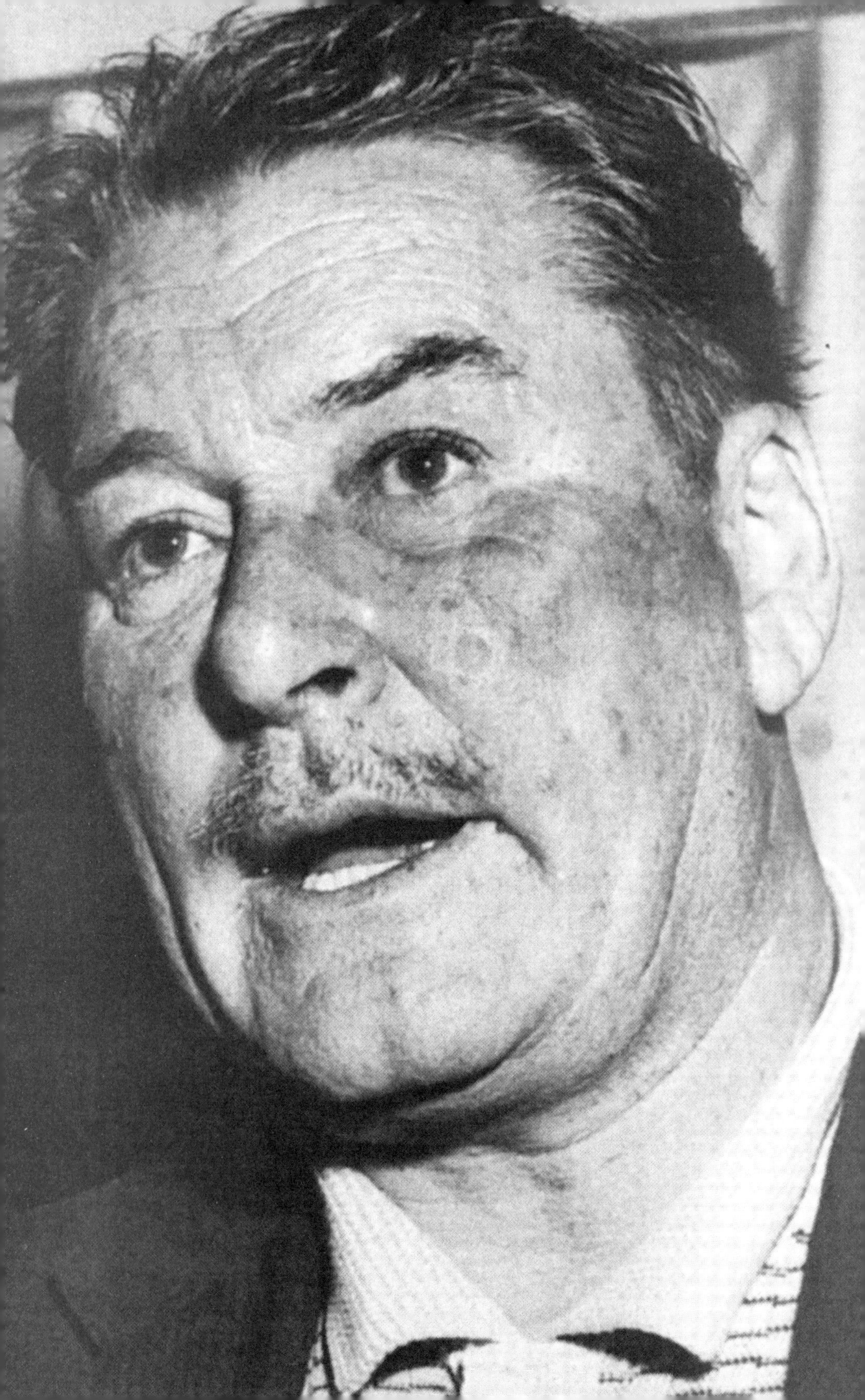

Chapter Twenty-One
Shuffling Off the Mortal Coil

The first to go after Decker was the patrician Roland Young, who died of natural causes June 5, 1953 at his home on West Ninth Street in Manhattan. When he died, the 65-year-old Bundy Drive Boy had his second wife, Dorothy Patience May DuCroz Young, whom he married in 1948, by his side.

Young had performed only occasionally during the last years of his life. Movie roles included *Bond Street* and *You Gotta Stay Happy* in 1948, *The Great Lover* in 1949, *Let's Dance* in 1950, and *St. Benny the Dip* in 1951. His final film performance was in the 1953 Spanish-made *Aquel Hombre de Tanger* (released in the U.S. as *That Man from Tangier*). TV appearances included *The Chevrolet Tele-Theatre*, *Pulitzer Prize Playhouse*, *Studio One* and *Lux Video Theatre*.

Few actors have ever captured Roland Young's humor and elegance.

The next to go — six years after Young and 12 years after John Decker — was Errol Flynn.

In those dozen years, Flynn seemed to imitate Barrymore's Jekyll-to-Hyde downfall, degenerating physically and emotionally before the public eye. The antics and publicity never ceased. In *The Intimate Sex Lives of Famous People,* Irving Wallace, Amy Wallace, David Wallechinsky and Sylvia Wallace reported:

Despite his constant sexual urges, Flynn rarely bragged about his endurance as a lover, but did claim to practice Oriental sexual techniques learned during a stay in Hong Kong. He was concerned about being able to perform whenever called upon, and was known to apply a pinch of cocaine to the tip of his penis as an aphrodisiac. His enjoyment of sex was heightened by watching other couples make love at the same time, and he also got a tremendous kick out of exhibiting himself — with a full erection — to his "straight" male friends. Flynn even installed a one-way mirror in his home so that he could observe his houseguests making love. He often indulged his taste for kinky sex in Mexico, where one could see men and women copulate on stage or have intercourse with animals. Flynn made no apologies for his self-proclaimed "wicked ways" and even urged his son, Sean, to follow in his footsteps, once sending the lad $25 for "condoms and/or flowers."

He married Patrice Wymore (his leading lady in 1950's *Rocky Mountain*) in Monte Carlo on October 23, 1950, the same day a 17-year-old French salesgirl accused him of rape. Five years later he sued *Confidential* magazine for $1,000,000 for claiming he'd left Wymore on their wedding night to romp with whores and drug addicts; he settled for $15,000. Flynn and Patrice had a daughter, Aranella, but Lili Damita was still reaping alimony, and Flynn's financial storms caused him to sell Mulholland Farm and his Gauguin. He took a stab at independent production in Europe, but a 1953 self-financed production of *William Tell*, conceived as being a Cinemascope color epic, went bust in the Alps. Bruce Cabot, Flynn's old "pal" whom he'd cast in *William Tell*, followed Flynn to Rome and sued him for salary, his lawyers attaching Flynn's car and Wymore's clothes. Flynn tried TV, hosting 1957's syndicated *The Errol Flynn Theatre*, sometimes guesting on episodes and always looking tired. Even his setting up quarters in Jamaica had its downside — his parents retired there, and Errol once again had to endure mother Marelle, who had not only retained her withering personality over the decades, but now had intensified her religious hysteria. The spiritual ranting hardly soothed her sad relationship with a son whose addictions besides alcohol and drugs now included screwing the native girls he collected in the Jamaican jungle. Flynn did enjoy the torchlit beach parties, singing along with the minstrels, belting out, for example, Conrad Mauge and Sean Altman's *Zombie Jamboree*:

> Back to back, ghoul, belly to belly
> Well, I don't give a damn 'cause I'm stone dead already, yeah
> Back to back, mon, belly to belly
> It's a zombie jamboree

There was a late-in-life respectability as an actor. Flynn received good reviews for his performance of dissolute Mike Campbell in *The Sun Also Rises*, 20th Century-Fox's 1957 version of the Hemingway novel. This led to Flynn's fortuitous casting as his old idol John Barrymore in *Too Much, Too Soon* (1958) based on the sordid best-selling memoir of Diana Barrymore (who would die in 1960). Dorothy Malone played Diana and Art Napoleon directed, careful to have Flynn underplay Barrymore. Under Napoleon's prosaic direction, Flynn avoided the posing, cackling, snorting and various Barrymore eccentricities that he in fact could expertly imitate, but was not allowed to do.

"They've great respect for the dead in Hollywood," Flynn told writer Charles Hamblett, who visited him on the *Too Much, Too Soon* set, "but none for the living."

It's an admirable, surely heartfelt performance, but Flynn was in no better shape filming it than Barrymore had been on *Playmates*. His heavy drinking constantly delayed shooting and ran the film over schedule. In one scene, his chauffeur, confident that Barrymore is on the wagon, was to leave him alone for the night. "You mean, I'm on parole?" Flynn as Barrymore was to say. Flynn kept saying "patrol." It required 17 takes before he finally said "parole."

Flynn disliked his director, and at one time responded to him with a Barrymore-style rant: "Are you, Art Napoleon, telling *me* how to play a drunk?" Yet his downfall was colossal, and Jack L. Warner — who'd personally offered Flynn the Barrymore role, and had felt magnanimous for having allowed him back into the Warner fold — now couldn't bear to watch him.

"He was one of the living dead," wrote Warner in his memoir.

Flynn's real-life Barrymore salute continued in 1958 as he disastrously starred in Huntington Hartford's pre-Broadway tryout of *The Master of Thornfield*, an adaptation of *Jane Eyre*. Flynn staggered through the Philadelphia run relying on Teleprompters, glasses of vodka strategically placed around the stage, and lame ad-libs. The play made it to Broadway without him, but only briefly.

Flynn was drunk again, on screen and off, in *The Roots of Heaven*, which 20th Century-Fox shot on location in Africa. Director John Huston remembered native girls coming in the night, and yowling like cats outside Flynn's hut — their signal that they had come for sex. There was one more film — *Cuban Rebel Girls* (1959), a semi-documentary embarrassment, memorable mainly for its promotion of Fidel Castro's revolution and its leading lady: Beverly Aadland, Flynn's new, blonde 15-year-old lover. Flynn called her "Woodsie," short for wood nymph. Still mirroring the Barrymore last act in the strangest ways, Flynn not only had a young lover, but the lover (à la Elaine) had a nightmarish mother. Beverly's mother, however, had her own special *accoutrement* — a wooden leg.

The shadows were darkening. Flynn completed his memoir, *My Wicked, Wicked Ways*. Fateful, philosophical, and at times still commanding, in September of 1959, Flynn talked with Vernon Scott of the *Los Angeles Herald-Express*:

> I've squandered seven million dollars. I'm going to have to sell the *Zaca*. I need the money, old bean. But don't grieve for me when I go. The way of a transgressor is not as hard as they claim...
>
> Years ago it was a matter of choosing which road to travel. After all, there is only one road to Hell, and there weren't any signposts along the way...
>
> "I hope I manage to face it all with a brave front," Flynn told Scott. "You shouldn't distress your friends or have them feel the disasters." Perhaps realizing he was speaking eulogistically, Flynn assured his interviewer, "I never felt better."

Nor had he ever looked worse. On September 29, 1959, he guest-starred as the "Gentleman Hobo" on *The Red Skelton Show*, clowning it up with Skelton's Freddie the Freeloader. There were jokes about the 1943 rape trial — Skelton notes a piece of junk is a "porthole," and Flynn replies, "Ah, memories, memories!" Even allowing for the hobo makeup, Flynn was so bloated he was almost unrecognizable. He played a guest star role on Ronald Reagan's *General Electric Theatre*, "The Golden Shanty." He couldn't remember the lines, and was so ill that director Arthur Hiller thought Flynn's agent wrong for even sending him out on a job. In a barroom sequence, as Flynn danced with his leading lady, Hill had several teleprompters so Flynn could read his lines from any angle. "He was hopelessly confused," said Hiller:

> After several minutes of this he put his head down on the bar, and when a few moments later he looked up at me he had tears in his eyes, and he said, "Arthur, I can't do it, I can't do it. I just don't know what I'm doing."

From *Too Much, Too Soon*. Errol Flynn plays John Barrymore and Dorothy Malone is Diana Barrymore

By the time "The Golden Shanty" was telecast November 9, 1959, Errol Flynn was dead.

Before heading to Vancouver, Flynn met with Nora, and advised her and their daughters that he had, according to a New York doctor, only a year to live. Nora said:

> I hadn't seen him in about a year and he looked like an old, old man, absolutely terrible, and I didn't think he could last six months. But he was strutting like a cock and trying to be debonair. He knew he was dying but he wasn't going to scream and yell about it. I started to cry and he said, "Don't be unhappy; you know I've lived twice and I've had a marvelous life."

In Vancouver to sell the *Zaca*, Flynn and Beverly stayed as houseguests of George Caldough. On Wednesday, October 14, 1959, they left to return home via Vancouver International Airport. Flynn was suffering from pains in his lower back and legs and asked Caldough to summon a doctor. Caldough took Flynn to the apartment of Dr. Grant Gould, where Flynn propped himself against a door and gallantly entertained, telling the assemblage about his days and nights as a Bundy Drive Boy. It was Errol Flynn's last performance.

Feeling worse, he lay on the floor and suffered a coronary. As Beverly became hysterical, an ambulance arrived, and Flynn was pronounced D.O.A. at Vancouver General Hospital. Post-mortem findings: Myocardial Infarction, Coronary Thrombosis, Coronary Atherosclerosis, Fatty Degeneration of the Liver, Portal Cirrhosis of the Liver and Diverticulosis of the Colon. The popular zinger that circulated was a coroner's observation that Flynn had the body of a "75-year-old man."

He was 50 years old.

As with John Barrymore, the funeral and burial were not precisely what the dearly departed had desired. Patrice Wymore, the official widow, took over the arrangements. Rather than have Flynn cremated and his ashes scattered in Jamaica as he had wished, she opted to bury him at Forest Lawn, Glendale. Flynn had mocked and despised Forest Lawn, but not as vehemently as he'd mocked and despised the man Patrice selected to deliver his eulogy — Jack L. Warner! Dennis Morgan sang "Home is the Sailor," and the pallbearers were Raoul Walsh, Mickey Rooney, Jack Oakie, Guinn "Big Boy" Williams, restaurateur Mike Romanoff and Flynn's lawyer Juston Golenbock — none of the surviving Bundy Drive Boys was in evidence. Patrice was the only Mrs. Errol Flynn to attend the funeral, and Beverly was also conspicuous by her discreet absence. There was no marker for 20 years — only in 1979 did daughters Rory, Deidre and Aranella place a tombstone over their father's grave in Forest Lawn's Garden of Everlasting Peace.

There were many ironies after Flynn's demise. And come February 27, 1961, Beverly Aadland and her mother sued the Flynn estate for $5,000,000, claiming that Flynn:

> ... had led Beverly along the byways of immorality, accustomed her to a life of frenzied parties, subjected her to immoral debauchery and sex orgies... and roused within her a lewd, wanton and wayward way of life, and deep unripened passions and unnatural desires...

Judge Samuel Hofstader got into the spirit of the trial, responding in prose that surely had the ghost of "Satan's Angel" howling with joy:

> Doubtless, the unfortunate young woman has been victimized — but by whom? To be sure, Flynn was the immediate occasion for her degradation.

But was he the sorcerer's apprentice who evoked a demon in her — or, was he not himself the issue of an evil spirit — one of the creatures which "never remains solitary (because) every demon evokes its counter demon" in an endless moral chain reaction? For we live in a climate of physical violence compounded by moral confusion...

In short, Judge Hofstader tossed out Beverly's claim. Beverly's mother was later charged with contributing to the delinquency of a minor after Beverly was raped at gunpoint, during which time the gun discharged a bullet into the rapist's brain. Florence allegedly watched while Beverly had sex and served the rest of her sentence in jail after attacking her janitor and shattering his shinbone with her wooden leg.

Sean Flynn, who'd worked a couple of episodes of *The Errol Flynn Theatre* and had a bit part in *Where the Boys Are* (1960), starred in *The Son of Captain Blood* (1962). He acted in some European films and gave it up to become a photographer for Time-Life. In April of 1970 he disappeared while on assignment in Viet Nam. Lili Damita, who had remarried three years after Flynn's death, spent great sums searching for her son, to no avail. In *Inherited Risk*, Jeffrey Meyers writes:

> Two months after Sean disappeared, Lili "received word that her son had been captured, tortured, executed and thrown into a ditch by the Vietcong." Rory Flynn, who noted that many other photographers had also died in captivity, heard that he was held for a year and, after going on a hunger strike to secure his release, was executed by a hoe that severed his neck.

Lili died in 1994 at age 89; Nora died in 2001 at age 77. Patrice Wymore, Flynn's widow, never remarried and turned 80 in 2006. Her daughter with Flynn, Arnella, died in 1998, the victim of drug abuse. Beverly "Woodsie" Aadland married three times and reportedly lives in North Hollywood.

Phil Rhodes' favorite Errol Flynn story involves taking a sexy female singer up to Mulholland Farm one time to meet Flynn — who answered the door stark naked. Sensing the young lady was agog and "a nice girl" — "I'd just like to talk with you," she sincerely insisted — Flynn decided not to have his wicked way with her. However, a carouser friend of the actor arrived, eyed the lady lasciviously and arranged to take her home.

The great star gave his on-the-make pal a warning:

"Listen, I want you to take this girl home. If you touch her, she will tell me. And as a result, I would fuck your wife — and you know I can do it!"

Gene Fowler never returned to the studios. He wrote the 1949 biography of Mayor James Walker of New York, *Beau James* (which became a 1957 movie, starring Bob Hope as Walker). In 1950 he received considerable attention when he was baptized a Roman Catholic at the Cathedral of the Immaculate Conception in his hometown of Denver. In 1951, Fowler published a biography of comedian Jimmy Durante, *Schnozzola*.

Minutes of the Last Meeting, Fowler's affectionate account of the Bundy Drive Boys, awarded the star spot to Sadakichi Hartmann, whose biography he had never completed. Predictably, Fowler's well-meaning gesture backfired. Harry Lawton, in his introduction to *The Sadakichi Hartmann Papers* catalogue for the University of California, Riverside, wrote about visiting "Catclaw Siding" in the Morongo Indian Reservation in 1954, after reading *Minutes of the Last Meeting*:

> I studied the shack, carefully jotting down descriptive notes for my story. Then I walked away from it and knocked on the door of a nearby adobe house. The door was opened by a hauntingly beautiful woman with coal-black hair framing an olive-hued face.
>
> She listened suspiciously as I explained that I was a reporter and wanted to do a story on her late father, Sadakichi Hartmann. Then she slammed the door in my face.
>
> That was my introduction to Wistaria Hartmann Linton, who was to become a close friend and future collaborator with Professor George Knox and me in research on her father.

Wistaria (and some others) saw Fowler's depiction of Sadakichi as a caricature. Surely, Fowler had realized that 1954 I-Like-Ike America was never going to take seriously a Japanese/German, truss-sporting savant who was infamous for pissing his pants. Nevertheless, on March 30, 1955, Wistaria, as administrator of Sadakichi's estate, sued Gene Fowler and *Minutes* publisher Viking Press for $300,000 each, claiming Fowler had "substantially copied, embodied and appropriated" material from Sadakichi's *Autobiography*, which he completed prior to 1940. Fowler, who was just recovering from another bout with serious illness, declared his innocence.

MINUTES of the LAST MEETING

or, some misadventures, both comic and melancholy, of JOHN BARRYMORE, W. C. FIELDS, and JOHN DECKER while helping the Author attempt to write the biography of SADAKICHI HARTMANN, poet, self-proclaimed genius, artful rogue, and moocher *sans pareil*.

by
GENE FOWLER

"But holy smoke, they're asking $300,000," chuckled Gene Fowler. "I'm deeply honored."

On August 28, 1955, Wistaria and her lawyers dropped the suit, releasing a statement that *Minutes of the Last Meeting* was entirely Fowler's original work and that he had full and exclusive rights to everything in it. Wistaria eventually donated her father's papers to UC Riverside, which awarded Sadakichi the respect he deserved.

Another blow for Fowler came after a film production of *Minutes of the Last Meeting*, set to star Red Skelton as W.C. Fields, crashed and burned after W.C.'s son Claude threatened a lawsuit.

Gene Fowler and wife Agnes lived at St. Helena Street, in Brentwood below Sunset. He was writing a new book, *Skyline*, about his years as a New York newspaperman, with a cat at his side whom he named "Frank Moran" (after the boxer turned character actor); Fowler was ill after years of serious heart trouble, and was sitting in his garden, having just read the proofs on the 19th chapter of *Skyline* when he suffered a fatal heart attack on Saturday, July 2, 1960. He was 70 years old, and survived by his wife of 44 years, Agnes, son Gene Jr. (who edited such films as *It's a Mad, Mad, Mad, Mad World*, and directed 1957's *I Was a Teenage Werewolf*), son Will (a reporter who had covered the famous Black Dahlia murder, a comedy writer for Red Skelton's TV show, and an author who wrote about the Bundy Boys in such books as *The Second Handshake* and *Reporters*), and daughter Jane, as well as seven grandchildren.

Before the undertakers removed the body, Agnes kissed him. "I want your lips to be the last to touch mine," he told her.

The Rosary was recited Tuesday night, July 5, at St. Martin of Tours Church in Brentwood, and a solemn Requiem Mass celebrated there the next day. The pallbearers included Bundy Boys Ben Hecht and Thomas Mitchell, as well as such celebrities as Jimmy Durante, Leo McCarey, Jack Dempsey, Westbrook Pegler and Red Skelton. Mourners included Pat O'Brien, Adolphe Menjou, Hedda Hopper and John Ford. Bishop Timothy Manning presided and delivered the final absolution, and the Rev. Edward Carney celebrated the Mass, calling Fowler a "genius" and a "lovable man" who was "masterful with words." He was buried at Holy Cross Cemetery, and his grave bears the words, "That Young Man from Denver."

Gene Fowler's will left his estate to his widow. He noted in the will that he had "missed opportunities for financial gain" so that he could "achieve my lifelong aspiration to write for my own soul's satisfaction instead of the possible applause of the larger audience." And he wrote to his children, "Remember me with a smile and never a tear. May God bless you in

Gene Fowler with Decker self-portrait hanging on his office wall

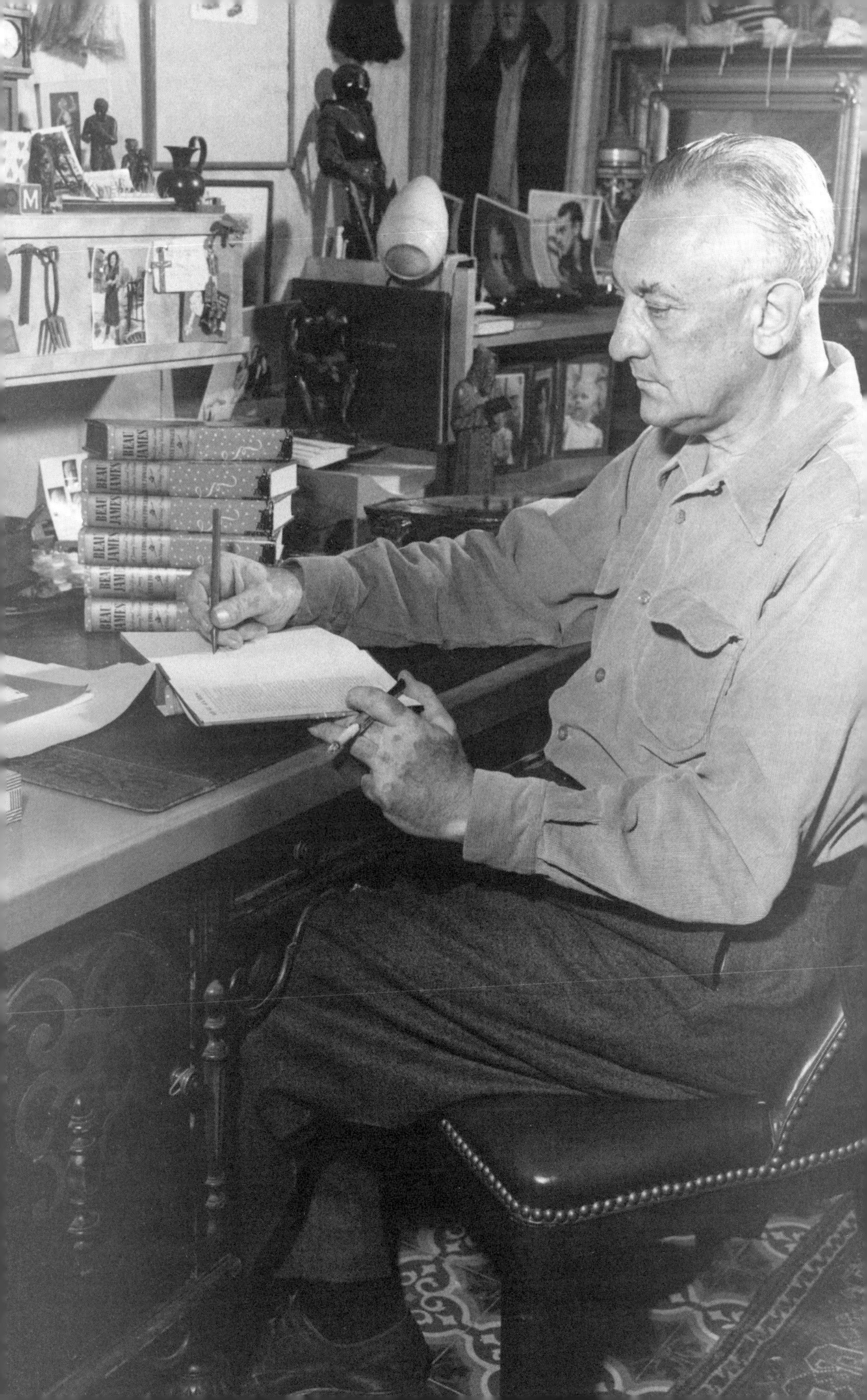
M
BEAU JAMES

DR. FRANK NOLAND   GEORGE POTNAM   BEN HECHT

Gene Fowler funeral with family annotations

every way and help you keep our great country forever free and in the right."

The phrase "in the right" might not be purely symbolic: Fowler, particularly in his late years, held very conservative political views, as did his good friends Pegler, Menjou and right-wing radio blowhard George Putnam.

Thomas Mitchell's career prospered in films such as *High Noon* (1952) and *Pocketful of Miracles* (1961). Broadway successes included replacing Lee J. Cobb as Willy Loman in *Death of a Salesman* (1949) and winning a Tony Award for the 1953 musical *Hazel Flagg* (based on Ben Hecht's 1937 film *Nothing Sacred* — Hecht wrote the book for the show, with music and lyrics by Jule Styne and Bob Hilliard). On television, he won the 1952 Best Actor Emmy Award and landed guest star roles on such shows as *Tales of Tomorrow* (as Captain Nemo in a two-part "20,000 Leagues Under the Sea"), *Climax!* (as the King in "The Adventures of Huckleberry Finn," with John Carradine as the Duke), and *The 20th Century-Fox Hour* (as Kris Kringle in "Miracle on 34th Street"). He also starred in his own series, 1955's *Mayor of the Town* and was host and occasional guest star on 1957's *The O. Henry Playhouse*.

"One thing about O. Henry," said Mitchell, "he could drink more than I can. But — I try!"

Thomas Mitchell died of cancer at 1:30 p.m., Monday December 17, 1962, at his home, 1013 North Roxbury Drive in Beverly Hills. He was 70 and survived by his wife and daughter, who were at his bedside when he died. A peculiarity about his death: Mitchell was cremated December 19, 1962 at the Chapel of the Pines in Los Angeles, and his ashes placed in "Vaultage" below the building. They have never been claimed, and remain there in rather celebrated if forlorn company — H.B. Warner (Christ in 1927's *The King of Kings*) and Helen Chandler (the heroine of 1931's *Dracula*) are among the "cremains" in Vaultage at the Chapel of the Pines.

Ben Hecht stayed prolific and hotheaded. Constantly racking up major screen credits — *Kiss of Death* (1947), *Monkey Business* (1952), *Miracle in the Rain*, based on his novel (1956), *A Farewell to Arms* (1957) — as well as uncredited work on everything from 1951's *The Thing* to 1963's *Cleopatra*. Hecht was also an outspoken champion of Irgun Zvei Leumji's terrorist organization for an independent Israel. In a 1947 newspaper advertisement, Hecht had written:

> Every time you blow up a British arsenal, or send a British railroad train sky-high, or rob a British bank, or let go with your guns and bombs at the British betrayers and invaders of your homeland, the Jews of America make a little holiday in their hearts.

When Britain retaliated and exhibitors refused to show his films, Hecht offered an apology — sort of: "The English are, with cavil, the nicest enemies the Jews have ever had." Indeed perhaps no honor (and surely not his Oscars) pleased Hecht more than the fact that Israel named a battleship *The Ben Hecht*.

He published his memoir, *A Child of the Century*, in 1954. His passion for the Israeli cause climaxed in 1961's wildly controversial *Perfidy*, in which he attacked Israel's "ruling clique." *Perfidy* accused Jewish leaders of "moral corruption," including Nazi collaboration and failure to stop the Holocaust. As he wrote in *Perfidy*:

> In my own time, governments have taken the place of people. They have also taken the place of God. Governments speak for people, dream for them, and determine, absurdly, their lives and deaths.
>
> This new worship of government is one of the subjects in this book. It is a worship I lack. I have no reverence for the all-powerful and bewildered face of Government. I see it as a lessening of the human being, and a final looting of his birthright — the survival of his young. I see it as an ogre with despair in its eyes.

David Ben-Gurion, outraged, denied Hecht the right to be buried in sacred ground in Israel.

Ben Hecht hosted a New York talk show in the 1950s/1960s and had just completed work on a musical based on his Academy Award-winning *Underworld* when, on the morning of Saturday April 18, 1964, Hecht died of a heart attack at his 14th-floor apartment, 39 West 67th Street in New York City. He was 70, and reportedly reading e.e. cummings when he suffered his fatal attack. Due to his political alienation from the "clique that ruled Israel," there were rumors of assassination.

He was survived by his wife Rose and daughter Jenny, an actress. In *Ben Hecht, The Man Behind the Legend*, William McAdams quotes Rose as saying she talked to him all the while she tried to revive him: "I talked to him while I tipped him backward, his head on the floor, his birthday pajama top of soft dark silk around his still warm body. I talked while getting him smelling salts and while beginning to work on his chest with respiratory rhythm. I only stopped talking to force my tongue into his mouth still sweeter than wine to me and then I breathed into him while keeping on with the artificial respiration...." Later, after the police had placed Hecht's body on the bed and Jenny and guests had come, Rose went back and told her husband in Yiddish how much she loved him.

"Except for a lullaby I used to sing to Jenny, I had never spoken of love in the mother tongue," said Rose Hecht. "I felt these words would reach his soul. I guess that is what it means to be a Jew."

The funeral took place at Temple Rodeph Sholom on West 83rd Street. The several hundred mourners included Helen Hayes to "Maurice," then New York's "Prince of Bohemia." George Jessel and Luther Adler provided eulogies, as did Mendham Beige, leader of Israel's Hero party (and formerly of the Argon terrorist organization), Samuel Tamer, leading Israeli lawyer, and Peter Bergson, investment broker and former chairman of the Hebrew Committee of National Liberation, who said:

> Ben attacked and derided the tinsel gods of his time. Ben's life was a permanent revolution against the errors of today and for a better tomorrow.

Outside the temple, Helen Hayes spoke about Hecht's friendship and professional relationship with her late husband, Charles MacArthur. "It is very curious," Ms. Hayes told the *New York Times*. "Their collaboration was so acute. It was nine years ago today that Charlie died." Denied burial in Israel, Ben Hecht was interred at Oak Hills Cemetery in Nyack, New York, near the grave of MacArthur.

"They are side by side again," said Helen Hayes.

Hecht's final book, *Letters from Bohemia*, which included a section on Gene Fowler, was published after his death. Several of his films have spawned remakes, including the 1983 *Scarface*, which director Brian De Palma dedicated to Ben Hecht.

Alan Mowbray remained a busy character player to the end of his life. He played in such films as *Wagon Master* (1950), *Blackbeard the Pirate* (1952), and *The King and I* (1956), and had his own 1953 TV series, *Colonel Humphrey Flack* — his role described by the *New York Times* as "a modern-day Robin Hood who outslicks swindlers and aids their innocent victims." The 39 episodes, originally aired live from New York, were kinescoped and played in syndication for years. He also was a regular on the 1960 TV series *Dante*.

On February 22, 1962, the 65-year-old Mowbray was jailed on a drunk charge after smashing a pane of glass in a Hollywood home. On the night of August 15 of that same year, he was arrested again, this time pleading guilty to drunken driving charges after driving into a curb at Hollywood Boulevard and Highland Avenue and blowing out a tire.

Come March 13, 1963, and Alan Mowbray, at age 66, enjoyed what had eluded him in his youth — a Broadway hit. The play was *Enter Laughing*, a comedy by Joseph Stein based on Carl Reiner's novel. Mowbray played Marlowe, a ham actor gone to seed who runs a fly-by-night drama school and fleeces aspiring young players. Directed by Gene Saks, the play also starred Alan Arkin, Vivian Blaine, and Sylvia Sidney. The show ran for a year, and if there was any disappointment for Mowbray, it was that Jose Ferrer played Marlowe in the 1967 film version.

Mowbray died at Hollywood Presbyterian Hospital on March 25, 1969, from a heart attack. He was 72 years old. His survivors included Lorayne (his wife of 42 years), a son Alan Jr., a daughter Patricia, two brothers and two grandchildren. There was also a son-in-law — Douglass Dumbrille, the veteran Hollywood heavy and an old friend of Alan's. Dumbrille was five years older than Mowbray and, as a 70-year-old widower in May of 1960, wed 28-year-old Patricia.

John Carradine continued pursuing acting as a holy cause, carrying his thespian cross though many hills and valleys. He had colorful roles in *The Ten Commandments* and *Around the World in Eighty Days* (both 1956), acted for John Ford again in *The Last Hurrah* (1958) and *Cheyenne Autumn* (1964), and enjoyed a long Broadway run as Lycus, "a buyer and seller of courtesans," in the 1962 musical comedy *A Funny Thing Happened on the Way to the Forum*. Pocking his reputation were dozens of low-grade horror films, perhaps none so infamous as 1966's *Billy the Kid vs. Dracula*.

His personal life was always rocky. He and Sonia, his "Ophelia" from his 1943 Shakespeare company, divorced in 1957 amidst sensational headlines; the marriage produced three sons, including actors Keith and Robert. His third wife Doris (whom he wed in 1957) died in a fire in 1971 and his fourth wife Emily (whom he married in 1975) became ill, prompting Carradine — old, desperate and gnarled by arthritis

— to lament to the *National Enquirer* that he was virtually destitute and unable to pay medical bills. The *Enquirer's* calls to his sons as to why they weren't helping the old man went unanswered.

Come the final years, John Carradine's life resembled a horror movie — reportedly living in a quonset hut in San Diego, represented by a deformed manager who delivered the venerable actor in a van to play in films such as *Death Farm* (1986, as the Judge of Hell). Fearing he'd go mad if he ever retired, Carradine would go anywhere to act, including South Africa, where, in 1988, he made *Buried Alive,* appearing in a few flashes of screen time as a cackling old geek in a wheelchair. Traveling back home he stopped in Milan, where, the story goes, the 82-year-old actor insisted he visit the Duomo, the medieval cathedral. There one can take an elevator to the top of the Gothic tower, where, in olden days, religious zealots performed penance by climbing the 328 steps on their knees as they flagellated themselves. When Carradine arrived, he learned the elevator was out of order.

"I'll walk up!" he announced.

So John Carradine, defiant, adventurous and still gloriously mad, made the ascent. He reached the top, looked at the view — and collapsed.

Various observers of the late-in-life Carradine find this account difficult to believe. (Director Fred Olen Ray, who loyally used Carradine whenever possible, told me he never filmed Carradine walking across a room — "I didn't have that much film!"). Whatever occurred, Carradine ended up in a pauper's ward in a Milan hospital. David and Keith flew to be at his side. Keith couldn't stay — he had to start a film — but David remained to read to his father his beloved Shakespeare. John Carradine died Sunday November 27, 1988 as David held him in his arms, heard the death rattle and closed his father's eyes.

In his final years, Carradine told David:

> Son, I've done everything I ever wanted to do. I have a few regrets, but I've had every woman I ever wanted. I played Hamlet. I skippered my own 70-foot schooner and I've raised a bunch of fine boys. Like every dog, I've had my day. I'm ready to go.

The funeral took place at Saint Thomas Episcopal Church in Hollywood, where Carradine had been a founder and where David had been baptized. A weeping David read Shakespeare and the words "Good Night, Sweet Prince, and may Flights of Angels Sing Thee to thy Rest." There was pomp and pageantry, the church was SRO and the funeral concluded with the hymn *Onward Christian Soldiers*.

Then came a postscript wake, worthy of the Bundy Drive Boys and almost a homage to them. As David (familiar with the kidnapping of Barrymore's corpse and "one final drink" story) wrote in his book *Endless Highway*:

> Afterward we carted the coffin over to our house and opened it up. I looked down at him and the undertakers had put a demonic, artificial grin on his face — like nothing I had ever seen him do in real life, except in a horror film. I reached out and using the sculptural skills I had learned from him, I remodeled his face to be more naturally him. Then I poured a half a bottle of J&B Scotch (his favorite) down his throat and we had the wake.

John Carradine was buried at sea — his activity in the 1941 coastal defense system allowed him this honor — complete with a 21-gun salute, a bugler playing taps and what David calls "the largest gathering of the Carradine clan that I can remember." A sailor tipped the coffin over the side into the Catalina Channel, where John Carradine had loved sailing his yacht *The Bali* in his glory years. David, as the eldest son, received the flag.

Phyllis Decker's choice in men had become more questionable when, on September 16, 1949 in Los Angeles, she married Jim Fleming, Errol Flynn's right-hand man. For a time things seemed rosy — they opened an art gallery in Del Monte, but as daughter Mary Lou Warn told me:

> Mother married this horrible, horrible person, Jim Fleming, Flynn's stand-in and — as I always said — procurer. He was terrible. What little Mother had, he blew. She was very jealous with him and got a little louder during those later years.

They parted four years later, but it wasn't until January 9, 1958 that finally received a divorce decree. She claimed that Fleming was content to live off the sale of John Decker's paintings (about $15,000 worth) and only worked about a fourth of the time. As Phyllis told the press:

> Mr. Fleming just sat around the house and drank whisky — a fifth a day. When I had to go to work, I thought it silly to carry him along and, besides, he had beaten me so severely that my front teeth were knocked loose.

Backing Phyllis' sad story was no less than Gloria Decker, John Decker's mysterious daughter by his first wife. A picture of Gloria and Phyllis made the *Los Angeles Times*, with both ladies looking as hard as actresses in a "B" women's prison melodrama, and Gloria actually appearing older than Phyllis. The divorcee settled with Jim Fleming for a token $1-per-month alimony. For a time, Thomas Mitchell and his family took Phyllis into their home in Beverly Hills.

Phyllis did marry again — for the fifth and final time — not to Marcel Grand, but to a nebbish. As Mary Lou remembers:

> I was married and traveled with my husband, a career Marine. We were always in these remote areas, and mother would come to visit. She had tough times after Jim, and went back to visit my aunt in Toledo, and this man who had just adored her for years from afar, a meek little man, five or six years younger than Mother, came along, and she married him for security. Every time anybody refers to him, it's as "Poor Louie" — it was never "Louie," it was just always "Poor Louie!"
>
> "Poor Louie" was a nice, sweet, quiet, little drunk. A beeraholic. We were living in Laguna Niguel, and our kids would all try to run and hide when they heard Grandpa Louie was coming, because he would just talk and talk — I mean, you'd go to the bathroom and shut the door in his face and he'd stand right there and he'd still keep talking!

Louie was a chemist for Union Oil in Toledo, which transferred him to Long Beach. His alcoholism was so severe that the company sent him as a patient to, as Mary Lou puts it, "the grand opening" of the Betty Ford Clinic. Louie died in 1988, and just before his death, Phyllis learned she had cancer. Mary Lou moved her to Bermuda Dunes, a golf course community near Riverside, California, where she managed an apartment complex. "She hated it," says Mary Lou. "She felt she was in prison. The end is very bad for cancer victims."

Phyllis died on her 72nd birthday, Wednesday, January 25, 1989.

Of all the Bundy Drive survivors, it was the youngest, Anthony Quinn, who most did the old gang proud.

He played Stanley Kowalski in the road company of Tennessee Williams' *A Streetcar Named Desire*, later replacing Marlon Brando on Broadway. He won a Best Supporting Actor Oscar for *Viva Zapata*, winning the same year his father-in-law Cecil B. DeMille finally won his Best Picture Oscar for *The Greatest Show on Earth*. Quinn won the Venice Film Festival award for his unforgettable sideshow strongman of Fellini's *La Strada* (1954), received a second Best Supporting Actor Oscar for *Lust for Life* (as Paul Gauguin, 1956) and won a Best Actor Academy nomination and the National Board of Review Best Actor award for his most famous performance, *Zorba the Greek* (1964). The actor's personal favorite, however, was his performance as Mountain Rivera in *Requiem for a Heavyweight* (1962).

There were also tepid efforts —as Quasimodo in 1957's *The Hunchback of Notre Dame* (with a script by Ben Hecht), directing 1958's *The Buccaneer* (the remake of DeMille's 1938 film — Quinn claimed DeMille recut his work and ruined the film) and co-starring as Henry II to Laurence Olivier's Becket in Broadway's 1960 *Becket* (with Olivier thoroughly intimidating him onstage). A 1971 TV series, *The Man and the City*, lasted one season.

Quinn was aware of his overpowering screen image. "I never get the girl," he joked. "I wind up with a country instead."

While starring in the title role of *Barabbas* (1962), Quinn met the 27-year-old costume designer Jolanda Addolori, and she bore him a son in March of 1963 (he was still married to Katherine), Quinn acknowledged his paternity and had the boy baptized at St. Peter's Basilica in Rome. "I want him to be loved," said Quinn, "and not to have to go to a psychiatrist at the age of 41 because he wasn't wanted." After Jolanda bore him a second son in April of 1964, Quinn bought a villa in Rome for his second family, and he and Katherine finally divorced ("for the good of *all* the children," said Katherine). In the early 1990s, after 30 years of living primarily in Italy, Quinn, nearly 80 years old, made another acknowledgment: his former secretary, Kathy Benvin, approximately 50 years his junior, had given birth to a daughter Antonia, and he was the father. Jolanda only reluctantly provided the divorce Quinn sought, and Quinn and Kathy became parents of son Ryan in July, 1996, three months after Quinn's 81st birthday. All in all, Anthony Quinn fathered 13 children.

An insight into Anthony Quinn came when, in 1982 at age 67, he began a four-year tour (including a Broadway engagement) in the musical *Zorba*. The show's anthem song, "Life Is," contained the lyric, "Life is what you do, while you're waiting to die." Quinn demanded the line be changed to "Life is what you do, till the moment you die." The producers granted his request.

Undoubtedly affected by John Decker and John Barrymore, Quinn became a fine visual artist, his paintings and sculptures winning exhibitions internationally.

1995 saw the publication of Quinn's memoir *One Man Tango*. The premise was interesting: Quinn, in Italy, had received a box from ex-wife Katherine, ill with Alzheimer's in the U.S. Quinn alternately probes into the box and bicycles around the Italian countryside, revealing his life story. His jealousy about Katherine was still seething, his sensitivity about C.B. DeMille still acute, his love for the Bundy Drive Boys was still strong. He couldn't resist boasting of his love affairs with Carole Lombard, Ingrid Bergman and Rita Hayworth, or bragging that his little daughter Antonia already had artistic talent.

"I never satisfied that kid," claimed Quinn, referring to his young self, "but I think he and I have made a deal now. It's like climbing a mountain. I didn't take him up Mount Everest, but I took him up Mount Whitney. And I think that's not bad."

Quinn had also made peace with approaching death, and wrote in his memoir:

> When my time is called I wish to go out in style. There will be no pine box sunk six feet under ground, no urn to be placed on a mantel and forgotten. No. I have thought this through. There will be my dozen children, carrying me up a hill in Chihuahua and leaving me to rot in the hot sun. I can picture the scene, transposed over the fertile ground of my youth. (I have the specific hill mapped for my executors.) I will be laid to rest at the top of the rise, a feast for the vultures. My children will go back to the rest of their lives, and the birds will peck at what is left of me. They will lift me up, piecemeal, and defecate me out all over the countryside, returning me to the earth from which I had sprung, leaving me forever a part of all Mexico.

For better or worse, this isn't the way it happened. Quinn's final film was 2001's *Avenging Angelo*, and he spent his final years at his Rhode Island estate, where he opened a restaurant. Aware of his approaching death, Quinn reconsidered those defecating vultures and requested the city of Bristol allow his burial on his estate. The city agreed, sanctioning the "Quinn Family Cemetery." On June 3, 2001, Anthony Quinn died in in Boston, finally brought down by lung cancer, renal failure and respiratory failure. He was 86. There was a private funeral on the estate with about 40 relatives and friends, and later a public memorial service at Bristol Baptist Church. Actor Franco Nero spoke, as did former New York mayor David Dinkins.

Anthony Quinn left his fortune only to widow Kathy and their two children; the other ten children received nothing. The Anthony Quinn Library stands on the site of his boyhood home in Los Angeles, on what is now Cesar Chavez Avenue. A branch of the L.A. library system, the building also houses the actor's collection of photos, memorabilia and scrapbooks.

There's also a famous Bundy Drive Boys relic — John Barrymore's Richard III black armor, which Quinn had bought at the auction of the actor's effects in 1942. A librarian there told me a ghost story, with true conviction, that the armor once escaped its plexiglas case and took a nocturnal stroll around the library.

Quinn's line in *Zorba the Greek* might have been a coat-of-arms motto for all the Bundy Drive Boys: "A man needs a little madness ... or else he never dares cut the rope and be free."

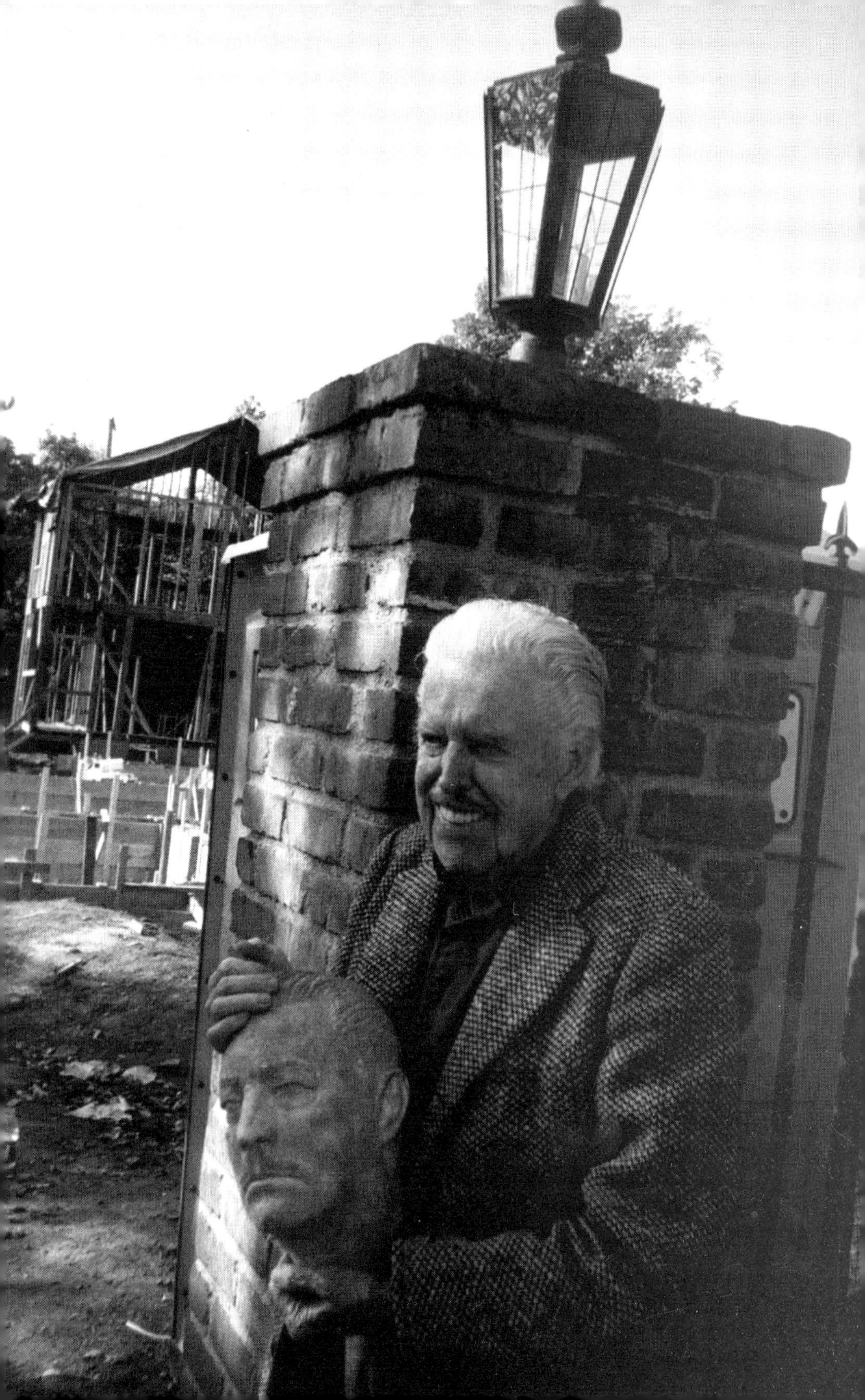

Chapter 22
Useless. Insignificant. Poetic.

May 2, 2006; As the May sun battles the Pacific clouds, Bundy Drive Boys historian and collector Bill Nelson and I drive west along Sunset, turn and park near 419 N. Bundy. The "For Sale" sign swings outside.

Rita Saiz has lived here for 25 years, has decided to move on. Caught on the freeway, she sanctions us by cellphone to enter the house — a trusting soul, she's left the back door unlocked.

The house has magic about it. It's changed — a pool now sparkles in the back yard, where Mary Lou's duck used to waken Decker from his hangovers, and there have been some additions made over the decades to indulge the Southern California mania for cubic space. Yet the old charm is still there, as is the fabled oak door with Decker's unicorns and motto. I climb the twisted steps to get an overview of the hearth and its mantel, the ancient chandelier and the old ceiling beams. We take a peek down at the catacombs-like cellar, where Decker kept his treasure chest.

Yes, the imagination goes amok, realizing that this is the old gathering spot of Decker, Barrymore, Flynn, Fields, Hecht, Fowler, Hartmann, Carradine, Quinn, Mitchell, Mowbray, Young... all of them at their best here. Yet something else is in the air... energy, a spirit, *spirits...*

Rita Saiz arrives, an auburn-haired dynamo adorned in a turquoise pants suit. Bill Nelson refers to her as a "Mexican Auntie Mame," and she has sold the house, but will

Phil Rhodes, John Barrymore, and the remains of 419 Bundy Drive be taking the historic Decker door with her. She changes from her black spiked heels to more comfortable shoes, and talks about 419 N. Bundy and, she insists, its ghosts.

"When did you first feel the presence of a ghost?" I ask.

"The first second I came here," Rita replies.

> The ghost is really sweet. After a while, when I caught on that he liked booze, I started lighting a candle and putting it on the fireplace mantel. And it would evaporate! If it were good whiskey, good Scotch, it would evaporate — but if I put in red wine, it would get full of fungus in one day. The ghost wants Scotch, expensive stuff... He ain't cheap!

Rita warms to her topic:

> I was always intrigued by the energy in here, because I'm intuitive and I've always known there's another life form of energy. I'd go into a trance, and a trance is your creative soul and you're connected with God. So I realized that all those guys are here — Decker, Flynn, Barrymore, the others — because they had found a matrix here, away from the reality of their lives. It was — and is — a safe haven for them.

Her excitement mounts and her eyes flash:

> Decker's ghost, Flynn's ghost, Barrymore's ghost — all of them are here! They're all partaking! Decker's the cool guy. Errol Flynn is the more social one — a trickster, always fooling around, dressing up, getting naked, being stupid — that's him. I think he's "bi" — "I'll be your girl, I'll be your boy, I'll be whatever you want me to be!" He's beautiful, like an angel. And Barrymore? He's like Lady Macbeth — very scandalous! I knew nothing about him, but by his energy – OH! Barrymore's a "tripper," the director, the conductor, the voyeur, because he's so flipped out! He's watching the circus. He is the circus!

She becomes more serious:

> In their time, these men had a lot of things going on — the Depression, and all that horrible stuff, and that's why they went cuckoo. But it wasn't really "cuckoo" — it was their essence. They've been telling me all these years — you don't die, there's another essence, a fifth dimension — a forever. We're going

to live just a temporary life here, 100 years or less — and they've been saying don't waste a minute in sadness. We're all going to have difficulties, but the difficulties are only to take you on to the next level.

They all saw the joke of life, and they teach us not to be scared. There is no bogeyman. Get the essence of love and happiness and joy, and share it with people. All that matters is to leave a legacy of happiness, and to give someone else an inspiration — like they gave us.

It's suddenly very still. The sunshine has finally fully emerged and fills the room.

We clown with Rita awhile, posing with foils (she fences) by the fireplace. As we drive away on Bundy Drive, I take one final look at the house that is knocked to the ground and becomes just a memory.

★

Rita Saiz and Mary Lou Warn

ACKNOWLEDGEMENTS

Researching and writing a book is often a great adventure, and sometimes these adventures seemed to have been fated to be.

My curiosity about the Bundy Drive Boys goes back to the mid-1960s, when I saw an old photograph of John Barrymore as *Svengali*. He seemed to epitomize, simply by his picture, the old-time theatrical spellbinder, and I soon learned he had been both the century's most exciting Shakespearean actor and a catastrophic self-destructive alcoholic. My 15-year-old morbid interest spiked when I saw the silent *Dr. Jekyll and Mr. Hyde*, and came away believing the passion and madness Barrymore conjured up in his magnificent dual performance exceeded anything the most daring rock bands of the '60s were offering.

His brilliance and tragedy also struck me as perhaps something very personal.

I visited the downtown Baltimore library to check out Gene Fowler's Barrymore biography, *Good Night, Sweet Prince*. On the bus, I glanced at a page mentioning the Bundy Drive Boys. For over 40 years, the various members of the gang who gathered at John Decker's studio fascinated me. Indeed, years ago on a research trip for another project, my wife and I drove up Bundy one morning to take a look at the house, and spent a few moments imagining all the genius and revelry that exploded there all those years ago.

Then came the night in 2006 when my friend and colleague Charles Heard called and said he and Bill Nelson were seeking a writer for a project on the Bundy Drive Boys. I instantly thought the quirks of fate that, for so many of us, seem to tag along faithfully with our favorite obsessions.

For all the decades of interest, this was a daunting project. Realistic assessment of the mythical gang was a challenge. Several books were more annoying than helpful. Some writers had seen the gang as no more than wicked, sybaritic creatures who egged on each other's slow suicides. Others chronicled their capers with a sophomoric I-love-bad-boys approach that missed the torment and genius that made them who they truly were. Even the brilliant Gene Fowler, Bundy Boys literary giant and charter member who wrote *Good Night, Sweet Prince* and *Minutes of the Last Meeting*, had a love and compassion for these men that caused him sometimes to pull his punches — and, through no fault of his own, was writing at a time when major publishers wouldn't have printed the gang's more baroque excesses.

What came clear throughout my research was the odd but touching mutual affection the Bundy Boys had for one another. These men both celebrated the demons that charged them, while they also tried to protect each other from them. As in any classical tragedy, catastrophe was inevitable. Of course, there was humor too, but for all the Comedy and Tragedy colliding and exploding in the book, the dominant theme was the love story.

My gratitude goes first to my co-authors. Charles Heard not only recruited me for this project, but also was a cordial host (along with his lovely wife Sherry) during my research trips to Dallas, including the icy night when I was stranded at their home and they insisted on sacking out on the floor so that I could have the bed. Charles provided me access to John Decker's own personal and voluminous scrapbooks, on loan to him from Decker's stepdaughter Mary Lou Warn. These, of course, were a major key to chronicling and fathoming the enigmatic Decker. Charles, who owns an impressive collection of Decker paintings, had many discussions with me about the book and he eloquently zeroed in on the fascination of the Bundy Drive Boys when he spoke of the Greek myth of Daedalus and Icarus. As Charles noted, Icarus' soaring flight on the wings crafted by his father Daedalus was inspiring, but what people remember most vividly in the ancient fable is Icarus' dizzying and fatal fall into the sea. I gratefully appreciate Charles' continuing trust and our ongoing friendship on this, our third project together.

Bill Nelson's enthusiasm for all things Bundy Boys never wavered through the surprises and crises of this book's writing and production. Bill's no-bounds generosity included, during my weeklong research trip to Los Angeles in May of 2006, actually moving out of his own quarters while I occupied his lodgings. (As such, I slept every night under John Decker's painting of Sadakichi Hartmann — which has, in its upper left corner, Decker's Barrymore-at-Calvary tribute — peacefully and with no nightmares.) Bill took me to the Bundy Drive house (which we visited just before its destruction), made several trips to Dallas and Pennsylvania to collaborate and shipped so many books cross-country. It was also Bill who found in the Irving Wallace Archives at Claremont College various interviews with John Decker, conducted in 1940/1941 for a magazine story called *Heroes With Hangovers* that presumably was never published. These invaluable interviews gave Decker a voice in our story. Bill's boundless energy and altruism on this project merit him the award for the project's true above-and-beyond-the-call-of-duty hero.

Adam Parfrey has been a cordial and encouraging publisher whose personal enthusiasm for this topic has been a great asset.

For their interviews, I thank:

• Ronald J. Fields, the grandson of W.C., Emmy winner for *W.C. Fields: Straight Up* and author of the books who spoke with me about of his celebrated ancestor with color and candor.

• Phil Rhodes, veteran actor, makeup man and Barrymore idolater, for a wealth of memories and his delightfully raucous Barrymore impression. Phil's trust and generosity included sending me one of John Barrymore's own oversized scrapbooks, which had been in the possession of John's ex-wife Dolores and now is part of Phil's awesome archive of Barrymorebilia.

• Rita Saiz, film producer/director and real estate agent, who gave us the run of her home, 419 N. Bundy Drive, and spoke sincerely and vivaciously of the ghosts and positive energy that romped there before the house's recent and lamentable destruction.

• Mary Lou Warn, John Decker's stepdaughter, who grew up in one of the strangest households anywhere, and emerged strong, confident and humorous, and provided unstinting help and encouragement along with her delightfully expressed memories and insights.

I'm also grateful to the late Constance Moore, leading lady of W.C. Fields' *You Can't Cheat an Honest Man*, who spoke with me about that film's chaotic shooting; and the late Marian Marsh, John Barrymore's leading lady of *Svengali* and *The Mad Genius*, who generously shared her memories of Barrymore with me.

James Bacon, veteran Hollywood columnist, provided co-authors Charles Heard and Bill Nelson an interview in October of 2006, for which we are grateful.

Ned Comstock, curator of the University of Southern California Performing Arts Archive, was invaluable as always, providing dozens of stories on Decker and the gang from the *Los Angeles Times*.

The late Will Fowler sat down for a videotaped interview with Bill Nelson, providing, among other things, a detailed eyewitness description of what very likely was John Decker's most infamous forgery.

The late Irving Wallace for his enormously helpful interviews with John Decker, titled *Heroes with Hangovers*.

G.D. Hamann's books *Hollywood Scandals in the 1930s* and *Hollywood Scandals in the 1940s* include the actual accounts from the various Los Angeles newspapers and were enormously helpful, especially in chronicling the Errol Flynn rape trial.

Roger Hurlburt loaned me the original personal correspondence between Gene Fowler and Dr. Harold Thomas Hyman, regarding Barrymore's private demons and his family history. Mr. Hurlburt, who also owns the original John Decker Barrymore Deathbed sketch, also provided the original hospital and autopsy reports related to Barrymore's final illness.

Leslee Mayo, now at work on her own book on Decker forgeries, was of enormous assistance in validating the details of Thomas Mitchell's "Rembrandt" and William

Goetz's "Van Gogh."

Scott Wilson, Indiana-based historian, was quite helpful with his information on the graves and final disposition of the various principals in this book, and revealed the sad-but-true account of John Decker's burial arrangement — at considerable odds with what has been routinely and erroneously reported elsewhere.

Valerie Yaros, curator of the Screen Actors Guild archive, kindly provided me copies of the SAG papers of Alan Mowbray, Bundy Drive Boy and SAG founder.

Thanks are due to Steve Beasley, the late DeWitt Bodeen, Richard Bojarski, the late Henry Brandon, Glenn Bray, Audrey Higer, Ron Hugo, Doug Norwine, Kelley Norwine, Victoria Price, Arianne Ulmer, Tom Weaver.

Finally, I must thank my wife Barbara, who worked with me around the clock to help make this book meet its deadline. It couldn't have been done without her, as is the case with all the books I've written over the past 30 years. The Bundy Drive Boys, as a group, have never been enormously appealing to women — in fact, most of the men's wives hated that they were a part of the pack. I was relieved when my wife came to appreciate the men and their madness.

My co-authors and I have referred to this work as *The Uncensored Minutes of the Last Meeting*, and the job at times has been an emotional wringer. Barrymore and Fowler were quick to lambaste anyone trying to "explain" them or pity them, so my apologies to their noble shades for any excesses in that area.

In a sense I feel as if I've lived with the ghosts of Barrymore, Decker, Flynn, Fields and the gang, and sharing their triumphs and disasters, even vicariously, has been a rollercoaster ride. With the book finally finished, we know better than to offer it to the ghosts with understanding or apologies.

Nevertheless, it surely comes with respect ... and affection.

Gregory William Mank
Delta, PA
March 16, 2007

Bibliography

Books

Astor, Mary, *A Life on Film.* New York: Delacorte Press, 1967, 1969, 1971.

Bacon, James, *Made in Hollywood.* Chicago: Contemporary Books, Inc., 1977.

Barrymore, Diana and Gerold Frank, *Too Much, Too Soon.* New York: Henry Holt and Company, 1957.

Barrymore, Elaine and Sandford Dody, *All My Sins Remembered.* New York: Appleton-Century, 1964.

Barrymore, Ethel, *Memories.* New York: Harper and Brothers, 1955.

Barrymore, John, *Confessions of an Actor.* Indianapolis: Bobbs-Merrill, 1926.

Barrymore, Lionel (with Cameron Shipp), *We Barrymores.* New York: Appleton-Century-Crofts, Inc., 1951.

Behlmer, Rudy (Editor), *Inside Warner Bros. (1935-1951).* New York: Viking Penguin Inc., 1985.

Bodenheim, Maxwell, *My Life and Loves in Greenwich Village.* New York: Bridgehead Books, 1954.

Bodenheim, Maxwell, *The Sardonic Arm.* Chicago: Covici-McGee, 1923.

Bret, David, *Errol Flynn: Satan's Angel.* London: Robson Books, 2000.

Brooks, Louise, *Lulu in Hollywood.* New York: Alfred A. Knopf, 1983.

Brown, Gene, *Movie Time.* New York: Macmillan, 1995.

Burke, Billie (with Cameron Shipp), *With a Feather on My Nose.* New York: Appleton-Century-Crofts, Inc. 1954.

Burke, Margaret and Gary Hudson, *Final Curtain.* Santa Ana, California, Minneapolis, MN and Washington, D.C.: Seven Locks Press, 1996.

Buscombe, Edward, *Stagecoach.* London: British Film Institute, 1992.

Carradine, David, *Endless Highway.* Boston: Journey Editions, 1995.

Casella, Frank A., *The Girls, Errol Flynn and Me.* Alhambra, CA: Anthony Press, 1980.

Castle, William, *Step Right Up! I'm Gonna Scare the Pants Off America.* New York: G.P. Putnam's Sons, Inc., 1976.

Cornwell, Patricia, *Portrait of a Killer: Jack the Ripper, Case Closed.* New York: G.P. Putnam's Sons, Inc., 2002.

Curtis, James, *W.C. Fields: A Biography.* New York: Alfred A. Knopf, 2003.

Davis, Ronald L., *John Ford: Hollywood's Old Master.* Norman and London: University of Oklahoma Press, 1995.

Deutsch, Armand, *Me and Bogie and Other Friends and Acquaintances from a Life in Hollywood and Beyond.* New York: G.P. Putnam's Sons, 1991.

Donati, William, *Ida Lupino, A Biography.* The University Press of Kentucky, 1996.

Endres, Stacy and Robert Cushman, *Hollywood's Chinese Theatre.* Los Angeles, London: Pomegranate Press, Ltd., 1992.

Fetherling, Doug, *The Five Lives of Ben Hecht.* Toronto, Lester and Orpen Limited, 1977.

Fields, Ronald J., *W.C. Fields: A Life on Film.* New York: St. Martin's Press, 1984.

Fields, Ronald J., *W.C. Fields by Himself.* Englewood Cliffs, NJ: Prentice-Hall, 1973.

Flynn, Errol, *My Wicked, Wicked Ways.* New York: Dell, 1959.

Flynn, Errol, *Showdown.* New York: Sheridan House, 1946.

Fowler, Gene, *Father Goose.* New York: Covici Friede, 1934.

Fowler, Gene, *Good Night, Sweet Prince.* New York: Viking, 1943 & 1944.

Fowler, Gene, *The Great Mouthpiece.* New York: Covici Friede Publishers, Inc., 1931.

Fowler, Gene, *Minutes of the Last Meeting.* New York: Viking, 1954.

Fowler, Gene, *Timberline.* New York: P.F. Collier & Son Corporation, 1933.

Fowler, Will, *Odyssey of a Spring Lamb, The Early Years of Legendary Reporter and Author Gene Fowler*, unpublished.

Fowler, Will, *Reporters.* Malibu, CA: Roundtable Publishing Company, 1991.

Fowler, Will, *The Second Handshake.* Secaucus, NJ: Lyle Stuart Inc., 1980.

Fowler, Will, *The Young Man from Denver.* Garden City, NY: Doubleday and Company, Inc., 1962.

Freedland, Michael, *The Two Lives of Errol Flynn.* New York: William Morrow, 1978.

Gehring, Wes D., *Groucho and W.C. Fields: Huckster Comedians.* University Press of Mississippi, 1994.

Gehring, Wes D., *W.C. Fields, A Bio-Bibliography.* Greenwood Press, 1984.

Gentry, Curt, *J. Edgar Hoover: The Man And His Secrets.* New York and London: W.W. Norton and Company, 1991.

Goodman, Dean, *Maria, Marlene, and Me.* San Francisco: Shadbolt Press, 1993.

Gordon, Mel, *The Seven Addictions and Five Professions of Anita Berber.* Los Angeles: Feral House, 2006.

Grady, Billy, *The Irish Peacock: The Confessions of A Legendary Talent Agent.* New Rochelle, NY: Arlington House, 1972.

Graham, Sheilah, *The Garden of Allah.* New York: Crown Publishers, Inc., 1970.

Hamann, G.D., *Hollywood Scandal in the 1930s.* Hollywood, CA: Filming Today Press, 2004.

Hamblett, Charles, *The Hollywood Cage.* New York: Hart Publishing Company, 1969.

Hartmann, Sadakichi, *A History of American Art*, Volume I. Boston: L.C. Page and Company, 1901.

Hartmann, Sadakichi, *A History of American Art*, Volume II. Boston: L.C. Page and Company, 1901.

Hartmann, Sadakichi, *The Last Thirty Days of Christ.* New York: Privately printed, 1920.

Hartmann, Sadakichi, *The Sadakichi Hartmann Papers, in the University of California, Riverside Library,* 1980.

Hartmann, Sadakichi, *Shakespeare in Art*. Boston: L.C. Page and Company, 1900.

Hartmann, Sadakichi, *The Whistler Book*. Boston: L.C. Page and Company, 1910.

Hartmann, Sadakichi, *White Chrysanthemums*, edited by George Knox and Harry W. Lawton. New York: Herder and Herder, 1971.

Hecht, Ben and Maxwell Bodenheim, *Cutie, A Warm Mamma*. Boar's Head Books, 1952.

Hecht, Ben, *1001 Afternoons in Chicago*. University of Chicago Press, 1992.

Hecht, Ben, *A Child of the Century*. New York: Simon and Schuster, 1954.

Hecht, Ben, *Fantazius Mallare, A Mysterious Oath*. New York: Harcourt Brace Jovanovich, 1978.

Hecht, Ben, *Gaily Gaily*. Garden City, NY: Doubleday and Company, Inc., 1963.

Hecht, Ben, *The Kingdom of Evil*. New York: Harcourt Brace Jovanovich, 1978.

Hecht, Ben, *Letters from Bohemia*. Garden City, NY: Doubleday, 1964.

Hecht, Ben, *Perfidy*. New York: Julian Messner, 1961.

Higham, Charles, *Errol Flynn: The Untold Story*. New York: Doubleday, 1980.

Jordan, Stephen C., *Bohemian Rogue: The Life of Hollywood Artist John Decker*. Lanham, MD, Toronto, Oxford: Scarecrow Press, 2005.

Kastor, Jacaber and Carlo McCormick, *Szukalski*. New York: Psy-Sol Word Press, 1989.

Kobler, John, *Damned in Paradise, The Life of John Barrymore*. New York: Atheneum, 1977.

Kotsilibas-Davis, James, *Great Times Good Times: The Odyssey of Maurice Barrymore*. Garden City, NY: Doubleday and Co., Inc., 1977.

Kovan, Florice Whyte, *Rediscovering Ben Hecht: Selling the Celluloid Serpent*, Snickersee Press, 1999.

Lambert, Gavin, *Nazimova*. New York: Alfred A. Knopf, 1997.

Louvish, Simon, *Man on the Flying Trapeze: The Life and Times of W.C. Fields*. New York: W.W. Norton and Company, 1997.

Lutyens, Mary, *Krishnamurti: The Years of Fulfillment*. New York: Avon Books, 1983.

MacAdams, William, *Ben Hecht: The Man Behind the Legend*. New York: Charles Scribner's Sons, 1990.

Martin, Pete, *Hollywood Without Make-Up*. Philadelphia and New York, J.P. Lippincott Company, 1948.

Marx, Samuel, *Mayer and Thalberg, The Make-Believe Saints*. New York: Random House, 1975.

Meyers, Jeffrey, *Inherited Risk: Errol and Sean Flynn in Hollywood and Vietnam*. New York: Simon & Schuster, 2002.

Monti, Carlota (with Cy Rice), *W.C. Fields and Me*. New York: Warner Books, 1971.

Morella, Joe, Edward G. Epstein and JohnGriggs, *The Films of World War II*. Secaucus, NJ: The Citadel Press, 1973.

Morrison, Michael A., *John Barrymore, Shakespearean Actor*. Cambridge University Press, 1997.

Murphy, Edwin, *After the Funeral*. New York: Barnes and Noble Books, 1995.

Napley, Sir David, *Rasputin in Hollywood*. London: Weidenfeld & Nicolson, 1989.

Nash, Jay Robert: *Zanies: The World's Greatest Eccentrics.* Piscataway, NJ: New Century Publishers, Inc., 1982.

Niven David, *Bring on the Empty Horses.* New York: G.P. Putnam's Sons, 1975.

Niven, David, *The Moon's a Balloon.* New York: G.P. Putnam's Sons, 1972.

Otash, Fred, *Investigation Hollywood!* Chicago: Henry Regnery Company, 1976.

Parish, James Robert, Alan G. Barbour and Alvin H. Marill, *Errol Flynn.* New York: Cinefax, 1969.

Parish, James Robert and William T. Leonard, with Gregory W. Mank and Charles Hoyt, *The Funsters.* New Rochelle, NY: Arlington House, 1979.

Paval, Philip, *Paval, Autobiography of a Hollywood Artist.* Hollywood, CA: Gunther Press, 1968.

Peary, Danny, *Alternate Oscars.* New York: Dell Publishing, 1993.

Peary, Danny, *Guide for the Film Fanatic.* New York: Simon & Schuster, Inc., 1986.

Peters, Margot, *The House of Barrymore.* New York: Alfred A. Knopf, 1990.

Price, Vincent, *I Like What I Know.* Garden City, NY: Doubleday, 1959.

Quinn, Anthony, (with Daniel Paisner), *One Man Tango.* New York: HarperCollins Publishing Company, 1995.

Quinn, Anthony, *The Original Sin, A Self-Portrait.* Boston: Little, Brown, 1972.

Rathbone, Basil, *In and Out of Character.* Garden City, NY: Doubleday, 1962

Sann, Paul, *The Lawless Decade.* Greenwich, CT: Fawcett Publications, Inc., 1971.

Seldes, George, *Witness to a Century.* Ballantine, 1987.

Stauffer, Teddy, *Forever Is a Hell of a Long Time.* Chicago: Henry Regnery, 1976.

Strange, Michael, *Who Tells Me True.* New York: Charles Scribner's Sons, 1940.

Thomas, Tony, Rudy Behlmer and Clifford McCarty, *The Films of Errol Flynn.* New York: Citadel Press, 1969.

Turk, Edward Baron, *Hollywood Diva, A Biography of Jeanette MacDonald.* University of California Press, 1998.

Vallee, Rudy, *Let the Chips Fall....* Harrisburg, PA: Stackpole Books, 1975.

Wallace, Irving, Amy Wallace, David Wallechinsky and Sylvia Wallace, *The Intimate Sex Lives of Famous People.* New York: Delacorte Press, 1981.

Weaver, Jane Calhoun (editor), *Sadakichi Hartmann, Critical Modernist.* Berkeley: University of California Press, 1991.

Weaver, Tom (with Gregory William Mank, Joe Dante and Fred Olen Ray), *John Carradine: The Films.* Jefferson, NC: McFarland, 1999.

Westmore, Frank and Muriel Davidson, *The Westmores of Hollywood.* New York: Berkley Medallion, 1977.

Wilson, Earl, *Pikes Peek or Bust.* Garden City, NY: Doubleday, 1946.

Wilkerson, Tichi and Marcia Borie, *Hollywood Legends: The Golden Years of The Hollywood Reporter.* Los Angeles: Tale Weaver Publishing, 1988.

Winokur, Jon, *The Portable Curmudgeon*. New York: New American Library, 1987.

Yurka, Blanche, *Bohemian Girl*. Ohio University Press, 1970.

Zolotow, Maurice, *Billy Wilder in Hollywood*. New York: G.P. Putnam's Sons, Inc., 1977.

Magazines and Periodicals

Beranger, Clara, "The Most Melancholy Funny Man on the Screen, *Liberty*, February 15, 1936.

Bodeen, DeWitt, "Evelyn Brent, 1899–1975," *Films in Review*, June-July 1976.

Bodeen, DeWitt, "John Barrymore and Dolores Costello," *Focus on Film*, Winter 1972.

Decker, John, "The Unpredictable Profile," *Esquire*, January, 1943.

Del Valle, David, "Shakespeare's Dracula," *Famous Monsters of Filmland*, No. 227, Aug/Sept 1999.

Fuller, Stanley, "Melville on the Screen," *Films in Review*, June-July, 1968.

Hecht, Ben, "John Decker's Hollywood," *Esquire*, December, 1945.

Hill, Richard, "The First Hippie," *Swank*, Volume 16, Number 2, April 1969.

Jean, Gloria (As Told To Gregory Lewis), "Gloria Jean Tells in Her Own Words What It Was Like To Be A Star at Twelve," *Films in Review*, November 1973.

Johnston, Alva, "Who Knows What Is Funny?" *The Saturday Evening Post*, August 6, 1938.

Marill, Alvin H., "Anthony Quinn," *Films in Review*, October 1968.

McEvoy, J.P., "W.C. Fields' Best Friend," unsourced article from Universal Pictures Co. Research Dept.

Rushfield, Richard, "The Rogues' Gallery," *Vlife*, April/May 2005.

Samuels, Charles, "Rabelais of the Rockies," unsourced magazine story, collection of Bill Nelson.

Sadakichi Hartmann Newsletter, University of California, Riverside, Fall, 1969.

_____, "The Little Bit of Rogue in All of Us," *TV Guide*, June 11, 1960.

Newspapers
The Los Angeles Daily News

"Half of Flynn's Jurors Dismissed in Second Day," January 13, 1943.

"Two Jurors in Flynn Case Charged with Perjury," January 16, 1943.

"Testimony of Doctor Aids Flynn Accuser," January 22, 1943.

"Errol Flynn Denies All on Stand," January 28, 1943.

"'Send Him to San Quentin, State Urges Errol Flynn Jury,'" February 3, 1943

"Girls Accuse Errol Flynn to Save Selves, Charges Geisler," February 4, 1943.

"W.C. Fields One Man Flask Force in Court," April 2, 1943.

"W.C. Fields Falls Off a Table," April 8, 1943.

The Los Angeles Evening Herald-Express

"Flynn Witness Attempts Suicide at Hall of Justice," January 15, 1943.

"W.C. Fields Guards on Snakes," April 1, 1943.

"W.C. Fields Mourns Loss of Gag Suit," April 10, 1943.
"Tell Errol Flynn Row At Party," April 30, 1945.

The Los Angeles Examiner
"Seek Jury to Try Errol Flynn," January 9, 1943.
"Flynn Case 'Lingering Kiss' Defined," by Marjorie Driscoll, January 15, 1943.
"Woman Juror in Flynn Case Replaced," by Marjorie Driscoll, January 19, 1943.
"Flynn Case Continues," by Marjorie Driscoll, January 20, 1943.

The Los Angeles Times
"College Boys in Film Are Real," May 8, 1929, p. A11.
"All-Star Cast," June 10, 1929, p. A7.
"Ex-Director Arrested in Theft Case," June 19, 1920, p. A11.
"New Revue at Pom Pom," June 25, 1929, p. A7.
"George Jessel Picked to Head New Late Show," August 8, 1929, p. A11.
"For Your Fancy," September 15, 1929, p. H8.
"Society of Cinemaland: Lingerie Shower," by Myra Nye, December 15, 1929, p. 22.
"Society of Cinemaland," by Myra Nye, April 6, 1930, p. B20.
"Sadakichi Hartmann, 'Ex-King of Bohemia,' Still a One-Man Show," by Arthur Millier, July 16, 1933.
"Tony Pastors's Planned Here," by John Scott, March 29, 1934, p. 12.
"Famous Theatre to Be Duplicated," April 8, 1934.
"Tony Pastor Theatre Club Novel Project," by Katherine T. Von Blon, May 7, 1934, pg. 8.
"Brush Strokes," by Arthur Millier, May 20, 1934, p. A8.
"Melodrama Near 'Century' Mark," August 19, 1934, p. A5.
"Brush Strokes," by Arthur Millier, June 9, 1935, p. A7.
"Around and About in Hollywood," by Read Kendall, April 23 1936, p. 10.
"Around and About in Hollywood," by Read Kendall, July 10, 1937, p. A7.
"Around and About in Hollywood," by Read Kendall, August 28, 1937, p. A7.
"Around and About in Hollywood," by Read Kendall, November 23, 1937, p. 10.
"Worship Him That Made Heart and Earth," December 4, 1937, p. A2.
Alice R. Rollins, "Antiques Santa Claus and Antiques," December 12, 1937, p. C11.
"Art Parade Reviewed," January 14, 1940, p. C8.
"Baroness Gives Dinner," January 5, 1941, p. D9.
"Grandchild of De Mille Dies in Pool," March 16, 1941.
"De Mille Grandson Funeral to Be Set," March 17, 1941.
"Town Called Hollywood," by Philip K. Scheuer, September 7, 1941, p. C3.
"Hedda Hopper's Hollywood," by Hedda Hopper, September 13, 1941, p. A6.
"Baby Showers Occupy Filmland's Coteries," by Maxine Bartlett, November 23, 1941, p. D10.

"Brush Strokes," November 23, 1941, p. C9.

"Chatterbox," December 9, 1941, p. A8.

"Joan, Olivia May Star in Warners' 'Devotion,'" by Edwin Schallert, February 25, 1942, p. A8.

"John Barrymore Taken By Death," May 30, 1942, p. 1.

"Barrymore's Funeral To Be Held Tomorrow," June 1, 1942, p. A1.

"Barrymore's Effects to be Sold, Give New Light on His Private Life," by Harold Mendelsohn, August 14, 1942, p. A1.

"Great Profile's Hidden Side Shown By Belongings Awaiting Sale," August 14, 1942, p. A1.

"All Barrymore's Clothing Sold Under Hammer," June 29, 1943, p. 14.

"Artist Divorces Wife in Enoch Arden Role," July 3, 1943, p. A1.

"Barrymore's Pet Dog Follows Actor in Death," December 22, 1943, p. A1.

"Virginia Medal Won by Hollywood Artist," March 19, 1944, p. B6.

"Artists' Row Rages After Judge's Wife Gets Prize," May 30, 1944, p. 7.

"Decker Displays Works Done in Five-Year Period," July 9, 1944, p. C6.

"Hartmann, 'King of Bohemia,' Taken by Death," November 23, 1944, p. 11.

"Actor Jack LaRue Hurt in Brawl Growing Out of Hollywood Party," January 19, 1946, p. 3.

"Movie Dillinger faces New Suit," February 21, 1946, p. 2.

"*Scarlet Street* Paintings Sent to Art Museum," March 7, 1946, p. A3.

"Darnell Prima Donna; New Actor Sidelighted," by Edwin Schallert, June 8, 1946, p. A5.

"John Decker Exhibits His Best Art Yet," June 23, 1946, p C4.

"Flynn's Scientist-Father Ready for Fish Study," August 8, 1946, p. 4.

"Flynn's Wife Parries Bligh Role Query," October 29, 1946, p. A1.

"Friends Say Farewell at W.C. Fields' Funeral," January 3, 1947, p. A1.

Obituary for John Decker, June 10, 1947, p. 10.

"Artist Speaks Via Recording at Own Funeral," June 11, 1947, p. A1.

"John Decker Studios Open Impressively," by Arthur Millier, August 17, 1947, p. C4.

"Painter John Decker Leaves Small Estate," October 18, 1947, p. 6.

"Stars of Filmdom Depicted in Paintings, Drawings," November 16, 1947, p. B4.

"Art of Late John Decker Being Shown," April 4, 1948, p. C4.

"Wife of Studio Director Gets Decree," December 17, 1948, p. A3.

"Dwelling Sold by Film Star," September 17, 1950, p. F2.

"Paulette Sandwiches Film Between Trips," by Philip K. Scheuer, January 11, 1953, p. E1.

"Fowler Introduces Another Pal," April 4, 1954, p. D6.

"Gene Fowler Scorns Pens That Drip Tears," by Cecil Smith, October 17, 1954, p. B4.

"Deckers Plan Art Colony at Del Mar," October 24, 1954, p. D7.

"O. Henry Series To See Mitchell in Title Role," by Cecil Smith, April 14, 1957, p. G3.

"Widow of John Decker Divorces Another Mate," January 10, 1958, p. 5.

"Quinn and Basehart Would Film 'Jest,'" by Hedda Hopper, February 18, 1958, p. A6.

"Fowler Recalls Days as Big City Reporter," by Jack Smith, February 3, 1959, p. B1.
"Not Only the Widow Was Merry Then!" by Philip K. Scheuer, February 5, 1963.
"The Second Handshake Really Gets to You," by Will Fowler, January 7, 1968, p. D7.
"Groucho's 3 Children to Get Bulk of Estate," by Myrna Oliver, August 26, 1977, p. B1.
"The Great Profile's Final Act," by Will Fowler, May 23, 1982, p. L28.
"The Late Great Days of Chasen's," by Rip Rense, March 31, 1995.
"Before the Rat Pack, Another Wild Bunch," by Richard Rushfield, July 30, 2005.

The New York Times
"Perfume Concert Fails," December 1, 1902, pg. 5.
"The Play." By Alexander Woollcott, September 13, 1922, p. 15.
"The Play," by John Colton, November 17, 1922, p. 22. *Underworld* advertisement, August 21, 1927.
"The Play," by Brooks Atkinson, August 16, 1929.
"The Play," by Brooks Atkinson, December 3, 1932.
"'The Profile' Names Actors Better Than He," June 27, 1940, p. 11.
"Gene Fowler Tells of His Writing Plans," by Robert Van Gelder, September 15, 1940, p. 94.
"Divorce Suit Is Filed by John Barrymore," September 24, 1940, p. 23.
"Roland Young Dies In Home Here At 65," June 7, 1953, p. 84.
"Gene Fowler Dead: Author and Newsman," July 3, 1960, p. 1.
"Rites For Fowler Set," July 4, 1960, p. 15.
"Rites Held For Fowler," July 7, 1960, p. 31.
"Gene Fowler Left Estate to Widow," July 19, 1960, p. 59.
"Thomas Mitchell Actor, Dead; Star of Stage and Screen, 70," December 18, 1962.
"The Theatre: 'Enter Laughing,'" March 15, 1963, p. 8.
"Ben Hecht, 70, Dies at His Home Here," April 19, 1964, p. 1.
"Hecht Completed Work on Musical," by Sam Zolotow, April 20, 1964, p. 35.
"Ben Hecht Is Buried in Nyack Near Charles MacArthur Grave," April 22, 1964, p. 47.
"Alan Mowbray, Character Actor Is Dead at 72," March 26, 1969.
"I Hate Hamlet Co-Star Walks Out," by Alex Witchel, May 4, 1991, p. 11.
"Anthony Quinn Dies at 86; Played Earthy Tough Guys," by Anita Gates, June 4, 2001, p. A1.

The New York Post
"King of the Bohemians, Past and Present," by William Bryk, (CQ), January 26, 2005.

Interviews
James Bacon, interview with Charles Heard and Bill Nelson, Northridge, California, October, 2006.
Henry Brandon, telephone interview with Gregory William Mank, West Hollywood, California, April 19, 1986 and April 26, 1986.

Ronald J. Fields, telephone interview with Gregory William Mank, La Selva Beach, California, October 27, 2006.

Will Fowler, interview with Bill Nelson.

Marian Marsh, interview with Gregory William Mank, Palm Desert, California, May 14, 1983 and December 15, 1992.

Constance Moore, telephone interview with Gregory William Mank, Los Angeles, California, August 28, 2000.

Phil Rhodes, interview with Gregory William Mank and Bill Nelson, Burbank, California, May 4, 2006.

Rita Saiz, interview with Gregory William Mank and Bill Nelson, Brentwood, California, May 2, 2006.

Mary Lou Warn, telephone interviews with Gregory William Mank, Clearwater, Florida, October 4, 2006 and March 5, 2007.

Personal Letters

John Barrymore to Laird Cregar, undated, circa Fall 1941.

John Decker to Phyllis Decker, undated, circa 1945.

Hubert Eaton, letters to Phyllis Decker and William R. Valentiner, respectively dated July 24, 1947 and July 21, 1947, collection of Charles Heard.

W.C. Fields to Jane Fowler, October 4, 1939.

W.C. Fields to Gene Fowler, September 6, no year (probably 1940).

W.C. Fields to Miss Elise Cavanna, April 7, 1942.

W.C. Fields to Gene Fowler, October 17, 1944.

Gene Fowler to John Barrymore, undated.

Gene Fowler to Dr. Harold Thomas Hyman, January 13, 1944.

Ben Hecht to Gene Fowler, February 8, 1933.

Dr. Harold Thomas Hyman, M.D., to Gene Fowler, January 12, 1943.

Dr. Harold Thomas Hyman to Gene Fowler, January 3, 1944.

Dr. Harold Thomas Hyman to Gene Fowler, January 17, 1944.

Legal Papers and Records

Death Certificate of John Barrymore, filed June 1, 1942.

Last Will and Testament of John Barrymore, December 30, 1941.

Death Certificate of John Decker, filed June 10, 1947.

Harriet V. Fields, Creditor's Claim and Disaffirmance, No. 264050, July 23, 1947.

Death Certificate of William Claude Fields, filed December 30, 1946.

Last Will and Testament of William C. Fields, April 28, 1943.

Death Certificate of Sadakichi Hartmann, filed November 24, 1944.

Death Certificate of Thomas Mitchell, registered December 19, 1962.

Death Certificate of Anthony Quinn, signed June 3, 2001.

Hospital Papers

Dr. V.L. Andrews, Autopsy Report on Mr. John Barrymore, undated.

Dr. Samuel Hirshfeld, Personal History of Mr. John Barrymore, May 14, 1934.

Dr. Hugo M. Kersten, Hollywood Hospital, Statement on the Death of
John Barrymore, undated.

Libraries

Claremont College, California. (From Irving Wallace's Archives, his interviews with
John Decker for the proposed magazine installments entitled *Heroes with Hangovers*.)

Billy Rose Library of Performing Arts, Lincoln Center, New York, New York.

Enoch Pratt Free Library, Baltimore, Maryland.

Margaret Herrick Library, Academy of Motion Pictures Arts and Sciences,
Los Angeles, California.

University of Southern California Performing Arts Library, Los Angeles, California.

Miscellaneous

Steve Beasley, e-mail to author, September 18, 2006.

James Card, program notes, *The Films of John Barrymore*, As Shown in the Dryden Theatre
Tribute Series, George Eastman House, Rochester, New York, May-June 1969.

John Decker, "Asylum" (also titled "James Felton, Insane"). Short story written by Decker
circa 1940.

Roby Heard, "Artist John Decker Revealed as German Baron by Widow," unsourced/undated
newspaper clipping, from John Decker's scrapbooks, Charles Heard collection.

"Decker Divorces Mate Thought Dead When He Wed Again," unsourced newspaper clipping,
Charles Heard collection.

Alan Mowbray, "Bits and Pieces," unsourced, November, 1945, from John Decker's scrapbooks.

Recording of *The Rudy Vallee Show*, May 1, 1941.

Sadakichi Hartmann "Perfume Concert" scrapbook and various unpublished works, from
Adam Parfrey collection.

Index

Anderson, John Murray 4, 237
Anderson, Sherwood 26
Barrie (Barrymore), Elaine 38, 40, 165–169, 171, 179, 182–183, 196, 202, 219, 221–222, 235, 239, 254, 258–261, 288, 344
Barrymore, Diana 10, 245–247, 249–254, 256–258, 260–261, 278–279, 308–310, 343, 345
Barrymore, John 10, 13–15, 20–21, 23–24, 27, 31–46, 48–49, 51–52, 60, 63–64, 68–69, 75, 78, 81–83, 86–87, 89–91, 93, 96–102, 108–110, 112–116, 121–122, 125–127, 130, 141, 143–145, 148–150, 153–154, 158–160, 163, 165–171, 173–175, 179–184, 200, 202, 208–209, 212–214, 219–225, 227–228, 230–233, 235–237, 239–265, 267, 274, 280, 284, 288, 292, 300, 309, 311, 314–315, 325–326, 329, 332, 336, 341, 343–346, 359, 361, 363–366
Brice, Fannie 68–69, 114, 126, 215, 240, 329
Brooks, Louise 65
Carradine, John 12, 147–150, 187–189, 206, 218–219, 240–241, 245–246, 253–254, 259–260, 280–285, 289–291, 300, 311–312, 354, 357–359, 365
Colbert, Claudette 182, 189
Costello (Barrymore), Dolores 23, 44, 47–49, 69, 90, 95, 100–102, 111–112, 122, 127, 167, 253–254, 259, 261, 264, 278
Decker, John 9–11, 13–15, 17–23, 25–29, 33, 49, 51–52, 60–61, 63, 69, 72, 78, 83, 91–93, 102, 104–106, 110–112, 118, 124, 129–130, 139, 148, 152, 154, 156, 158–160, 162, 172–174, 181–182, 184–185, 191–197, 199–200, 202–204, 206, 208–210, 212, 214, 218–222, 224–225, 227, 230, 233–234, 237, 239–241, 243, 248, 250, 252–254, 256, 258, 260, 274–280, 284, 286–289, 294, 297, 299–300, 302–311, 313–317, 320–321, 325–330, 332–337, 341, 359, 361, 365–366
    419 Bundy Drive 9, 200, 202, 204, 206, 208–210, 212–214, 219–220, 222, 224, 227, 233, 237, 247–248, 252, 260, 278, 286, 287–289, 364–366
    Alta Loma Studio 9, 13, 203, 213, 289, 304, 306–309, 320, 325–326, 330, 332–335
    Rembrandt *Bust of Christ* 11, 192–195, 334
Decker, Phyllis 14, 20–21, 194, 196, 207, 209–210, 214, 222, 227, 233, 237, 240, 278, 288, 302–303, 305, 308, 317, 326, 329–332, 334–336, 359–360
DeMille, Cecil B. 13, 148, 150, 161, 190, 204, 228–229, 259, 295, 361
DeMille (Quinn), Katherine 13, 161, 163, 190, 225, 228–229, 295, 325, 361–362
Dentist, The 68–69
Dvorak, Ann 107
Fallon, Joseph 110
Father Goose 124
Fields, W.C. 3–4, 11, 24, 61, 63–70, 78, 83, 93, 117–118, 120, 122–124, 135, 139, 172, 178–180, 184–186, 202, 204–206, 212, 216, 218, 220, 222, 228–230, 233, 234, 237–241, 251, 254, 258–260, 273–274, 288, 292, 294, 298, 300–302, 318, 320–324, 332, 350, 365
Flynn, Errol 11, 20, 128–135, 142–143, 150, 176–178, 186–187, 202, 204, 206, 211, 213–215, 234–235, 239, 241, 247, 251–252, 257, 261, 268–272, 274, 278, 289, 291, 295, 300, 306, 308–313, 315–317, 320, 332, 335–337, 341–347, 359, 365–366
Fowler, Gene 12–14, 20–21, 33, 38, 43, 52, 61, 66, 81–87, 90, 93, 110–111, 114, 116–117, 124, 136, 145, 154, 159, 165, 174–176, 181–182, 184, 186, 190–191, 200, 202, 204, 206, 219–222, 224, 226–227, 230, 233–234, 237, 239–241, 244–245, 253–261, 284–289, 294, 296–297, 300, 302, 306, 308, 311, 321, 325, 328–329, 332, 337, 348, 350, 353–354, 356, 365
Fowler, Will 79, 83, 191–192, 194–195, 276, 286, 296, 314, 316, 321–322, 328, 332, 334–335, 350,

Frankenstein 77, 154, 289–291, 305, 326
Front Page, The 12, 77–78, 208
Gable, Clark 102–104, 117, 122, 126, 163
Garbo, Greta 10, 93, 98, 108–110, 168, 240
Gone With the Wind 12, 154, 181, 188, 190
Great Magoo, The 114, 117
Great Mouthpiece, The 110
Harlow, Jean 121, 153, 322
Hartmann, Sadakichi 3, 11, 49–61, 78, 83, 93, 119–121, 182, 206, 213, 217, 219–221, 226–227, 234, 240, 258, 260–261, 263, 286–289, 296–297, 325–326, 336, 348, 350, 365
Hecht, Ben 10, 12, 14, 25–26, 70–79, 81–82, 84, 93, 107, 114, 116–117, 125–126, 129, 135–136, 145, 175–176, 190, 208, 240, 248, 250, 258, 284–285, 297, 300, 308, 312, 321, 325, 329–330, 336–337, 339, 350, 354–356, 361
Hepburn, Katharine 10, 112, 115, 150–152, 208
Karloff, Boris 108, 117, 150, 153, 289
Louvish, Simon 118
MacArthur, Charles 10, 77, 81–82, 85, 114, 116, 125–126, 135–136, 145, 175, 190, 208, 258, 356
Macbeth 13, 220–221, 366
Mannix, Eddie 144, 258
Marx, Harpo 10, 106, 280, 308, 316
Minutes of the Last Meeting 12, 20–21, 52, 154, 190, 220, 297, 308, 328, 348, 350
Mitchell, Thomas 11, 154, 156, 187–188, 192, 194–197, 202, 208, 218, 231, 240, 251, 254, 258, 273, 275, 279, 295, 300, 311–312, 325, 332, 334, 336, 350, 354, 360, 365
Mowbray, Alan 12, 15, 152–155, 218, 240, 254, 258, 275, 306, 308, 310, 312, 325, 330, 332–334, 356–357, 365
Muni, Paul 107, 219
Nagel, Anne 238
Pangborn, Franklin 117, 216, 237
Paval, Philip 15, 206, 320, 325–326, 328–330, 332–334, 335–336
Peary, Danny 126, 135, 238
Perfidy 355
Peters, Margot 90, 102, 254, 257, 260
Price, Vincent 15, 279–280, 294, 325, 332
Richards, Frank 228
Queen Victoria 11, 63, 184, 280, 321
Quinn, Anthony 13, 15, 159–161, 163, 190, 213, 218–219, 224–225, 228–230, 234, 241, 254, 259–260, 294–295, 300, 308–309, 312, 325, 327, 330, 332–333, 336, 360–363, 365
Roosevelt, Eleanor 205–206
Sennett, Mack 69, 124
Sheridan, Ann 130, 219
Sherlock Holmes 13, 158
Stagecoach 11–12, 147, 154, 156, 181, 187–188, 190
Swall, Dr. Vernon 325
Topper 158
Underworld 12, 72, 78, 355
Vagabond King, The 253
Van Gogh, Vincent 13, 23, 204, 311, 326, 330
Wuthering Heights 12, 181, 190
Young, Roland 13, 157–159, 208, 212, 219–221, 224, 240, 251, 258, 300, 325, 341, 365

Hollywood's Hellfire Club: The Misadventures of John Barrymore, W.C. Fields, Errol Flynn and "The Bundy Drive Boys"
© 2007 by Gregory William Mank and Feral House

The photographs, research material, paintings, previously unpublished manuscripts are courtesy of the collections of Charles Heard, Bill Nelson, Phil Rhodes, Adam Parfrey, Gregory William Mank, Ronald J. Fields.

The publisher wishes to thank Anton Szandor LaVey for initially charming us with stories of the Bundy Drive boys.

All rights reserved.

No part of this book may be used or reproduced in any manner whatsoever without written permission from the publisher. No part of this book may be stored in a retrieval system or transmitted in any form or by any means including electronic, electrostatic, magnetic tape, mechanical, photocopying, recording, or otherwise without prior permission in writing from the publisher.

For information contact Feral House, P.O. Box 39910, Los Angeles, CA 90039

www.FeralHouse.com

Designer: Dana Collins

10 9 8 7 6 5 4 3 2 1